Professional Examinations

PART 2

Paper 2.4

Financial Management and Control

EXAM KIT

ACCA

Approved Publisher

KAPLAN PUBLISHING

FOULKS LYNCH

British Library Cataloguing-in-Publication Data

A catalogue record for this book is available from the British Library.

Published by:
Kaplan Publishing Foulks Lynch
Unit 2 The Business Centre
Molly Millars Lane
Wokingham
RG41 2QZ

ISBN 978 1 84390 891 3

Printed and bound in Great Britain by William Clowes Ltd, Beccles, Suffolk

Acknowledgements

The past ACCA exam questions are the copyright of the Association of Chartered Certified Accountants. The original answers to the questions from June 1994 onwards were produced by the examiners themselves and have been adapted by Kaplan Publishing Foulks Lynch.

We are grateful to the Chartered Institute of Management Accountants and the Institute of Chartered Accountants in England and Wales for permission to reproduce past exam questions. The answers have been prepared by Kaplan Publishing Foulks Lynch.

CONTENTS

INDEX TO QUESTIONS AND ANSWERS

PRACTICE QUESTIONS

SCENARIO-BASED QUESTIONS

SYLLABUS AND EXAM FORMAT

Format of the exam

		Number of marks
Section A:	One compulsory scenario-based question	50
Section B:	Choice of 2 from 4 questions (25 marks each)	50
		100
Total time allowed: 3 hours		

Aim

To develop knowledge and understanding of financial management methods for analysing the benefits of various sources of finance and capital investment opportunities, and of the application of management accounting techniques for business planning and control.

Objectives

On completion of this paper candidates should be able to:

- explain the role and purpose of financial management
- evaluate the overall management of working capital
- evaluate appropriate sources of finance for particular situations
- appraise capital investment through the use of appropriate methods
- identify and discuss appropriate costing systems and techniques
- prepare budgets and use them to control and evaluate organisational performance
- understand the basic principles of performance management
- critically assess the tools and techniques of financial management and control
- demonstrate the knowledge, understanding, skills, abilities and critical evaluation expected in Part 2.

Position of the paper in the overall syllabus

Students must have a thorough knowledge of the material in Paper 1.2 Financial Information for Management and a good knowledge of other Part 1 papers.

Financial Management and Control is integrated with other Part 2 papers by providing a management decision framework within which some aspects of the Part 2 syllabus are developed. The effects of capital allowances and corporation tax on capital investment appraisal are examinable. Knowledge gained from Paper 2.3 Business Taxation (UK) will be useful in this respect.

Financial Management and Control is developed in Part 3 into advanced study of Performance Management (Paper 3.3) and Strategic Financial Management (Paper 3.7).

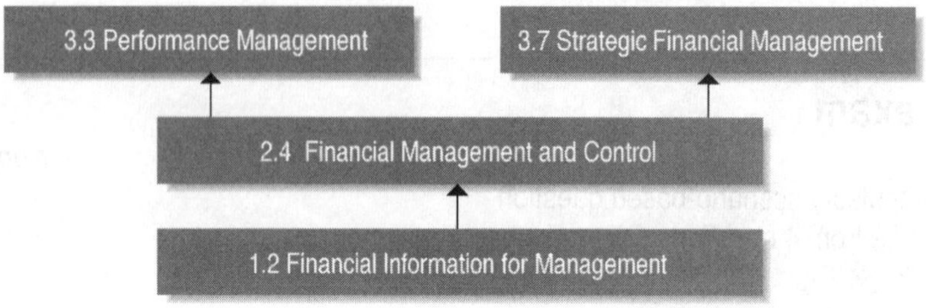

Syllabus content

1 Financial management objectives

(a) The nature, purpose and scope of financial management.

(b) The relationship between financial management, management accounting and financial accounting.

(c) The relationship of financial objectives and organisational strategy.

(d) Problems of multiple stakeholders in financial management and the consequent multiple objectives.

(e) Objectives (financial and otherwise) in not-for-profit organisations.

2 The financial management environment

(a) Financial intermediation and credit creation.

(b) Money and capital markets

- (i) Domestic and international
- (ii) Stock markets (both major markets and small firm markets).

(c) The Efficient Markets Hypothesis.

(d) Rates of interest and yield curves.

(e) The impact of fiscal and monetary policy on business.

(f) Regulation of business (for example, pricing restrictions, green policies and corporate governance).

3 Management of working capital

(a) The nature and scope of working capital management.

(b) Funding requirements for working capital.

(c) Working capital needs of different types of business.

(d) The relationship of working capital management to business solvency.

(e) Management of stock, debtors, short term funds, cash, overdrafts and creditors.

(f) Techniques of working capital management (including ratio analysis, EOQ, JIT, credit evaluation, terms of credit, cash discounts, factoring and invoice discounting, debtors cycles, efficient short-term fund investing, cash forecasting and budgets, Miller-Orr model, basic foreign exchange methods, probabilities and risk assessment, terms of trade with creditors).

4 Sources of finance

(a) Sources and relative costs (including issue costs) of various types of finance and their suitability to different circumstances and organisations (large and small, listed and unlisted) including:

(i) access to funds and the nature of business risk

(ii) the nature and importance of internally generated funds

(iii) capital markets (types of share capital, new issues, rights issues, loan capital, convertibles, warrants)

(iv) the effect of dividend policy on financing needs

(v) bank finance (short, medium and long term, including leasing)

(vi) trade credit

(vii) government sources: grants, regional and national aid schemes and tax incentives

(viii) problems of small company financing (collateral, maturity funding gap, risk)

(ix) problems of companies with low initial earnings (R&D, Internet, and other high-technology businesses)

(x) venture capital and financial sources particularly suited to the small company

(xi) international money and capital markets, including an introduction to international banking and the finance of foreign trade.

(b) Requirements of finance (for what purpose, how much and for how long) in relation to business operational and strategic objectives.

(c) The importance of the choice of capital structure: equity versus debt and basic analysis of the term profile of funds.

(d) Financial gearing and other key financial ratios and analysis of their significance to the organisation.

(e) Appropriate sources of finance, taking into account:

(i) cost of finance

(ii) timing of cash payments

(iii) business risk and financial risk

(iv) effect on gearing and other ratios

(v) effect on company's existing investors.

5 Capital investment appraisal

(a) Discounted cash flow techniques

(i) simple and compound interest

(ii) net present value

(iii) annuities and perpetuities

(iv) internal rate of return

(v) future value

(vi) nominal interest

(b) Appraisal of domestic capital investment opportunities for profit making and not-for-profit organisations through the use of appropriate methods and techniques

(i) the risk / return relationship

(ii) return on capital employed

(iii) payback

(iv) internal rate of return

(v) net present value

(vi) single and multi-period capital rationing

(vii) lease or buy decisions

(viii) asset replacement using equivalent annual cost. Including (in categories (i)-(viii)) the effects of taxation, inflation, risk and uncertainty (probabilities, sensitivity analysis, simulation).

6 Costing systems and techniques

(a) The purpose of costing as an aid to planning, monitoring and control of business activity.

(b) Different approaches to costing.

(c) Costing information requirements and limitations in not-for-profit organisations.

(d) Behavioural implications of different costing approaches including performance evaluation.

(e) Implications of costing approaches for profit reporting, the pricing of products and internal activities/ services.

7 Standard costing and variance analysis

(a) Standard costing

(i) determination of standards

(ii) identification and calculation of sales variances (including quantity and mix), cost variances (including mix and yield); absorption and marginal approaches

(iii) significance and relevance of variances

(iv) operating statements

(v) interpretation and relevance of variance calculations to business performance.

(b) Planning and operational variances.

(c) Behavioural implications of standard costing and variance reporting.

8 Budgeting and budgetary control

(a) Objectives of budgetary planning and control systems including aspects of behavioural implications.

(b) Evaluation of budgetary systems such as fixed and flexible, zero based and incremental, periodic, continuous and activity based.

(c) Development, implementation and coordination of budgeting systems: functional, subsidiary and master/ principal budgets (including cash budgeting); budget review.

(d) Calculation and cause of variances as aids to controlling performance.

(e) Quantitative aids to budgeting and the concepts of correlation, basic time series analysis (seasonality) and forecasting; use of computer based models.

(f) Behavioural implications of budgeting and budgetary control.

9 Performance measurement

(a) Measurement of productivity, activity, profitability and quality of service

(b) Relationship of measure to type of entity and range of measures, both monetary and non-monetary

(c) Indices to allow for price and performance changes through time

(d) Evaluating performance against objectives and plans, and identifying areas of concern from the information produced

(e) The impact of cost centres, revenue centres, profit centres and investment centres on management appraisal

(f) Difference between business performance and management performance

(g) Benchmarking

Excluded topics

The following topics are specifically excluded from the syllabus:

- Calculations involving the derivation of cost of capital in discounting problems. Candidates will always be supplied with an appropriate discount rate.
- Calculations relating to Modigliani and Miller propositions.

Additional information

Present value and annuity tables will be provided in the exam.

ANALYSIS OF PAST PAPERS

June 2003

Section A

1 NPV calculation with writing down allowances and sensitivity analysis. Ratio analysis. Method of financing proposed investment.

Section B

2 Sales forecasting: trend line and seasonal variations. Top-down and bottom-up budgeting.

3 Early settlement discount (evaluation). Financing working capital.

4 Stock market efficient. Value for money (VFM) and maximisation of shareholder wealth.

5 Limiting factor analysis. Make-or-buy decision. Limitations of marginal costing for decision-making.

December 2003

Section A

1 Working capital management: overtrading, using a factor. Lease or buy decision.

Section B

2 Budgeting. Production and cash budgets. Periodic and continuous budgets. Budgetary slack.

3 Capital rationing.

4 Problems of monopoly. Raising long-term finance.

5 Variance analysis, including materials mix and yield variances.

June 2004

Section A

1 NPV, IRR and accounting rate of return, with inflation and taxation (including capital allowances) and the use of investment appraisal methods. Assessing risk and uncertainty for investment decision-making. Sources of finance for a machine.

Section B

2 Factors affecting loan interest rates. Long-term and short-term funding to finance working capital. Cash operating cycle and working capital investment.

3 Activity-based costing and its uses

4 Financing an expansion with debt capital or equity capital: financial and operational gearing, interest cover, earnings per share; business risk and financial risk

5 Planning and operational variances. Factors in a decision whether or not to investigate a variance.

December 2004

Section A

1 Planning and operational variances.

DCF: equivalent annual cost, investment appraisal with taxation and inflation.

Conflicting corporate objectives.

Lifecycle costing and target costing.

Section B

2 Flexible budget. Variance analysis. Purpose of budgeting.

3 Rights issue. Effect of a rights issue on EPS, shareholder wealth, gearing and interest cover.

4 Activity-based costing. Financial and non-financial performance measures for organisational and management performance.

5 Risk and uncertainty in investment appraisal: payback, sensitivity analysis, expected NPV.

June 2005

Section A

1 A wide-ranging question covering NPV with inflation and taxation (including capital allowances), limitations of the method used, evaluation of financing method, ABC, forward contracts and bills of exchange.

Section B

2 Applying costing methods to not-for-profit organisations, including ZBB. Using ABB in a manufacturing business.

3 Variances, including sales mix. Standard costing.

4 Performance appraisal of a quoted company, total shareholder return and directors' remuneration.

5 Inventory management, including EOQ. Evaluation of a discount.

December 2005

Section A

1 (a) Investment appraisal calculation – NPV

(b) Investment appraisal decision – discussion aspects

(c) Additional NPV calculations

(d) Analysis of current financial position and likelihood of raising a bank loan

(e) Variances – calculation and comment

Section B

2 Discussion question on divisional performance appraisal

3 Activity based costing – calculations and discussion

4 Finance – buy v lease and calculations for a bank loan

5 Cash management

June 2006

Section A

1 A wide-ranging question on financing covering
 (a) ratio analysis
 (b) debt factoring
 (c) rights issues
 (d) dividend valuation model

Section B

2 Financial objectives for a NFP organisation, EMH, financing gap for small companies.
3 Variances (operating statement with discussion)
4 Budgeting (calculation plus discussion).
5 Investment appraisal (NPV, IRR and discussion of techniques)

REVISION GUIDANCE

Planning your revision

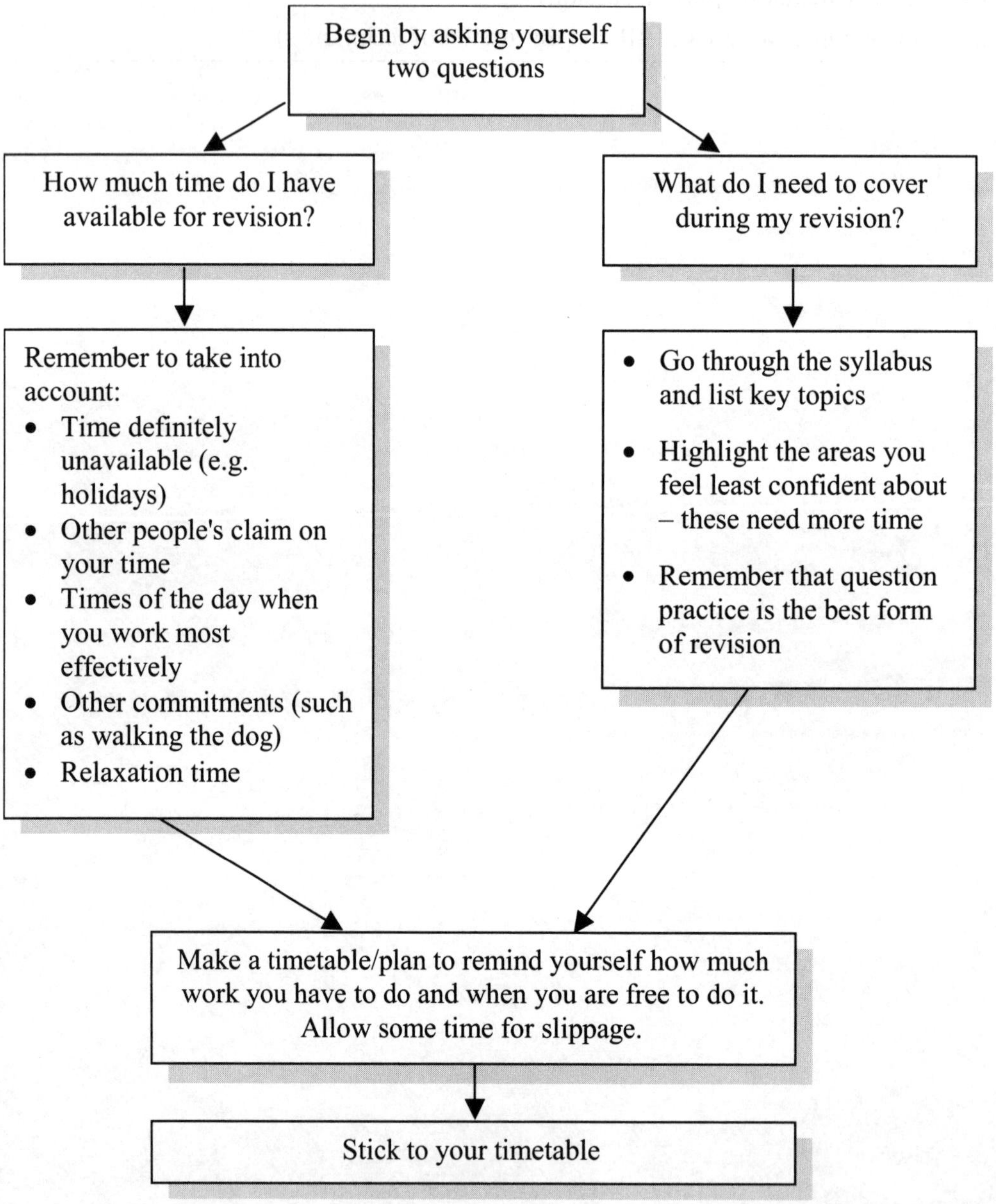

Revision techniques

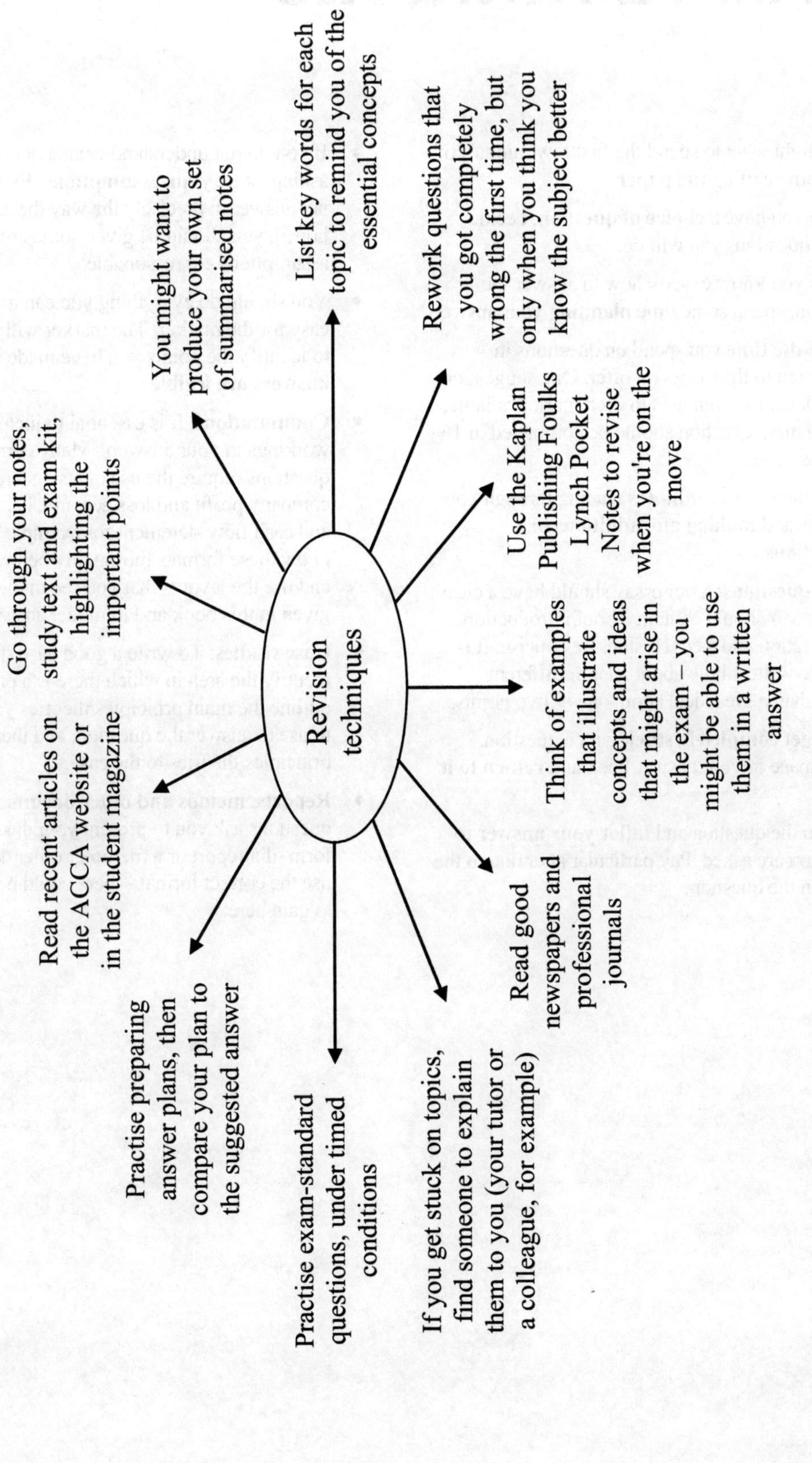

EXAM TECHNIQUES

- You might want to spend the first few minutes of the exam **reading the paper**.
- Where you have a **choice of question**, decide which questions you will do.
- Unless you know exactly how to answer the question, spend some time **planning** your answer.
- **Divide the time** you spend on questions in proportion to the marks on offer. One suggestion is to allocate 1½ minutes to each mark available, so a 10 mark question should be completed in 15 minutes.
- Spend the last **five minutes** reading through your answers and **making any additions or corrections**.
- **Essay questions**: Your essay should have a clear structure. It should contain a brief introduction, a main section and a conclusion. Be concise. It is better to write a little about a lot of different points than a great deal about one or two points.
- If you **get completely stuck** with a question, leave space in your answer book and **return to it later.**
- Stick to the question and **tailor your answer** to what you are asked. Pay particular attention to the verbs in the question.
- If you do not understand what a question is asking, **state your assumptions**. Even if you do not answer in precisely the way the examiner hoped, you should be given some credit, if your assumptions are reasonable.
- You should do everything you can to make things easy for the marker. The marker will find it easier to identify the points you have made if your **answers are legible**.
- **Computations**: It is essential to include all your workings in your answers. Many computational questions require the use of a standard format: company profit and loss account, balance sheet and cash flow statement for example. Be sure you know these formats thoroughly before the exam and use the layouts that you see in the answers given in this book and in model answers.
- **Case studies**: To write a good case study, first identify the area in which there is a problem, outline the main principles/theories you are going to use to answer the question, and then apply the principles/theories to the case.
- **Reports, memos and other documents**: Some questions ask you to present your answer in the form of a report or a memo or other document. So use the correct format - there could be easy marks to gain here.

MATHEMATICAL TABLES

Formulae sheet

Economic order quantity $= \sqrt{\dfrac{2C_oD}{C_H}}$

Discount factor $= \dfrac{1}{(1+r)^n}$

Annuities

Future value $= A\left(\dfrac{(1+r)^n - 1}{r}\right)$

Present value $= \dfrac{A}{r}\left(1 - \dfrac{1}{(1+r)^n}\right)$

Dividend growth model

$$P_0 = \left(\frac{D_0(1+g)}{(r-g)}\right)$$

Miller Orr Model

Return point = Lower limit + ($\frac{1}{3}$ × spread)

$$\text{Spread} = 3\left[\frac{\frac{3}{4} \times \text{transaction cost} \times \text{variance of cashflows}}{\text{interest rate}}\right]^{\frac{1}{3}}$$

Linear regression

y = a + bx

$$b = \frac{n\sum xy - \sum x \sum y}{n\sum x^2 - \left(\sum x\right)^2}$$

$$a = \frac{\sum y}{n} - \frac{b\sum x}{n}$$

$$r = \frac{n\sum xy - \sum x \sum y}{\sqrt{\left(n\sum x^2 - \left(\sum x\right)^2\right)\left(n\sum y^2 - \left(\sum y\right)^2\right)}}$$

Indices

Laspeyre price index = $\dfrac{\sum (p_1 \times q_0)}{\sum (p_0 \times q_0)} \times 100$

Paasche price index = $\dfrac{\sum (p_1 \times q_1)}{\sum (p_0 \times q_1)} \times 100$

Laspeyre quantity index = $\dfrac{\sum (q_1 \times p_0)}{\sum (q_0 \times p_0)} \times 100$

Paasche quantity index = $\dfrac{\sum (q_1 \times p_1)}{\sum (q_0 \times p_1)} \times 100$

Present value table

Present value of 1 i.e. $(1 + r)^{-n}$

Where r = discount rate

n = number of periods until payment

Periods ***Discount rate (r)***

(n)	1%	2%	3%	4%	5%	6%	7%	8%	9%	10%	
1	0.990	0.980	0.971	0.962	0.952	0.943	0.935	0.926	0.917	0.909	1
2	0.980	0.961	0.943	0.925	0.907	0.890	0.873	0.857	0.842	0.826	2
3	0.971	0.942	0.915	0.889	0.864	0.840	0.816	0.794	0.772	0.751	3
4	0.961	0.924	0.888	0.855	0.823	0.792	0.763	0.735	0.708	0.683	4
5	0.951	0.906	0.863	0.822	0.784	0.747	0.713	0.681	0.650	0.621	5
6	0.942	0.888	0.837	0.790	0.746	0.705	0.666	0.630	0.596	0.564	6
7	0.933	0.871	0.813	0.760	0.711	0.665	0.623	0.583	0.547	0.513	7
8	0.923	0.853	0.789	0.731	0.677	0.627	0.582	0.540	0.502	0.467	8
9	0.914	0.837	0.766	0.703	0.645	0.592	0.544	0.500	0.460	0.424	9
10	0.905	0.820	0.744	0.676	0.614	0.558	0.508	0.463	0.422	0.386	10
11	0.896	0.804	0.722	0.650	0.585	0.527	0.475	0.429	0.388	0.350	11
12	0.887	0.788	0.701	0.625	0.557	0.497	0.444	0.397	0.356	0.319	12
13	0.879	0.773	0.681	0.601	0.530	0.469	0.415	0.368	0.326	0.290	13
14	0.870	0.758	0.661	0.577	0.505	0.442	0.388	0.340	0.299	0.263	14
15	0.861	0.743	0.642	0.555	0.481	0.417	0.362	0.315	0.275	0.239	15

(n)	11%	12%	13%	14%	15%	16%	17%	18%	19%	20%	
1	0.901	0.893	0.885	0.877	0.870	0.862	0.855	0.847	0.840	0.833	1
2	0.812	0.797	0.783	0.769	0.756	0.743	0.731	0.718	0.706	0.694	2
3	0.731	0.712	0.693	0.675	0.658	0.641	0.624	0.609	0.593	0.579	3
4	0.659	0.636	0.613	0.592	0.572	0.552	0.534	0.516	0.499	0.482	4
5	0.593	0.567	0.543	0.519	0.497	0.476	0.456	0.437	0.419	0.402	5
6	0.535	0.507	0.480	0.456	0.432	0.410	0.390	0.370	0.352	0.335	6
7	0.482	0.452	0.425	0.400	0.376	0.354	0.333	0.314	0.296	0.279	7
8	0.434	0.404	0.376	0.351	0.327	0.305	0.285	0.266	0.249	0.233	8
9	0.391	0.361	0.333	0.308	0.284	0.263	0.243	0.225	0.209	0.194	9
10	0.352	0.322	0.295	0.270	0.247	0.227	0.208	0.191	0.176	0.162	10
11	0.317	0.287	0.261	0.237	0.215	0.195	0.178	0.162	0.148	0.135	11
12	0.286	0.257	0.231	0.208	0.187	0.168	0.152	0.137	0.124	0.112	12
13	0.258	0.229	0.204	0.182	0.163	0.145	0.130	0.116	0.104	0.093	13
14	0.232	0.205	0.181	0.160	0.141	0.125	0.111	0.099	0.088	0.078	14
15	0.209	0.183	0.160	0.140	0.123	0.108	0.095	0.084	0.074	0.065	15

Annuity table

Present value of an annuity of 1 i.e. $\frac{1-(1+r)^{-n}}{r}$

Where r = discount rate

n = number of periods

Periods (n)	Discount rate (r) 1%	2%	3%	4%	5%	6%	7%	8%	9%	10%	
1	0.990	0.980	0.971	0.962	0.952	0.943	0.935	0.926	0.917	0.909	1
2	1.970	1.942	1.913	1.886	1.859	1.833	1.808	1.783	1.759	1.736	2
3	2.941	2.884	20829	2.775	2.723	2.673	2.624	2.577	2.531	2.487	3
4	3.902	3.808	3.717	3.630	3.546	3.465	3.387	3.312	3.240	3.170	4
5	4.853	4.713	4.580	4.452	4.329	4.212	4.100	3.993	3.890	3.791	5
6	5.795	5.601	5.417	5.242	5.076	4.917	4.767	4.623	4.486	4.355	6
7	6.728	6.472	6.230	6.002	5.786	5.582	5.389	5.206	5.033	4.868	7
8	7.652	7.325	7.020	6.733	6.463	6.210	5.971	5.747	5.535	5.335	8
9	8.566	8.162	7.786	7.435	7.108	6.802	6.515	6.247	5.995	5.759	9
10	9.471	8.983	8.530	8.111	7.722	7.360	7.024	6.710	6.418	6.145	10
11	10.37	9.787	9.253	8.760	8.306	7.887	7.499	7.139	6.805	6.495	11
12	11.26	10.58	9.954	9.385	8.863	8.384	7.943	7.536	7.161	6.814	12
13	12.13	11.35	10.63	9.986	9.394	8.853	8.358	7.904	7.487	7.103	13
14	13.00	12.11	11.30	10.56	9.899	9.295	8.745	8.244	7.786	7.367	14
15	13.87	12.85	11.94	11.12	10.38	9.712	9.108	8.559	8.061	7.606	15

(n)	11%	12%	13%	14%	15%	16%	17%	18%	19%	20%	
1	0.901	0.893	0.885	0.877	0.870	0.862	0.855	0.847	0.840	0.833	1
2	1.713	1.690	1.668	1.647	1.626	1.605	1.585	1.566	1.547	1.528	2
3	2.444	2.402	2.361	2.322	2.283	2.246	2.210	2.174	2.140	2.106	3
4	3.102	3.037	2.974	2.914	2.855	2.798	2.743	2.690	2.639	2.589	4
5	3.696	3.605	3.517	3.433	3.352	3.274	3.199	3.127	3.058	2.991	5
6	4.231	4.111	3.998	3.889	3.784	3.685	3.589	3.498	3.410	3.326	6
7	4.712	4.564	4.423	4.288	4.160	4.039	3.922	3.812	3.706	3.605	7
8	5.146	4.968	4.799	4.639	4.487	4.344	4.207	4.078	3.954	3.837	8
9	5.537	5.328	5.132	4.946	4.772	4.607	4.451	4.303	4.163	4.031	9
10	5.889	5.650	5.426	5.216	5.019	4.833	4.659	4.494	4.339	4.192	10
11	6.207	5.938	5.687	5.453	5.234	5.029	4.836	4.656	4.486	4.327	11
12	6.492	6.194	5.918	5.660	5.421	5.197	4.988	4.793	4.611	4.439	12
13	6.750	6.424	6.122	5.842	5.583	5.342	5.118	4.910	4.715	4.533	13
14	6.982	6.628	6.302	6.002	5.724	5.468	5.229	5.008	4.802	4.611	14
15	7.191	6.811	6.462	6.142	5.847	5.575	5.324	5.092	4.876	4.675	15

Section 1

PRACTICE QUESTIONS

FINANCIAL MANAGEMENT OBJECTIVES AND ENVIRONMENT

1 TAGNA

Tagna is a medium-sized company that manufactures luxury goods for several well-known chain stores. In real terms, the company has experienced only a small growth in turnover in recent years, but it has managed to maintain a constant, if low, level of reported profits by careful control of costs. It has paid a constant nominal (money terms) dividend for several years and its managing director has publicly stated that the primary objective of the company is to increase the wealth of shareholders. Tagna is financed as follows:

	£m
Overdraft	1.0
10 year fixed-interest bank loan	2.0
Share capital and reserves	4.5
	7.5

Tagna has the agreement of its existing shareholders to make a new issue of shares on the stock market but has been informed by its bank that current circumstances are unsuitable. The bank has stated that if new shares were to be issued now they would be significantly under-priced by the stock market, causing Tagna to issue many more shares than necessary in order to raise the amount of finance it requires. The bank recommends that the company waits for at least six months before issuing new shares, by which time it expects the stock market to have become strong-form efficient.

The financial press has reported that it expects the Central Bank to make a substantial increase in interest rate in the near future in response to rapidly increasing consumer demand and a sharp rise in inflation. The financial press has also reported that the rapid increase in consumer demand has been associated with an increase in consumer credit to record levels.

Required:

(a) Discuss the meaning and significance of the different forms of market efficiency (weak, semi-strong and strong) and comment on the recommendation of the bank that Tagna waits for six months before issuing new shares on the stock market. **(9 marks)**

(b) On the assumption that the Central Bank makes a substantial interest rate increase, discuss the possible consequences for Tagna in the following areas:

(i) sales

(ii) operating costs, and

(iii) earnings (profit after tax). **(10 marks)**

(c) Explain and compare the public sector objective of 'value for money' and the private sector objective of 'maximisation of shareholder wealth'. **(6 marks)**

(Total: 25 marks)

2 STAKEHOLDERS

Private sector companies have multiple stakeholders who are likely to have divergent interests.

Required:

(a) Identify five stakeholder groups and briefly discuss their financial and other objectives. **(12 marks)**

(b) Examine the extent to which good corporate governance procedures can help manage the problems arising from the divergent interests of multiple stakeholder groups in private sector companies in the UK. **(13 marks)**

(Total: 25 marks)

3 MANAGEMENT ACCOUNTING

(a) Some writers have suggested that the purposes of management accounting systems are costing and management control.

Required:

Briefly discuss whether this satisfactorily describes the purposes of management accounting systems. **(6 marks)**

(b) A company, which is engaged in retailing food and household products, has stores in many towns. These stores, whilst managed locally, report to a Head Office and are served from a few strategically located warehouses by the company's own transport fleet.

Required:

Discuss the management accounting information which is likely to be provided in such a company. **(14 marks)**

(Total: 20 marks)

4 NEWS FOR YOU

News For You operate a chain of newsagents and confectioner's shops in the south of England, and are considering the possibility of expanding their business across a wider geographical area. The business was started in 20X2 and annual turnover grew to £10 million by the end of 20X6. Between 20X6 and 20X9 turnover grew at an average rate of 2% per year.

The business still remains under family control, but the high cost of expansion via the purchase or building of new outlets would mean that the family would need to raise at least £2 million in equity or debt finance. One of the possible risks of expansion lies in the fact that both tobacco and newspaper sales are falling. New income is being generated by expanding the product range stocked by the stores, to include basic foodstuffs such as bread and milk. News For You purchases all of its products from a large wholesale distributor which is convenient, but the wholesale prices leave News For You with a relatively small gross margin. The key to profit growth for News For You lies in the ability to generate sales growth, but the company recognises that it faces stiff competition from large food retailers in respect of the prices that it charges for several of its products.

In planning its future, News For You was advised to look carefully at a number of external factors which may affect the business, including government economic policy and, in recent months, the following information has been published in respect of key economic data:

(i) Bank base rate has been reduced from 5% to 4.5%, and the forecast is for a further 0.5% reduction within six months.

(ii) The annual rate of inflation is now 1.2%, down from 1.3% in the previous quarter, and 1.7% 12 months ago. The rate is now at its lowest for 25 years, and no further falls in the rate are expected over the medium/long term.

(iii) Personal and corporation tax rates are expected to remain unchanged for at least 12 months.

(iv) Taxes on tobacco have been increased by 10% over the last 12 months, although no further increases are anticipated.

(v) The government has initiated an investigation into the food retail sector focusing on the problems of 'excessive' profits on certain foodstuffs created by the high prices being charged for these goods by the large retail food stores.

Required:

(a) Explain the relevance of each of the items of economic data listed above to News For You. **(10 marks)**

(b) Explain whether News For You should continue with their expansion plans. Clearly justify your arguments for or against the expansion. **(10 marks)**

(Total: 20 marks)

5 DISCOURAGING MONOPOLY AND AVAILABILITY OF FINANCE

Two important elements in the economic and financial management environment of companies are the regulation of markets to discourage monopoly and the availability of finance to fund growth and development.

Required:

(a) Outline the economic problems caused by monopoly and explain the role of government in maintaining competition between companies. **(9 marks)**

(b) Describe the methods of raising new equity finance that can be used by an unlisted company. **(8 marks)**

(c) Discuss the factors to be considered by a listed company when choosing between an issue of debt and an issue of equity finance. **(8 marks)**

(Total: 25 marks)

6 PLANKERS LTD

Assume that 'now' is June 20X3.

You are in charge of developing long term plans for your business, Plankers Ltd. Plans are developed on the basis that the business has a single objective and seeks to maximise its profits as measured by profit after tax.

The company has a loan facility from its bank of £8m at 8% annually. The outstanding liability at 31 May 20X3 is £7m. It is possible to extend the facility up to £12m but only at an interest cost of 9% on the whole outstanding balance. The condition attached to this loan is that interest cover should at least be equal to 3: that is, profit before interest and tax (PBIT) should be at least three times the interest. If the condition is breached then the loan becomes repayable immediately.

Interest charges in the profit and loss accounts are calculated on year-end balances (at 31 May each year). For example, interest charges in the year-end 31 May 20X3 profit and loss account were based on year-end balances at 31 May 20X3.

Targets set by the directors of Plankers are as follows:

1 cash balances must not fall below £1m, and

2 it is desirable that Basic Earnings per Share should not fall below 20p per share. The company has in issue 4m £1 ordinary shares.

The constraint set by the bank and the targets set by the directors are measured and assessed at each year-end. The summary profit and loss account for the year just ended (31 May 20X3) and a summary balance sheet are shown below along with forecasts for the next 2 years:

	31 May 20X3	*31 May 20X4*	*31 May 20X5*
	£m	£m	£m
PBIT	1.71	1.80	1.89
Interest charges	(0.56)	(0.56)	(0.56)
Profit before tax	1.15	1.24	1.33
Tax	(0.35)	(0.37)	(0.40)
Profit after tax	0.80	0.87	0.93
Dividends	(0.40)	(0.44)	(0.47)
Retained	0.40	0.43	0.46
Non-cash net assets	5.25	5.57	5.91
Cash	8.25	8.36	8.48
Loan liabilities	(7.00)	(7.00)	(7.00)
Shareholders' funds	6.50	6.93	7.39

Forecasts are based on the assumption that PBIT is likely to grow at a rate of 5% per annum. The forecasts of PBIT growth include the effect of the building programme and the depreciation on it. The corporation tax rate is 30%.

The company is planning a major building programme on 1 June 20X5 at which time a cash outflow of £12m would have to be paid. 50% of this expenditure will be depreciated at the rate of 15% per annum (the company has no other depreciable assets). This depreciation has been agreed as allowable for tax purposes with the tax authorities.

The directors of Plankers are considering utilising the loan facility to help meet the funding requirements of the building programme, but are wondering whether their targets will be met or whether the loan conditions will be breached. They have asked you to conduct an analysis of the company's financial position at 31 May 20X6 assuming the building programme begins on the 1 June 20X5. For 20X6 only, the company will not pay any dividends to minimise its refinancing needs.

Required:

(a) (i) Prepare a forecast summary profit and loss account for the year to 31 May 20X6 assuming that the building programme is undertaken at 1 June 20X5 and that any additional funds are provided by an extension of the bank loan.

Assume that tax is paid in the year in which incurred.

Work to 3 decimal places of £m in your answer. **(5 marks)**

(ii) Assess whether, at 31 May 20X6 and based on the scenario in (i) above, the loan condition would be breached and whether the directors' targets would be achieved.

Work to 3 decimal places of £m in your answer. **(3 marks)**

(iii) Identify 5 options the company could use, assuming it faced a cash shortfall, to ease any cash shortage. **(5 marks)**

(iv) Explain, without further computations, whether each of the options in (a)(iii) is likely to meet Planker's requirements for additional capital and also the constraint set by the bank. **(3 marks)**

(b) Whilst the financial plans of the business are based on a single objective, it faces a number of constraints that put pressure on the company to address more than one objective simultaneously.

Required:

What types of constraints might the company face when assessing its long-term plans? Specifically refer in your answer to:

(i) responding to various stakeholder groups, and **(4 marks)**

(ii) the difficulties associated with managing organisations with multiple objectives.

(5 marks)

(Total: 25 marks)

7 RZP CO

As assistant to the Finance Director of RZP Co, a company that has been listed on the London Stock Market for several years, you are reviewing the draft Annual Report of the company, which contains the following statement made by the chairman:

'This company has consistently delivered above-average performance in fulfilment of our declared objective of creating value for our shareholders. Apart from 20X2, when our overall performance was hampered by a general market downturn, this company has delivered growth in dividends, earnings and ordinary share price. Our shareholders can rest assured that my directors and I will continue to deliver this performance in the future'.

The five-year summary in the draft Annual Report contains the following information:

Year	20X4	20X3	20X2	20X1	20X0
Dividend per share	2.8p	2.3p	2.2p	2.2p	1.7p
Earnings per share	19.04p	14.95p	11.22p	15.84p	13.43p
Price/earnings ratio	22.0	33.5	25.5	17.2	15.2
General price index	117	113	110	105	100

A recent article in the financial press reported the following information for the last five years for the business sector within which RZP Co operates:

Share price growth	average increase per year of 20%
Earnings growth	average increase per year of 10%
Nominal dividend growth	average increase per year of 10%
Real dividend growth	average increase per year of 9%

You may assume that the number of shares issued by RZP Co has been constant over the five-year period. All price/earnings ratios are based on end-of-year share prices.

Required:

(a) Analyse the information provided and comment on the views expressed by the chairman in terms of:

(i) growth in dividends per share;

(ii) share price growth;

(iii) growth in earnings per share.

Your analysis should consider both arithmetic mean and equivalent annual growth rates. **(13 marks)**

(b) Calculate the total shareholder return (dividend yield plus capital growth) for 20X4 and comment on your findings. **(3 marks)**

(c) Discuss the factors that should be considered when deciding on a management remuneration package that will encourage the directors of RZP Co to maximise the wealth of shareholders, giving examples of management remuneration packages that might be appropriate for RZP Co. **(9 marks)**

(Total: 25 marks)

MANAGEMENT OF WORKING CAPITAL

8 HEXICON PLC

(a) Give reasons, with a brief explanation, why the net present value (NPV) method of investment appraisal is thought to be superior to other approaches. **(5 marks)**

(b) Hexicon plc manufactures and markets automatic washing machines. Among the many hundreds of components which it purchases each year from external suppliers for assembling into the finished article are drive belts, of which it uses 40,000 units pa. It is considering converting its purchasing, delivery and stock control of this item to a just-in-time system. This will raise the number of orders placed but lower the administrative and other costs of placing and receiving orders. If successful, this will provide the model for switching most of its inwards supplies on to this system. Details of actual and expected ordering and carrying costs are given in the table below.

			Actual	*Proposed*
O	=	Ordering cost per order	£100	£25
P	=	Purchase cost per item	£2.50	£2.50
I	=	Inventory holding cost (as a percentage of the purchase cost)	20%	20%

To implement the new arrangements will require 'one-off' reorganisation costs estimated at £4,000 which will be treated as a revenue item for tax purposes. The rate of corporation tax is 33% and Hexicon can obtain finance at 12%. The effective life span of the Determine new system can be assumed to be eight years.

Required:

(i) Determine the effect of the new system on the economic order quantity (EOQ).

(ii) Determine whether the new system is worthwhile in financial terms.

Note: EOQ is given by $Q = \sqrt{\dfrac{2 \times D \times O}{I \times P}}$ where D = demand, or usage. **(10 marks)**

(c) **You are required** to briefly explain the nature and objectives of JIT purchasing agreements concluded between components users and suppliers. **(5 marks)**

(Total: 20 marks)

9 BLIN

Blin is a company listed on a European stock exchange, with a market capitalisation of €6m, which manufactures household cleaning chemicals. The company has expanded sales quite significantly over the last year and has been following an aggressive approach to working capital financing. As a result, Blin has come to rely heavily on overdraft finance for its short-term needs. On the advice of its finance director, the company intends to take out a long-term bank loan, part of which would be used to repay its overdraft.

Required:

(a) Discuss the factors that will influence the rate of interest charged on the new bank loan, making reference in your answer to the yield curve. **(9 marks)**

(b) Explain and discuss the approaches that Blin could adopt regarding the relative proportions of long- and short-term finance to meet its working capital needs, and comment on the proposed repayment of the overdraft. **(9 marks)**

(c) Explain the meaning of the term 'cash operating cycle' and discuss its significance in determining the level of investment in working capital. Your answer should refer to the working capital needs of different business sectors. **(7 marks)**

(Total: 25 marks)

10 VELM PLC

Velm plc sells stationery and office supplies on a wholesale basis and has an annual turnover of £4,000,000. The company employs four people in its sales ledger and credit control department at an annual salary of £12,000 each. All sales are on 40 days' credit with no discount for early payment. Bad debts represent 3% of turnover and Velm plc pays annual interest of 9% on its overdraft. The most recent accounts of the company offer the following financial information:

Velm plc: Balance Sheet as at 31 December 20X2

	£000	£000	£000
Fixed assets			17,500
Current assets			
Stock of goods for resale		900	
Debtors		550	
Cash		120	
		1,570	
Creditors: amounts falling due within one year			
Trade creditors	330		
Overdraft	1,200		
		1,530	
			40
			17,540
Creditors: amounts falling due after more than one year			
12% Debenture due 20X9			2,400
			15,140
Ordinary shares			3,500
Reserves			11,640
			15,140

Velm plc is considering offering a discount of 1% to customers paying within 14 days, which it believes will reduce bad debts to 2.4% of turnover. The company also expects that offering a discount for early payment will reduce the average credit period taken by its customers to 26 days. The consequent reduction in the time spent chasing customers where payments are overdue will allow one member of the credit control team to take early retirement. Two -thirds of customers are expected to take advantage of the discount.

Required:

(a) Using the information provided, determine whether a discount for early payment of one per cent will lead to an increase in profitability for Velm plc. **(5 marks)**

(b) Discuss the relative merits of short-term and long-term debt sources for the financing of working capital. **(6 marks)**

(c) Discuss the different policies that may be adopted by a company towards the financing of working capital needs and indicate which policy has been adopted by Velm plc. **(7 marks)**

(d) Outline the advantages to a company of taking steps to improve its working capital management, giving examples of steps that might be taken. **(7 marks)**

(Total: 25 marks)

11 SPECIAL GIFT SUPPLIES PLC

Special Gift Supplies plc is a wholesale distributor of a variety of imported goods to a range of retail outlets. The company specialises in supplying ornaments, small works of art, high value furnishings (rugs, etc) and other items that the chief buyer for the company feels would have a market in the UK. In seeking to improve working capital management, the financial controller has gathered the following information.

	Months
Average period for which items are held in stock	3.5
Average debtors collection period	2.5
Average creditors payment period	2.0

Required:

(a) Calculate Special Gift Supplies' funding requirements for working capital measured in terms of months. **(2 marks)**

(b) In looking to reduce the working capital funding requirement, the financial controller of Special Gift Supplies is considering factoring credit sales. The company's annual turnover is £2.5m of which 90% are credit sales. Bad debts are typically 3% of credit sales. The offer from the factor is conditional on the following:

(1) The factor will take over the sales ledger of Special Gift Supplies completely.

(2) 80% of the value of credit sales will be advanced immediately (as soon as sales are made to the customer) to Special Gift Supplies, the remaining 20% will be paid to the company one month later. The factor charges 15% per annum on credit sales for advancing funds in the manner suggested. The factor is normally able to reduce the debtors' collection period to one month.

(3) The factor offers a 'no recourse' facility whereby they take on the responsibility for dealing with bad debts. The factor is normally able to reduce bad debts to 2% of credit sales.

(4) A charge for factoring services of 4% of credit sales will be made.

(5) A one-off payment of £25,000 is payable to the factor.

The salary of the Sales Ledger Administrator (£12,500) would be saved under the proposals and overhead costs of the credit control department, amounting to £2,000 per annum, would have to be reallocated. Special Gift Supplies' cost of overdraft finance is 12% per annum. Special Gift Supplies pays its sales force on a commission only basis. The cost of this is 5% of credit sales and is payable immediately the sales are made. There is no intention to alter this arrangement under the factoring proposals.

Required:

Evaluate the proposal to factor the sales ledger by comparing Special Gift Supplies' existing debtor collection costs with those that would result from using the factor (assuming that the factor can reduce the debtors' collection period to one month). **(8 marks)**

(c) As an advisor to Special Gift Supplies plc, write a report to the financial controller that outlines:

(i) how a credit control department might function

(ii) the benefits of factoring and

(iii) how the financing of working capital can be arranged in terms of short and long term sources of finance.

In particular, make reference to: the financing of working capital or net current assets when short term sources of finances are exhausted; and the distinction between fluctuating and permanent current assets. **(15 marks)**

(Total: 25 marks)

12 TNG

TNG Co expects annual demand for product X to be 255,380 units. Product X has a selling price of £19 per unit and is purchased for £11 per unit from a supplier, MKR Co. TNG places an order for 50,000 units of product X at regular intervals throughout the year. Because the demand for product X is to some degree uncertain, TNG maintains a safety (buffer) stock of product X which is sufficient to meet demand for 28 working days. The cost of placing an order is £25 and the storage cost for Product X is 10 pence per unit per year.

TNG normally pays trade suppliers after 60 days but MKR has offered a discount of 1% for cash settlement within 20 days.

TNG Co has a short-term cost of debt of 8% and uses a working year consisting of 365 days.

Required:

(a) Calculate the annual cost of the current ordering policy. Ignore financing costs in this part of the question. **(4 marks)**

(b) Calculate the annual saving if the economic order quantity model is used to determine an optimal ordering policy. Ignore financing costs in this part of the question. **(5 marks)**

(c) Determine whether the discount offered by the supplier is financially acceptable to TNG Co. **(4 marks)**

(d) Critically discuss the limitations of the economic order quantity model as a way of managing stock. **(4 marks)**

(e) Discuss the advantages and disadvantages of using just-in-time stock management methods. **(8 marks)**

(Total: 25 marks)

SOURCES OF FINANCE

13 ASSOCIATED INTERNATIONAL SUPPLIES LTD

The following are summary financial statements for Associated International Supplies Ltd.

	20X4	*20X9*
	£000	£000
Fixed assets	115	410
Current assets	650	1,000
Current liabilities	513	982
Long-term liabilities	42	158
Total	210	270
Capital and reserves	210	270

	20X4	*20X9*
	£000	£000
Sales	1,200	3,010
Cost of sales, expenses and interest	1,102	2,860
Profit before tax	98	150
Tax and distributions	33	133
Retained earnings	65	17

Notes: Cost of sales was £530,000 for 20X4 and £1,330,000 for 20X9.

Debtors are 50% of current assets and trade creditors are 25% of current liabilities for both years.

Required:

(a) You are a consultant advising Associated International Supplies Ltd. Using suitable financial ratios, and paying particular attention to growth and liquidity, write a report on the significant changes faced by the company since 20X4. The report should also comment on the capacity of the company to continue trading, together with any other factors considered appropriate.

An appendix to the report should be used to outline your calculations. **(17 marks)**

(b) Explain and evaluate the sources of finance available to small businesses for fixed assets. **(8 marks)**

(Total: 25 marks)

14 ARWIN

Arwin plans to raise £5m in order to expand its existing chain of retail outlets. It can raise the finance by issuing 10% debentures redeemable in ten years' time, or by a rights issue at £4.00 per share. The current financial statements of Arwin are as follows.

Profit and loss account for the last year	£000
Sales	50,000
Cost of sales	30,000
Gross profit	20,000
Administration costs	14,000
Profit before interest and tax	6,000
Interest	300

Profit before tax	5,700
Taxation at 30%	1,710
Profit after tax	3,990
Dividends	2,394
Retained earnings	1,596

Balance sheet	£000
Net fixed assets	20,100
Net current assets	4,960
12% debentures (redeemable in six years)	2,500
	22,560
Ordinary shares, par value 25p	2,500
Retained profit	20,060
	22,560

The expansion of business is expected to increase sales revenue by 12% in the first year. Variable cost of sales makes up 85% of cost of sales. Administration costs will increase by 5% due to new staff appointments. Arwin has a policy of paying out 60% of profit after tax as dividends and has no overdraft.

Required:

(a) For each financing proposal, prepare the forecast profit and loss account after one additional year of operation. **(5 marks)**

(b) Evaluate and comment on the effects of each financing proposal on the following:

(i) Financial gearing;

(ii) Operational gearing;

(iii) Interest cover;

(iv) Earnings per share. **(12 marks)**

(c) Discuss the dangers to a company of a high level of gearing, including in your answer an explanation of the following terms:

(i) Business risk;

(ii) Financial risk. **(8 marks)**

(Total: 25 marks)

15 JERONIMO PLC

Jeronimo plc currently has 5 million ordinary shares in issue, which have a market value of £1.60 each. The company wishes to raise finance for a major investment project by means of a rights issue, and is proposing to issue shares on the basis of 1 for 5 at a price of £1.30 each.

James Brown currently owns 10,000 shares in Jeronimo plc and is seeking advice on whether or not to take up the proposed rights.

Required:

(a) Explain the difference between a rights issue and a scrip issue. Your answer should include comment on the reasons why companies make such issues and the effect of the issues on private investors. **(6 marks)**

(b) Calculate:

(i) the theoretical value of James Brown's shareholding if he takes up his rights

(ii) the theoretical value of James Brown's rights if he chooses to sell them. **(4 marks)**

(c) Using only the information given below, and applying the dividend growth model formula, calculate the required return on equity for an investor in Jeronimo plc.

Jeronimo plc:

Current share price:	£1.60
Number of shares in issue:	5 million
Current earnings:	£1.5 million
Dividend Paid	(Pence per share):
20X5:	8
20X6:	9
20X7:	11
20X8:	11
20X9:	12

The formula for the dividend growth model is as follows: $R = \left(\frac{D_1}{MV} + g\right) \times 100$

(4 marks)

Where R = Percentage required return on equity

(d) If the stock market is believed to operate with a strong level of efficiency, what effect might this have on the behaviour of the finance directors of publicly quoted companies? **(6 marks)**

(Total: 20 marks)

16 TECHFOOLS

Techfools.com has just issued convertible debentures with an 8% per annum coupon to the value of £5 million. The nominal value of the debentures is £100 and the issue price was £105. The conversion details are that 45 shares will be issued for every £100 convertible debentures held with a date for conversion in five years exactly. Redemption, should the debenture not be converted, will also take place in exactly five years. Debentures will be redeemed at £110 per £100 nominal convertibles held. It is widely expected that the share price of the company will be £4 in five years' time.

Assume an investor required return of 15%.

Ignore taxation in your answer.

Required:

(a) Briefly explain why convertibles might be an attractive source of finance for companies. **(4 marks)**

(b) (i) Estimate the current market value of the debentures, assuming conversion takes place, using net present value methods and assess if it is likely that conversion will take place. **(5 marks)**

(ii) Identify and briefly comment on a single major reservation you have with your evaluation in part b (i). **(2 marks)**

(c) Explain why an issuing company seeks to maximise its conversion premium and why companies can issue convertibles with a high conversion premium. **(4 marks)**

(d) Explain what is meant by the concept of intermediation (the role of a banking sector) and how such a process benefits both investors and companies. **(10 marks)**

(Total: 25 marks)

17 TIRWEN PLC

Tirwen plc is a medium-sized manufacturing company which is considering a 1 for 5 rights issue at a 15% discount to the current market price of £4.00 per share. Issue costs are expected to be £220,000 and these costs will be paid out of the funds raised. It is proposed that the rights issue funds raised will be used to redeem some of the existing debentures at par. Financial information relating to Tirwen plc is as follows:

Current balance sheet

	£000	£000	£000
Fixed assets			6,550
Current assets			
Stock		2,000	
Debtors		1,500	
Cash		300	
		3,800	
Current liabilities			
Trade creditors	1,100		
Overdraft	1,250		
		2,350	
Net current assets			1,450
Total assets less current liabilities			8,000
12% debentures 2012			4,500
			3,500
Ordinary shares (per value 50p)			2,000
Reserves			1,500
			3,500

Other information:

Price/earnings ratio of Tirwen plc:		15.24
Overdraft interest rate:		7%
Corporation tax rate:		30%
Sector advantages:	debt/equity ratio (book value):	100%
	interest cover:	6 times

Required:

(a) Ignoring issue costs and any use that may be made of the funds raised by the rights issue, calculate:

(i) the theoretical ex rights price per share;

(ii) the value of rights per existing share. **(3 marks)**

(b) What alternative actions are open to the owner of 1,000 shares in Tirwen plc as regards the rights issue? Determine the effect of each of these actions on the wealth of the investor. **(6 marks)**

(c) Calculate the current earnings per share and the revised earnings per share if the rights issue funds are used to redeem some of the existing debentures. **(6 marks)**

(d) Evaluate whether the proposal to redeem some of the debentures would increase the wealth of the shareholders of Tirwen plc. Assume that the price/earnings ratio of Tirwen plc remains constant. **(3 marks)**

(e) Discuss the reasons why a rights issue could be an attractive source of finance for Tirwen plc. Your discussion should include an evaluation of the effect of the rights issue on the debt/equity ratio and interest cover. **(7 marks)**

(Total: 25 marks)

CAPITAL INVESTMENT APPRAISAL

18 INVESTMENT APPRAISAL

(a) Explain and illustrate (using simple numerical examples) the Accounting Rate of Return and Payback approaches to investment appraisal, paying particular attention to the limitations of each approach. **(6 marks)**

(b) (i) Explain the differences between NPV and IRR as methods of Discounted Cash Flow analysis. **(6 marks)**

(ii) A company with a cost of capital of 14% is trying to determine the optimal replacement cycle for the laptop computers used by its sales team. The following information is relevant to the decision:

The cost of each laptop is £2,400. Maintenance costs are payable at the end of *each full year* of ownership, but not in the year of replacement, e.g. if the laptop is owned for two years, then the maintenance cost is payable at the end of year 1.

Interval between replacement (years)	*Trade-in value (£)*	*Maintenance cost*
1	1,200	Zero
2	800	£75 (payable at end of Year 1)
3	300	£150 (payable at end of Year 2)

Required:

Ignoring taxation, calculate the equivalent annual cost of the three different replacement cycles, and recommend which should be adopted. What other factors should the company take into account when determining the optimal cycle? **(8 marks)**

(Total: 20 marks)

19 BREAD PRODUCTS LTD

Bread Products Ltd is considering the replacement policy for its industrial size ovens which are used as part of a production line that bakes bread. Given its heavy usage each oven has to be replaced frequently. The choice is between replacing every two years or every three years. Only one type of oven is used, each of which costs £24,500. Maintenance costs and resale values are as follows:

Year	*Maintenance per annum*	*Resale value*
	£	£
1	500	
2	800	15,600
3	1,500	11,200

Original cost, maintenance costs and resale values are expressed in current prices. That is, for example, maintenance for a two year old oven would cost £800 for maintenance undertaken now. It is expected that maintenance costs will increase at 10% per annum and oven replacement cost and resale values at 5% per annum. The money discount rate is 15%.

Required:

(a) Calculate the preferred replacement policy for the ovens in a choice between a two-year or three-year replacement cycle. **(12 marks)**

(b) Identify the limitations of Net Present Value techniques when applied generally to investment appraisal. **(13 marks)**

(Total: 25 marks)

20 HOWDEN PLC

(a) Explain how inflation affects the rate of return required on an investment project, and the distinction between a real and a nominal (or 'money terms') approach to the evaluation of an investment project under inflation. **(6 marks)**

(b) Howden plc is contemplating investment in an additional production line to produce its range of compact discs. A market research study, undertaken by a well-known firm of consultants, has revealed scope to sell an additional output of 400,000 units p.a. The study cost £0.1 m but the account has not yet been settled.

The price and cost structure of a typical disc (net of royalties), is as follows:

	£	£
Price per unit		12.00
Costs per unit of output		
Material cost per unit	1.50	
Direct labour cost per unit	0.50	
Variable overhead cost per unit	0.50	
Fixed overhead cost per unit	1.50	
		(4.00)
Profit		8.00

The fixed overhead represents an apportionment of central administrative and marketing costs. These are expected to rise in total by £500,000 pa as a result of undertaking this project. The production line is expected to operate for five years and require a total cash outlay of £11m, including £0.5m of materials stocks. The equipment will have a residual value of £2m. Because the company is moving towards a JIT stock management policy, it is expected that this project will involve steadily reducing working capital needs, expected to decline at about 3% pa by volume. The production line will be accommodated in a presently empty building for which an offer of £2m has recently been received from another company. If the building is retained, it is expected that property price inflation will increase its value to £3m after five years.

While the precise rates of price and cost inflation are uncertain, economists in Howden's corporate planning department make the following forecasts for the average annual rates of inflation relevant to the project:

Retail Price Index	6% pa
Disc prices	5% pa
Material prices	3% pa
Direct labour wage rates	7% pa
Variable overhead costs	7% pa
Other overhead costs	5% pa

Note: you may ignore taxes and capital allowances in this question.

Required:

Given that Howden's shareholders require a real return of 8.5% for projects of this degree of risk, assess the financial viability of this proposal. **(13 marks)**

(c) Briefly discuss how inflation may complicate the analysis of business financial decisions. **(6 marks)**

(Total: 25 marks)

21 FILTREX PLC

(a) Distinguish between 'hard' and 'soft' capital rationing, explaining why a company may deliberately choose to restrict its capital expenditure. **(6 marks)**

(b) Filtrex plc is a medium-sized, all equity-financed, unquoted company which specialises in the development and production of water- and air-filtering devices to reduce the emission of effluents. Its small but ingenious R & D team has recently made a technological breakthrough which has revealed a number of attractive investment opportunities. It has applied for patents to protect its rights in all these areas. However, it lacks the financial resources required to exploit all of these projects, whose required outlays and post-tax NPVs are listed in the table below. Filtrex's managers consider that delaying any of these projects would seriously undermine their profitability, as competitors bring forward their own new developments. All projects are thought to have a similar degree of risk.

Project	*Required outlay*	*NPV*
	£	£
A	150,000	65,000
B	120,000	50,000
C	200,000	80,000
D	80,000	30,000
E	400,000	120,000

The NPVs have been calculated using as a discount rate the 18% post-tax rate of return which Filtrex requires for risky R & D ventures. The maximum amount available for this type of investment is £400,000, corresponding to Filtrex's present cash balances, built up over several years' profitable trading. Projects A and C are mutually exclusive and no project can be sub-divided. Any unused capital will either remain invested in short-term deposits or used to purchase marketable securities, both of which offer a return well below 18% post-tax.

Required:

(i) Advise Filtrex plc, using suitable supporting calculations, which combination of projects should be undertaken in the best interests of shareholders.

(ii) Suggest what further information might be obtained to assist a fuller analysis. **(12 marks)**

(c) Explain how, apart from delaying projects, Filtrex plc could manage to exploit more of these opportunities. **(7 marks)**

(Total: 25 marks)

22 ARMCLIFF LTD

Armcliff Ltd is a division of Shevin plc which requires each of its divisions to achieve a rate of return on capital employed of at least 10% pa. For this purpose, capital employed is defined as fixed capital and investment in stocks. This rate of return is also applied as a hurdle rate for new investment projects. Divisions have limited borrowing powers and all capital projects are centrally funded.

The following is an extract from Armcliff's divisional accounts:

Profit and loss account for the year ended 31 December 20X4

	£m
Turnover	120
Cost of sales	(100)
Operating profit	20

Assets employed as at 31 December 20X4

	£m	£m
Fixed (net)		75
Current assets (including stocks £25m)	45	
Current liabilities	(32)	
		13
Net capital employed		88

Armcliff's production engineers wish to invest in a new computer-controlled press. The equipment cost is £14m. The residual value is expected to be £2m after four years operation, when the equipment will be shipped to a customer in South America.

The new machine is capable of improving the quality of the existing product and also of producing a higher volume. The firm's marketing team is confident of selling the increased volume by extending the credit period. The expected additional sales are:

Year 1	2,000,000 units
Year 2	1,800,000 units
Year 3	1,600,000 units
Year 4	1,600,000 units

Sales volume is expected to fall over time due to emerging competitive pressures. Competition will also necessitate a reduction in price by £0.5 each year from the £5 per unit proposed in the first year. Operating costs are expected to be steady at £1 per unit, and allocation of overheads (none of which are affected by the new project) by the central finance department is set at £0.75 per unit.

Higher production levels will require additional investment in stocks of £0.5m, which would be held at this level until the final stages of operation of the project. Customers at present settle accounts after 90 days on average.

Required:

(a) Determine whether the proposed capital investment is attractive to Armcliff, using the average rate of return on capital method, as defined as average profit-to-average capital employed, ignoring debtors and creditors.

Note: Ignore taxes. **(10 marks)**

(b) (i) Suggest three problems which arise with the use of the average return method for appraising new investment. **(3 marks)**

(ii) In view of the problems associated with the ARR method, why do companies continue to use it in project appraisal? **(3 marks)**

(c) Briefly discuss the dangers of offering more generous credit, and suggest ways of assessing customers' creditworthiness. **(9 marks)**

(Total: 25 marks)

23 SLUDGEWATER PLC

Sludgewater plc, a furniture manufacturer, has been reported to the anti-pollution authorities on several occasions in recent years, and fined substantial amounts for making excessive toxic discharges into the air. Both the environmental lobby and Sludgewater's shareholders have demanded that it clean up its operations.

If no clean up takes place, Sludgewater estimates that the total fines it would incur over the next three years can be summarised by the following probability distribution (all figures are expressed in present values.)

Level of fine	*Probability*
£1.0m	0.3
£1.8m	0.5
£2.6m	0.2

A firm of environmental consultants has advised that spray painting equipment can be installed at a cost of £4m to virtually eliminate discharges. Unlike fines, expenditure on pollution control equipment is tax-allowable via a 25% writing-down allowance (reducing balance, based on gross expenditure). The rate of corporation tax is 30%, paid with a one-year delay. The equipment will have no scrap or resale value after its expected three year working life. The equipment can be in place ready for Sludgewater's next financial year.

A European Union grant of 25% of gross expenditure is available, but with payment delayed by a year. The consultant's charge is £200,000 and the new equipment will raise annual production costs by 2% of sales revenue. Current sales are £15 million per annum, and are expected to grow by 5% per annum compound. No change in working capital is envisaged.

Sludgewater applies a discount rate of 10% after tax on investment projects of this nature. All cash inflows and outflows occur at year ends.

Required:

(a) Calculate the expected net present value of the investment.

Briefly comment on your results. **(12 marks)**

(b) Write a memorandum to Sludgewater's management in respect of the potential investment taking into account both financial and non-financial criteria. **(8 marks)**

(Total: 20 marks)

24 LEAMINGER PLC

Leaminger plc has decided it must replace its major turbine machine on 31 December 20X2. The machine is essential to the operations of the company. The company is, however, considering whether to purchase the machine outright or to use lease financing.

Purchasing the machine outright

The machine is expected to cost £360,000 if it is purchased outright, payable on 31 December 20X2. After four years the company expects new technology to make the machine redundant and it will be sold on 31 December 20X6 generating proceeds of £20,000. Capital allowances for tax purposes are available on the cost of the machine at the rate of 25% per annum reducing balance. A full year's allowance is given in the year of acquisition but no writing down allowance is available in the year of disposal. The difference between the proceeds and the tax written down value in the year of disposal is allowable or chargeable for tax as appropriate.

Leasing

The company has approached its bank with a view to arranging a lease to finance the machine acquisition. The bank has offered two options with respect to leasing which are as follows:

	Finance lease	*Operating lease*
Contract length (years)	4	1
Annual rental	£135,000	£140,000
First rent payable	31 December 20X3	31 December 20X2

General

For both the purchasing and the finance lease option, maintenance costs of £15,000 per year are payable at the end of each year. All lease rentals (for both finance and operating options) can be assumed to be allowable for tax purposes in full in the year of payment. Assume that tax is payable one year after the end of the accounting year in which the transaction occurs. For the operating lease only, contracts are renewable annually at the discretion of either party. Leaminger plc has adequate taxable profits to relieve all its costs. The rate of corporation tax can be assumed to be 30%. The company's accounting year-end is 31 December. The company's annual after tax cost of capital is 10%.

Required:

(a) Calculate the net present value at 31 December 20X2, using the after tax cost of capital, for:

(i) purchasing the machine outright

(ii) using the finance lease to acquire the machine

(iii) using the operating lease to acquire the machine.

Recommend the optimal method. **(12 marks)**

(b) Assume now that the company is facing capital rationing up until 30 December 20X3 when it expects to make a share issue. During this time the most marginal investment project, which is perfectly divisible, requires an outlay of £500,000 and would generate a net present value of £100,000. Investment in the turbine would reduce funds available for this project. Investments cannot be delayed.

Calculate the revised net present values of the three options for the turbine given capital rationing. Advise whether your recommendation in (a) would change.

(5 marks)

(c) As their business advisor, prepare a report for the directors of Leaminger plc that assesses the issues that need to be considered in acquiring the turbine with respect to capital rationing. **(8 marks)**

(Total: 25 marks)

25 CAPITAL RATIONING

Basril plc is reviewing investment proposals that have been submitted by divisional managers. The investment funds of the company are limited to £800,000 in the current year. Details of three possible investments, none of which can be delayed, are given below.

Project 1

An investment of £300,000 in work station assessments. Each assessment would be on an individual employee basis and would lead to savings in labour costs from increased efficiency and from reduced absenteeism due to work-related illness. Savings in labour costs from these assessments in money terms are expected to be as follows:

Year	1	2	3	4	5
Cash flows (£000)	85	90	95	100	95

Project 2

An investment of £450,000 in individual workstations for staff that is expected to reduce administration costs by £140,800 per annum in money terms for the next five years.

Project 3

An investment of £400,000 in new ticket machines. Net cash savings of £120,000 per annum are expected in current price terms and these are expected to increase by 3.6% per annum due to inflation during the five-year life of the machines.

Basril plc has a money cost of capital of 12% and taxation should be ignored.

Required:

(a) Determine the best way for Basril plc to invest the available funds and calculate the resultant NPV:

(i) on the assumption that each of the three projects is divisible;

(ii) on the assumption that none of the projects are divisible. **(10 marks)**

(b) Explain how the NPV investment appraisal method is applied in situations where capital is rationed. **(3 marks)**

(c) Discuss the reasons why capital rationing may arise. **(7 marks)**

(d) Discuss the meaning of the term 'relevant cash flows' in the context of investment appraisal, giving examples to illustrate your discussion. **(5 marks)**

(Total: 25 marks)

26 UMUNAT PLC

Umunat plc is considering investing £50,000 in a new machine with an expected life of five years. The machine will have no scrap value at the end of five years. It is expected that 20,000 units will be sold each year at a selling price of £3·00 per unit. Variable production costs are expected to be £1·65 per unit, while incremental fixed costs, mainly the wages of a maintenance engineer, are expected to be £10,000 per year. Umunat plc uses a discount rate of 12% for investment appraisal purposes and expects investment projects to recover their initial investment within two years.

Required:

(a) Explain why risk and uncertainty should be considered in the investment appraisal process. **(5 marks)**

(b) Calculate and comment on the payback period of the project. **(4 marks)**

(c) Evaluate the sensitivity of the project's net present value to a change in the following project variables:

(i) sales volume;

(ii) sales price;

(iii) variable cost;

and discuss the use of sensitivity analysis as a way of evaluating project risk. **(10 marks)**

(d) Upon further investigation it is found that there is a significant chance that the expected sales volume of 20,000 units per year will not be achieved. The sales manager of Umunat plc suggests that sales volumes could depend on expected economic states that could be assigned the following probabilities:

Economic state	*Poor*	*Normal*	*Good*
Probability	0.3	0.6	0.1
Annual sale volume (units)	17,500	20,000	22,500

Calculate and comment on the expected net present value of the project. **(6 marks)**

(Total: 25 marks)

27 AGD CO

AGD Co is a profitable company which is considering the purchase of a machine costing £320,000. If purchased, AGD Co would incur annual maintenance costs of £25,000. The machine would be used for three years and at the end of this period would be sold for £50,000. Alternatively, the machine could be obtained under an operating lease for an annual lease rental of £120,000 per year, payable in advance.

AGD Co can claim capital allowances on a 25% reducing balance basis. The company pays tax on profits at an annual rate of 30% and all tax liabilities are paid one year in arrears. AGD Co has an accounting year that ends on 31 December. If the machine is purchased, payment will be made in January of the first year of operation. If leased, annual lease rentals will be paid in January of each year of operation.

Required:

(a) Using an after-tax borrowing rate of 7%, evaluate whether AGD Co should purchase or lease the new machine. **(12 marks)**

(b) Explain and discuss the key differences between an operating lease and a finance lease. **(8 marks)**

(c) The after-tax borrowing rate of 7% was used in the evaluation because a bank had offered to lend AGD Co £320,000 for a period of five years at a before-tax rate of 10% per year with interest payable every six months.

Required:

(i) Calculate the annual percentage rate (APR) implied by the bank's offer to lend at 10% per year with interest payable every six months. **(2 marks)**

(ii) Calculate the amount to be repaid at the end of each six-month period if the offered loan is to be repaid in equal instalments. **(3 marks)**

(Total: 25 marks)

COSTING SYSTEMS AND TECHNIQUES

28 BUD PLC

A division of Bud plc is engaged in the manual assembly of finished products F1 and F2 from bought-in components. These products are sold to external customers. The budgeted sales volumes and prices for Month 9 are as follows:

Product	*Units*	*Price*
Fl	34,000	£50.00
F2	58,000	£30.00

Finished goods stockholding budgeted for the end of Month 9, is 1,000 units of F1 and 2,000 units of F2, with no stock at the beginning of that month. The purchased components C3 and C4 are used in the finished products in the quantities shown below. The unit price is for just-in-time delivery of the components; the company holds no component stocks.

	Component	
Product	*C3*	*C4*
F1 (per unit)	8 units	4 units
F2 (per unit)	4 units	3 units
Price (each)	£1.25	£1.80

The standard direct labour times and labour rates and the budgeted monthly manufacturing overhead costs for the assembly and finishing departments for Month 9 are given below:

Product	*Assembly*	*Finishing*
Fl (per unit)	30 minutes	12 minutes
F2 (per unit)	15 minutes	10 minutes
Labour rate (per hour)	£5.00	£6.00
Manufacturing overhead cost for the month	£617,500	£204,000

Every month a predetermined direct labour hour recovery rate is computed in each department for manufacturing overhead and applied to items produced in that month.

The selling overhead of £344,000 per month is applied to products based on a predetermined percentage of the budgeted sales value in each month.

Required:

(a) Prepare summaries of the following budgets for Month 9:

(i) component purchase and usage (units and value)

(ii) direct labour (hours and value)

(iii) departmental manufacturing overhead recovery rates

(iv) selling overhead recovery rate

(v) stock value at the month-end. **(8 marks)**

(b) Tabulate the standard unit cost and profit of each of F1 and F2 in Month 9. **(3 marks)**

(c) Prepare a budgeted profit and loss account for Month 9 which clearly incorporates the budget values obtained in (a) above. **(3 marks)**

(d) Explain clearly the implications of the company's treatment of manufacturing overheads, i.e. computing a monthly overhead rate, compared to a predetermined overhead rate prepared annually. **(6 marks)**

(Total: 20 marks)

29 ABC

(a) Discuss the conditions under which the introduction of ABC is likely to be most effective, paying particular attention to:

- product mix
- the significance of overheads and the ABC method of charging costs
- the availability of information collection procedures and resources, and
- other appropriate factors. **(17 marks)**

(b) Explain why ABC might lead to a more accurate assessment of management performance than absorption costing. **(8 marks)**

(Total: 25 marks)

30 ABKABER PLC

Abkaber plc assembles three types of motorcycle at the same factory: the 50cc Sunshine; the 250cc Roadster and the 1000cc Fireball. It sells the motorcycles throughout the world. In response to market pressures Abkaber plc has invested heavily in new manufacturing technology in recent years and, as a result, has significantly reduced the size of its workforce.

Historically, the company has allocated all overhead costs using total direct labour hours, but is now considering introducing Activity Based Costing (ABC). Abkaber plc's accountant has produced the following analysis.

	Annual output (units)	*Annual direct labour hours*	*Selling price (£ per unit)*	*Raw material cost (£ per unit)*
Sunshine	2,000	200,000	4,000	400
Roadster	1,600	220,000	6,000	600
Fireball	400	80,000	8,000	900

The three cost drivers that generate overheads are:

Deliveries to retailers	–	the number of deliveries of motorcycles to retail showrooms
Set-ups	–	the number of times the assembly line process is re-set to accommodate a production run of a different type of motorcycle
Purchase orders	–	the number of purchase orders.

The annual cost driver volumes relating to each activity and for each type of motorcycle are as follows:

	Number of deliveries to retailers	*Number of set-ups*	*Number of purchase orders*
Sunshine	100	35	400
Roadster	80	40	300
Fireball	70	25	100

The annual overhead costs relating to these activities are as follows:

	£
Deliveries to retailers	2,400,000
Set-up costs	6,000,000
Purchase orders	3,600,000

All direct labour is paid at £5 per hour. The company holds no stocks.

At a board meeting there was some concern over the introduction of activity based costing.

The finance director argued: 'I very much doubt whether selling the Fireball is viable but I am not convinced that activity based costing would tell us any more than the use of labour hours in assessing the viability of each product.'

The marketing director argued: 'I am in the process of negotiating a major new contract with a motorcycle rental company for the Sunshine model. For such a big order they will not pay our normal prices but we need to at least cover our incremental costs. I am not convinced that activity based costing would achieve this as it merely averages costs for our entire production'.

The managing director argued: 'I believe that activity based costing would be an improvement but it still has its problems. For instance if we carry out an activity many times surely we get better at it and costs fall rather than remain constant. Similarly, some costs are fixed and do not vary either with labour hours or any other cost driver.'

The chairman argued: 'I cannot see the problem. The overall profit for the company is the same no matter which method of allocating overheads we use. It seems to make no difference to me.'

Required:

(a) Calculate the total profit on each of Abkaber plc's three types of product using each of the following methods to attribute overheads:

(i) the existing method based upon labour hours

(ii) activity based costing. **(13 marks)**

(b) Write a report to the directors of Abkaber plc, as its management accountant. The report should:

(i) evaluate the labour hours and the activity based costing methods in the circumstances of Abkaber plc; and

(ii) examine the implications of activity based costing for Abkaber plc, and in so doing evaluate the issues raised by each of the directors.

Refer to your calculations in requirement (a) above where appropriate. **(12 marks)**

(Total: 25 marks)

31 ADMER

Admer owns several home furnishing stores. In each store, consultations, if needed, are undertaken by specialists, who also visit potential customers in their homes, using specialist software to help customers realise their design objectives. Customers visit the store to make their selections from the wide range of goods offered, after which sales staff collect payment and raise a purchase order. Customers then collect their self-assembly goods from the warehouse, using the purchase order as authority to collect. Administration staff process purchase orders and also arrange consultations.

Each store operates an absorption costing system and costs other than the cost of goods sold are apportioned on the basis of sales floor area.

Results for one of Admer's stores for the last three months are as follows:

Department	*Kitchens*	*Bathrooms*	*Dining Rooms*	*Total*
	£	£	£	£
Sales	210,000	112,500	440,000	762,500
Cost of goods sold	63,000	37,500	176,000	276,500
Other costs	130,250	81,406	113,968	325,624
Profit	16,750	(6,406)	150,032	160,376

The management accountant of Admer is concerned that the bathrooms department of the store has been showing a loss for some time, and is considering a proposal to close the bathrooms department in order to concentrate on the more profitable kitchens and dining rooms departments. He has found that other costs for this store for the last three months are made up of:

	£	*Employees*
Sales staff wages	64,800	12
Consultation staff wages	24,960	4
Warehouse staff wages	30,240	6
Administration staff wages	30,624	4
General overheads (light, heat, rates, etc.)	175,000	
	325,624	

He has also collected the following information for the last three months:

Department	*Kitchens*	*Bathrooms*	*Dining Rooms*
Number of items sold	1,000	1,500	4,000
Purchase orders	1,000	900	2,500
Floor area (square metres)	16,000	10,000	14,000
Number of consultations	798	200	250

The management accountant believes that he can use this information to review the store's performance in the last three months from an activity-based costing (ABC) perspective.

Required:

(a) Discuss the management accountant's belief that the information provided can be used in an activity-based costing analysis. **(4 marks)**

(b) Explain and illustrate, using supporting calculations, how an ABC profit statement might be produced from the information provided. Clearly explain the reasons behind your choice of cost drivers. **(8 marks)**

(c) Evaluate and discuss the proposal to close the bathrooms department. **(6 marks)**

(d) Discuss the advantages and disadvantages that may arise for Admer from introducing activity-based costing in its stores. **(7 marks)**

(Total: 25 marks)

32 BML

BML has three product lines: P1, P2 and P3. Since its creation the company has been using a single direct labour cost percentage to assign overhead costs to products.

Despite P3, a relatively new line, attracting additional business, increasing overhead costs and a loss of market share, particularly for P2, a major product, have convinced the management that the costing system is in need of some development. A team, led by the management accountant was established to develop an improved system of costing based on activities. The team spent several weeks collecting data (see tables below) for the different activities and products. For the accounting period in question, given in the tables below is data on BML's three product lines and overhead costs:

	P1	*P2*	*P3*
Production volume	7,500 units	12,500 units	4,000 units
Direct labour cost per unit	£4	£8	£6.40
Material cost per unit	£18	£25	£16
Selling price per unit	£47	£80	£68
Materials movements (in total)	4	25	50
Machine hours per unit	0.5	0.5	0.2
Set-ups (in total)	1	5	10
Proportion of engineering work	30%	20%	50%
Orders packed (in total)	1	7	22

Activities	*Overhead cost*
	£
Material receiving and handling	150,000
Machine maintenance and depreciation	390,000
Set-up labour	18,688
Engineering	100,000
Packing	60,000
Total	718,688

Required:

(a) Calculate the overhead rate and the product unit costs under the existing costing system. **(4 marks)**

(b) Identify for each overhead activity, an appropriate cost driver from the information supplied, and then calculate the product unit costs using a system that assigns overheads on the basis of the use of activities. **(9 marks)**

(c) Comment on the results of the two costing systems in (a) and (b) above. **(7 marks)**

(Total: 20 marks)

33 ABC PLC

ABC plc, a group operating retail stores, is compiling its budget statements for 20X8. In this exercise revenues and costs at each store A, B and C are predicted. Additionally, all central costs of warehousing and a head office are allocated across the three stores in order to arrive at a total cost and net profit of each store operation.

In earlier years the central costs were allocated in total based on the total sales value of each store. But as a result of dissatisfaction expressed by some store managers alternative methods are to be evaluated.

The predicted results before any re-allocation of central costs are as follows:

	A	*B*	*C*
	£000	£000	£000
Sales	5,000	4,000	3,000
Costs of sales	2,800	2,300	1,900
Gross margin	2,200	1,700	1,100
Local operating expenses			
Variable	660	730	310
Fixed	700	600	500
Operating profit	840	370	290

The central costs which are to be allocated are:

	£000
Warehouse costs:	
Depreciation	100
Storage	80
Operating and despatch	120
Delivery	300
Head office:	
Salaries	200
Advertising	80
Establishment	120
Total	1,000

The management accountant has carried out discussions with staff at all locations in order to identify more suitable 'cost drivers' of some of the central costs. So far the following has been revealed.

	A	*B*	*C*
Number of despatches	550	450	520
Total delivery distances (thousand miles)	70	50	90
Storage space occupied (%)	40	30	30

1 An analysis of senior management time revealed that 10% of their time was devoted to warehouse issues with the remainder shared equally between the three stores.

2 It was agreed that the only basis on which to allocate the advertising costs was sales revenue.

3 Establishment costs were mainly occupancy costs of senior management.

This analysis has been carried out against a background of developments in the company, for example, automated warehousing and greater integration with suppliers.

Required:

(a) As the management accountant prepare a report for the management of the group which:

(i) computes the budgeted net profit of each store based on the *sales value* allocation base originally adopted *and* explains 'cost driver', 'volume' and 'complexity' issues in relation to cost allocation commenting on the possible implications of the dissatisfaction expressed **(7 marks)**

(ii) computes the budgeted net profit of each store using the additional information provided, discusses the extent to which an improvement has been achieved in the information on the costs and profitability of running the stores and comments on the results. **(14 marks)**

(b) Explain briefly how regression analysis and coefficient of determination (r^2) could be used in confirming the delivery mileage allocation method used in (a) above. **(4 marks)**

(Total: 25 marks)

34 PARSER LTD

The managing director of Parser Ltd, a small business, is considering undertaking a one-off contract and has asked her inexperienced accountant to advise on what costs are likely to be incurred so that she can price at a profit. The following schedule has been prepared:

Costs per special order:	*Notes*	£
Direct wages	1	28,500
Supervisor costs	2	11,500
General overheads	3	4,000
Machine depreciation	4	2,300
Machine overheads	5	18,000
Materials	6	34,000
		98,300

Notes

1 Direct wages comprise the wages of two employees, particularly skilled in the labour process for this job, who could be transferred from another department to undertake work on the special order. They are fully occupied in their usual department and sub-contracting staff would have to be brought in to undertake the work left behind. Sub-contracting costs would be £32,000 for the period of the work. Different sub-contractors who are skilled in the special order techniques are available to work on the special order and their costs would amount to £31,300.

2 A supervisor would have to work on the special order. The cost of £11,500 is comprised of £8,000 normal payments plus £3,500 additional bonus for working on the special order. Normal payments refer to the fixed salary of the supervisor. In addition, the supervisor would lose incentive payments in his normal work amounting to £2,500. It is not anticipated that any replacement costs relating to the supervisor's work on other jobs would arise.

3 General overheads comprise an apportionment of £3,000 plus an estimate of £1,000 incremental overheads.

4 Machine depreciation represents the normal period cost based on the duration of the contract. It is anticipated that £500 will be incurred in additional machine maintenance costs.

5 Machine overheads (for running costs such as electricity) are charged at £3 per hour. It is estimated that 6,000 hours will be needed for the special order. The machine has 4,000 hours available capacity. The further 2,000 hours required will mean an existing job is taken off the machine resulting in a lost contribution of £2 per hour.

6 Materials represent the purchase cost of 7,500 kg bought some time ago. The materials are no longer used and are unlikely to be wanted in the future except on the special order. The complete stock of materials (amounting to 10,000 kg), or part thereof, could be sold for £4.20 per kg. The replacement cost of material used would be £33,375.

Because the business does not have adequate funds to finance the special order, a bank overdraft amounting to £20,000 would be required for the project duration of three months. The overdraft would be repaid at the end of the period. The company uses a cost of capital of 20% to appraise projects. The bank's overdraft rate is 18%.

The managing director has heard that, for special orders such as this, relevant costing should be used that also incorporate opportunity costs. She has approached you to create a revised costing schedule based on relevant costing principles.

Required:

(a) Briefly explain what is meant by opportunity cost. **(2 marks)**

(b) Adjust the schedule prepared by the accountant to a relevant cost basis, incorporating appropriate opportunity costs. **(11 marks)**

(c) Explain why very Small to Medium-sized Enterprises (SMEs), such as Parser Ltd, might face problems in obtaining appropriate sources of finance. In your answer pay particular attention to problems and issues associated with:

(i) uncertainty concerning the business

(ii) assets available to offer as collateral or security, and

(iii) potential sources of finance for very new SMEs excluding sources from capital markets. **(12 marks)**

(Total: 25 marks)

35 ALBION PLC

The managers of Albion plc are reviewing the operations of the company with a view to making operational decisions for the next month. Details of some of the products manufactured by the company are given below.

Product	*AR2*	*GL3*	*HT4*	*XY5*
Selling price (£/unit)	21.00	28.50	27.30	
Material R2 (kg/unit)	2.0	3.0	3.0	
Material R3 (kg/unit)	2.0	2.2	1.6	3.0
Direct labour (hours/unit)	0.6	1.2	1.5	1.7
Variable production overheads (£/unit)	1.10	1.30	1.10	1.40
Fixed production overheads (£/unit)	1.50	1.60	1.70	1.40
Expected demand for next month (units)	950	1,000	900	

Products AR2, GL3 and HT4 are sold to customers of Albion plc, while Product XY5 is a component that is used in the manufacture of other products. Albion plc manufactures a wide range of products in addition to those detailed above.

Material R2, which is not used in any other of Albion's products, is expected to be in short supply in the next month because of industrial action at a major producer of the material. Albion plc has just received a delivery of 5,500 kg of Material R2 and this is expected to be the amount held in stock at the start of the next month. The company does not expect to be able to obtain further supplies of Material R2 unless it pays a premium price. The normal market price is £2.50 per kg.

Material R3 is available at a price of £2.00 per kg and Albion plc does not expect any problems in securing supplies of this material. Direct labour is paid at a rate of £4.00 per hour.

Folam Limited has recently approached Albion plc with an offer to supply a substitute for Product XY5 at a price of £10.20 per unit. Albion plc would need to pay an annual fee of £50,000 for the right to use this patented substitute.

Required:

(a) Determine the optimum production schedule for Products AR2, GL3 and HT4 for the next month, on the assumption that additional supplies of Material R2 are not purchased. **(8 marks)**

(b) If Albion plc decides to purchase further supplies of Material R2 to meet demand for Products AR2, GL3 and HT4, what should be the maximum price per kg that the company is prepared to pay? **(3 marks)**

(c) Discuss whether Albion plc should manufacture Product XY5 or buy the substitute offered by Folam Limited.

Your answer must be supported by appropriate calculations. **(7 marks)**

(d) Discuss the limitations of marginal costing (variable costing) as a basis for making short-term decisions. **(7 marks)**

(Total: 25 marks)

36 THROUGHPUT

MN Ltd manufactures automated industrial trolleys, known as TRLs. Each TRL sells for £2,000 and the material cost per unit is £600. Labour and variable overhead are £5,500 and £8,000 per week respectively. Fixed production costs are £450,000 per annum and marketing and administrative costs are £265,000 per annum.

The trolleys are made on three different machines. Machine X makes the four frame panels required for each TRL. Its maximum output is 180 frame panels per week. Machine X is old and unreliable and it breaks down from time to time. It is estimated that, on average, between 15 and 20 hours of production are lost per month. Machine Y can manufacture parts for 52 TRLs per week and machine Z, which is old but reasonably reliable, can process and assemble 30 TRLs per week.

The company has recently introduced a just-in-time (JIT) system and it is company policy to hold little work-in-progress and no finished goods stock from week to week. The company operates a 40-hour week, 48 weeks a year (12 months × 4 weeks) but cannot meet demand. The demand for the next year is predicted to be as follows. This is expected to be typical of the demand for the next four years:

Units per week		*Units per week*	
January	30	July	48
February	30	August	45
March	33	September	42
April	36	October	40
May	39	November	33
June	44	December	30

The production manager has suggested that the company replaces machine Z with machine G. Machine G can process 45 TRLs per week and costs £550,000. It is estimated that the variable overhead cost per week will increase by £4,500 if TRLs are made on machine G. The maintenance manager is keen to spend £100,000 on a major overhaul of machine X – he says this will make it 100% reliable.

Required:

(a) Calculate the throughput accounting ratio for MN (defined below) for the key resource for an average hour next year.

$$\text{Throughput accounting ratio} = \frac{\text{Return per factory hour}}{\text{Cost per factory hour}}$$

Where

$$\text{Return per factory hour} = \frac{\text{Sales price - material cost}}{\text{Time on key resource}}$$

(6 marks)

(b) Explain the concept of throughput accounting. **(4 marks)**

(c) To what use might the throughput accounting the ratio be put? Use the case of MN Ltd where appropriate to illustrate your answer. **(4 marks)**

(d) Explain how the concept of contribution in throughput accounting differs from that in marginal costing. **(6 marks)**

(e) If MN Ltd has decided to purchase machine G and spend £100,000 on a major overhaul of machine X, the accountant and the production manager should collaborate to ensure a new focus for monitoring and reporting production activities. What is the new focus? Explain what should be monitored and reported.

(5 marks)

(Total: 25 marks)

37 SPRING PLC

At a recent board meeting of Spring plc, there was a heated discussion on the need to improve financial performance. The Production Director argued that financial performance could be improved if the company replaced its existing absorption costing approach with an activity-based costing system. He argued that this would lead to better cost control and increased profit margins. The Managing Director agreed that better cost control could lead to increased profitability, but informed the meeting that he believed that performance needed to be monitored in both financial and non-financial terms. He pointed out that sales could be lost due to poor product quality or a lack of after-sales service just as easily as by asking too high a price for Spring plc's products. He suggested that while the board should consider introducing activity-based costing, it should also consider ways in which the company could monitor and assess performance on a wide basis.

Required:

(a) Describe the key features of activity-based costing and discuss the advantages and disadvantages of adopting an activity-based approach to cost accumulation.

(14 marks)

(b) Explain the need for the measurement of organisational and managerial performance, giving examples of the range of financial and non-financial performance measures that might be used. **(11 marks)**

(Total: 25 marks)

38 LINEACRE CO

Linacre Co operates an activity-based costing system and has forecast the following information for next year.

Cost Pool	*Cost*	*Cost Driver*	*Number of Drivers*
Production set-ups	£105,000	Set-ups	300
Product testing	£300,000	Tests	1,500
Component supply and storage	£25,000	Component orders	500
Customer orders and delivery	£112,500	Customer orders	1,000

General fixed overheads such as lighting and heating, which cannot be linked to any specific activity, are expected to be £900,000 and these overheads are absorbed on a direct labour hour basis. Total direct labour hours for next year are expected to be 300,000 hours.

Linacre Co expects orders for Product ZT3 next year to be 100 orders of 60 units per order and 60 orders of 50 units per order. The company holds no stocks of Product ZT3 and will need to produce the order requirement in production runs of 900 units. One order for components is placed prior to each production run. Four tests are made during each production run to ensure that quality standards are maintained. The following additional cost and profit information relates to product ZT3:

Component cost:	£1.00 per unit
Direct labour:	10 minutes per unit at £7.80 per hour
Profit mark up:	40% of total unit cost

Required:

(a) Calculate the activity-based recovery rates for each cost pool. **(4 marks)**

(b) Calculate the total unit cost and selling price of Product ZT3. **(9 marks)**

(c) Discuss the reasons why activity-based costing may be preferred to traditional absorption costing in the modern manufacturing environment. **(12 marks)**

(Total: 25 marks)

STANDARD COSTING AND VARIANCE ANALYSIS

39 STANDARD COSTING

(a) Outline the uses of standard costing and discuss the reasons why standards have to be reviewed. **(13 marks)**

(b) Standard costs are a detailed financial expression of organisational objectives. What non-financial objectives might organisations have? In your answer, identify any stakeholder group that may have a non-financial interest. **(12 marks)**

(Total: 25 marks)

40 MATERIAL VARIANCES

A company makes a product using two materials, X and Y, in the production process. A system of standard costing and variance analysis is in operation. The standard material requirement per tonne of mixed output is 60% material X at £30 per tonne and 40% material Y at £45 per tonne, with a standard yield of 90%.

The following information has been gathered for the three months January to March:

	January	*February*	*March*
Output achieved (tonnes)	810	765	900
Actual material input:			
X (tonnes)	540	480	700
Y (tonnes)	360	360	360
Actual material cost (X plus Y) (£)	32,400	31,560	38,600

The actual price per tonne of material Y throughout the January to March period was £45.

Required:

(a) Prepare material variance summaries for each of January, February and March which include yield and mix variances in total plus usage and price variances for each material and in total. **(15 marks)**

(b) Prepare comments for management on each variance including variance trend. **(6 marks)**

(c) Discuss the relevance of the variances calculated above in the light of the following additional information. The company has an agreement to purchase 360 tonnes of material Y each month and the perishable nature of the material means that it must be used in the month of purchase and additional supplies in excess of 360 tonnes per month are not available. **(4 marks)**

(Total: 25 marks)

41 PERSEUS CO LTD

The Perseus Co Ltd a medium sized company, produces a single product in its one overseas factory. For control purposes, a standard costing system was recently introduced and is now in operation.

The standards set for the month of May were as follows:

Production and sales	16,000 units
Selling price (per unit)	£140

Materials

Material 007	6 kilos per unit at £12.25 per kilo
Material XL90	3 kilos per unit at £3.20 per kilo

Labour

4.5 hours per unit at £8.40 per hour

Overheads (all fixed)

£86,400 per month. They are not absorbed into the product costs.

The actual data for the month of May, is as follows.

Produced 15,400 units which were sold at £138.25 each.

Materials

Used 98,560 kilos of material 007 at a total cost of £1,256,640 and used 42,350 kilos of material XL90 at a total cost of £132,979.

Labour

Paid an actual rate of £8.65 per hour to the labour force. The total amount paid out, amounted to £612,766.

Overheads (all fixed)

£96,840

Required:

(a) Prepare a standard costing profit statement, and a profit statement based on actual figures for the month of May. **(6 marks)**

(b) Prepare a statement of the variances which reconciles the actual with the standard profit or loss figure. (Mix and yield variances are not required.) **(9 marks)**

(c) Explain briefly the possible reasons for inter-relationships between material variances and labour variances. **(5 marks)**

(Total: 20 marks)

42 WOODEEZER LTD

Woodeezer Ltd makes quality wooden benches for both indoor and outdoor use. Results have been disappointing in recent years and a new managing director, Peter Beech, was appointed to raise production volumes. After an initial assessment Peter Beech considered that budgets had been set at levels which made it easy for employees to achieve. He argued that employees would be better motivated by setting budgets which challenged them more in terms of higher expected output.

Other than changing the overall budgeted output, Mr. Beech has not yet altered any part of the standard cost card. Thus, the budgeted output and sales for November 20X2 was 4,000 benches and the standard cost card below was calculated on this basis:

		£
Wood	25 kg at £3.20 per kg	80.00
Labour	4 hours at £8 per hour	32.00
Variable overheads	4 hours at £4 per hour	16.00
Fixed overhead	4 hours at £16 per hour	64.00
		192.00
Selling price		220.00
Standard profit		28.00

Overheads are absorbed on the basis of labour hours and the company uses an absorption costing system. There were no stocks at the beginning of November 20X2. Stocks are valued at standard cost.

Actual results for November 20X2 were as follows:

		£
Wood	80,000 kg at £3.50	280,000
Labour	16,000 hours at £7	112,000
Variable overheads		60,000
Fixed overhead		196,000
Total production cost (3,600 benches)		648,000
Closing stock (400 benches at £192)		76,800
		571,200
Sales (3,200 benches)		720,000
Actual profit		148,800

The average monthly production and sales for some years prior to November 20X2 had been 3,400 units and budgets had previously been set at this level. Very few operating variances had historically been generated by the standard costs used.

Mr. Beech has made some significant changes to the operations of the company. However, the other directors are now concerned that Mr. Beech has been too ambitious in raising production targets. Mr. Beech had also changed suppliers of raw materials to improve quality, increased selling prices, begun to introduce less skilled labour, and significantly reduced fixed overheads.

The finance director suggested that an absorption costing system is misleading and that a marginal costing system should be considered at some stage in the future to guide decision-making.

Required:

(a) Prepare an operating statement for November 20X2. This should show all operating variances and should reconcile budgeted and actual profit for the month for Woodeezer Ltd. **(14 marks)**

(b) In so far as the information permits, examine the impact of the operational changes made by Mr. Beech on the profitability of the company. In your answer, consider each of the following:

(i) motivation and budget setting

(ii) possible causes of variances. **(6 marks)**

(c) Re-assess the impact of your comments in part (b), using a marginal costing approach to evaluating the impact of the operational changes made by Mr Beech.

Show any relevant additional calculations to support your arguments. **(5 marks)**

(Total: 25 marks)

43 BICYCLES

It is the quarter-end at a UK company which sells bicycles throughout Europe. One model produced in a dedicated plant had a budgeted column of 20,000 units of production and sales for the quarter. The budgeted/standard manufacturing and selling costs, applicable to this one model, for the quarter are shown in Table 1 below:

Table 1

	Per unit	*Total*
	£	£000
Manufacturing:		
Material	45	900
Labour and variable overhead	15	300
Fixed overhead		1,200
Total manufacturing cost		2,400
Selling:		
Variable overhead	15	300
Fixed overhead		340
Total selling overhead		640

1 The fixed manufacturing overheads are recovered, at a rate per unit, based on the budgeted volume levels.

2 Variable selling overheads are incurred in proportion to units sold.

3 The standard selling price is £190 per unit.

For reporting purposes and identifying stock values the company operates a standard absorption costing system. For the quarter in question the production was 16.800 units, however sales were only 11,800 units.

In order to undertake some basic sales and marketing planning, costs are analysed into variable and fixed elements in order to compute the break-even point and profits at various sales volumes. The Sales Manager had calculated the break-even point as 1,339 units and for the 11,800 units sold in this quarter had predicted a loss. He was surprised therefore to see that the statement of actual profit/loss just produced for the quarter (Table 2) revealed a small profit as follows:

Table 2

Production 16,800 units
Sales 11,800 units

	£000	£000
Sales:		2,242
Manufacturing costs		
Standard cost of production		
16,800 units	2,016	
Less: increase in stock 5,000 units	600	
Cost of sales		1,416
Manufacturing margin		826
Less: Manufacturing variances		
Fixed overhead volume	192	
Expenditure	48	
		240
		586
Selling overheads		
Variable	138	
Fixed	376	
		514
Net profit		72

Required:

(a) Using marginal costing:

(i) illustrate the calculation of the break-even point undertaken by the Sales Manager

(ii) calculate the loss predicted by the Sales Manager based on the actual units sold of 11,800.

For part (a) use the budgeted/standard costs given for the quarter in Table 1. **(4 marks)**

(b) (i) Demonstrate how the value of the manufacturing fixed overhead volume variance, shown in Table 2, has been computed and briefly explain its significance. **(5 marks)**

(ii) Calculate the expenditure and volume variances which apply to the selling overheads in this quarter. **(3 marks)**

(c) Reconcile the loss calculated in (a) (ii) with the profit for the quarter shown in Table 2 indicating all relevant differences. Briefly explain why an actual profit is revealed when a loss was anticipated by the Sales Manager. **(8 marks)**

(Total: 20 marks)

44 PAN-OCEAN CHEMICALS

Pan-Ocean Chemicals has one product which requires inputs from three types of material to produce batches of product Synthon. Standard cost details for a single batch are shown below:

	Materials		*Labour*	
Material type	*Standard kgs*	*Standard price per kg (£)*	*Standard hours*	*Standard rate per hour (£)*
S1	8	0.3	1	5.00
S2	5	0.5		
S3	3	0.4		

A standard loss of 10% of input is expected. Actual production was 15,408 kgs for the previous week. Details of the materials used were:

Actual material used (kg)	
S1	8,284
S2	7,535
S3	3,334

Total labour cost for the week was £6,916 for 1,235 hours worked.

Required:

(a) Calculate:

(i) total material mix, yield and usage variances **(9 marks)**

(ii) labour rate and efficiency variances. **(2 marks)**

(b) Explain why the sum of the mix variances for materials measured in kg should be zero. **(3 marks)**

(c) Write a report to management which explains and interprets your results in part (a). The report should pay particular attention to:

– explaining what is meant by mix and yield variances in respect of materials, and

– possible reasons for all the results you have derived. **(11 marks)**

(Total: 25 marks)

45 CARAT

Carat plc, a premium food manufacturer, is reviewing operations for a three-month period of 20X3. The company operates a standard marginal costing system and manufactures one product, ZP, for which the following standard revenue and cost data per unit of product is available:

Selling price	£12.00
Direct material A	2.5 kg at £1.70 per kg
Direct material B	1.5 kg at £1.20 per kg
Direct labour	0.45 hrs at £6.00 per hour

Fixed production overheads for the three-month period were expected to be £62,500.

Actual data for the three-month period was as follows:

Sales and production	48,000 units of ZP were produced and sold for £580,800.
Direct material A	121,951 kg were used at a cost of £200,000.
Direct material B	67,200 kg were used at a cost of £84,000.
Direct labour	Employees worked for 18,900 hours, but 19,200 hours were paid at a cost of £117,120.
Fixed production overheads	£64,000

Budgeted sales for the three-month period were 50,000 units of Product ZP.

Required:

(a) Calculate the following variances:

(i) sales volume contribution and sales price variances

(ii) price, mix and yield variances for each material

(iii) labour rate, labour efficiency and idle time variances. **(8 marks)**

(b) Prepare an operating statement that reconciles budgeted gross profit to actual gross profit with each variance clearly shown. **(5 marks)**

(c) Suggest possible explanations for the following variances:

(i) material price, mix and yield variances for material A

(ii) labour rate, labour efficiency and idle time variances. **(5 marks)**

(d) Critically discuss the types of standard used in standard costing and their effect on employee motivation. **(7 marks)**

(Total: 25 marks)

46 FOOD MANUFACTURER

A food manufacturer specialises in the production of frozen cakes and sweet products, selling mainly to supermarkets. The following monthly budget applies to one of its products.

Original budget

	£000	£000
Sales		1,000
Costs:		
Ingredients	400	
Labour and energy	100	
Fixed overheads	300	
		800
Profit		200

For the ingredients, a standard quantity of 5 kg per pack is required; a standard price of 40p per kg applies in the original budget.

Considerable attention has been given to increasing the market share of this product whilst attempting to maintain its profitability. Consequently, since the preparation of the budget the management team implemented some changes to the manufacture and sale of this product. These changes were as follows:

(i) The product was budgeted to sell for £5.00 per pack but, to promote sales, a price reduction on all sales to £4.50 per pack was made.

(ii) The supplier of ingredients was changed and this secured a price reduction to 37.5p per kg on all ingredient supplies in return for a long-term contract.

(iii) The method of working was changed in order to reduce the direct labour and energy costs which are regarded as variable.

All of the above changes applied for the whole of the month just ended and are reflected in the actual results shown below. The management intend, however, to use the original budget, for both cost and volume, as a reference point until the effect of the changes has been evaluated.

The following actual results have just been reported for the month:

Actual results

	£000	£000
Sales		1,080
Costs:		
Ingredients	520	
Labour and energy	110	
Fixed overheads	340	
		970
Profit		110

Required:

(a) Prepare a flexible budget (for the actual quantity sold in the month just ended) based on the original budgeted unit costs and selling price. **(3 marks)**

(b) Using variances, reconcile the original budget profit with the actual profit. You should use a contribution approach to variance analysis. **(9 marks)**

(c) Provide a commentary on the variances you have produced. Within this commentary refer to possible interrelationships between the variances and how the level of fixed overheads may be reduced. **(8 marks)**

(Total: 20 marks)

47 LINSIL

Linsil has produced the following operating statement reconciling budgeted and actual gross profit for the last three months, based on actual sales of 122,000 units of its single product:

Operating statement	£	£	£
Budgeted gross profit			800,000
Budgeted fixed production overhead			352,000
Budgeted contribution			1,152,000
Sales volume contribution variance		19,200	
Sales price variance		(61,000)	
			(41,800)
Actual sales less standard variable cost of sales			1,110,200
Planning variances			
Variable cost variances	**Favourable**	**Adverse**	
Direct material price		23,570	
Direct material usage	42,090		
Direct labour rate		76,128	
Direct labour efficiency		203,333	
	42,090	303,031	(260,941)
Operational variances			
Variable cost variances	**Favourable**	**Adverse**	
Direct material price		31,086	
Direct material usage	14,030		
Direct labour rate		19,032	
Direct labour efficiency	130,133		
	144,163	50,118	94,045
Actual contribution			943,304
Budgeted fixed production overhead		(352,000)	
Fixed production overhead expenditure variance		27,000	
Actual fixed production overhead			(325,000)
Actual gross profit			618,304

The standard direct costs and selling price applied during the three-month period and the actual direct costs and selling price for the period were as follows:

	Standard	*Actual*
Selling price (£/unit)	31.50	31.00
Direct material usage (kg/unit)	3.00	2.80
Direct material price (£/kg)	2.30	2.46
Direct labour efficiency (hrs/unit)	1.25	1.30
Direct labour rate (£/hr)	12.00	12.60

After the end of the three-month period and prior to the preparation of the above operating statement, it was decided to revise the standard costs retrospectively to take account of the following:

1 A 3% increase in the direct material price per kilogram

2 A labour rate increase of 4%

3 The standard for labour efficiency had anticipated buying a new machine leading to a 10% decrease in labour hours; instead of buying a new machine, existing machines had been improved, giving an expected 5% saving in material usage.

Required:

(a) Using the information provided, demonstrate how each planning and operational variance in the operating statement has been calculated. **(11 marks)**

(b) Calculate direct labour and direct material variances based on the standard cost data applied during the three-month period. **(4 marks)**

(c) Explain the significance of separating variances into planning and operational elements, using the operating statement above to illustrate your answer. **(5 marks)**

(d) Discuss the factors to be considered in deciding whether a variance should be investigated. **(5 marks)**

(Total: 25 marks)

48 MERMUS PLC

Mermus plc is comparing budget and actual data for the last three months.

	Budget		*Actual*	
	£	£	£	£
Sales		950,000		922,500
Cost of sales				
Raw materials	133,000		130,500	
Direct labour	152,000		153,000	
Variable production overheads	100,700		96,300	
Fixed production overheads	125,400		115,300	
		511,100		495,100
		438,900		427,400

The budget was prepared on the basis of 95,000 units produced and sold, but actual production and sales for the three-month period were 90,000 units.

Mermus uses standard costing and absorbs fixed production overheads on a machine hour basis. A total of 28,500 standard machine hours were budgeted. A total of 27,200 machine hours were actually used in the three-month period.

Required:

(a) Prepare a revised budget at the new level of activity using a flexible budgeting approach. **(4 marks)**

(b) Calculate the following:

(i) raw material total cost variance;

(ii) direct labour total cost variance;

(iii) fixed overhead efficiency variance;

(iv) fixed overhead capacity variance;

(v) fixed overhead expenditure variance. **(8 marks)**

(c) Suggest possible explanations for the following variances:

(i) raw materials total cost variance;

(ii) fixed overhead efficiency variance;

(iii) fixed overhead expenditure variance. **(6 marks)**

(d) Explain three key purposes of a budgeting system. **(7 marks)**

(Total: 25 marks)

49 BRK

BRK Co operates an absorption costing system and sells three products, B, R and K which are substitutes for each other. The following standard selling price and cost data relate to these three products:

Product	*Selling price per unit*	*Direct material per unit*	*Direct labour per unit*
B	£14.00	3.00 kg at £1.80 per kg	0.5 hrs at £6.50 per hour
R	£15.00	1.25 kg at £3.28 per kg	0.8 hrs at £6.50 per hour
K	£18.00	1.94 kg at £2.50 per kg	0.7 hrs at £6.50 per hour

Budgeted fixed production overhead for the last period was £81,000. This was absorbed on a machine hour basis. The standard machine hours for each product and the budgeted levels of production and sales for each product for the last period are as follows:

Product	*B*	*R*	*K*
Standard machine hours per unit	0.3 hrs	0.6 hrs	0.8 hrs
Budgeted production and sales (units)	10,000	13,000	9,000

Actual volumes and selling prices for the three products in the last period were as follows:

Product	*B*	*R*	*K*
Actual selling price per unit	£14.50	£15.50	£19.00
Actual production and sales (units)	9,500	13,500	8,500

Required:

(a) Calculate the following variances for overall sales for the last period:

(i) sales price variance;

(ii) sales volume profit variance;

(iii) sales mix profit variance;

(iv) sales quantity profit variance and reconcile budgeted profit for the period to actual sales less standard cost. **(13 marks)**

(b) Discuss the significance of the sales mix profit variance and comment on whether useful information would be obtained by calculating mix variances for each of these three products. **(4 marks)**

(c) Describe the essential elements of a standard costing system and explain how quantitative analysis can assist in the preparation of standard costs. **(8 marks)**

(Total: 25 marks)

BUDGETING, BUDGETARY CONTROL AND DECISION-MAKING

50 ALL PREMIER SERVICES PLC

All Premier Services plc is a fee charging hospital that has two specialist wards, X and Y. A third ward, Z, is used for patients who are well enough to leave Wards X and Y but who require a short period of hospital rest before being discharged. It is intended that Ward Z will be only occupied by patients transferred from the other wards. Budgeted details relating to the wards are as follows (fixed and variable costs are for a complete week).

Ward:	*X*	*Y*	*Z*
Number of beds	60	40	45
Budgeted fee per bed per night (£)	225	200	170
Budgeted occupancy %	65	80	100
Budgeted costs:		£	
Fixed overheads		127,300	
Variable overheads		42,412	

Fixed overheads are allocated to the wards on the basis of the number of beds available in each ward. Variable overheads are allocated to beds in proportion to the fees earned per ward.

Required:

(a) (i) Prepare a budgeted profit/loss statement (based on one week) for each of the wards and for the three wards combined. Calculate the total cost incurred per bed occupied per week (seven nights). **(5 marks)**

(ii) A proposal has been put forward to increase the number of beds in ward Z to 75. This proposal would be expected to increase occupancy in wards X and Y to 80% and 95%, respectively. Budgeted occupancy in ward Z will remain at 100%. It is expected that total variable overheads would increase to £57,881 as a result.

Evaluate this proposal on the same basis as your answer to part (a) (i).

(5 marks)

(b) (i) In making decision about expanding Ward Z, comment on the fact that it is only occupied by patients from wards X and Y. **(2 marks)**

(ii) Briefly assess the relevance of the allocation bases for fixed and variable overheads. **(3 marks)**

(c) Describe the characteristics of a responsibility accounting system and discuss what factors exist in non-profit organisations that make responsibility accounting difficult to implement. **(10 marks)**

(Total: 25 marks)

51 ACRED LIMITED

Acred Ltd manufactures a single product. It is preparing monthly budgets for the six months from July to December 20X4. The following standard revenue and cost data is available:

Selling price	£12.00 per unit
Materials	2 kg per unit at £2.40 per kg
Labour	£1.80 per unit
Direct expenses	£1.20 per unit

Sales in June 20X4 and July 20X4 are forecast to be 10,000 units in each month. As a direct result of marketing expenditure of £95,000 in August 20X4, sales are expected to be 11,000 units in August 20X4 and to increase by 1,000 units in each month from September to December. Sales after December 20X4 are expected to remain at the December 20X4 level.

25% of sales are paid for when they occur and 75% of sales are paid for in the month following sale. Stocks of finished goods at the end of each month are required to be 20% of the expected sales for the following month. Stocks of materials at the end of each month are required to be 50% of the materials required for the following month's production.

Materials are paid for in the month following purchase. Labour and direct expenses are paid for in the month in which they occur. Overheads for production, administration and distribution will be £34,000 per month, including depreciation of £12,000 per month. These overheads are payable in the month in which they occur. Acred Ltd has a £750,000 bank loan at 8% per annum on which it pays interest twice per year, in March and September.

The cash balance at the end of June 20X4 is expected to be £50,000.

Required:

(a) Prepare the following budgets for Acred Ltd on a month by month basis for the six month period from July to December 20X4:

(i) production budget (units)

(ii) cash budget. **(13 marks)**

(b) Critically discuss the relative merits of periodic budgeting and continuous budgeting. **(7 marks)**

(c) Discuss the consequences of budget bias (budgetary slack) for cost control. **(5 marks)**

(Total: 25 marks)

52 PRIVATE HOSPITAL

A private hospital is organised into separate medical units which offer specialised nursing care (e.g. maternity unit, paediatric unit). Figures for the paediatric unit for the year to 31 May 20X3 have just become available. For the year in question the paediatric unit charged patients £200 per patient day for nursing care and £4.4m in revenue was earned.

Costs of running the unit consist of variable costs, direct staffing costs and allocated fixed costs. The charges for variable costs such as catering and laundry are based on the number of patient days spent in hospital. Staffing costs are established from the personnel requirements applicable to particular levels of patient days. Charges for fixed costs such as security administration etc, are based on bed capacity, currently 80 beds.

The number of beds available to be occupied is regarded as bed capacity and this is agreed and held constant for the whole year. There was an agreement that a bed capacity of 80 beds would apply to the paediatric unit for the 365 days of the year to 31 May 20X3.

The tables below show the variable, staffing and fixed costs applicable to the paediatric unit for the year to 31 May 20X3.

Variable costs (based on patient days)

	£
Catering	450,000
Laundry	150,000
Pharmacy	500,000
	1,100,000

Staffing costs

Each speciality recruits its own supervisors and assistants. The staffing requirements for the paediatric unit are based on the actual patient day, see the following table:

Patient days per annum	*Supervisors*	*Nurses*	*Assistants*
Up to 20,500	4	10	20
20,500 to 23,000	4	13	24
Over 23,000	4	15	28

The annual costs of employment are: supervisors £22,000 each, nurses £16,000 each and assistants £12,000 each.

Fixed costs (based on bed capacity)

	£
Administration	850,000
Security	80,000
Rent and property	720,000
	1,650,000

During the year to 31 May 20X3 the paediatric unit operated at 100% occupancy (i.e. all 80 beds occupied) for 100 days of the year. In fact the demand on these days was for at least 20 beds more.

As a consequence of this, in the budget for the following year to 31 May 20X4, an increase in the bed capacity has been agreed. 20 extra beds will be contracted for the whole of the year. It is assumed that the 100 beds will be fully occupied for 100 days, rather than being restricted to 80 beds on those days. An increase of 10% in employment costs for the year to 31 May 20X4, due to wage rate rises, will occur for all personnel. The revenue per patient day, all other cost factors and the remaining occupancy will be the same as the year to 31 May 20X3.

Required:

(a) Determine for the year to 31 May 20X3, the actual number of patient-days, the bed occupancy percentage, the net profit/loss and the break-even number(s) of patient days for the paediatric unit. **(6 marks)**

(b) Determine the budget for the year to 31 May 20X4 showing the revised number of patient-days, the bed occupancy percentage, the net profit/loss and the number of patient-days required to achieve the same profit/loss as computed in (a) above. **(5 marks)**

(c) Comment on your findings from (a) and (b) offering advice to the management of the unit. **(6 marks)**

(d) A business or operating unit can have both financial and social objectives and at times these can be in conflict. Briefly explain and give an example. **(3 marks)**

(Total: 20 marks)

53 PUBLIC SECTOR ORGANISATION

A public sector organisation is extending its budgetary control and responsibility accounting system to all departments. One such department concerned with public health and welfare is called 'Homecare'. The department consists of staff who visit elderly 'clients' in their homes to support them with their basic medical and welfare needs.

A monthly cost control report is to be sent to the department manager, a copy of which is also passed to a Director who controls a number of departments. In the system, which is still being refined, the budget was set by the Director and the manager had not been consulted over the budget or the use of the monthly control report.

Shown below is the first month's cost control report for the Homecare department

Cost Control Report - Homecare Department
Month ending May 20X0

	Budget	*Actual*	*(Overspend)/ Underspend*
Visits	10,000	12,000	(2,000)
	£	£	£
Department expenses:			
Supervisory salary	2,000	2,125	(125)
Wages (Permanent staff)	2,700	2,400	300
Wages (Casual staff)	1,500	2,500	(1,000)
Office equipment depreciation	500	750	(250)
Repairs to equipment	200	20	180
Travel expenses	1,500	1,800	(300)
Consumables	4,000	6,000	(2,000)
Administration and telephone	1,000	1,200	(200)
Allocated administrative costs	2,000	3,000	(1,000)
	15,400	19,795	(4,395)

In addition to the manager and permanent members of staff, appropriately qualified casual staff are appointed on a week to week basis to cope with fluctuations in demand. Staff use their own transport, and travel expenses are reimbursed. There is a central administration overhead charge over all departments. Consumables consist of materials which are used by staff to care for clients. Administration and telephone are costs of keeping in touch with the staff who often operate from their own homes.

As a result of the report, the Director sent a memo to the manager of the Homecare department pointing out that the department must spend within its funding allocation and that any spending more than 5% above budget on any item would not be tolerated. The Director requested an immediate explanation for the serious overspend.

You work as the assistant to the Directorate Management Accountant. On seeing the way the budget system was developing, he made a note of points he would wish to discuss and develop further, but was called away before these could be completed.

Required:

(a) Develop and explain the issues concerning the budgetary control and responsibility accounting system which are likely to be raised by the management accountant. You should refer to the way the budget was prepared, the implications of a 20% increase in the number of visits, the extent of controllability of costs, the implications of the funding allocation, social aspects and any other points you think appropriate. You may include numerical illustrations and comment on specific costs, but you are not required to reproduce the cost control report. **(14 marks)**

(b) Briefly explain Zero-Based Budgeting (ZBB), describe how (in a situation such as that above) it might be implemented, and how as a result it could improve the budget setting procedure. **(6 marks)**

(Total: 20 marks)

54 ZERO BASED BUDGETING

(a) Explain why Zero Based Budgeting might be a useful tool to employ to ensure that budgetary requirements are kept up to date. **(4 marks)**

(b) Describe the steps needed to be undertaken in order to implement a Zero Based Budgeting system in respect of:

- the questioning of why expenditure needs to be incurred
- how a decision is made as to which activities should be provided with a budget, and
- what questions should be asked when budgeted activities need to be ranked to allocate scarce resources. **(8 marks)**

(c) Critically assess the use of Zero Based Budgeting as a tool that might be used to motivate employees. **(6 marks)**

(d) Explain the advantages of encouraging employee participation in budget setting. **(7 marks)**

(Total: 25 marks)

55 ROLLING BUDGETS

A company operates a system of quarterly rolling budgets. Budgets for the next three quarters have been prepared. The figures below reflect the likely cost behaviour of each element of cost. Quarter four is being developed based on these budgets and other information available.

Budget Quarters 1 to 3

	Q1 (000)	*Q2* (000)	*Q3* (000)
Activity:			
Sales (units)	18	34	30
Production (units)	20	40	30
Costs:	£000	£000	£000
Direct materials	50	100	75
Production labour	180	280	230
Factory overheads (excluding indirect labour)	170	200	185
Administration	30	30	30
Selling and distribution	29	37	35

In the current planning stage for quarter four, flexible budgets are to be developed for low, most likely and high sales volumes (38,000, 44,000 and 50,000 units respectively). The company wishes to have a closing stock (end of quarter four) equal to the opening stock for quarter one. Management will therefore adjust the production levels to fall in line with this policy.

Cost structures as for quarters one to three will apply to quarter four except that:

(i) raw material prices are expected to rise by 10%

(ii) production labour rates will increase by 2.5%. However, management have declared that all labour rate increases must be matched by increased efficiency so that labour costs (both total fixed and variable per unit) are unaltered.

(iii) a quarterly bonus payment, of 50% of the variable labour cost per unit, will apply for all production above 40,000 units.

(iv) fixed factory overheads and fixed selling and distribution expenses will rise by 5%.

The expected selling price per unit is £18. Stock is valued at full factory cost of £13 per unit. This has been established using absorption principles and based on long run cost and capacity predictions. Small fluctuations in cost prices or volumes will not cause this unit cost to be amended.

Required:

(a) Explain what is meant by a 'rolling budget' and what additional benefit may be claimed for this compared to the annual style of budget. **(4 marks)**

(b) Summarise the variable cost per unit and the total fixed cost, for each cost heading, that will apply to quarter four, for production below 40,000 units. **(6 marks)**

(c) Prepare detailed flexed budget profit statements for quarter four under the separate assumptions of low, most likely and high levels of sales and corresponding production volumes. **(8 marks)**

(d) Produce in *summary form only* a statement of the likely change in profit for quarter four if management change their policy on stock levels so as to manufacture the same volume as the forecast sales for the quarter. Comment on the reason for the profit change and how this might motivate management regarding production levels in the future. **(7 marks)**

(Total: 25 marks)

56 STORRS PLC

It is mid-June and the new managing director of Storrs plc is reviewing sales forecasts for Quarter 3 of 20X3, which begins on 1 July, and for Quarter 4. The company manufactures garden furniture and experiences seasonal variations in sales, which has made forecasting difficult in the past. Sales for the last two calendar years were as follows:

Year	*Quarter 1*	*Quarter 2*	*Quarter 3*	*Quarter 4*
20X1	£2,700,000	£3,500,000	£3,400,000	£3,000,000
20X2	£3,100,000	£3,900,000	£3,600,000	£3,400,000

Sales in Quarter 1 of 20X3 were £3,600,000. There is two weeks to go until the end of Quarter 2 and the managing director of Storrs plc is confident that it will achieve sales of £4,400,000 in this quarter.

The existing sales forecasts for the two remaining quarters of the year were made by the sales director (who has been with the company for several years) during last year's budget-setting process. These forecasts are £3,800,000 for Quarter 3 and £3,600,000 for Quarter 4. Budgets within Storrs plc have traditionally been prepared and agreed by the directors of the company before being implemented by junior managers.

As a basis for revising the sales forecasts for the two remaining quarters of 20X3, the management accountant of Storrs plc has begun to apply time series analysis in order to identify the seasonal variations in sales. He has so far calculated the following centred moving averages, using a base period of four quarters.

Year	*Quarter 1*	*Quarter 2*	*Quarter 3*	*Quarter 4*
20X1			£3,200,000	£3,300,000
20X2	£3,375,000	£3,450,000	£3,562,500	£3,687,500

Required:

(a) Using the sales information and centred moving averages provided, and assuming an additive model, forecast the sales of Storrs plc for Quarter 3 and Quarter 4 of 20X3, and comment on the sales forecasts made by the sales director.

(Note that you are NOT required to use regression analysis) **(8 marks)**

(b) Discuss the limitations of the sales forecasting method used in part (a). **(5 marks)**

(c) Discuss the relative merits of top-down and bottom-up approaches to budget setting. **(12 marks)**

(Total: 25 marks)

57 BUDGET BEHAVIOUR

For many organisations in both the private and public sectors the annual budget is the basis of much internal management information. When preparing and using budgets, however, management and the accountant must be aware of their behavioural implications.

Required:

(a) Briefly discuss four purposes of budgets. **(8 marks)**

(b) Explain the behavioural factors which should be borne in mind and the difficulties of applying them in the process of budgeting and budgetary control. **(12 marks)**

(Total: 20 marks)

58 NOT-FOR-PROFIT ORGANISATIONS

Required:

(a) Discuss how costing information and principles may be applied in a not-for-profit organisation in the following areas:
  (i) the selection of cost units;
  (ii) the use of performance measures to measure output and quality;
  (iii) the comparison of planned and actual performance. **(10 marks)**

(b) Discuss the key features of zero-based budgeting and explain how it may be applied in a not-for-profit organisation. **(8 marks)**

(c) Briefly discuss how activity-based budgeting might be introduced into a manufacturing organisation and the advantages that might arise from the use of activity-based budgeting in such an organisation. **(7 marks)**

(Total: 25 marks)

59 THORNE CO

Thorne Co values, advertises and sells residential property on behalf of its customers. The company has been in business for only a short time and is preparing a cash budget for the first four months of 2006. Expected sales of residential properties are as follows.

	2005	*2006*	*2006*	*2006*	*2006*
Month	December	January	February	March	April
Units sold	10	10	15	25	30

The average price of each property is £180,000 and Thorne Co charges a fee of 3% of the value of each property sold. Thorne Co receives 1% in the month of sale and the remaining 2% in the month after sale. The company has nine employees who are paid on a monthly basis. The average salary per employee is £35,000 per year. If more than 20 properties are sold in a given month, each employee is paid in that month a bonus of £140 for each additional property sold.

Variable expenses are incurred at the rate of 0.5% of the value of each property sold and these expenses are paid in the month of sale. Fixed overheads of £4,300 per month are paid in the month in which they arise. Thorne Co pays interest every three months on a loan of £200,000 at a rate of 6% per year. The last interest payment in each year is paid in December.

An outstanding tax liability of £95,800 is due to be paid in April. In the same month Thorne Co intends to dispose of surplus vehicles, with a net book value of £15,000, for £20,000. The cash balance at the start of January 2006 is expected to be a deficit of £40,000.

Required:

(a) Prepare a monthly cash budget for the period from January to April 2006. Your budget must clearly indicate each item of income and expenditure, and the opening and closing monthly cash balances. **(10 marks)**

(b) Discuss the factors to be considered by Thorne Co when planning ways to invest any cash surplus forecast by its cash budgets. **(5 marks)**

(c) Discuss the advantages and disadvantages to Thorne Co of using overdraft finance to fund any cash shortages forecast by its cash budgets. **(5 marks)**

(d) Explain how the Baumol model can be employed to reduce the costs of cash management and discuss whether the Baumol cash management model may be of assistance to Thorne Co for this purpose. **(5 marks)**

(Total: 25 marks)

PERFORMANCE MEASUREMENT

60 PERFORMANCE APPRAISAL

Required:

(a) Identify the types of responsibility centres used in responsibility accounting and discuss how the performance of each responsibility centre type might be measured, including in your discussion examples of controllable and non-controllable factors. **(12 marks)**

(b) Critically discuss whether return on investment or residual income should be used to assess managerial performance in an investment centre. **(13 marks)**

(Total: 25 marks)

61 WINDERMERE

Windermere operates a divisional organisation structure. The performance of each division is assessed on the basis of the Return on Capital Employed (ROCE) that it generates.

For this purpose the ROCE of a division is calculated by dividing its 'trading profit' for the year by the 'book value of net assets' that it is using at the end of the year. Trading profit is the profit earned excluding non-recurring items. Book value of net assets excludes any cash, bank account balance or overdraft because Windermere plc uses a common bank account (under the control of its head office) for all divisions.

At the start of every year each division is given a target ROCE. If the target is achieved or exceeded than the divisional executives are given a large salary bonus at the end of the year.

In 20X1, Windermere plc's division A was given a target ROCE of 15%. On 15 December 20X1 A's divisional manager receives a forecast that trading profit for 20X1 would be £120,000 and net assets employed at the end of 20X1 would be £820,000. This would give an ROCE of 14.6% which is slightly below A's target.

The divisional manager immediately circulates a memorandum to his fellow executives inviting proposals to deal with the problem. By the end of the day he has received the following proposals from those executives (all of whom will lose their salary bonus if the ROCE target is not achieved):

(1) from the Works Manager: that £100,000 should be invested in new equipment resulting in cost savings of £18,000 per year over the next fifteen years;

(2) from the Chief Accountant: that payment of a £42,000 trade debt owed to a supplier due on 16 December 20X1 be deferred until 1 January 20X2. This would result in a £1,000 default penalty becoming immediately due;

(3) from the Sales Manager: that £1,500 additional production expenses be incurred and paid in order to bring completion of an order forward to 29 December 20X1 from its previous scheduled date of 3 January 20X2. This would allow the customer to be invoiced in December, thereby boosting 20X1 profits by £6,000, but would not accelerate customer payment due on 1 February 20X2.

(4) From the Head of Internal Audit: That a regional plant producing a particular product be closed allowing immediate sale for £120,000 of premises having a book value of £90,000. This would result in £50,000 immediate redundancy payments and a reduction in profit of £12,600 per year over the next fifteen years.

(a) **You are required** to assess each of the above four proposals having regard to:

(i) their effect on divisional performance in 20X1 and 20X2 as measured by Windermere plc's existing criteria,

(ii) their intrinsic commercial merits,

(iii) any ethical matters that you consider relevant.

You should ignore taxation and inflation. **(20 marks)**

(b) **You are required** to discuss what action Windermere plc's Finance Director should take when the situation at division A and the above four proposals are brought to his attention. **(5 marks)**

(Total: 25 marks)

62 KDS LTD

KDS Ltd is an engineering company which is organised for management purposes in the form of several autonomous divisions. The performance of each division is currently measured by calculation of its return on capital employed (ROCE). KDS Ltd's existing accounting policy is to calculate ROCE by dividing the net assets of each division at the end of the year into the operating profit generated by the division during the year. Cash is excluded from net assets since all divisions share a bank account controlled by KDS Ltd's head office. Depreciation is on a straight-line basis.

The divisional management teams are paid a performance-related bonus conditional upon achievement of a 15% ROCE target. On 20 December 20X5 the divisional managers were provided with performance forecasts for 20X5 which included the following:

Forecast	*Net assets at 31 December 20X5*	*20X5 operating profit*	*ROCE*
	£	£	
Division K	4,400,000	649,000	14.75%
Division D	480,000	120,000	25.00%

Subsequently, the manager of Division K invited members of her management team to offer advice. The responses she received included the following:

From the divisional administrator:

'We can achieve our 20X5 target by deferring payment of a £90,000 trade debt payable on 20 December until 1 January. I should add that we will thereby immediately incur a £2,000 late payment penalty.'

From the works manager:

'We should replace a number of our oldest machine tools (which have nil book value) at a cost of £320,000. The new equipment will have a life of eight years and generate cost savings of £76,000 per year. The new equipment can be on site and operational by 31 December 20X5.'

From the financial controller:

'The existing method of performance appraisal is unfair. We should ask head office to adopt residual income (RI) as the key performance indicator, using the company's average 12% cost of money for a finance charge.'

Required:

(a) Compare and appraise the proposals of the divisional administrator and the works manager, having regard to the achievement of the ROCE performance target in 20X5 and to any longer term factors you think relevant. **(9 marks)**

(b) Explain the extent to which you agree or disagree with the financial controller's proposal. **(7 marks)**

(c) Explain the value and use of non-financial performance measures. **(4 marks)**

(Total: 20 marks)

63 PROPOSALS FOR DIVISION X

Division X is in a stable market. The first draft of its plan for the next three years is regarded as unacceptable to group management because it shows a slow decline in profit and return on investment:

	Year 1	*Year 2*	*Year 3*
	£m	£m	£m
Profit before interest and tax (PBIT)	3.0	2.7	2.4
Asset base (at beginning of year)	24.0	25.0	26.0

Proposals which may improve the situation in the next three years are being discussed; ONLY ONE can be accepted because of cash limitations. Projects are evaluated with a 10% required return on investment. These proposed projects are shown below.

(i) **Special-purpose machine**

Capital expenditure in years 1 and 2, followed by operating cash flow in year 3:

Year 1	*Year 2*	*Year 3*	*NPV*
£m	£m	£m	£m
-0.5	-0.5	2.0	0.634

(ii) **R&D project**

Revenue expenditure in years 1 and 2, followed by operating cash flow in year 3:

Year 1	*Year 2*	*Year 3*	*NPV*
£m	£m	£m	£m
-1.0	-1.0	4.0	1.269

(iii) **Advertising**

This can be done in each year if required. Each annual campaign costs £1m, but produces additional contributions of £0.4m in the year of the campaign and £1.1m in the subsequent year. A decision has been made to run annual campaigns in years 1 and 2 only. The combined cash flows are:

Year 1	*Year 2*	*Year 3*	*NPV*
£m	£m	£m	£m
-0.6	+0.5	+1.1	0.694

Managers are currently evaluated on return on investment (ROI), and are paid bonuses when this reaches or exceeds 10%. At 10% ROI the manager of division X will receive 25% of his salary of £50,000 pa. For each 1 % increase in ROI above 10%, and *pro rata*, he will receive an additional 2.5% of basic salary with an upper bonus limit of 50% of salary for that year.

Thus, for the first draft of the plan, the bonus based on the ROI has been correctly calculated as:

	Year 1	*Year 2*	*Year 3*
Bonus	£15,625	£13,500	£ zero

Calculations ignore tax and depreciation. The asset base represents the assets employed in the division at the beginning of each year, and excludes cash balances which are transferred to the group, and is used for the calculation of residual income (Rl) and ROI.

Required:

(a) Calculate the ROI, and the manager's bonus each year for the three alternative proposals. Comment on the effects of the bonus system on the manager's choice of project. **(14 marks)**

(b) A proposal is under consideration to change the bonus scheme to 2% of residual income (RI) with a limit of 50% of salary. A 10% rate of interest would be used in the calculation of RI.

For the plan including the special-purpose machine, the bonus, based on the Rl, has been correctly calculated as:

	Year 1	*Year 2*	*Year 3*
Bonus	£12,000	£3,000	£25,000

Required:

(i) Calculate the RI and bonuses each year, both for the first draft of the plan and for the R&D and Advertising alternatives.

(ii) Comment on whether the proposed revised bonus system would influence the manager's choice of project in a different way from that based on the ROI.

(10 marks)

(c) Explain whether the manager's project choices are beneficial to the company, under the current bonus scheme and under the proposed bonus scheme. If not, what would be the requirements for a bonus scheme which would produce better decision-making?

(6 marks)

(Total: 30 marks)

Section 2

SCENARIO-BASED QUESTIONS

64 FRANTIC LTD

Frantic Ltd is a specialist car manufacturer and is a member of a group of companies that provides a range of automobile products and services. It is currently facing difficulties in the management of its working capital and the financial controller of Frantic Ltd is to investigate the situation with a view to optimising creditor payments, stock ordering and debtor discounts to ease projected cash flow problems.

Creditors

Creditors arise only for engine purchases. Engine suppliers have offered an early settlement discount of 1.5% if invoices are settled within one month of delivery. If the settlement discount is not taken, normal payment terms of two months from delivery apply.

Stock

Frantic has a budgeted production of 800 cars for the year. The most expensive bought-in components for the cars are engines. Other components are either made in-house or are minor items which are bought-in but which do not require special stock management. Engine purchase prices are subject to quantity discounts according to the following schedule:

Order quantity	*Order quantity*
0-49 units	0%
50-249 units	2%
above 249 units	3%

Other details are:

Engine price (before discounts):	£1,300
Stock holding costs per annum (as a percentage of engine costs):	22%
Delivery costs per order:	£1,200

There is zero lead-time on engine orders.

Debtors

The cars are sold at £42,500 each and unit sales are equal to the units produced in each month. 50% of the cars are made to order and payment is on a cash on delivery basis. The remaining cars are sold to specialist retailers who take two months' credit. Frantic is considering offering the specialist retailers a 2% discount for payments made within one month of sale. It is expected that 75% of the retailers would take up the offer.

Other factors

A budget forecast is to be prepared for a six-month period. Other variable costs (including the other components) represent 65% of sales value and are payable immediately. Fixed costs are £18,000 per month for the first three months, rising to £22,000 per month thereafter. The first instalment of £3.2 million for a major re-tooling operation will be paid in month three of the budget forecast.

Assume that the opening bank overdraft is £25,000 and that there are creditors outstanding to the value of £97,500 which will be paid in the first month of the budget plan. It is expected that debtors payments of £1,062,500 will be received in each of the first two months.

The company uses its bank overdraft rate of 15% as its discount rate. Assume one month comprises 30 days, that no opening stock of engines is held and that production is evenly spread throughout the year.

Required:

(a) Calculate:

(i) if it is beneficial for Frantic to change from a two month payment period to a one month payment period for creditors **(3 marks)**

(ii) the optimal ordering policy for engines **(6 marks)**

(iii) if it is beneficial for Frantic to implement the 2% discount for debtors. **(3 marks)**

(b) On the basis of your answer to part (a), and the information given above, prepare the cash budget for Frantic for each of the next six months. **(18 marks)**

(c) Write a report to the Managing Director which identifies:

– how cash flow problems can arise

– the methods available for easing cash shortages

– the techniques, besides cash budgeting, that could be used to monitor and manage cash resources

– the benefits of centralising cash management in a treasury department for group companies. **(20 marks)**

In all your answers clearly state any assumptions you make. **(Total: 50 marks)**

65 JACK GEEP

Jack Geep will set up a new business as a sole trader on 1 January 20X3 making decorative glassware. Jack is in the process of planning the initial cash flows of the business. He estimates that there will not be any sales demand in January 20X3 so production in that month will be used to build up stocks to satisfy the expected demand in February 20X3. Thereafter it is intended to schedule production in order to build up sufficient finished goods stock at the end of each month to satisfy demand during the following month. Production will, however, need to be 5% higher than sales due to expected defects that will have to be scrapped. Defects are only discovered after the goods have been completed. The company will not hold stocks of raw materials or work in progress.

As the business is new, demand is uncertain, but Jack has estimated three possible levels of demand in 20X3 as follows:

	High demand	*Medium demand*	*Low demand*
	£	£	£
February	22,000	20,000	19,000
March	26,000	24,000	23,000
April	30,000	28,000	27,000
May	29,000	27,000	26,000
June	35,000	33,000	32,000

Demand for July 20X3 onwards is expected to be the same as June 20X3. The probability of each level of demand occurring each month is as follows:

High 0.05; Medium 0.85; Low 0.10.

It is expected that 10% of the total sales value will be cash sales, mainly being retail customers making small purchases. The remaining 90% of sales will be made on two months' credit. A 2.5% discount will, however, be offered to credit customers settling within one month. It is estimated that customers, representing half of credit sales by value, will take advantage of the discount while the remainder will take the full two months to pay.

Variable production costs (excluding costs of rejects) per £1,000 of sales are as follows:

	£
Labour	300
Materials	200
Variable overhead	100

Labour is paid in the month in which labour costs are incurred. Materials are paid one month in arrears and variable overheads are paid two months in arrears. Fixed production and administration overheads, excluding depreciation, are £7,000 per month and are payable in the same month as the expenditure is incurred.

Jack employed a firm of consultants to give him initial business advice. Their fee of £12,000 will be paid in February 20X3. Smelting machinery will be purchased on 1 January 20X3 for £200,000 payable in February 20X3. Further machinery will be purchased for £50,000 in March 20X3 payable in April 20X3. This machinery is highly specialized and will have a low net realisable value after purchase.

Jack has redundancy money from his previous employment and savings totalling £150,000, which he intends to pay into his bank account on 1 January 20X3 as the initial capital of the business. He realises that this will be insufficient for his business plans, so he is intending to approach his bank for finance in the form of both a fixed term loan and an overdraft. The only asset Jack has is his house that is valued at £200,000, but he has an outstanding mortgage of £80,000 on this property.

The consultants advising Jack have recommended that rather than accumulating sufficient stock to satisfy the following month's demand he should not maintain any stock levels but merely produce sufficient in each month to meet the expected demand for that month.

Jack's production manager objected: 'I need to set up my production schedule based on the expected average demand for the month. I will reduce production in the month if it seems demand is low. However, there is no way production can be increased during the month to accommodate demand if it happens to be at the higher level that month. As a result, under this new system, there would be no stocks to fall back on and the extra sales, when monthly demand is high, would be lost, as customers require immediate delivery.' In respect of this, an assessment of the impact of the introduction of just-in-time stock management on cash flows has been made that showed the following:

	January	*February*	*March*	*April*	*May*	*June*
Net cash flow (£)	143,000	(223,279)	(7,587)	(50,667)	1,843	1,704
Month-end balance (£)	143,000	(80,279)	(87,866)	(138,533)	(136,690)	(134,986)

Required:

(a) Prepare a monthly cash budget for Jack Geep's business for the six month period ending 30 June 20X3. Calculations should be made on the basis of the expected values of sales. The cash budget should show the net cash inflow or outflow in each month and the cumulative cash surplus or deficit at the end of each month.

For this purpose ignore bank finance and the suggested use of just-in-time stock management. **(17 marks)**

(b) Assume now that just-in-time stock management is used in accordance with the recommendations of the consultants. Calculate for EACH of the six months ending 30 June 20X3:

(i) receipts from sales

(ii) payments to labour. **(6 marks)**

(c) Evaluate the impact for Jack Geep of introducing just-in-time stock management. This should include an assessment of the wider implications of just-in-time stock management in the particular circumstances of Jack Geep's business. **(10 marks)**

(d) Write a report to Jack Geep which identifies the financing needs of the company. It should consider the following:

(i) the extent of financing required

(ii) the factors that should be considered in determining the most appropriate mix of short-term financing (e.g. overdraft) and long-term financing (e.g. fixed term bank loan)

(iii) the extent to which improved working capital management (other than just-in-time stock management) might reduce the company's financing needs and describe how this might be achieved.

Where appropriate, show supporting calculations. **(17 marks)**

(Total: 50 marks)

66 DOE LIMITED

Assume that 'now' is December 20X3.

At a recent meeting of the Board of Doe Ltd, a supplier of industrial and commercial clothing, it was suggested that the company might be suffering liquidity problems as a result of overtrading, despite encouraging growth in turnover. The Finance Director was instructed to report to the next Board meeting on this matter.

Extracts from the financial statements of Doe Ltd for 20X2, and from the forecast financial statements for 20X3, are given below.

Profit and Loss Account extracts for years ending 31 December

	20X3	*20X2*
	£000	£000
Turnover	8,300	6,638
Cost of sales	4,900	3,720
Gross profit	3,400	2,918
Administration and distribution expenses	2,700	2,318
Operating profit	700	600
Interest	125	100
Profit before tax	575	500

Balance Sheet extracts as at 31 December

		20X3			*20X2*	
	£000	£000	£000	£000	£000	£000
Fixed assets			1,650			1,500
Current assets						
Stocks		3,200			2,700	
Debtors		2,750			2,000	
		5,950			4,700	
Creditors: amounts due within 1 year						
Trade creditors	2,550			1,800		
Bank overdraft	2,750			2,300		
Other liabilities	500			400		
		5,800			4,500	
Net current assets			150			200
Total assets less current liabilities			1,800			1,700
Capital and reserves						
Ordinary shares			400			400
Reserves			1,400			1,300
			1,800			1,700

The Finance Director had reported to the recent board meeting that the bank was insisting the company reduce its overdraft as a matter of urgency. It was suggested that the company could consider factor finance as an alternative source of funds for working capital investment. The Production Director insisted that a new machine would be needed to maintain growth in turnover and the Finance Director agreed to investigate how this might be financed.

Factoring

The Finance Director has found a factor who would take over administration of the company's debtors on a non-recourse basis for an annual fee of 1.0% of turnover. The factor would advance 80% of the book value of debts at an annual interest rate 2% above the company's current overdraft rate. The factor expects to reduce the average debtor period to 90 days. The company estimates that Doe Ltd could save £15,000 per year in administration costs. No redundancy costs are expected.

The new machine

The new machine wanted by the Production Director would cost £365,000 if purchased. The Finance Director is confident this purchase could be financed by a medium-term bank loan at an annual interest cost of 10% before tax.

Alternatively, the machine could be leased for £77,250 per annum, payable annually in advance. The machine has an expected life of five years, at the end of which it would have zero scrap value.

Sales and costs of new machine output

The Finance Director has commissioned research that shows growth in sales of the output produced by the new machine depends on the sales price, as follows:

Sales price	*New sales in year 1*	*Expected annual growth in sales*
£70 per unit	10,000 units	20%
£67 per unit	11,000 units	23%

Variable costs of production are £42 per unit and incremental fixed production overheads arising from the use of the machine are expected to be £85,000 per annum. The maximum capacity of the new machine is 20,000 units per annum.

Other information

Doe Ltd pays tax one year in arrears at a rate of 30% and can claim annual writing down allowances (tax-allowable depreciation) on a 25% reducing balance basis. The company pays interest on its overdraft at approximately 6% per annum before tax.

Average ratios for the business sector in which Doe Ltd operates are as follows:

Stock days	210 days	Current ratio	1.35
Debtor days	100 days	Quick ratio	0.55
Creditor days	120 days		

Required:

(a) Write a report to the board of Doe Ltd that analyses and discusses the suggestion that the company is overtrading. **(12 marks)**

(b) (i) Determine whether Doe Ltd should accept the factor's offer. **(7 marks)**

(ii) What are the advantages to Doe Ltd of factoring its debtors? **(8 marks)**

(c) Discuss three ways (other than factoring) by which Doe Ltd might improve the management of its debtors. **(8 marks)**

(d) Evaluate whether Doe Ltd should buy or lease the new machine, using an after-tax discount rate of 7%.

(Assume that payment for the purchase, or the first lease payment, would take place on 1 January 20X4.) **(9 marks)**

(e) Calculate the optimum sales price for the output from the new machine. (Taxation and the time value of money should be ignored.) **(6 marks)**

(Total: 50 marks)

67 NESPA

Nespa is a profitable medium-sized toy manufacturer that has been listed on a stock exchange for three years. Although the company has an overdraft, it has no long-term debt and its current interest cover is high compared to similar companies. Its return on capital employed, however, is close to the average for its business sector. One of its machines is leased under an operating lease, but the company has no other leasing or hire purchase commitments. The company owns two factories and the land on which they are built, as well as a small fleet of delivery vehicles. The company does not own any retail outlets through which to distribute its manufactured output.

Nespa is considering an investment in a new machine, with a maximum output of 200,000 units per annum, in order to manufacture a new toy. Market research undertaken for the company indicated a link between selling price and demand, and the research agency involved has suggested two sales strategies that could be implemented, as follows:

	Strategy 1	Strategy 2
Selling price (in current price terms)	£8.00 per unit	£7.00 per unit
Sales volume in first year	100,000 units	110,000 units
Annual increase in sales volume after first year	5%	15%

The services of the market research agency have cost £75,000 and this amount has yet to be paid.

Nespa expects economies of scale to reduce the variable cost per unit as the level of production increases. When 100,000 units are produced in a year, the variable cost per unit is expected to be £3.00 (in current price terms). For each additional 10,000 units produced in excess of 100,000 units, a reduction in average variable cost per unit of £0.05 is expected to occur. The average variable cost per unit when production is between 110,000 units and 119,999 units, for example, is expected to be £2.95 (in current price terms); and the average variable cost per unit when production is between 120,000 units and 129,999 units is expected to be £2.90 (in current price terms), and so on.

The new machine would cost £1,500,000 and would not be expected to have any resale value at the end of its life. Capital allowances would be available on the investment on a 25% reducing balance basis. Although the machine may have a longer useful economic life, Nespa uses a five-year planning period for all investment projects. The company pays tax at an annual rate of 30% and settles tax liabilities in the year in which they arise.

Operation of the new machine will cause fixed costs to increase by £110,000 (in current price terms). Inflation is expected to increase these costs by 4% per year. Annual inflation on the selling price and unit variable costs is expected to be 3% per year. For profit reporting purposes Nespa depreciates machinery on a straight-line basis over its planning period.

Nespa applies three investment appraisal methods to new projects because it believes that a single investment appraisal method is unable to capture the true value of a proposed investment. The methods it uses are net present value, internal rate of return and return on capital employed (accounting rate of return). The company believes that net present value measures the potential increase in company value of an investment project: that a high internal rate of return offers a margin of safety for risky projects; and that a project's before-tax return on capital employed should be greater than the company's before-tax return on capital employed, which is 20%. Nespa does not use any explicit method of assessing project risk and has an average cost of capital of 10% in money (nominal) terms.

The company has not yet decided on a method of financing the purchase of the new machine, although the finance director believes that a new issue of equity finance is appropriate given the amount of finance required.

Required:

(a) Determine the sales strategy which maximizes the present value of total contribution. Ignore taxation in this part of the question. **(9 marks)**

(b) Evaluate the investment in the new machine using internal rate of return. **(12 marks)**

(c) Evaluate the investment in the new machine using return on capital employed (accounting rate of return) based on the average investment. **(5 marks)**

(d) Critically discuss the relative advantages and disadvantages of internal rate of return and return on capital employed (accounting rate of return), and comment on Nespa's views on investment appraisal methods. **(8 marks)**

(e) Discuss TWO methods that could be used to assess the risk or level of uncertainty associated with an investment project. **(8 marks)**

(f) Discuss the factors that Nespa should consider when selecting an appropriate source of finance for the new machine. **(8 marks)**

(Total: 50 marks)

68 SPENDER CONSTRUCTION PLC

Assume that 'now' is the end of December 20X0.

Spender Construction plc is an expanding UK based building company wishing to raise funds to invest in building a new headquarters and IT centre with upgraded facilities for its logistics and project management business. The total investment required is estimated to be £7 million. The financial justification for the investment is based upon estimates that the new centre will cut fixed administration costs by approximately £500,000 per annum, and reduce the cost of sales by 2%. Sales for the year to 31 December 20X1 are forecast to rise 15% above 20X0 levels (regardless of the investment decision), and so the company anticipates a need for higher working capital funding, in addition to finance for the capital expenditure.

Spender's finance director has commented that in raising funds the Board need to be conscious of the fact that the company operates in a sector which is notorious for its volatility of demand, and also that the company has relatively high levels of fixed operating costs. The industry average is for fixed operating costs to equal 7% of sales revenue. Summarised financial statement for Spender Construction plc are shown below:

Profit and loss account, year ending 31 December 20X0

	£000
Turnover	55,258
Cost of sales	41,827
Gross profit	13,431
Selling and distribution costs	348
Administration costs	8,250
Operating profit	4,833
Interest charges	327
Profit before tax	4,506
Corporation tax payable	1,352
Profit after tax	3,154
Dividend payable	1,520
Retained profit	1,634

Balance sheet as at 31 December 20X0

	£000
Fixed assets	5,800
Current assets	27,928
Current liabilities	20,076
Net current assets	7,852
Total assets less Current liabilities	13,652
10% Debentures 20X6	1,200
Net assets	12,452
Capital and reserves	
Ordinary share capital	4,000
Share premium account	800
Profit and loss account	7,652
Equity shareholders' funds	12,452

Additional information

(1) The nominal value of ordinary share capital is 50 pence per share.

(2) Costs are classified as fixed or variable as follows:

Cost of sales: 100% variable

Selling and distribution: £100,000 per annum fixed, balance variable

Administration costs: £7 million per annum fixed, balance variable.

(3) The current rate of corporation tax is 30%.

(4) Current liabilities as at 31 December 20X0 includes a £2 million overdraft, and a £450,000 VAT bill.

(5) The current market price of ordinary shares in Spender plc is £6.50.

(6) Working capital needs are expected to rise in line with sales.

(7) The dividend forecast for year ending 31 December 20X1 is 25 pence per share.

(8) Bank interest charges for the year to 31 December 20X1 are forecast to be £280,000. Interest is charged at 12.5% per annum.

(9) Depreciation charges on fixed assets for the year to 31 December 20X0 are £435,000.

(10) Assume that payments totalling £2.5 million were made during 20X0 in respect of creditors outstanding at the end of the previous year.

(11) Working capital requirements for 20X0 were the same as those for the previous year.

Required:

(a) Explain and illustrate, using the above data, each of the following terms and comment upon the implications of these two forms of gearing for the equity investors in Spender Construction plc:

(i) operational gearing

(ii) financial gearing. **(14 marks)**

(b) Calculate how much external finance Spender must raise in order to finance the planned sales growth and the investment in the new HQ and IT centre. Assume that both additional working capital and the capital funds are required in full immediately, i.e. on 1 January 20X1. **(8 marks)**

(c) Given that it currently has an overdraft of £2 million, under what circumstances would it be prudent for Spender plc to replace this short-term funding with long-term debt finance? **(5 marks)**

(d) Evaluate (by comparison of shareholder risks and returns, including EPS) the relative merits of raising the £7 million required for the capital investment via a 1 for 6 rights issue priced at £5.25, or a 10% debenture issue redeemable in 20 years time. Ignore issue costs. **(10 marks)**

(e) Explain the meaning of the term dividend cover and, using the forecast figures for the year ending 31 December 20X1, calculate the dividend cover for Spender plc assuming the debenture issue is made. **(3 marks)**

(Total: 40 marks)

69 STADIUM EATS

Stadium Eats is a themed football (soccer) restaurant, seating 150 people, which was set up four years ago by a partnership of two graduate caterers. The restaurant has proved very popular, and sales are now (20X8) averaging £8,500 per week for the 50 weeks of the year that the restaurant is open. The average spend per customer is £15 per head on Saturdays and Sundays, and £12 per head on weekdays. The gross profit margin is 20% and the operating profit margin is 11%.

Stadium Eats is now facing the problem of having to turn customers away on Saturdays and Sundays, as demand is starting to exceed the capacity. Customers are finding that they are needing to place bookings around eight weeks ahead in order to be certain of getting a table at the required time on these days.

In order to overcome the capacity problem, and expand the business further, Stadium Eats are planning to open a second restaurant. They have already identified a suitable site, and drawn up a simple forecast profit and loss account for the new outlet for the first year of trading and an end of year balance sheet. The forecasts are *loosely* based on the revenues and costs of the existing outlet, and are detailed below.

Forecast profit and loss account for the year ended 30 June 20X9

	£000
Sales	600
Operating profit	135
Interest payable	18
Profit before tax	117
Taxation	35
Profit after tax	82

Notes

(1) In calculating operating profit, the two owners have not allowed for any salary costs for themselves, as they already draw a salary of £22,000 each from the existing business.

(2) The new restaurant will be able to seat 180 people, and will be open 50 weeks of the year.

(3) The tax rate is assumed to be 30%.

(4) After tax profit is shared equally between the two partners, but will be wholly re-invested in the business. To date, the partners have made no drawings other than the salaries indicated above.

(5) The current cash balance in the existing business amounts to £45,000, and it is expected that £25,000 of this will be required for refurbishment of the premises for the new restaurant.

(6) The two partners will own equal shares in the new concern.

Forecast balance sheet as at 30 June 20X9

	£000	£000
Assets employed:		
Fixed (net)		
Premises		280
Fixtures and fittings		75
		355

Current assets		
Food stocks	3	
Debtors	7	
Cash	18	
	—	
		28
Current liabilities		
Creditors	12	
	—	
Net current assets		16
		—
Total assets less current liabilities		371
Long-term creditors		195
		—
Net assets		176
		—
Financed by:		
Ordinary shares (25p nominal)		94
Profit & loss account		82
		—
		176

Notes

(1) The long-term creditors would be made up of bank loans and a mortgage against the premises. The mortgage outstanding at 30 June 20X9 would be £184,000 and the balance of the long-term creditors represents a bank loan at 10% interest (fixed rate). The loan would be repaid in monthly instalments, and the balance cleared after five years.

(2) Stadium Eats is currently run as a partnership, but it is intended that the new restaurant will be operated as a private limited company.

(3) In order to raise the cash for their equity investment in the new venture, the two partners would need to raise loans totalling £75,000 against their own homes. They have been assured that the loans will be available but are a little concerned at the risk that they may be taking in borrowing so much to invest in a new business.

Required:

(a) State and explain any reservations that you may have regarding the figures in the forecast profit and loss account, and draft a revised version, adjusted to take account of your criticisms. **(10 marks)**

(b) A bank may be concerned about the level of gearing in a business which has applied for additional loan finance. Explain the meaning of the term capital gearing, and why a lender/investor should be wary of further borrowing when gearing is already high. **(10 marks)**

(c) Calculate and comment on the level of gearing based on the 20X9 forecast balance sheet. (Note that this excludes the proposed £75,000 personal loans for the new restaurant). **(4 marks)**

(d) Given that Stadium Eats are already operating successfully, what other sources of long-term finance might be available to the new business? **(8 marks)**

(e) An accountant has advised the partners that it might be best for them to combine the two restaurants under the umbrella of a single company, and seek a flotation on AIM in five years' time.

Explain the role of AIM within the financial markets, and identify the factors to be considered in seeking a stock market quotation. **(8 marks)**

(Total: 40 marks)

70 WATER SUPPLY SERVICES PLC

Water Supply Services plc is a small regional supplier of water to domestic premises. The company has been operating for a number of years. Its sole customer is the Regional Water Authority (RWA), which allows the company to charge a 25% mark up of agreed costs. The agreed costs that can be incorporated into any calculation of mark up are only labour costs, materials costs, variable overheads, fixed overheads and machine rentals.

Water Supply Services has been approached by RWA with a proposal to increase output to meet a further domestic customer base not previously supplied with water. The company would have to increase its capacity to meet this demand and increased demand from existing customers. Water output is measured in units, with each unit being 1,000 litres. Water Supply Services is currently operating at capacity which is 80,000 units per annum as determined by processing capability.

Increasing processing capability would require the rental of further machines that are involved in the chemical cleaning of water. There is an overall maximum capacity of 200,000 units beyond which the company cannot produce water because of physical limitations of its production site. Each water-cleaning machine has the following rental and unit capacity details.

Water cleaning machine	
Annual rental (£)	22,000
Maximum annual capacity (units)	45,000

Water Supply Services has an existing budgeted direct cost structure based on its current level of output of 80,000 units, as follows:

	£/unit
Labour grade 1	45.00
Labour grade 2	64.00
Material A costs	23.85
Material B costs	62.25

Variable overheads (electricity, maintenance etc.) are absorbed at the rate of £2 per kg of material B used. 5kg of material B is used in the manufacture of 1,000 litres of water. Fixed overheads are based on an existing output of 80,000 units and are absorbed at the rate of £10.20 per unit. Above 160,000 units, fixed overheads would be expected to increase at the rate of £50,000 per annum for every additional 40,000 units produced, or part thereof.

The existing agreement that Water Supply Services will charge a 25% mark up of agreed costs will apply for this proposal. The acceptance of this proposal would not affect any charges relating to the existing supply of 80,000 units.

Domestic demand for water in the next year, if the customer base is expanded, is estimated to total 110,000 units rising by 15% per annum thereafter. This level of demand growth is expected to continue for the foreseeable future.

Working capital requirements are estimated at 15% of sales value and are required to be in place at the start of the period to which the sales relate. Capital investment of £7·5m would be required in order to provide the necessary support facilities to expand capacity to 200,000 units per annum. Thereafter, updating costs of £30,000 would be required at the end of every four years. The cost of capital used in appraising projects is 20% per annum.

All sales and costs should be assumed to arise at the end of the year unless otherwise identified. Ignore the impact of taxation in your answer.

Required:

(a) Evaluate the proposal to expand capacity using present value methods. Make your evaluation on the basis of a five-year period only.

Express all calculations in this part of the question to the nearest £1,000. You are advised to state any assumptions made. **(20 marks)**

(b) In your capacity as Senior Accountant, draft a report to the Board of Directors that considers the following:

(i) the limitations of the five year period of analysis

(ii) the problems and difficulties associated with forecasting

(iii) the choice of an appropriate discount rate, and

(iv) any non-quantifiable factors you feel might influence the decision to accept the proposal. **(20 marks)**

(c) The sales director believes that quarterly forecasts of demand would provide better information for planning purposes. He has asked you, in your capacity as senior company accountant, to forecast demand for the 1st quarter of year 6. In forecasting quarterly demand the following quarterly seasonal adjustments should be made to the basic trend:

Quarter	1	2	3	4
Percentage adjustment	- 8	+ 2	+ 15	- 9

Required:

On the assumption that capacity is expanded to 200,000 units per annum and that growth in demand continues at 15% per annum, estimate output for the 1st quarter of year 6. Briefly comment on your results. **(5 marks)**

(d) The production director has heard that regression analysis is an alternative to seasonal forecasting by time series and wondered if it might be useful in forecasting costs faced by the company. She has had one of her team look at this and has produced the following linear equation:

Total costs (£) = 816,000 + 205·1x

Required:

(i) Describe what is meant by each of the following components of the linear equation:

– 816,000

– 205.1

– x **(2 marks)**

(ii) Comment on your interpretation of the figure 816,000 and whether it is likely to be relevant for year 6. **(3 marks)**

(Total: 50 marks)

71 TOWER RAILWAYS PLC

Assume that 'now' is December 20X3.

Tower Railways plc, which has a financial year-end of 31 December, operates a rail passenger service between the major cities in England. It is currently negotiating with the regulatory authorities about a five-year extension and enhancement of its existing contract. Tower Railways has forecast passenger use over the next five-year period to 31 December 20X8 and, based on its proposed carriage capacity, has calculated the following figures:

Five year projections:

Number of carriages used on the line:	8
Maximum passengers per carriage:	55
Average occupancy rate:	60%
Average number of return journeys per day:	10
Average price per return trip:	£12
Number of days operating per year:	340

Contribution per unit (sales price less variable costs) is expected to remain at a constant 35% of price over the period. Additional fixed costs of £1m per annum will be incurred on the new project. The management accountant has suggested that, in addition, the existing fixed overhead apportionment be increased by £200,000 per annum to reflect the increased activities relating to this part of the business. If the contract is renewed, other services offered by Tower Railways will be reduced to enable capacity expansion on the new contract. This will involve the loss of a long-standing contract, which was expected to continue indefinitely, worth £250,000 in pre-tax cash inflows per annum.

One of the conditions of a successful new bid is that a minimum investment of £5m, in support equipment to enhance the existing service, is required at the start of the new contract on 31 December 20X3. This equipment will no longer be needed to support the contract after four years and will be disposed of for £0.5m on 31 December 20X7. Capital allowances are available for these transactions. A balancing charge or allowance would arise on disposal of the asset. The investment in this asset should be treated separately from any other asset investment for tax purposes (ignore any pooling requirements). Assume all tax payments and allowances arise at the end of the year in which the taxable transactions arise (in other words, not delayed). Assume that all operating cash inflows arise at the relevant year-end.

Other relevant information:

After tax discount rate per annum:	10%
Corporation tax rate:	30%
Writing down allowance:	25% per annum, reducing balance

Required:

(a) Calculate separately the present value of the net operating cash flows (after payment of corporation tax and using annuities and perpetuities where appropriate), and the capital flows (investment, disposal and related tax flows). Assess if it is beneficial for Tower Railways to begin the new contract on 31 December 20X3.

Express all calculations in this and other parts of the question to the nearest £1,000. State any assumptions you make. **(18 marks)**

(b) The Chairman of Tower Railways is concerned about the risk of the project, particularly with respect to the average price charged.

Calculate the sensitivity of the project in relation to the average price charged. **(4 marks)**

Assume, in your answer that all other factors are as per your analysis in part (a).

(c) On reviewing the initial proposal from your answer to part (a), the regulatory authorities are now insisting that further investment of £7m be made to ensure carriage availability to meet targets for the level of proposed service provision. This would not involve the purchase of additional carriages. Assume that by incorporating the additional £7m investment on top of the existing £5m, a total NPV at 31 December 20X3 of £9.220m (negative) for the capital cash flows only will arise.

Required:

(i) Calculate the occupancy rate required to break even (that is, to produce a zero NPV). **(4 marks)**

(ii) Calculate the length of the contract required to break even (that is, to produce a zero NPV). **(4 marks)**

Assume, in your answers to each case, that all other factors are as per your analysis in part (a).

(d) Write a report to the Chairman of Tower Railways, in your capacity as an external consultant, explaining:

(i) what is meant by business risk

(ii) the methods of estimating business risk in the context of NPV, and

(iii) the methods of reducing business risk. **(20 marks)**

(Total: 50 marks)

72 AMBER PLC

Amber plc operates a daily return high-speed train service between the UK and mainland Europe, via the Channel Tunnel. In an attempt to reduce overheads, the company is considering using an outside supplier to take over responsibility for all on-train catering services. Amber invited tenders for a five-year contract, and at the same time the senior management accountant drafted a schedule of costs for in-house provision of an equivalent service. This cost schedule, together with the details of the lowest price tender which was received, are given below. (See Table 1 and additional information).

Table 1: In-house provision of train catering services

Schedule of costs, Amber plc

	Pence per £ sales
Variable costs	
Direct material	55
Variable overhead	12
Fixed costs (allocated to products)	
Labour (Year 1)	10
Purchase/storage management	3
Depreciation (catering equipment)	4
Insurance	2
Total cost	86

The train service operates 360 days per year and a single restaurant carriage is adequate to service the catering needs of a train carrying up to 600 passengers. The tendered contract (and the in-house schedule of costs) is for the provision of one catering carriage per train. Past sales data indicates that 45% of passengers will use the catering service, spending an average of £4.50 each per single journey or £9.00 per return journey. This is expected to remain unchanged over the next five years, unless Amber invests in quality improvements.

Statistical forecasts of the level of demand for the train service, under differing average weather conditions and average exchange rates over the next five years, are shown in Table 2.

Table 2: Forecast passenger figures (per single journey)

	UK weather conditions		
Exchange rate: € per £1	*Poor*	*Reasonable*	*Good*
1.52	500	460	420
1.54	550	520	450
1.65	600	580	500

The differing weather conditions are all assumed to be equally likely.

Based on historical trends, the probability of each different exchange rate occurring is estimated as follows:

Exchange rate *€ per £1*	*Probability*
1.52	0.2
1.54	0.5
1.65	0.3

Additional information

(1) Labour costs are expected to rise at a rate of 5% per year over the next five years.

(2) Variable costs per £ sales are expected to remain unchanged over the next five years.

(3) Some catering equipment will need to be replaced at the end of Year 2 at a cost of £500,000. This would increase the depreciation charge on catering equipment to 5 pence per £ sales. The equipment value at the end of Year 5 is estimated to be £280,000.

(4) The outside supplier (lowest price tender) has agreed to purchase immediately (for cash) the existing catering equipment owned by Amber plc at a price equal to the current book value i.e. £650,000. The supplier would charge Amber a flat fee of £250 per day for the provision of this catering service, and Amber would receive 5% of gross catering receipts where these exceeded an average of £2,200 per day in each 360 day period. The quality of the catering service is expected to be unaffected by the contracting out.

(5) In the event of Amber deciding to contract out the catering, the following fixed costs will be saved:

Depreciation	£35,000 per year
Purchasing/storage costs	£18,000 per year
Insurance	£3,000 per year
Labour costs	£74,844 (Year 1)

(6) The cost of capital for Amber plc is 12%.

Assume that all cash flows occur at the end of each year. Taxation may be ignored in answering this question.

Required:

(a) Calculate the expected number of passengers per single journey for the train service. **(5 marks)**

(b) Draft a table of annual cash flows and, using discounted cash flow analysis, determine which of the two alternatives (in-house provision or contracting out) is preferred. **(16 marks)**

(c) Calculate and comment upon the financial effect on the decision of a forecast ten per cent increase in the number of passengers purchasing food and beverages on each train if the in-house catering service were to be improved. Any such improvement would require Amber investing £10,000 per year over five years on staff training. **(7 marks)**

(d) Comment on the limitations of using demand forecasts, such as that given in Table 2, for the purposes of the decision in question. **(5 marks)**

(e) Identify and critically comment upon three non-financial factors which need to be taken into account when a business is considering this type of decision. **(7 marks)**

(Total: 40 marks)

73 SPRINGBANK PLC

Springbank plc is a medium-sized manufacturing company that plans to increase capacity by purchasing new machinery at an initial cost of £3 million. The following are the most recent financial statements of the company:

Profit and loss accounts for years ending 31 December

	20X2	*20X1*
	£000	*£000*
Sales	5,000	5,000
Cost of sales	3,100	3,000
Gross profit	1,900	2,000
Administration and distribution expenses	400	250
Profit before interest and tax	1,500	1,750
Interest	400	380
Profit before tax	1,100	1,370
Tax	330	400
Profit after tax	770	970
Dividends	390	390
Retained earnings	380	580

Balance Sheets as at 31 December

	20X2		20X1	
	£000	£000	£000	£000
Fixed assets		6,500		6,400
Current assets				
Stock	1,170		1,000	
Debtors	850		900	
Cash	130		100	
	2,150		2,000	
Current liabilities	1,150		1,280	
		1,000		720
		7,500		7,120
10% Debentures 20X7		3,500		3,500
		4,000		3,620
Capital and reserves		4,000		3,620

The investment is expected to increase annual sales by 5,500 units. Investment in replacement machinery would be needed after five years. Financial data on the additional units to be sold is as follows:

	£
Selling price per unit	500
Production costs per unit	200

Variable administration and distribution expenses are expected to increase by £220,000 per year as a result of the increase in capacity. In addition to the initial investment in new machinery, £400,000 would need to be invested in working capital. The full amount of the initial investment in new machinery of £3 million will give rise to capital allowances on a 25% per year reducing balance basis. The scrap value of the machinery after five years is expected to be negligible. Tax liabilities are paid in the year in which they arise and Springbank plc pays tax at 30% of annual profits.

The Finance Director of Springbank plc has proposed that the £3.4 million investment should be financed by an issue of debentures at a fixed rate of 8% per year.

Springbank plc uses an after tax discount rate of 12% to evaluate investment proposals. In preparing its financial statements, Springbank plc uses straight-line depreciation over the expected life of fixed assets.

Average data for the business sector in which Springbank operates is as follows:

Gearing (book value of debt/book value of equity)	100%
Interest cover	4 times
Current ratio	2:1
Stock days	90 days
Return before interest and tax/Capital employed	25%

Required:

(a) Calculate the net present value of the proposed investment in increased capacity of Springbank plc, clearly stating any assumptions that you make in your calculations. **(11 marks)**

(b) Calculate the increase in sales (in units) that would produce a zero net present value for the proposed investment. **(4 marks)**

(c) (i) Calculate the effect on the gearing and interest cover of Springbank plc of financing the proposed investment with an issue of debentures and compare your results with the sector averages. **(6 marks)**

(ii) Analyse and comment on the recent financial performance of the company. **(13 marks)**

(iii) On the basis of your previous calculations and analysis, comment on the acceptability of the proposed investment and discuss whether the proposed method of financing can be recommended. **(10 marks)**

(d) Briefly discuss the possible advantages to Springbank plc of using an issue of ordinary shares to finance the investment. **(6 marks)**

(Total: 50 marks)

74 SASSONE PLC

Sassone plc is a medium-sized profitable company that manufactures engineering products. Its stated objectives are to maximise shareholder wealth and to maintain an ethical approach to the production and distribution of engineering products. It has in issue two million ordinary shares, held as follows:

	Number of shares
Pension funds	550,000
Insurance companies	250,000
Investment trusts	200,000
Unit trusts	100,000
Directors of Sassone	350,000
Other shareholders	550,000
	2,000,000

The Managing Director of Sassone plc is considering three items that have been placed on the agenda of the next

Board Meeting:

1 **Complaint by institutional investors**

A number of institutional investors complained at the recent Annual General Meeting of the company that expenditure on environmentally-friendly and socially responsible projects was at too high a level, resulting in a less than acceptable increase in annual dividend payments. They had warned that they would vote against the re-appointment of directors if matters had not improved by the next Annual General Meeting.

2 **Proposal to change variance reporting procedure**

The Production Director has asked that the company amend its current variance reporting procedures in order to report planning and operational variances rather than variances based only on start-of-period standard costing information. In support of his request he has highlighted a £33,000 adverse direct material usage variance for the last period for Product Z, which he claims is not the responsibility of his staff since he believes that most of this variance is due to the use of an out-of-date standard.

The Production Director states that the standard cost of materials of Product Z at the start of the period was 5 kg per unit at £7.50 per kg, and that budgeted production and sales of Product Z for the period were 11,000 units. During the period, actual production and sales of Product Z were 10,000 units and 54,400 kg of materials were used at a cost of £408,000. The Production Director believes that, due to the age of the machinery used to make

Product Z, the standard usage of materials should be revised to 5.3 kg per unit.

3 **Proposal to increase manufacturing capacity**

The directors of Sassone plc need to increase capacity in order to meet expected demand for a new product, Product G, which is to be used in the manufacture of new-generation personal computers. Product G cannot be manufactured on existing machines. The directors have identified two machines which can manufacture Product G, each with a capacity of 60,000 units per year, as follows:

Machine One

This machine will cost £238,850 and last for five years, at the end of which time it will have zero scrap value. Maintenance costs will be £10,000 in the first year of operation, increasing by £3,000 per year for each year of operation.

Machine Two

This machine will cost £215,000 and last for four years, at the end of which time it will have zero scrap value. Maintenance costs will be £10,000 in the first year of operation, increasing by £5,000 per year for each year of operation.

Sassone plc expects demand for Product G to be 30,000 units per year in the first year, and to increase by a further 10,000 units per year in each subsequent year. Selling price is expected to be £10.00 per unit and the marginal cost of production is expected to be £7.80 per unit. Incremental fixed production overheads of £10,000 per year will be incurred. Selling price and costs are all in current price terms.

Annual inflation rates are expected to be as follows:

Selling price of Product G:	4% per year
Marginal cost of production:	4% per year
Maintenance costs:	5% per year
Fixed production overheads:	6% per year

Other information

Sassone plc has a real cost of capital of 8% and uses a nominal (money) cost of capital of 11% in investment appraisal. The company pays tax one year in arrears at an annual rate of 30% and can claim capital allowances on a 25% reducing balance basis, with a balancing allowance at the end of the life of the machines. The company depreciates fixed assets on a straight-line basis over the life of the asset and has a target before-tax return on capital employed (accounting rate of return) of 25%.

Required:

(a) Calculate the planning and operational direct material usage variances for Product Z and comment on the views of the Production Director. **(4 marks)**

(b) Using equivalent annual cost and considering machine purchase prices and maintenance costs only, determine which machine should be purchased by Sassone. Ignore inflation and taxation in this part of the question only. **(6 marks)**

(c) Calculate the net present value of the incremental cash flows arising from purchasing Machine Two and advise on its acquisition. **(18 marks)**

(d) Calculate the before-tax return on capital employed (accounting rate of return) of the incremental cash flows arising from purchasing Machine Two based on the average investment and comment on your findings. **(4 marks)**

(e) Discuss the conflict that may arise between corporate objectives, using the information provided on Sassone plc to illustrate your answer. **(10 marks)**

(f) Discuss how lifecycle costing and target costing may assist Sassone plc in controlling costs and pricing engineering products. **(8 marks)**

(Total: 50 marks)

75 ARG CO

ARG Co is a leisure company that is recovering from a loss-making venture into magazine publication three years ago. Recent financial statements of the company are as follows.

Profit and loss account for year ending 30 June 20X5

	£000
Turnover	140,400
Cost of sales	112,840
Gross profit	27,560
Administration costs	23,000
Profit before interest and tax	4,560
Interest	900
Profit before tax	3,660
Taxation	1,098
Profit after taxation	2,562
Dividends	400
Retained profit	2,162

Balance sheet as at 30 June 20X5

	£000	£000
Fixed assets		50,000
Current assets		
Stock	2,400	
Debtors	20,000	
Cash	1,500	
	23,900	
Current liabilities	33,000	
		(9,100)
		40,900
9% Debentures 2014		10,000
		30,900
Financed by:		
Ordinary shares, £1 par value		2,000
Reserves		27,000
Profit and loss		1,900
		30,900

The company plans to launch two new products, Alpha and Beta, at the start of July 2005, which it believes will each have a life-cycle of four years. Alpha is the deluxe version of Beta. The sales mix is assumed to be constant. Expected sales volumes for the two products are as follows.

Year	*1*	*2*	*3*	*4*
Alpha	60,000	110,000	100,000	30,000
Beta	75,000	137,500	125,000	37,500

The standard selling price and standard costs for each product in the first year will be as follows.

Product	*Alpha*	*Beta*
	£/unit	£/unit
Direct material costs	12.00	9.00
Incremental fixed production costs	8.64	6.42
Total absorption cost	20.64	15.42
Standard mark-up	10.36	7.58
Selling price	31.00	23.00

ARG traditionally operates a cost-plus approach to product pricing.

Incremental fixed production costs are expected to be £1 million in the first year of operation and are apportioned on the basis of sales value. Advertising costs will be £500,000 in the first year of operation and then £200,000 per year for the following two years. There are no incremental non-production fixed costs other than advertising costs.

In order to produce the two products, investment of £1 million in premises, £1 million in machinery and £1 million in working capital will be needed, payable at the start of July 2005. The investment will be financed by the issue of £3 million of 9% debentures, each £100 debenture being convertible into 20 ordinary shares of ARG Co after 8 years or redeemable at par after 12 years.

Selling price per unit, direct material cost per unit and incremental fixed production costs are expected to increase after the first year of operation due to inflation:

Selling price inflation	3.0% per year
Direct material cost inflation	3.0% per year
Fixed production cost inflation	5.0% per year

These inflation rates are applied to the standard selling price and standard cost data provided above. Working capital will be recovered at the end of the fourth year of operation, at which time production will cease and ARG Co expects to be able to recover £1·2 million from the sale of premises and machinery. All staff involved in the production and sale of Alpha and Beta will be redeployed elsewhere in the company.

ARG Co pays tax in the year in which the taxable profit occurs at an annual rate of 25%. Investment in machinery attracts a first-year capital allowance of 100%. ARG Co has sufficient profits to take the full benefit of this allowance in the first year. For the purpose of reporting accounting profit, ARG Co depreciates machinery on a straight line basis over four years. ARG Co uses an after-tax discount rate of 13% for investment appraisal.

Other information

Assume that it is now 30 June 2005

The ordinary share price of ARG Co is currently £4.00

Average interest cover for ARG Co's sector is 7

Average gearing for ARG Co's sector is 45% (long-term debt/equity using book values)

Required:

(a) Calculate the net present value of the proposed investment in products Alpha and Beta. **(17 marks)**

(b) Identify and discuss any likely limitations in the evaluation of the proposed investment in Alpha and Beta. **(6 marks)**

(c) Evaluate and discuss the proposal to finance the investment with a £3 million 9% convertible debenture issue. **(8 marks)**

(d) A detailed evaluation of the incremental fixed costs for the first year of producing Alpha and Beta reveals the following information on the composition of the fixed costs and their associated cost drivers.

Fixed cost	£	*Cost driver*	*Alpha*	*Beta*
Power, heating, etc.	505,000	Floor area	3,500 m^2	6,500 m^2
Salaries	300,000	Labour hours	10,000	15,000
Inspection costs	67,500	Inspections	3,000	3,750
Order processing	67,500	Orders	3,000	1,500
Maintenance	26,000	Maintenance hours	625	1,875
Set-up costs	34,000	Set-ups	120	50
	1,000,000			

Calculate activity-based recovery rates for each fixed cost and calculate the total standard cost per unit for each product using an activity-based approach. Comment on the implications of your findings for product pricing. **(11 marks)**

(e) Included in the debtors of ARG Co is an expected receipt of $500,000 payable in three months' time. The following exchange rates are available:

	$/£
Spot	1.7642 – 1.7962
Three months forward	1.7855 – 1.8174

Explain why ARG Co might wish to hedge its expected three-month dollar receipt using the forward market and calculate the sterling value arising from a forward market hedge. **(4 marks)**

(f) Discuss how bills of exchange can be used to reduce the risk associated with the overseas debtors of ARG Co. **(4 marks)**

(Total: 50 marks)

76 BFD CO

BFD Co is a private company formed three years ago by four brothers who, as directors, retain sole ownership of its ordinary share capital. One quarter of the initial share capital was provided by each brother. The company has returned a profit in each year of operation as shown by the following financial statements.

Profit and Loss Accounts for years ending 30 November

	2005	*2004*	*2003*
	£000	£000	£000
Turnover	5,200	3,400	2,600
Cost of sales	4,570	2,806	2,104
Profit before interest and tax	630	594	496
Interest	70	34	3

	2005	2004	2003
	£000	£000	£000
Profit before tax	560	560	493
Tax	140	140	123
Profit after tax	420	420	370
Dividends	20	20	20
Retained profit	400	400	350

Balance Sheets as at 30 November

		2005		2004		2003
	£000	£000	£000	£000	£000	£000
Fixed assets		1,600		1,200		800
Current assets						
Stock	1,450		1,000		600	
Debtors	1,400		850		400	
	2,850		1,850		1,000	
Current liabilities	2,300		1,300		450	
Net current assets		550		550		550
		2,150		1,750		1,350
Ordinary shares (£1 par)		1,000		1,000		1,000
Reserves		1,150		750		350
		2,150		1,750		1,350

BFD Co has an overdraft limit of £1.25 million and pays interest on its overdraft at a rate of 6% per year. Current liabilities consist of trade creditors and overdraft finance in each of the three years.

The directors are delighted with the rapid growth of BFD Co and are considering further expansion through buying new premises and machinery to manufacture Product FT7. This new product has only just been developed and patented by BFD Co. Test marketing has indicated considerable demand for the product, as shown by the following research data.

Year of operation	*1*	*2*	*3*	*4*
Accounting year	2005/6	2006/7	2007/8	2008/9
Sales volume (units)	100,000	120,000	130,000	140,000

Sales after 2008/9 (the fourth year of operation) are expected to continue at the 2008/9 level in perpetuity.

Initial investment of £3,000,000 would be required in new premises and machinery, as well as an additional £200,000 of working capital. The directors have no further financial resources to offer and are considering approaching their bank for a loan to meet their investment needs. Selling price and standard cost data for Product FT7, based on an annual budgeted volume of 100,000 units, are as follows.

	£ *per unit*
Selling price	18.00
Direct material	7.00
Direct labour	1.50
Fixed production overhead	4.50

The fixed production overhead is incurred exclusively in the production of Product FT7 and excludes depreciation. Selling price and standard unit variable cost data for Product FT7 are expected to remain constant.

BFD Co expects to be able to claim writing down allowances on the initial investment of £3,000,000 on a straightline basis over 10 years. The company pays tax on profit at an annual rate of 25% in the year in which the liability arises and has an after-tax cost of capital of 12%.

Average data for companies similar to BFD Co

Net profit margin:	9%	Creditor days:	70 days
Interest cover:	15 times	Current ratio:	2.1 times
Stock days: 85 days	Quick ratio:	0.8 times	
Debtor days:	75 days	Debt/equity ratio:	40% (using book values)

Required:

(a) Calculate the net present value of the proposed investment in Product FT7. Assume that it is now 1 December 2005. **(16 marks)**

(b) Comment on the acceptability of the proposed investment in Product FT7 and discuss what additional information might improve the decision-making process. **(7 marks)**

(c) BFD Co has received an offer from a rival company of £300,000 per year for 10 years for the manufacturing rights for Product FT7. If BFD Co accepts this offer, it would not be able to manufacture Product FT7 for the duration of the agreement.

Required:

Determine whether BFD Co should accept the offer for the manufacturing rights to Product FT7. In this part of the question only, ignore cash flows occurring after the ten-year period of the offer. Assume that it is 1 December 2005. **(6 marks)**

(d) As the newly-appointed finance director of BFD Co, write a report to the board which discusses whether the company is likely to be successful if it approaches its bank for a loan. Your discussion should include an analysis of the current financial position and recent financial performance of the company. **(16 marks)**

(e) On the basis that BFD Co decided to invest and manufacture Product FT7, the actual data for the first year of operation (2005/6) is now available and is as follows:

Number of units produced and sold	110,000
Selling price (£ per unit)	18.20
Direct material (£ per unit)	7.10
Direct labour (£ per unit)	1.70
Fixed production overhead (£ per unit)	4.50

Required:

Calculate the following variances using marginal costing and absorption costing:

(i) sales price variance;

(ii) sales volume profit variance;

and comment on the relative values obtained. **(5 marks)**

(Total: 50 marks)

RFD Co [illegible] of [illegible] £ [illegible] years. The company [illegible] of 12%.

Average data for companies similar to RFD Co

[illegible]

Required:

[illegible] (3 marks)

[illegible] (7 marks)

[illegible]

Required:

[illegible]

[illegible]

Required:

[illegible]

(i) [illegible]

(ii) [illegible]

[illegible] (9 marks)

(Total 15 marks)

Section 3

ANSWERS TO PRACTICE QUESTIONS

FINANCIAL MANAGEMENT OBJECTIVES AND ENVIRONMENT

1 TAGNA

(a) Market efficiency is commonly discussed in terms of pricing efficiency.

A stock market is described as efficient when share prices fully and fairly reflect relevant information.

Weak form efficiency occurs when share prices fully and fairly reflect all past information, such as share price movements in preceding periods. If a stock market is weak-form efficient, investors cannot make abnormal gains by studying and acting upon past information.

Semi-strong form efficiency occurs when share prices fully and fairly reflect not only past information, but all publicly available information as well, such as the information provided by the published financial statements of companies or by reports in the financial press. If a stock market is semi-strong-form efficient, investors cannot make abnormal gains by studying and acting upon publicly available information.

Strong form efficiency occurs when share prices fully and fairly reflect not only all past and publicly available information, but all relevant private information as well, such as confidential minutes of board meetings. If a stock market is strong-form efficient, investors cannot make abnormal gains by acting upon any information, whether publicly available or not. There is no empirical evidence supporting the proposition that stock markets are strong form efficient and so the bank is incorrect in suggesting that in six months the stock market will be strong-form efficient. However, there is a great deal of evidence suggesting that stock markets are semi-strong-form efficient and so Tagna's share are unlikely to be under-priced.

(b) A **substantial interest rate increase** may have several consequences for Tagna in the areas indicated.

(i) As a manufacturer and supplier of luxury goods, it is likely that Tagna will experience a **sharp decrease in sales** as a result of the increase in interest rates. One reason for this is that sales of luxury goods will be more sensitive to changes in disposable income than sales of basic necessities, and disposable income is likely to fall as a result of the interest rate increase. Another reason is the likely effect of the interest rate increase on consumer demand. If the increase in demand has been supported, even in part, by the increase in consumer credit, the substantial interest rate increase will have a negative effect on demand as the cost of consumer credit increases. It is also likely that many chain store customers will buy Tagna's goods by using credit.

(ii) Tagna may experience an **increase in operating costs** as a result of the substantial interest rate increase, although this is likely to be a smaller effect and one that occurs more slowly than a decrease in sales. As the higher cost of borrowing moves through the various supply chains in the economy, producer prices may increase and the cost of materials and other inputs Tagna may rise by more than the current rate of inflation. Labour costs may also increase sharply if the recent sharp rise in inflation leads to high inflationary expectations being built into wage demands. Acting against this will be the deflationary effect on consumer demand of the interest rate increase. If the Central Bank has made an accurate assessment of the economic situation when determining the interest rate increase, both the growth in consumer demand and the rate of inflation may fall to more acceptable levels, leading to a lower increase in operating costs.

(iii) The **earnings (profit after tax)** of Tagna are likely to fall as a result of the interest rate increase. In addition to the decrease in sales and the possible increase in operating costs discussed above, Tagna will experience an increase in interest costs arising from its overdraft. The combination of these effects is likely to result in a sharp fall in earnings. The level of reported profits has been low in recent years and so Tagna may be faced with insufficient profits to maintain its dividend, or even a reported loss.

(c) The objectives of public sector organisations are often difficult to define. Even though the cost of resources used can be measured, the benefits gained from the consumption of those resources can be difficult, if not impossible, to quantify. Because of this difficulty, public sector organisations often have financial targets imposed on them, such as a target rate of return on capital employed. Furthermore, they will tend to focus on maximising the return on resources consumed by producing the best possible combination of services for the lowest possible cost. This is the meaning of **'value for money'**, often referred to as the pursuit of economy, efficiency and effectiveness.

Economy refers to seeking the lowest level of input costs for a given level of output. **Efficiency** refers to seeking the highest level of output for a given level of input resources. **Effectiveness** refers to the extent to which output produced meets the specified objectives, for example in terms of provision of a required range of services.

In contrast, private sector organisations have to compete for funds in the capital markets and must offer an adequate return to investors. The objective of **maximisation of shareholder wealth** equates to the view that the primary financial objective of companies is to reward their owners. If this objective is not followed, the directors may be replaced or a company may find it difficult to obtain funds in the market, since investors will prefer companies that increase their wealth. However, shareholder wealth cannot be maximised if companies do not seek both economy and efficiency in their business operations.

ACCA marking scheme

		Marks
(a)	Pricing efficiency	1
	Meaning and significance of weak form	2
	Meaning and significance of semi strong form	2
	Meaning and significance of strong form	2
	Comments on banks recommendation	2
		9
(b)	Up to 2 marks for each detailed consequence	10
(c)	Value for money	3
	Maximization of shareholder wealth	3
		6
Total		25

2 STAKEHOLDERS

(a) Stakeholders in a company include: shareholders, directors/managers, lenders, employees, suppliers and customers. These groups are likely to share in the wealth and risk generated by a company in different ways and thus conflicts of interest are likely to exist. Conflicts also exist not just between groups but within stakeholder groups. This might be because sub-groups exist, for example preference shareholders and equity shareholders within the overall category of shareholders. Alternatively individuals within a stakeholder group might have different preferences (e.g. to risk and return, short term and long term returns). Good corporate governance is partly about the resolution of such conflicts. Financial and other objectives of stakeholder groups may be identified as follows:

Shareholders

Shareholders are normally assumed to be interested in wealth maximisation. This, however, involves consideration of potential return and risk. For a listed company, this can be viewed in terms of the changes in the share price and other market-based ratios using share price (e.g. price/earnings ratio, dividend yield, earnings yield).

Where a company is not listed, financial objectives need to be set in terms of other financial measures, such as return on capital employed, earnings per share, gearing, growth, profit margin, asset utilisation, and market share. Many other measures also exist which may collectively capture the objectives of return and risk.

Shareholders may have other objectives for the company and these can be identified in terms of the interests of other stakeholder groups. Thus, shareholders as a group may be interested in profit maximisation; they may also be interested in the welfare of their employees, or the environmental impact of the company's operations.

Directors and managers

While executive directors and managers should attempt to promote and balance the interests of shareholders and other stakeholder groups, it has been argued that they also promote their own individual interests and should be seen as a separate stakeholder group.

This problem arises from the divorce between ownership and control. The behaviour of managers cannot be fully observed by the shareholders, giving them the capacity to take decisions which are consistent with their own reward structures and risk preferences. Directors may therefore be interested in their own remuneration package. They may also be interested in building empires, exercising greater control, or positioning themselves for their next promotion. Non-financial objectives of managers are sometimes inconsistent with what the financial objectives of the company ought to be.

Lenders

Lenders are concerned to receive payment of interest and eventually re-payment of the capital at maturity. Unlike the ordinary shareholders, they do not share in the upside (profitability) of successful organisational strategies. They are therefore likely to be more risk averse than shareholders, with an emphasis on financial objectives that promote liquidity and solvency with low risk (e.g. low gearing, high interest cover, security, strong cash flow).

Employees

The primary interests of employees are their salary/wage and their security of employment. To an extent there is a direct conflict between employees and shareholders as wages are a cost to the company and income to employees.

Performance-related pay based on financial or other quantitative objectives may, however, go some way toward drawing the divergent interests together.

Suppliers and customers

Suppliers and customers are external stakeholders with their own set of objectives (profit for the supplier and, possibly, customer satisfaction with the good or service from the customer) that, within a portfolio of businesses, are only partly dependent on the company in question. Nevertheless it is important to consider and measure the relationship in term of financial objectives relating to quality, lead times, volume of business, price and a range of other variables in considering any organisational strategy.

(b) Corporate governance is the system by which organisations are directed and controlled.

Where the power to direct and control an organisation is given, a duty of accountability exists to those who have devolved that power. Part of that duty of accountability is discharged by disclosure of both performance in the annual report and accounts and also the governance procedures themselves.

Corporate governance codes in the UK are voluntary, and operate on a comply or explain basis. Thus, any requirements are to disclose governance procedures in relation to best practice, rather than comply with best practice, and to explain/justify any divergence from best practice.

The decision-making powers in a company rest mainly with the board of directors. Much of the corporate governance regulation in the UK has therefore focused on governance principles and best practice relating to this stakeholder group. The principles and guidelines in the Combined Code are aimed largely at trying to ensure that the directors act responsibly and in the interests of the other stakeholder groups, particularly the shareholders, rather than themselves. Ideally, the interests of directors and other stakeholders should be aligned and consistent with each other.

A feature of UK companies is a unitary board structure, with one board consisting of both executive and non-executive directors. This contrasts with the two-tier board structure in Germany for instance where there is more independence between the two groups of directors. In a two-tier structure, non-executives on a supervisory board and executive directors on a management board which reports to the supervisory board.

Particular corporate governance proposals in the UK written into the Combined Code include:

(1) Independence of the board with no covert financial reward

(2) Adequate quality and quantity of non-executive directors to act as a counterbalance to the power of executive directors.

(3) Remuneration committee controlled by non-executives, to decide the remuneration of the executive directors.

(4) Appointments committee consisting of non-executives, to recommend new appointments to the board.

(5) Audit committee consisting of non-executives, with responsibilities for audit matters, including negotiating the fee of the external auditors.

(6) Separation of the roles of chairman and chief executive to prevent concentration of power in one person.

(7) Full disclosure of all forms of director remuneration including shares and share options.

(8) Better communication between the board of directors and the shareholders, particularly institutional investors.

(9) Greater prominence for risk management, which is specified as a particular board responsibility.

Overall, the visibility given by corporate governance procedures goes some way toward discharging the directors' duty of accountability to stakeholders and makes more transparent the underlying incentive systems of directors.

ACCA marking scheme		
		Marks
(a)	Explanation of financial and other objectives 3 marks for each explained point: maximum awarded	12
(b)	Outline of good corporate governance practices with appropriate references to elements of Combined Code Up to 2 marks for each point	13
Total		25

3 MANAGEMENT ACCOUNTING

(a) The accuracy of the statement depends on the interpretation of the terms **costing** and **management control**.

Costing can involve the ascertainment of costs, for example, of products, services, activities, machines, departments or divisions. Typical purposes of ascertaining these costs may be stock valuation, pricing, make-or-buy decisions or judgement of operating efficiency. For such purposes they may be full costs, variable costs or some permutation of decision-relevant costs. In this wide context it embraces much of the management accountant's work. This could either be part of a regular routine, as in many standard costing systems, or part of an ad hoc reporting procedure.

Control in the enterprise implies the provision of information so that management may take some corrective action, where necessary, to bring events back on track. That is the aim of regular reporting of events and deviations on an exception basis. This suggests the existence of a plan and a desired course of action, against which control may be exercised. The plan will have been specified by the longer-term objectives of the organisation and its strategy for attaining these objectives. This would be envisaged to take place within a framework of responsibility accounting and management by objectives including both financial and non-financial information.

In this light, the terms costing and management control include the preparation of costs for various decision purposes and of information to support organisational planning and control activities. It therefore covers, to quite a large extent, the purpose of management accounting systems. However, it doesn't make reference to activities related to drawing data from the external environment or using insights into competitor's activities, which are increasingly common in the context of Strategic Management Accounting.

(b) **Examiner's comment**

It will be the responsibility of the management accountant to serve the information needs of three management groups identified in the question – retail stores, transport and warehouse. Other functions not specifically mentioned could involve personnel and training, purchasing and marketing. We have no information regarding the extent to which this company undertakes these other functions, so detailed comment will not be made here. (However, the sort of information would follow the pattern for the other functions described below.)

Retail stores

Costing information would provide a basis for **pricing decisions**, e.g. setting minimum prices, making special offers and the range of mark-up possibilities. Such decisions would be likely to apply to major lines and be based on predicted sales volumes and perceived minimum or break-even levels of demand for each store and the company as a whole. Any sales promotions by product manufacturers or competitive moves against other retailers would be taken into account. The extent to which individual stores had discretion to make pricing decisions would dictate the degree of detail available in stores, or whether this information is maintained centrally. If this was a centralised function, greater detail would be maintained at head office, and the dictated policy would be confirmed by regular reports of gross margin by store and by major product group.

Retail store management would require regular **reports on controllable costs** (wages and some overheads) compared with a flexible budget. Some store costs may be fixed and hence not amenable to the use of a flexed budget. There should be scope, however, to manage staff levels to cope with busy and slack periods. **Sales** in total and by major product line should be monitored and compared with both a budget and last year's sales. A **monthly profit and loss summary** should be provided focusing on controllable profit, with any head office cost allocations shown separately.

Stores would have responsibility for **some parts of the company's working capital**, for example, regular banking or takings for transmission to a central bank account and management of stock. Local stock levels and the rate and frequency of replenishment of major lines would also be the subject of regular reporting. Sales per square foot of floor space would be an example of a useful statistic for each store and major product line.

Transport

The responsibility of the transport fleet is to **supply stores efficiently** and **run the transport fleet as economically as possible**. Cost reports on wages, vehicle repairs and other running costs in comparison with budget would be required. Statistics would be required for measuring vehicle use and mileage travelled, in addition to data to select the most cost-effective delivery routes. Some of this information would probably be located in the head office to enable some central direction of transport to take place.

Warehouse

The attention of the warehouse management must **focus on efficient stock control**. The right products must be delivered to store when required, yet they should not hold too much in stock, as this ties up capital. Stock in hand could also eventually deteriorate if held too long. Some inputs for the mathematical stock control models that help with stock management could fall within the remit of the management accountant. Reports on stock levels and rate of stock turnover should therefore be a priority, in addition to the monitoring of costs. It is also likely that for some products, direct delivery from the supplier would be the practice, and information to confirm the cost effectiveness of this practice should be maintained.

Head Office

The overall direction of the company will take place from the Head Office. This would involve senior management receiving information on the performance of their functional areas in a **more aggregated form** and of **a more strategic nature** than at individual locations.

A centralised sales and marketing function governing price setting, advertising and sales promotion could be envisaged. In addition to summary sales statistics provided as routine to individual stores management (see above), information from sources external to the company would be desirable, for example covering market size or competitors' price levels. Additionally, data would be required to plot longer-term trends such as market size, changing tastes, population trends and demographic statistics. This data would inform future development, and decisions about stores extensions and the building of new stores, as well as the management of the use of existing space in stores. Some of this information will be generated by market researchers, however, and will not be the remit of the management accountant alone.

ACCA marking scheme		
		Marks
(a)	Explain and develop costing	2
	Explain and develop control	2
	Other issues/evidence of judgement	2
		6
(b)	2 marks for development of applied points on costing, control, strategy, non-financial measures etc for each function mentioned and Head Office	14
Total		20

4 NEWS FOR YOU

(a) Economic opinion on the effect of an **interest rate change** on News For You might vary. Keynesian economists argue that if base rate (and other interest rates) fall, this will lead to an increase in consumer demand (i.e. consumer spending). Unfortunately, however, even if the recent drop in the base rate increases consumer demand, it is unlikely to have any significant impact on the particular business of News For You. Sales are likely to remain unchanged, because newspapers and small confectionery items are low cost purchases, often bought on impulse. Interest rate movements will not make such items suddenly affordable where before they were not.

News For You needs to think about other ways in which the interest rate change might affect its business, and particularly its impact on business costs. If the company has an overdraft facility, its cost of borrowing will have been reduced. At the same time, the expansion plans require the business to raise £2 million, and changes in interest rates affect the cost of all types of capital, both loans and equity. Corporate borrowing rates are generally linked to the prevailing base rate or inter-bank lending rate, with companies paying a premium above base or interbank rate for their loans. The drop in interest rates will therefore affect the required return on the finance needed to fund the proposed expansion. If News For You uses Discounted Cash Flow analysis for investment appraisals, the fall in the cost of capital resulting from the drop in the base rate will mean that a lower discount rate can be applied to the investment evaluation. A lower rate of discount will result in a higher Net Present Value for any given proposal.

Keynesian economists, however, do not agree that changes in interest rates affect corporate investment decisions. They argue that investments are more dependent on the level of business confidence. It might be possible to suggest that News For You will see the fall in the base rate as stimulating general economic confidence. If so, it will be more confident about the future of its business, and so regardless of any changes in the cost of capital, it might be more willing to undertake the expansionary investment. (On the other hand, a fall in interest rates could be a response to a deterioration in the economy, and a loss of business confidence.)

The **inflation figures** are useful to News For You because they can directly affect profit and cash flow forecasts. The impact of inflation on cash flows and profit will be dependent to a large degree on the relative rates of increase in wages, the cost of wholesale supplies for the shop, and the prices that News For You can charge its customers. The quoted rate of inflation is very low at just over 1% per year and, although the rate is not expected to fall any further, its current level is unlikely to have a dramatic effect on the ability of the business to trade profitably. The greater risk for the business might come from the problem that, because inflation is so low, customers are not prepared to tolerate any price rises at all. If so, News For You might become more vulnerable to loss of business to the large food stores which can draw away customers via price cutting campaigns.

Personal and corporation tax rates are relevant to the owners of News For You because they will affect the net gain to the business that may be generated by expansion. As with interest rates, tax rates can affect personal spending patterns and therefore affect the turnover of a particular business. News For You, however, is unlikely to have a business that is sensitive to tax rates, because its products are basic essentials and low cost items. Nonetheless, the information that tax rates will remain unchanged is useful because it allows the business to be certain of the amount of tax relief that may be available on loan finance, and the relief that equity investors may claim for investing in a small unquoted company. This information might be useful in deciding whether or not to go ahead with the expansion, because it may affect the relative cost and availability of capital.

The **changes in taxes on tobacco** might be expected to have had a significant effect on News For You because it is one of the relatively high value products sold by the stores. The question indicates that tobacco sales have been falling, but it is unclear whether this drop is linked to the 10% rise in tax over the last twelve months, or simply a result of the population becoming more health conscious and so buying fewer cigarettes. If customers are price-sensitive in their purchasing of tobacco, News For You might once again find itself vulnerable to competition from the food retailers that can exercise greater buying power and sell similar products at lower prices. The high cost of these items also means that stocking costs are high, and if stock turnover is reduced because of tax increase, then the amount of working capital required by News For You will rise.

The **investigation into the food sector** might prove detrimental to News For You if it serves to initiate a price war amongst the retailers, all of whom will be anxious to prove that they look after their customers. The business grew very quickly between 20X2 and 20X6, but since then turnover has increased by just 2% per year, and the owners must be concerned that further growth potential is limited, at least within the existing outlets. Moving into the sale of basic foodstuffs has been used as a strategy to compensate for loss of sales in other products such as tobacco, but in many countries a large proportion of people do their food shopping in large retail outlets. By expanding their product range, News For You has also created for itself another set of competitors in the form of food retailers. The only way in which the business might gain from this investigation is if it also covers food wholesaling, and the result is a drop in the prices that News For You have to pay for their stock.

(b) **Arguments in favour of the expansion include the following:**

- The turnover figures suggest that there is only limited opportunity for the business to continue to grow organically. The business is seeking to replace sales of tobacco and newspapers with sales of foods, but as suggested in answer to (a), the potential of this side of the business may be limited. News For You may be advised to try to grow sales turnover by means of acquiring new outlets instead.

- If News For You is being forced into paying relatively high prices for supplies from a local wholesaler, then expansion may allow it to gain more bargaining power, and purchase at reduced rates from a national wholesale chain. Increased size will offer the opportunity to take advantage of possible economies of scale via bulk ordering. In this way, margins could be widened and the overall business made more profitable.

- With a larger number of stores covering a wider geographic area, News For You will be able to broaden the nature of their business base, so that it will be less vulnerable to regional economic trends.

Arguments against any expansion include the following:

- The potential to increase sales substantially via food sales is very limited. The majority of people purchase most of their food from larger stores, and will only use a local shop for small low cost items, for which it is not worthwhile making a special car journey to the supermarket. It is unlikely a profitable business can be created based on this type of sale.
- The widespread ownership of televisions and access to differing forms of mass media communications is likely to mean that fewer people will purchase newspapers on a daily basis. This is particularly true of those papers that are also published in electronic form. Many newsagents are dependent for the bulk of their sales on customers who come into the shop to buy a newspaper and then purchase additional items at the same time. If customers do not come in for a newspaper, then the associated sales income will also be lost. Expanding a business where there is such a risk of demand falling away may be regarded as very risky.
- The information in the question suggests that the competitive environment for News For You is becoming much tougher on a number of different fronts simultaneously, with rising excise duties, powerful food retailers and a reduction in tobacco and newspaper purchases. Expansion usually occurs because a business is very confident of the future, but in this case it is questionable whether News For You has much about which to be confident.

It would therefore seem advisable for News For You to postpone its expansion plans, and perhaps look at ways of using its existing outlets to sell very different products, thereby 're-inventing' their business, perhaps by moving completely away from confectionery and into, for example, video rental.

5 DISCOURAGING MONOPOLY AND AVAILABILITY OF FINANCE

Key answer tips

To answer part (a), a knowledge of basic economics would be helpful, but common sense and an awareness of the business environment could help you to provide a reasonable answer. Don't let part (a) put you off the question. Part (b) and part (c) are both relatively straightforward. The answer provided here discusses obtaining a listing to issue shares on a main stock market, as well as private sources of equity finance. It would also be reasonable to make the point that companies whose shares are traded on a junior market, such as AIM in the UK, are not 'listed' companies, and an unlisted company could therefore raise equity by issuing shares on the junior market.

(a) Many governments consider it necessary to prevent or control monopolies.

A **pure monopoly** exists when one organisation controls the production or supply of a good that has no close substitute. In practice, legislation may consider a monopoly situation to occur when there is limited competition in a particular market. For example, UK legislation considers a monopoly to occur if an organisation controls 25% or more of a particular market.

Governments consider it necessary to act against an existing or potential monopoly because of the economic problems that can arise through the abuse of a dominant market position. Monopoly can lead to *economic inefficiency in the use of resources*, so that output is at a higher cost than necessary. Further inefficiency can arise as a monopoly *may lack the incentive to innovate*, to research technological improvements, or to eliminate unnecessary managers, since it can always be sure of passing on the cost of its inefficiencies to its customers. Inefficiencies such as these have been seen as major problems in state-owned monopolies and have fuelled the movement towards privatisation in recent years. It has been expected that the competition arising following privatisation will lead to the elimination of these kinds of inefficiency.

Monopoly can also result in *high prices* being charged for output, so that the cost to customers is higher than would be the case if significant competition existed, allowing monopolies to generate monopoly profits.

The government can prevent monopolies occurring by *monitoring proposed takeovers and mergers*, and acting when it decides that a monopoly situation may occur. This monitoring is carried out in the UK by the Office of Fair Trading, which can refer takeovers and mergers that are potentially against the public interest to the Competition Commission for detailed investigation.

The Competition Commission has the power to prevent a proposed takeover or merger, or to allow it to proceed with conditions attached, such as disposal of a portion of the business in order to preserve competition.

Tutorial note

Your answer might refer to legislation or regulations in a country other than the UK.

(b) In the UK, a company is required by law to offer an issue of new shares to raise cash on a pro-rata basis to its existing shareholders. This ensures that the existing pattern of ownership and control will not be affected if all shareholders take up the new shares offered. Because this right of existing shareholders to be offered new equity is a legal one, such an issue is called a **rights issue**. (However, shareholders can vote to waive their rights, such as when the company wishes to obtain a stock market quotation for the shares.)

If an unlisted company decides that it needs to raise a large amount of equity finance and provided existing shareholders have agreed, it can decide to obtain a listing for its shares, and offer ordinary shares to new investors (the public at large) via an **offer for sale**. Such an offer is usually part of the process of seeking a stock exchange quotation, and it leads to the wider spread of ownership that is needed to meet the requirements of the listing regulations and the stock exchange concerned. An offer for sale may be either at a fixed price, where the offer price is set in advance by the issuing company, or by tender, where investors are invited to submit bids for shares. (***Tutorial note***: Offers for sale by tender are uncommon.) An offer for sale will result in a significant change to the shareholder structure of the company, for example by bringing in institutional investors. In order to ensure that the required amount of finance is raised, offers for sale are underwritten by institutional investors who guarantee to buy any unwanted shares.

A **placing** is cheaper than an offer for sale. In a placing, large blocks of shares are placed with institutional investors, so that the spread of new ownership is not as wide as with an offer for sale. While a placing may be part of seeking a listing and a stock exchange quotation (for example, it is very popular with companies wanting to float on markets for smaller companies such as the Alternative Investment Market in the UK), it can also provide equity finance for a company that wishes to remain unlisted.

New shares can also be sold by an unlisted company by **private negotiation,** to individual investors or a venture capital organisation. While the amount of equity finance raised by this method is small, it has been supported in the UK in recent years by government initiatives such as the Enterprise Investment Scheme and Venture Capital Trusts schemes in the UK.

(c) The factors that should be considered by a company when choosing between an issue of debt and issue of equity finance could include the following:

Risk and return

Raising debt finance will increase the gearing and the financial risk of the company, while raising equity finance will lower gearing and financial risk.

Financial risk arises since raising debt brings a commitment to meet regular interest payments, whether fixed or variable. Failure to meet these interest payments gives debt holders the right to appoint a receiver to recover their investment. In contrast, there is no right to receive dividends on ordinary shares, only a right to participate in any dividend (share of profit) declared by the directors of a company. If profits are low, then dividends can be passed, but interest must be paid regardless of the level of profits. Furthermore, increasing the level of interest payments will increase the volatility of returns to shareholders, since only returns in excess of the cost of debt accrue to shareholders.

Cost

Debt is cheaper than equity because debt is less risky from an investor point of view. This is because it is often secured by either a fixed or floating charge on company assets and ranks above equity on liquidation, and because of the statutory requirement to pay interest. Debt is also cheaper than equity because interest is an allowable deduction in calculating taxable profit. This is referred to as the tax efficiency of debt.

Ownership and control

Issuing equity can have ownership implications for a company, particularly if the finance is raised by means of a placing or offer for sale. Shareholders also have the right to appoint directors and auditors, and the right to attend general meetings of the company. While issuing debt has no such ownership implications, an issue of debt can place restrictions on the activities of a company by means of restrictive covenants included in the issue documents. For example, a restrictive covenant may specify a maximum level of gearing or a minimum level of interest cover which the borrowing company must not exceed, or a covenant may forbid the securing of further debt on particular assets.

Redemption

Equity finance is permanent capital that does not need to be redeemed, while debt finance will need to be redeemed at some future date. Redeeming a large amount of debt can place a severe strain on the cash flow of a company, although this can be addressed by refinancing or by using convertible debt.

Flexibility

Debt finance is more flexible than equity, in that various amounts can be borrowed, at a fixed or floating interest rate and for a range of maturities, to suit the financing need of a company. If debt finance is no longer required, it can more easily be repaid (depending on the issue terms).

Availability

A new issue of equity finance may not be readily available to a listed company or may be available on terms that are unacceptable with regards to issue price or issue quantity, if the stock market is depressed (a bear market). Current shareholders may be unwilling to subscribe to a rights issue, for example if they have made other investment plans or if they have urgent calls on their existing finances. A new issue of debt finance may not be available to a listed company, or available at a cost considered to be unacceptable, if it has a poor credit rating, or if it faces trading difficulties.

ACCA marking scheme		
		Marks
(a)	Meaning of monopoly	1
	Discussion of economic problems of monopoly	5
	Discussion of role of government	3
		9
(b)	Rights issue	2
	Offer for sale	2
	Placing	2
	Private sale to individuals or institutions	2
		8
(c)	Up to 2 marks for each well discussed factor	8
Total		25

6 PLANKERS LTD

(a) (i)

	£m
Cash brought forward at 1 June 20X5:	8.48
Building programme investment	(12.00)
Minimum cash balance requirement	1.00
Additional loan required at 1 June 20X5:	4.52

The cash balance needed for 31 May 20X6 will be added to by cash retentions during the year. This can be found from the P&L account for 31 May 20X6.

Projected P&L for the year to 31 May 20X6

	£m
PBIT before depreciation	1.980
(£1.71m × 1.05 × 1.05 × 1.05)	
Extra depreciation (15% of (50% of £12m)	(0.900)
Interest charges (see note)	(1.037)
Profit before tax	0.043
Tax (30%)	0.013
Profit after tax	0.030
Cash available in profit after tax:	
Profit after tax	0.030
Add back depreciation (non-cash expense)	0.900
	0.930

Note on interest charges:

Total loans = £7m + £4.52m = £11.52m

Interest rate = 9%

Interest = £11.52m × 0.09 = £1.037m.

(ii) **Check on cash balances at 31 May 20X6**

Cash ledger	DR	CR
	£m	£m
Brought forward 1 June 20X5	8.48	
Cash retentions	0.93	
Additional loan financing	4.52	
Building programme expenditure		12.00
Carried forward balance 31 May 20X6		1.93

The conditions of the loan and the other targets can then be checked:

Interest cover: = (1.98 – 0.9)/1.037: = 1.041 times

EPS: (Profit after tax/number of shares = £0.03m/4m shares): 0.75p

The minimum cash balance target is met. However, the target minimum interest cover (3 times) and the target minimum EPS (20 pence) are not met.

(iii) **Options**

1 Delay the building programme until sufficient funds are available from cash retentions

2 Re-negotiate the terms of the long-term loan

3 Pay out less in dividends

4 Leasing assets rather than buying them

5 Raise further equity capital

6 Sell assets

7 Reduce working capital investments

8 Combinations of the above

(iv) The only condition satisfied is that relating to the minimum cash balance. Both the interest cover and the EPS conditions are breached. The scale of the building programme suggests that options 1, 3, 4, 6 and 7 are very unlikely to provide sufficient additional capital. Extending the loan facilities in option 2 would likely make worse the interest cover and EPS figures. The only viable option appears to be an equity issue.

(b) (i) **Responding to various stakeholder groups**

If a company has a single objective in terms of maximising profitability then it is only responding to one stakeholder group, namely shareholders. However, companies can no longer fail to respond to the interests and concerns of a wider range of groups, particularly with respect to those who may have a non-financial interest in the organisation. Stakeholder groups with a non-financial interest can therefore generate for companies non-financial objectives and place constraints on their operations to the extent that the company is prepared to respond to such groups.

Various stakeholder groupings can emerge. The following represents examples of likely groups, their non-financial objectives and/or the constraints they may place on a business:

Stakeholder	*Objective*	*Constraints*
Employees	Employee welfare	Maximum hours worked
Community	Responding to community concerns	Limits on activities
Customers	Product or service levels	Minimum quality standards

Stakeholder	*Objective*	*Constraints*
Suppliers	Good trading relationships	
Government	Protecting the consumer	Minimum standards on products or services
Trade bodies	Protecting professional reputation	Minimum standards on products or services

(ii) **The difficulties associated with managing organisations with multiple objectives**

To the extent that an organisation faces a range of stakeholders, then they also face multiple objectives. This would not particularly be a problem if the multiple objectives were congruent, but they normally are not. There are a number of difficulties:

- Multiple stakeholders imply multiple objectives. To the extent that they conflict then compromises must be made. This will lead potentially to opportunity costs in that maximisation of profitability will potentially be reduced.
- Responding to stakeholders other than shareholders involves costs, either in management time or in directly responding to their needs.
- Some objectives are not clearly defined, for example what is actually meant by 'protecting the consumer'? It will therefore not always be clear to the organisation that they have met the needs of all of their stakeholders.
- Some of the objectives may actually be conflicting where compromise is not possible. Prioritisation and ranking will then have to take place. Questions then arise as to who is the most important stakeholder or what ranking should be assigned?
- New stakeholder groups often emerge. This can create a problem of longer-term strategic management in that plans can be diverted if new pressures arise. For example, environmental issues were not so important 20 years ago.
- Management of the organisation becomes complex when multiple objectives have to be satisfied. Each managerial decision is likely to face many constraints.

ACCA marking scheme

				Marks
(a)	(i)	Additional loan required		2
		Projected P&L		1
		Cash retention		2
	(ii)	Cash carried forward		1
		Assessment of constraints		2
	(iii)	1 mark each for five realistic options		5
	(iv)	Relevant comments	up to	3
				16
(b)	(i)	1 mark each for identified constraint	up to	4
	(ii)	2 marks for each detailed point on multiple objectives	up to	5
Total				25

7 RZP CO

(a) Analysis of data provided

Year	*20X4*	*20X3*	*20X2*	*20X1*	*20X0*
Dividend per share	2.8p	2.3p	2.2p	2.2p	1.7p
Annual dividend growth	21.7%	4.5%	Nil	29.4%	
Earnings per share	19.04p	14.95p	11.22p	15.84p	13.43
Annual earnings growth	27.3%	33.2%	-29.2%	17.9%	
Price/earnings ratio	22.0	33.5	25.5	17.2	15.2
Share price	418.9p	500.8p	286.1p	272.4p	204.1p
Annual share price growth	-16.3%	75.0%	5.0%	33.5%	
Dividend per share	2.8p	2.3p	2.2p	2.2p	1.7p
General price index	117	113	110	105	100
Real dividend per share	2.4p	2.0p	2.0p	2.1p	1.7p
Annual dividend growth	20.0%	Nil	-4.8%	23.5%	

Average dividend growth:

Arithmetic mean = (21.7 + 4.5 + 0 + 29.4)/4 = 55.6/4 = 13.9%

Equivalent annual growth rate = [(2.8/1.7)0.25 – 1] × 100 = 13.3%

Average earnings per share growth:

Arithmetic mean = (27.3 + 33.2 – 29.2 + 17.9)/4 = 49.2/4 =12.3%

Equivalent annual growth rate = [(19.04/13.43)0.25 – 1] × 100 = 9.1%

Average share price growth:

Arithmetic mean = (–16.3 + 75.0 + 5.0 + 33.5)/4 = 97.2/4 = 24.3%

Equivalent annual growth rate = [(418.9/204.1)0.25 – 1] × 100 = 19.7%

Average real dividend growth:

Arithmetic mean = (20.0 + 0 – 4.8 + 23.5)/4 = 38.7/4 = 9.7%

Equivalent annual growth rate = [(2.4/1.7)0.25 – 1] × 100 = 9.0%

Discussion of analysis and views expressed by chairman

The chairman's statement claims that RZP Co has delivered growth in every year in dividends, earnings and ordinary share price, apart from 20X2. Analysis shows that the chairman is correct in excluding 20X2, when no growth occurred in dividends, earnings fell by 29.2%, and real dividends fell by 4.8%. Analysis also shows that no growth in real dividends occurred in 20X3 and that the company's share price fell by 16.3% in 20X4. It is possible the chairman may not have been referring to real dividend growth, in which case his statement could be amended. However, shareholders will be aware of the decline in share price in 20X4 or could calculate the decline from the information provided, so the chairman cannot claim that RZP Co has delivered share price growth in 20X4. In fact, the statement could explain the reasons for the decline in share price in order to reassure shareholders. It also possible for the five-year summary to be extended to include annual share price data, such as maximum, minimum and average share price, so that shareholders have this information readily available.

The chairman's statement claims that RZP Co has consistently delivered above-average performance. The company may have delivered above- or below-average performance in individual years but without further information in the form of sector averages for individual years, it is not possible to reach a conclusion on this point. The average growth rates for the sector cannot therefore be used to comment on the performance of RZP Co in individual years. If the company has consistently delivered above-average performance, however, the company's average annual growth rates should be greater than the sector averages.

The growth rates can be compared as follows:

	Arithmetic mean	*Equivalent annual rate*	*Sector*
Nominal dividends	13.9%	13.3%	10%
Real dividends	9.7%	9.0%	9%
Earnings per share	12.3%	9.1%	10%
Share price	24.3%	19.7%	20%

It can be seen that if the sector average growth rates are arithmetic mean growth rates, the chairman's statement is correct. If the sector average growth rates are equivalent annual growth rates, however, only the nominal dividend growth rate is greater than the sector average. The basis on which the sector average growth rates have been prepared should therefore be clarified in order to determine whether the chairman's statement is correct.

(b) The dividend yield and capital growth for 20X4 must be calculated with reference to the 20X3 end-of-year share price. The dividend yield is 0.56% (100 × 2.8/500.8) and the capital growth is –16.35% (100 × (418.9 – 500.8)/500.8), so the total shareholder return is –15.79% or –15.8% (0.56 – 16.35). A negative return of 15.8% looks even worse when it is noted that annual inflation for 20X4 was 3.5% (117/113).

While the negative total shareholder return is at odds with the chairman's claim to have delivered growth in dividends and share price in 20X4, a different view might have emerged if average share prices had been used, since the return calculation ignores share price volatility. The chairman should also be aware that share prices may be affected by other factors than corporate activity, so a good performance in share price terms may not be due to managerial excellence. It also possible that the negative return may represent a good performance when compared to the sector as a whole in 20X4: further information is needed to assess this.

Note that total shareholder return can also be found as (100 × (2.8 + 418.9 – 500.8)/500.8).

(c) The objectives of managers may conflict with the objectives of shareholders, particularly with the objective of maximisation of shareholder wealth. Management remuneration package are one way in which goal congruence between managers and shareholders may be increased. Such packages should motivate managers while supporting the achievement of shareholder wealth maximisation. The following factors should be considered when deciding on a remuneration package intended to encourage directors to act in ways that maximise shareholder wealth.

Clarity and transparency

The terms of the remuneration package should be clear and transparent so that directors and shareholders are in no doubt as to when rewards have been earned or the basis on which rewards have been calculated.

Appropriate performance measure

The managerial performance measure selected for use in the remuneration package should support the achievement of shareholder wealth maximisation. It is therefore likely that the performance measure could be linked to share price changes.

Quantitative performance measure

The managerial performance measure should be quantitative and the manner in which it is to be calculated should be specified. The managerial performance measure should ideally be linked to a benchmark comparing the company's performance with that of its peers. The managerial performance measure should not be open to manipulation by management.

Time horizon

The remuneration package should have a time horizon that is linked to that of shareholders. If shareholders desire long-term capital growth, for example, the remuneration package should discourage decisions whose objective is to maximise short-term profits at the expense of long-term growth.

Impartiality

In recent years there has been an increased emphasis on decisions about managerial remuneration packages being removed from the control of managers who benefit from them. The use of remuneration committees in listed companies is an example of this. The impartial decisions of non-executive directors, it is believed, will eliminate or reduce managerial self-interest and encourage remuneration packages that support the achievement of shareholder rather than managerial goals.

Appropriate management remuneration packages for RZP Co

Remuneration packages may be based on a performance measure linked to values in the profit and loss account. A bonus could be awarded, for example, based on growth in turnover, profit before tax, or earnings (earnings per share). Such performance measures could lead to maximisation of profit in the short-term rather than in the long-term, for example by deferring capital expenditure required to reduce environmental pollution, and may encourage managers to manipulate reported financial information in order to achieve bonus targets. They could also lead to sub-optimal managerial performance if managers do enough to earn their bonus, but then reduce their efforts once their target has been achieved.

RZP Co has achieved earnings growth of more than 20% in both 20X3 and 20X4, but this is likely to reflect in part a recovery from the negative earnings growth in 20X1, since over the five-year period its earnings growth is not very different from its sector's (it may be worse). If annual earnings growth were to be part of a remuneration package for RZP Co, earnings growth could perhaps be compared to the sector and any bonus made conditional upon ongoing performance in order to discourage a short-term focus.

Remuneration packages may be based on a performance measure linked to relative stock market performance, e.g. share price growth over the year compared to average share price growth for the company's sector, or compared to growth in a stock market index, such as the FTSE 100. This would have the advantage that managers would be encouraged to make decisions that had a positive effect on the company's share price and hence are likely to be consistent with shareholder wealth maximisation. However, as noted earlier, other factors than managerial decisions can have a continuing effect on share prices and so managers may fail to be rewarded for good performance due to general economic changes or market conditions.

RZP Co recorded negative share price growth in 20X4 and the reasons for this should be investigated. In the circumstances, a remuneration package linked to benchmarked share price growth could focus the attention of RZP managers on decisions likely to increase shareholder wealth. The effect of such a remuneration package could be enhanced if the reward received by managers were partly or wholly in the form of shares or share options. Apart from emphasising the focus on share price growth, such a reward scheme would encourage goal congruence between shareholders and managers by turning managers into shareholders.

ACCA marking scheme		
		Marks
(a)	Growth in dividends per share: analysis/discussion	4-5
	Share price growth: analysis/discussion	4-5
	Growth in earnings per share: analysis/discussion	4-5
	Maximum	13
(b)	Calculation of total shareholder return	2
	Comment	1
	Maximum	3
(c)	Discussion of factors	5-6
	Examples of appropriate remuneration packages	4-5
	Maximum	9
Total		25

MANAGEMENT OF WORKING CAPITAL

8 HEXICON PLC

Key answer tips

Part (a) is standard textbook material. For five marks, you should give at least five reasons, and don't forget a brief explanation: 'it uses cash flows' will not get the full marks available. As the question mentions other approaches, you should structure your answer around direct comparisons with alternative methods of investment appraisal.

In part (b) you are applying the familiar EOQ model in the context of a change to a just-in-time system. To answer both parts, you need to assess the 'before' and 'after' positions, evaluating the changes between the two. Note that the question includes information on tax and discount rates, so you are clearly intended to take account of both of these in your evaluation (particularly in the light of part (a)). You should be prepared for the examiner to include various syllabus areas and techniques within one question.

Part (c) first requires an explanation of JIT agreements ('the nature of') and then a discussion as to the reasons for such agreements ('the objectives of').

(a) The following reasons may be cited for using the net present value (NPV) method of investment appraisal:

(i) Compared to accounting rate of return (ARR), it discounts real cash flows as opposed to accounting profits which are affected by non-cash items.

(ii) Compared to measuring internal rate of return (IRR), the NPV method only gives one solution. In some circumstances, (when there are a number of outflows occurring at different times), multiple IRR solutions are possible.

(iii) Compared to the payback method, NPV considers all of the cash flows of a project.

(iv) By using a discount rate it measures the opportunity cost of the money invested by a person in a project.

(v) The interest rate used can be increased/decreased depending upon the level of perceived risk in the investment.

(vi) The NPV of a project can be shown to be equal to the increase in the value of shareholder's equity in the company. Thus the method is consistent with the objective of shareholder wealth maximisation.

(b) (i) The **present EOQ** is $\sqrt{\dfrac{2\times £100\times 40{,}000}{20\%\times £2.50}}$ = 4,000 units/order

The **revised EOQ** = $\sqrt{\dfrac{2\times £25\times 40{,}000}{20\%\times £2.50}}$ = 2,000 units/order

From this it can be seen that the EOQ is halved.

(ii) The number of orders has increased from (40,000/4,000) 10 orders to (40,000/2,000) 20 orders. However, ordering costs are reduced by:

(10 × £100) - (20 × £25) = £500 per annum

Average stocks have also reduced from $\dfrac{4{,}000}{2}$ (2,000 units) to $\dfrac{2{,}000}{2}$ (1,000 units). Consequently carrying costs have reduced by 20% × £2.50 × 1,000 = £500 per annum.

Total inventory costs are thereby reduced by £1,000 per annum (before tax).

Assuming that Hexicon plc pays tax in the same year as it earns profits, the present value of the proposal is found by comparing the outflow cost with the discounted after-tax savings over the eight-year life of the proposal (using a 12% discount rate). The after-tax savings are £1,000 × 67% = £670.

Discounted savings:

Year	*Item*	*Cash flow*	*Discount factor at 12%*	*Present value*
		£		£
1 - 8	After-tax savings	670	4.968	3,329
0	Cost of reorganisation	(4,000)	1.000	(4,000)
0	Tax saving (assume same year: 33% × £4,000)	1,320	1.000	1,320
	Net benefit			649

As the present value of the proposal is positive, it is worthwhile.

(c) The **main objective of Just In Time (JIT) purchasing** is to match the delivery of components from suppliers to their usage in production. If this is achieved there are significant benefits to be gained by both the supplier and the customer.

The customer is likely to use only one supplier for each component and to build up a relationship with the supplier which encourages communication thus enabling the supplier to benefit from advanced production planning and economies of scale. To enhance this relationship, the customer makes a long-term commitment to future orders.

The supplier guarantees to deliver goods of an appropriate quality in accordance with an agreed delivery schedule. The benefit to the customer is thereby a reduction (or elimination) of stockholding and significant cost savings. These arise in both holding costs and also in materials handling, because goods are transferred directly from goods inwards to production.

9 BLIN

Key answer tips

Parts (a) and (c) of this question should be fairly straightforward. For part (a), your answer should give some emphasis to the yield curve. Part (b) is probably more difficult, because it is not necessarily easy to see what the examiner had in mind with 'approaches'. Thinking about the question logically might help you to construct an answer. You are asked to comment on approaches to the mix of long-term and short-term funding to finance working capital. Logically, the approaches are (1) to have mainly long-term capital and not much short-term capital, (2) to have mainly short-term capital and not much long-term capital, and (3) to have a more balanced mixture of short-term and long-term capital. These are the approaches in the solution.

However, the distinction between 'permanent' levels of current assets and 'fluctuating' levels of current assets is a useful distinction, which the solution in part (b) uses as a basis for analysis. A company's current assets are continually changing in total amount, up and down, but there is usually a 'permanent' amount below which the total of current assets does not fall. Fluctuating current assets are current assets in excess of the minimum level.

(a) The following factors will influence the rate of interest charged on the new bank loan.

General level of interest rates

Interest rates charged on loans will depend on the general level of interest rates. Typically, interest rates on a bank loan are set at a margin above a 'base rate' or 'prime rate' or at a margin above a money market benchmark rate such as LIBOR. Similarly, longer-term fixed interest rates are at a margin above either a government bond rate or the swap rate. When the general level of interest rates goes up, rates on new lending will also rise.

Risk of default

The bank providing the loan to Blin will make an assessment of the risk that the company might default on its loan commitments and charge an interest rate that reflects this risk. Since Blin is listed on a stock exchange it will be seen as less risky than an unlisted company and will pay a lower interest rate as a result. The period of time that the company has been listed may also be an influential factor.

Since Blin has expanded sales significantly and relies heavily on overdraft finance, it may be overtrading. This could increase the risk of default and so increase the rate of interest charged on the loan. The bank would need to be convinced through financial information supporting the loan application, such as cash flow forecasts, that Blin would be able to meet future interest payments and repayments of principal.

Security offered

The rate of interest charged on the loan will be lower if the debt is secured against an asset or assets of the company. It is likely in Blin's case that the loan will carry a fixed charge on particular assets, such as land or buildings. In the event of default by the company, the bank can recover its loan by selling the secured assets.

Duration of loan

The longer the period of the loan taken out by Blin, the higher the interest rate that will be charged. This reflects the shape of the normal yield curve.

Yield curve

The normal yield curve shows that the yield required on debt increases in line with the term to maturity. One reason for this is that loan providers require compensation for deferring their use of the cash they have lent, and the longer the period for which they are deprived of their cash, the more compensation they require. This is described as the liquidity preference explanation for the shape of the normal yield curve.

Other explanations for the shape of the normal yield curve are expectations theory and market segmentation theory. Expectations theory suggests that interest rates rise with maturity because rates of interest are expected to rise in the future, for example due to an expected increase in inflation. Market segmentation theory suggests that the market for long-term debt differs from the market for short-term debt.

Amount borrowed

The rate of interest charged on the new loan could be lower if the amount borrowed is not a small sum. It is more convenient from an administrative point of view for a bank to lend a large sum rather than several small amounts.

(b) The approaches that Blin could adopt regarding the relative proportions of long- and short-term finance to meet its working capital needs could be described as conservative, moderate and aggressive.

The assets of a business are categorised into current assets and fixed assets. Current assets are used up on a regular basis within a single accounting period and fixed assets benefit a business for several accounting periods. Current assets can be further categorised into permanent current assets and fluctuating current assets. Permanent current assets represent the core level or minimum level of investment in current assets needed for a given level of business activity, and arise from the need for businesses to carry stock and to extend credit. Fluctuating current assets represent a variable need for investment in current assets, arising from either seasonal or unpredictable variations in business activity.

With a ***conservative* approach** to the financing mix, long-term finance is the main source of working capital funds. Long-term finance is used to finance fixed assets, permanent current assets and some fluctuating current assets.

Long-term debt finance is less risky to a company than short-term debt finance, since once in place it is not subjected to the dangers of renewal or immediate repayment. However, it is more expensive in that the rate of interest charged normally increases with maturity. A conservative approach would therefore increase the amount of lower-risk long-term debt finance used by the company, but would also incur higher total interest payments than an approach emphasizing the use of short-term debt. This approach will therefore lead to relatively lower profitability. A similar argument can be made when equity finance is used as long-term finance; equity requires an even higher return than long-term debt finance.

With an ***aggressive* approach** to the financing mix, short-term finance is the main source of working capital funds. This approach, which is currently being used by Blin, uses short-term finance for fluctuating current assets and some permanent current assets, with long-term finance being used for the balance of permanent current assets and fixed assets. This increases the relative amount of higher-risk short-term finance used by the company, but will also incur lower total interest payments than the conservative approach discussed above, leading to relatively higher profitability.

Between these two approaches lies a **moderate or matching approach**. This approach applies the matching principle, whereby the maturity of the funding is matched with life of the assets financed. Here, long-term finance is used for permanent current assets and fixed assets, while short-term finance is used for fluctuating current assets.

The repayment of the overdraft will result in Blin adopting a conservative approach to the mix of long- and short-term finance. This will resolve an overtrading situation, if it exists. However, it may reduce profitability more than necessary. If Blin continues to expand sales, or reintroduces overdraft finance, the conservative position will only be temporary and a moderate position may arise in the future. The speed with which this happens will depend on the size of the loan taken out, and whether a moderate position is desirable will depend on the company's attitude to risk and return. It may be preferable to reduce the overdraft to a lower level rather than repaying it completely. A clearer picture would emerge if we knew the intended use for, and the amount of, the balance of the loan not being used to repay the overdraft.

(c) The **cash operating cycle** is the length of time between paying trade creditors and receiving cash from debtors. It can be calculated by adding together the average stock holding period and the average time for debtors to pay, and then subtracting the average time taken to pay trade creditors. The stock holding period may be subdivided into the holding periods for raw materials, work-in-progress and finished goods. Using accounting ratios, the cash operating cycle can be approximated by adding together stock days and debtor days (debtors' ratio) and subtracting creditor days (creditors' ratio). If creditors are paid before cash is received from debtors, the cash operating cycle is positive; if debtors pay before trade creditors are paid, the cycle is negative.

The significance of the cash operating cycle in determining the level of investment in working capital is that the longer the cash operating cycle, the higher the investment in working capital.

The length of the cash operating cycle varies between industries: for example, a service organization may have no stock holding period, a retail organization will have a stock holding period based almost entirely on finished goods and a very low level of debtors, and a manufacturing organization will have a stock holding period based on raw materials, work-in-progress and finished goods. The level of investment in working capital will therefore depend on the nature of business operations.

The cash operating cycle and the resulting level of investment in working capital does not depend only on the nature of the business, however. Companies within the same business sector may have different levels of investment in working capital, measured for example by the accounting ratio of sales/net working capital, as a result of adopting different working capital policies. A relatively aggressive policy on the level of investment in working capital is characterised by lower levels of stock and debtors: this lower level of investment increases profitability but also increases the risk of running out of stock, or of losing potential customers due to better credit terms being offered by competitors. A relatively conservative policy on the level of investment in working capital has higher levels of investment in stock and debtors: profitability is therefore reduced, but the risk of stock-outs is lower and new credit customers may be attracted by more generous terms.

It is also possible to reduce the level of investment in working capital by reducing the length of the cash operating cycle. This is achieved by reducing the stock holding period (for example by using JIT methods), by reducing the average time taken by debtors to pay (for example by improving debtor management), or by increasing the length of credit period taken from suppliers (for example by settling invoices as late as possible). In this way an understanding of the cash operating cycle can assist in taking steps to improve working capital management and profitability.

ACCA marking scheme		
		Marks
(a)	Risk of default	2
	Security	2
	Duration	1
	Yield curve	3
	Amount borrowed	1
		9

(b)	Relative risk of long- and short-term finance	1
	Discussion of aggressive approach	2
	Discussion of conservative approach	2
	Discussion of moderate/matching approach	2
	Comment on repayment of overdraft	2
		9
(c)	Meaning of cash operating cycle	2
	Significance re level of working capital investment	5
		7
Total		25

10 VELM PLC

(a) The benefits of the proposed policy change are as follows.

Trade terms are 40 days, but debtors are taking 365 × 550,000/4 million = 50 days. Current level of debtors = £550,000.

Cost of 1% discount = 0.01 × 4m × 2/3 = £26,667.

Proposed level of debtors = (4,000,000 – 26,667) × (26/365) = £283,000.

Reduction in debtors = 550,000 – 283,000 = £267,000.

Debtors appear to be financed by the overdraft at an annual rate of 9%.

		£
Reduction in financing cost	£267,000 × 9%	24,030
Reduction of 0.6% in bad debts	0.6% × £4 million	24,000
Salary saving from early retirement		12,000
Total benefits		60,030
Cost of 1% discount (see above)		(26,667)
Net benefit of discount		33,363

A discount for early payment of one per cent will therefore lead to an increase in profitability for Velm plc.

(b) **Short-term sources of debt finance** include overdrafts and short-term loans. An **overdraft** offers flexibility but it is technically repayable on demand. Consequently it is a relatively risky source of finance. A company could experience liquidity problems if an overdraft were called in, until an alternative source of finance were found. The danger with a **short-term loan** as a source of finance is that it may be renewed at maturity on less favourable terms if economic circumstances have deteriorated and short-term interest rats are higher.

Short-term finance should be cheaper than long-term finance, based on the assumption of a normal shape to the yield curve. Economic circumstances could invert the yield curve, for example if short-term interest rates have been increased in order to curb economic growth or to dampen inflationary pressures.

Long-term sources of debt finance include loan stock, debentures and long-term loans. These are relatively secure forms of finance. For example if a company meets its contractual obligations on debentures in terms of interest payments and loan covenants, it will not have to repay the finance until maturity. The risk for the company is therefore lower if it finances working capital from a long-term source.

However, long-term finance is usually more expensive than short-term finance. The shape of the normal yield curve indicates that providers of debt finance will expect compensation for deferred consumption and default risk, as well as protection against expected inflation.

The choice between short-term and long-term debt for the financing of working capital is hence a choice between cheaper but riskier short-term finance and more expensive but less risky long-term debt.

(c) Working capital policies on the method of financing working capital can be characterised as conservative, moderate and aggressive. A **conservative financing policy** would involve financing working capital needs predominantly from long-term sources of finance. If current assets are analysed into permanent and fluctuating current assets, a conservative policy would use long-term finance for permanent current assets and some of the fluctuating current assets. Such a policy would increase the amount of lower-risk finance used by the company, at the expense of increased interest payments and lower profitability.

Velm plc is clearly not pursuing a conservative financing policy, since long-term debt only accounts for 2.75% (40/1,450) of non-cash current assets. Rather, it seems to be following an **aggressive financing policy**, characterised by short-term finance being used for all of fluctuating current assets and most of the permanent current assets as well. Such a policy will decrease interest costs and increase profitability, but at the expense of an increase in the amount of higher-risk finance used by the company.

Between these two extremes in policy terms lies a **moderate or matching approach**, where short-term finance is used for fluctuating current assets and long-term finance is used for permanent current assets. This is an expression of the matching principle, which holds that the maturity of the finance should match the maturity of the assets.

(d) The objectives of working capital management are often stated to be profitability and liquidity. These objectives are often in conflict, since liquid assets earn the lowest return and so liquidity is achieved at the expense of profitability. However, liquidity is needed in the sense that a company must meet its liabilities as they fall due if it is to remain in business. For this reason cash is often called the lifeblood of the company, since without cash a company would quickly fail. Good working capital management is therefore necessary if the company is to survive and remain profitable.

The fundamental objective of the company is to maximise the wealth of its shareholders and good working capital management helps to achieve this by **minimising the cost of investing in current assets**. **Good credit management**, for example, aims to minimise the risk of bad debts and expedite the prompt payment of money due from debtors in accordance with agreed terms of trade. Taking steps to optimise the level and age of debtors will minimise the cost of financing them, leading to an increase in the returns available to shareholders.

A similar case can be made for the **management of stock**. It is likely that Velm plc will need to have a good range of stationery and office supplies on its premises if customers' needs are to be quickly met and their custom retained. Good stock management, for example using techniques such as the economic order quantity model, ABC analysis, stock rotation and buffer stock management can minimise the costs of holding and ordering stock. The application of just-in-time methods of stock procurement and manufacture can reduce the cost of investing in stock. Taking steps to improve stock management can therefore reduce costs and increase shareholder wealth.

Cash budgets can help to determine the transactions need for cash in each budget control period, although the optimum cash position will also depend on the precautionary and speculative need for cash. Cash management models such as the Baumol model and the Miller-Orr model can help to maintain cash balances close to optimum levels.

The different elements of good working capital management therefore combine to help the company to achieve its primary financial objective.

ACCA marking scheme		
		Marks
(a)	Reduction in debtors	1
	Cost of discount	1
	Reduction in financing costs	1
	Reduction in bad debts	1
	Calculation of net benefit and conclusion	1
		5
(b)	Risks of short-term finance	2
	Cost of short-term finance	1
	Risks of long-term finance	1
	Cost of long-term finance	1
	Discussion and conclusion	1
		6
(c)	Permanent and fluctuating current assets	2
	Explanation of financing policies	4
	Discussion and link to Velm plc	1
		7
(d)	Objectives of working capital management	2
	Credit management	2
	Stock management	2
	Discussion and link to Velm plc	1
		7
Total		25

11 SPECIAL GIFT SUPPLIES PLC

(a) The funding requirements for working capital is the sum of:

	Months
Stock holding period	3.5
Debtors collection period	2.5
Creditors payment period	(2.0)
Working capital funding period	4.0

Diagrammatically, the funding requirement may be represented as follows.

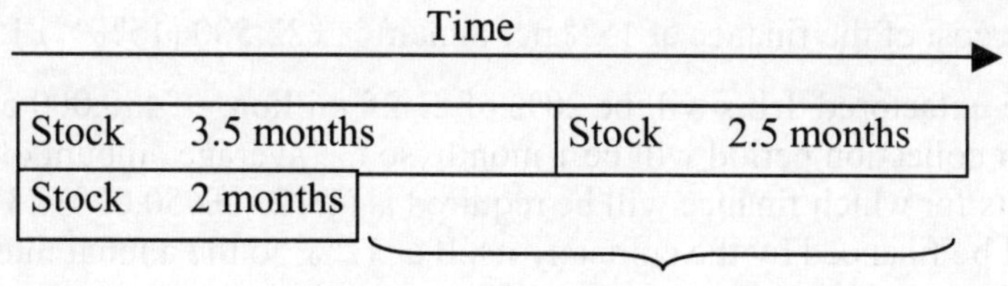

Funding requirement = 4 months

(b) Annual sales: £2.5m

Credit sales: £2.5m × 90% = £2.25m

Commission charges payable to the sales force are ignored in the following calculations since they are common to both. The allocated overheads are also irrelevant for the evaluation. The factor's better record with bad debts is not part of the evaluation of the proposal in terms of the benefits to Special Gift Supplies, because the factor's service will be provided without recourse (i.e. the factor will take on the bad debt risk).

Existing position	£
Credit control salary	12,500
Bad debts 3% × £2.25m =	67,500
Annual funding costs for debtors £468,750 × 12% (see note below)	56,250
Total costs	136,250

Note:

Average debtors are currently (2.5/12) × £2.25 million = £468,750.

The annual cost of financing these debtors at 12% per annum is:

12% × £468,750 = £56,250.

Factor's offer:	£
Factor finance charge (see note 1 below)	22,500
Unfactored funding costs (see note 2 below)	4,500
Factor service charge: 4% × £2.25m	90,000
One-off payment funding costs: £25,000 × 12% (note 3 below)	3,000
	120,000

Conclusion

It is worthwhile to factor the debts because it will be less costly.

Notes

(1) The debtors for which the factor will provide finance at 15% = 80% of £2.25 million = £1.8 million.

The average debt collection period will be 1 month, so the average amount of debtors for which the factor will provide finance is (1/12 × £1.8 million) = £150,000.

The cost of the finance at 15% per annum is £22,500 (15% × £150,000).

(2) The unfactored debts will be 20% of £2.25 million = £450,000 each year. The debt collection period will be 1 month, so the average amount of unfactored debts for which finance will be required is (1/12 × £450,000) £37,500. These will be financed by the company itself at 12%, so the annual interest cost will be £4,500.

(3) ***Tutorial note*:** The one-off payment of £25,000 to the factor has to be converted into an annual cost, for comparison purposes (i.e. comparing costs with the existing position). Here the cost has been established using the assumption that the annual cost is the interest cost on the £25,000 using the company's overdraft rate (12%) as the cost of capital. You might prefer to make a different assumption. The assumption used here is the one preferred by the examiner when this question was set in the examination.

(c) **Report on the credit control, factoring of debtors and the financing of working capital**

To: Financial Controller, Special Gift Supplies plc

From: A Student

Date: xx/xx/xx

Subject: **Credit control**

A good credit control department would exhibit a number of characteristics, some of which are included in the list below:

1 Preferably have a cash business relationship with customers to begin with

2 Obtain references for new customers and possibly visit their premises

3 Access the services of a credit rating agency

4 Only incrementally raise credit limits to that preferred by the customer

5 Maintain a history of transactions with each customer

6 Have documented procedures that explain to credit control employees credit limits and duration with clear action plans when these limits are breached

7 Create good reporting controls, such as aged list of debtors, and ensure the line of reporting is clear so that senior management are aware of problem cases

8 Ensure the credit control reports form part of the monitoring of the working capital cycle as a whole so that imbalances do not arise

9 Access published information on customers, particularly through financial statements or through information services via credit or other agencies

10 Ensure all customers' credit limits are periodically reviewed

The benefits of factoring

A list of the benefits of factoring might include:

1 Access to flexible sources of finance. This is important for small businesses that experience rapid growth since the facility would normally grow with the business.

2 Sales ledger expertise. Factors can often bring a level of expertise to debtor management that small businesses may not have, either in skills or resources, thus making them more effective.

3 Factors can bring economies of scale to debtor management thus making them more efficient than a single small company could be.

4 The business can pay its own debts more promptly, thus ensuring continued supply of goods, for example and also in being able to access early payment discounts which may be substantial.

5 Stock levels may be optimally managed since they will be unencumbered by restrictions relating to payment difficulties. For example, it may be optimal for stock management purposes to reorder stock at lower, more expensive levels so that the whole of the stock related costs are minimised.

6 Debt factoring is a source of funds that ensure adequate financing for growing businesses. By facilitating this, one of the key issues involved in over trading is addressed.

7 Costs of sales ledger administration are avoided.

Financing of working capital

The financing of the components of working capital is not always undertaken on a completely maturity-matched basis. That is, whilst working capital is regarded as net current assets that arguably should be funded by short-term sources of finance, this is not always the case for two reasons. First, by construction, net current assets are funded by long-term sources of finance to the extent that all short-term sources of finance have been exhausted. This can be demonstrated from a characterisation of a typical balance sheet.

Fixed assets + net current assets – long term loans = capital and reserves

By simply re-arranging we see that:

Net current assets = capital and reserves + long term loans – fixed assets

That is, net current assets are funded by long-term sources of finance not otherwise tied up in fixed assets. This amount will vary day to day because the components of working capital vary from day to day. However, to the extent that there exists positive net current assets, then adequate long term financing needs have to be considered.

Second, the liabilities components of working capital (trade creditors and bank overdrafts) represent sources of finance. As such, they are normally regarded as short-term sources of finance. In reality for many businesses, there is likely to be a core of current assets that will always need funding: whilst the components of current assets will change on a day to day basis, their level – to an extent – will remain predictable. It is this predictable component that enables managers to utilise longer term sources of finance in the knowledge that the finance will always be required. The distinction is often made between **fluctuating current assets** and **permanent current assets**. To the extent that current assets are permanent, they are more efficiently financed by longer-term sources (because these are usually cheaper). This will help avoid the higher interest costs (implicit or explicit) in shorter term sources of finance. The distinction between fluctuating and permanent current assets is illustrated in the following diagram that indicates the relationship between asset variability and funding maturity.

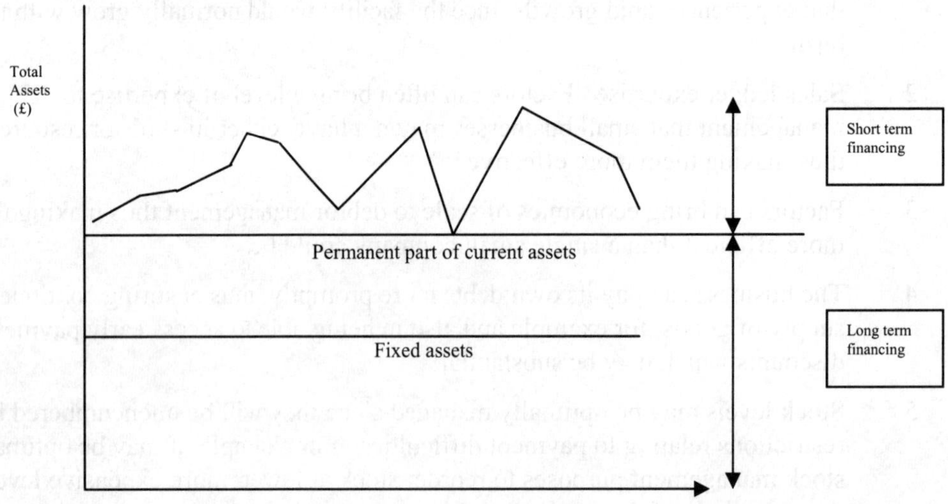

ACCA marking scheme			
			Marks
(a)	Calculation of funding requirements in months		2
(b)	Evaluation of existing position	2	
	Evaluation of factor's offer	4	
	Omission of overheads from evaluation	1	
	Omission of factor's bad debt record	1	
			8
(c)	1 mark for each item characterising good credit control	5	
	1 mark for each benefit of factoring	5	
	Up to 2 marks for each detailed point on financing	6	
	Presentation and quality of argument	2	
	Maximum marks available	18	
	Maximum marks awarded		15
Total			25

12 TNG

(a) TNG has a current order size of 50,000 units

Average number of orders per year = demand/order size = 255,380/50,000 = 5.11 orders
Annual ordering cost = 5.11 × 25 = £127.75

Buffer stock held = 255,380 × 28/365 = 19,591 units
Average stock held = 19,591 + (50,000/2) = 44,591 units
Annual holding cost = 44,591 × 0.1 = £4,459.10

Annual cost of current ordering policy = 4,459.10 + 127.75 = £4,587

(b) We need to calculate the economic order quantity:
EOQ = ((2 × 255,380 × 25)/0.1)0.5 = 11,300 units
Average number of orders per year = 255,380/11,300 = 22.6 orders
Annual ordering cost = 22.6 × 25 = £565.00

Average stock held = 19,591 + (11,300/2) = 25,241 units
Annual holding cost = 25,241 × 0.1 = £2,524.10

Annual cost of EOQ ordering policy = 2,524.10 + 565.00 = £3,089

Saving compared to current policy = 4,587 – 3,089 = £1,498

(c) Annual credit purchases = 255,380 × 11 = £2,809,180
Current creditors = 2,809,180 × 60/365 = £461,783
Creditors if discount is taken = 2,809,180 × 20/365 = £153,928
Reduction in creditors = 461,783 – 153,928 = £307,855
Finance cost increase = 307,855 × 0.08 = £24,628

Discount gained = 2,809,180 × 0.01 = £28,091
Net benefit of taking discount = 28,091 – 24,628 = £3,463
The discount is financially acceptable.

An alternative approach is to calculate the annual percentage benefit of the discount. This can be done on a simple interest basis:

(1/(100 – 1)) × (365/40) = 9.2%

Alternatively, the equivalent annual rate can be calculated:
(100/(100 – 1))365/40 – 1 = 9.6%

Both methods indicate that the annual percentage benefit is greater than the current cost of short-term debt (8%) of TNG and hence can be recommended on financial grounds.

(d) The economic order quantity (EOQ) model is based on a cost function for holding stock which has two terms: holding costs and ordering costs. With the EOQ, the total cost of having stock is minimised when holding cost is equal to ordering cost. The EOQ model assumes certain knowledge of the variables on which it depends and for this reason is called a deterministic model. Demand for stock, holding cost per unit per year and order cost are assumed to be certain and constant for the period under consideration. In practice, demand is likely to be variable or irregular and costs will not remain constant. The EOQ model also ignores the cost of running out of stock (stockouts). This has caused some to suggest that the EOQ model has little to recommend it as a practical model for the management of stock.

The model was developed on the basis of zero lead time and no buffer stock, but these are not difficulties that prevent the practical application of the EOQ model. As our earlier analysis has shown, the EOQ model can be used in circumstances where buffer stock exists and provided that lead time is known with certainty it can be ignored.

The EOQ model also serves a useful purpose in directing attention towards the costs that arise from holding stock. If these costs can be reduced, working capital tied up in stock can be reduced and overall profitability can be increased.

If uncertainty exists in terms of demand or lead time, a more complex stock management model using probabilities (a stochastic model) such as the Miller-Orr model can be used. This model calculates control limits that give guidance as to when an order should be placed.

(e) Just-in-time (JIT) stock management methods seek to eliminate any waste that arises in the manufacturing process as a result of using stock. JIT purchasing methods apply the JIT principle to deliveries of material from suppliers. With JIT production methods, stock levels of raw materials, work-in-progress and finished goods are reduced to a minimum or eliminated altogether by improved work-flow planning and closer relationships with suppliers.

Advantages

JIT stock management methods seek to eliminate waste at all stages of the manufacturing process by minimising or eliminating stock, defects, breakdowns and production delays[3]. This is achieved by improved workflow planning, an emphasis on quality control and firm contracts between buyer and supplier.

One advantage of JIT stock management methods is a stronger relationship between buyer and supplier. This offers security to the supplier, who benefits from regular orders, continuing future business and more certain production planning. The buyer benefits from lower stock holding costs, lower investment in stock and work in progress, and the transfer of stock management problems to the supplier. The buyer may also benefit from bulk purchase discounts or lower purchase costs.

The emphasis on quality control in the production process reduces scrap, reworking and set-up costs, while improved production design can reduce or even eliminate unnecessary material movements. The result is a smooth flow of material and work through the production system, with no queues or idle time.

Disadvantages

A JIT stock management system may not run as smoothly in practice as theory may predict, since there may be little room for manoeuvre in the event of unforeseen delays. There is little room for error, for example, on delivery times.

The buyer is also dependent on the supplier for maintaining the quality of delivered materials and components. If delivered quality is not up to the required standard, expensive downtime or a production standstill may arise, although the buyer can protect against this eventuality by including guarantees and penalties in to the supplier's contract. If the supplier increases prices, the buyer may find that it is not easy to find an alternative supplier who is able, at short notice, to meet his needs.

ACCA marking scheme			
		Marks	
(a)	Annual ordering cost	1	
	Annual holding cost	2	
	Annual cost of current policy	1	
			4
(b)	Calculation of economic order quantity	1	
	Annual ordering cost	1	
	Annual holding cost	1	
	Annual cost of EOQ policy	1	
	Saving from using EOQ policy or discussion	1	
			5
(c)	Analysis	2-3	
	Discussion	1-2	
	Maximum		4
(d)	Discussion of limitations of EOQ model		4
(e)	Advantages of JIT stock management methods	4-5	
	Disadvantages of stock management methods	4-5	
	Maximum		8
TOTAL			25

SOURCES OF FINANCE

13 ASSOCIATED INTERNATIONAL SUPPLIES LTD

(a) **Analysis of company position**

Associated International Supplies Ltd

Circulation: Associated International Supplies Ltd (AIS Ltd)

Author:

Date: xx/xx/xx

General appraisal

The first point to note is that, by most standards, the company would be regarded as small, and is therefore likely to exhibit many of the problems typical of the small company sector. Generally, small companies which are characterised by strong growth also usually exhibit substantial borrowings in relation to equity funds. It is likely, therefore, that the appropriate mix of financing for the business becomes a critical issue in the appraisal of AIS Ltd.

Growth and liquidity

In the five year period from 20X4 to 20X9 sales for AIS have grown by 150%. In terms of supporting the business with adequate working capital, the pressures of such growth can be substantial. Thus, in the same period we see that current assets have expanded by 54% and current liabilities by 91%. Whilst this aspect of the business will be dealt-with in more detail below, it is worthwhile questioning at this stage whether sufficient funding for working capital is available to support the growth in sales.

Whilst there has been significant growth in sales during the period, profit before tax (PBT) as a percentage of sales has actually declined from 8% to about 5%. This must call into question either the management of costs (operational or financial) or whether the company is unable to force price increases on to customers. Given the information available, the most likely source of this problem appears to relate to interest costs. Both current and long term liabilities have increased substantially (91% and 276%, respectively) against a background of barely increased equity funding. Debt funding (both long and short term) looks to have increased (see detail below) and this will have an associated interest burden. This has an importance in relation to the sustainability of the business.

Earnings retentions do not appear sufficient to fund business growth, and hence it is clear that **borrowings have been increased** to deal with this problem. However, a balance must be kept in the business between its earnings capability and its capacity to service its debt commitments. Whilst PBT has increased by 53% over the period, retentions have declined by about 74%. This may be partly explained by an increased tax burden, but is obviously due mainly to excessive distributions. In other words, not enough funds are being retained in the business to support its growth or funded from increased equity issues.

The impact of excessive growth in relation to its funding base might have a severe impact on liquidity. **Net current assets** are not seriously out of line if a ratio of current assets to current liabilities of 1.0 (unity) is considered acceptable. However, when current assets are looked at in relation to sales a different picture emerges. The ratio was 54% in 20X4 and only 33% in 20X9. This suggests, in combination with the other information, that stocks, debtors and cash resources might be insufficient to support the volume of sales. It might be argued that this reflects greater efficiency in current asset management. This is indeed the case when debtor days are compared over the period (they declined from 99 to 61), but it is not in relation to creditor days which also declined (from 88 to 67 during the period). When working capital is measured as a proportion of sales, we observe a decline from 11.4% in 20X4 to 0.5% in 20X9. This appears to be a reflection of reduced current asset investment and overdraft increases.

Because it is debt rather than equity funding that has grown, the business faces a potentially critical situation. We know that current assets consist mainly of stock and debtors (because the business has substantial borrowings, it is unlikely to simultaneously have large cash balances) and that this is being funded by borrowing rather than retained earnings. The reason why this is the case is because the business is **not generating adequate profits** and it is distributing too much of post tax earnings. The outlook is for greater borrowing. The poor profit figures suggest that **a critical point has been reached in terms of liquidity and solvency**. This is reflected in debt/equity ratios which have increased from 2.19 in 20X4 to 4.22 in 20X9 (current and long term liabilities used as debt and capital and reserves used as equity). Unless a capital reorganisation can take place quickly, either through injected funds or conversion of debt into equity, the business is likely to become insolvent.

Company capacity to continue trading

Given the points made above, it is unlikely that the business can continue in its current form. The trading performance is obviously very strong when measured in terms of its sales capacity and growth. This indicates a good customer base and the ability to service customer needs. The markets the company serves suggest a long-term future for its product or service.

However, it is likely that the company's cost base will be overwhelmed by interest charges, which is resulting in reduced PBT/Sales ratios over the period in spite of significant sales growth. If that is the case, it may well be that the underlying trading profitability is good. If it is not found to be good after further investigation then additional action may need to be taken. For example if low profitability is due to aggressive pricing, an investigation into alternative marketing strategies may be appropriate. In addition, given the significant growth, it may now be an appropriate time to look at the customer base and withdraw service from those customers who are either unprofitable or otherwise difficult (late payers, for example). Product mix might be usefully assessed to focus on higher-margin sales activities and to decrease effort on lower-margin activities. A business plan describing the customer base and the strategy for greater profitability will underpin any bid for a reorganisation of AIS Ltd's finances.

Bank support is crucial to long term survival if the debt is in the form of bank related lending. Alternative sources of finance should also be considered, particularly in the form of equity which is required to re-balance the business.

Other factors

(i) Venture capitalists might be interested in the business because of its significant growth but poorly structured finance. An equity injection would stabilise the business' finances.

(ii) Future projections of growth might provide a clearer picture of how to respond to the situation the business is now in.

(iii) The maturity of the debt obligations would indicate any critical repayments that may be due.

(iv) Comparisons with other businesses in the sector may provide some assurance as to the debt levels if high debt is a characteristic of the sector.

(v) Investigation of possible renegotiation of the debt to ease the interest burden.

(vi) Investigation of potential sale of the business or merger with a large partner with a view to securing a realistic equity base.

(vii) Information on detailed trading results would enable an accurate assessment of the profitability of AIS Ltd.

(viii) Working capital management needs to be investigated to assess if it is being efficiently organised.

Appendix to report: Ratio calculations

Sales growth:	(3,010 – 1,200)/1,200 = 150%
Current asset growth:	(1,000 – 650)/650 = 54%
Current liability growth:	(982 – 513)/513 = 91%
Long term liabilities growth:	(158 – 42)/42 = 276%
PBT growth:	(150 – 98)/98 = 53%
Retained earnings decline:	(65 – 17)/65 = 74%

	20X4	*20X9*
PBT/Sales	98/1,200 = 8%	150/3,010 = 5%
Current assets/ Current liabilities	650/513 = 1.3	1,000/982 = 1.0
Current assets / Sales	650/1,200 = 54%	1,000/3,010 = 33%
Working capital/Sales	(650–513)/1,200 = 11.4%	(1,000–982)/3,010 = 0.5%
Debt/Equity	(513 + 42)/210 = 2.64	(982 + 158)/270 = 4.22
Debtors at 50% of current assets	£325,000	£500,000
Sales per day (365 days)	£3,288	£8,247
Debtor days	325,000/3,288 = 99	500,000/8,247 = 61
Creditors at 25% of current liabilities	£128,000	£245,500
Cost of sales per day (365 days)	£1,452	£3,643
Creditor days	128,000/1,452 = 88	245,500/3,643 = 67

(b) **General**

Funds for fixed assets would normally be **long term in nature** in order to match asset use with funding maturity. Moreover, if the asset is a building or other major asset which has a secondary market value, then secured lending may be arranged where lower rates of interest are accessible. In particular, **specific asset financing** may be available (such as for fleet cars) which may represent an efficient source of funds. In general, the **finance leasing** option is available and represents a significant source of flexibility to the business. Fixed assets with secondary market values may also be subject to **sale and leaseback** arrangements.

Long-term sources of finance would typically be either **equity funds** (either injections or dividend retentions), **bank debt** or **possibly venture capital** equity interests for small businesses. What would not be appropriate are debentures, convertibles, warrants, equity public issues, and listings (with the potential exception of a small company stock market like AIM).

The most significant barrier to secure external equity funding for small firms is the lack of liquidity, or the inability to either find a market or buyer for the shares when the time arrives when the investor wishes to sell. There is evidence that small companies tend to have low gearing ratios when long-term debt finance to long-term finance plus equity is used as the measure of gearing. Moreover, a large proportion of the debt finance, in general, comes from overdrafts and short-term loans.

Sources of finance

No details are given concerning the nature of a business to comment on, and hence only general recommendations can be made. Given that fixed asset finance is required, long-term finance that is likely to be the most appropriate. Below are listed some ideas of what might be most suitable:

(i) If the fixed asset is substantial, such as a new building, or tooling for a new product, then the Alternative Investment Market may be suitable. AIM is directed largely at small and growing companies who do not qualify for the main stock market. The restrictions for admission are not that binding and may suit a company such as AIS Ltd. In particular, there are no eligibility criteria for new entrants in terms of size, profitability or existence. By listing on AIM, a company would address the market liquidity issue of equity investments for small firms.

(ii) Venture capital may also be suitable. This would be desirable from the point of view that, whilst venture capitalists may take an equity participation, they are likely to liquidate their shareholders to the owners of the business and hence ownership dilution would not occur.

(iii) Cash or dividend retentions. This would clearly take time for major asset purchases and may not be suitable for companies that face a funding shortfall in any case (the costs required in asset purchase may simply be too big for any realistic retention timescale).

(iv) Entering a merger or partnership, or accessing 'Business Angel' funding.

(v) Leasing the asset or arranging secured loans at lower interest rates.

(vi) Possible mortgages for buildings, or specialist financing for cars (for example hire purchase, leasing).

(vii) Availability of government grants, European funding or other agency assistance.

ACCA marking scheme		
		Marks
(a)	1 mark each for relevant ratio, up to a maximum of:	6
	Analysis of company position	6
	Comments on the capacity to continue trading	2
	Other relevant factors	2
	Quality of presentation of report	1
		17
(b)	2 marks for each identified appropriate sources of finance, up to max of	8
Total		25

14 ARWIN

Key answer tips

Part (a) should be straightforward, except that you need to be careful with the calculation of the fixed costs in the cost of sales. These are not expected to rise next year, and so should be calculated using the current year figures. For part (b), the question does not state how financial gearing or operational gearing should be measured: there are different methods of calculation. Make clear the method of calculation you are using. (The solution here gives two methods of measuring financial gearing and three methods of measuring operational gearing, but your answer only needs one of each.) For part (c), you need to discuss the problems of high gearing, and you need to spot that 'gearing' in this question refers to both financial gearing and operational gearing. The question hints at this strongly, by referring to both business risk and financial risk. Unfortunately, an unwary student will overlook operational gearing and business risk entirely.

(a) The forecast profit and loss accounts are as follows:

	Debt finance	*Equity finance*
	£000	£000
Sales (50,000 × 1.12)	56,000	56,000
Variable cost of sales (85% × sales)	28,560	28,560
Fixed cost of sales (15% × 30,000)	4,500	4,500
Gross profit	22,940	22,940
Administration costs (14,000 × 1.05)	14,700	14,700
Profit before interest and tax	8,240	8,240
Interest (see working)	800	300
Profit before tax	7,440	7,940
Taxation at 30%	2,232	2,382
Profit after tax	5,208	5,558
Dividends paid (60%)	3,125	3,335
Retained earnings	2,083	2,223

Working:

Interest under debt financing = £300,000 + (£5,000,000 × 0.10) = £800,000.

(b) **Financial gearing**

If financial gearing is measured as the debt: equity ratio:

Using debt/equity ratio:	*Current*	*Debt finance*	*Equity finance*
Debt	2,500	7,500	2,500
Share capital and reserves	22,560	24,643	29,783
Debt/equity ratio (%)	11.1	30.4	8.4

Workings:

Share capital and reserves (debt finance) = 22,560 + 2,083 = £24,643

Share capital and reserves (equity finance) = 22,560 + 5,000 + 2,223 = £29,783.

If financial gearing is measured as the ratio of debt capital to total capital:

Using capital (total) gearing:	*Current*	*Debt finance*	*Equity finance*
Debt	2,500	7,500	2,500
Total long-term capital	25,060	32,143	32,283
Capital (total) gearing (%)	10.0	23.3	7.7

Operational gearing:

If operational gearing is measured as the ratio of fixed costs to total costs:

Using fixed costs/total costs:	*Current*	*Debt finance*	*Equity finance*
Fixed costs	18,500	19,200	19,200
Total costs	44,000	47,760	47,760
Operational gearing (%)	42.0%	40.2%	40.2%

Total costs are assumed to consist of cost of sales plus administration costs.

If operational gearing is measured as the ratio of fixed costs to variable costs:

Using fixed costs/variable costs:	*Current*	*Debt finance*	*Equity finance*
Fixed costs	18,500	19,200	19,200
Variable costs	25,500	29,560	28,560
Operational gearing (%)	0.73	3.3	3.3

If operational gearing is measured as the ratio of contribution to profit before interest and tax (PBIT):

Using contribution/PBIT	*Current*	*Debt finance*	*Equity finance*
Contribution	24,500	27,440	27,440
PBIT	6,000	8,240	8,240
Operational gearing	4.1	3.3	3.3

Contribution is sales revenue minus the variable cost of sales.

Interest cover:

	Current	*Debt finance*	*Equity finance*
Profit before interest and tax	6,000	8,240	8,240
Debt interest	300	800	300
Interest cover	20	10.3	27.5

Earnings per share:

	Current	*Debt finance*	*Equity finance*
Profit after tax	3,990	5,208	5,558
Number of shares	10,000	10,000	11,250
Earnings per share (pence)	39.9	52.1	49.4

Comment:

The debt finance proposal leads to the largest increase in earnings per share, but results in an increase in financial gearing and a decrease in interest cover. Whether these changes in financial gearing and interest cover are acceptable depends on the attitude of both investors and managers to the new level of financial risk; a comparison with sector averages would be helpful in this context. The equity finance proposal leads to a decrease in financial gearing and an increase in interest cover. The expansion leads to a decrease in operational gearing, whichever measure of operational gearing is used, indicating that fixed costs have decreased as a proportion of total costs.

(c) **Business risk** could be described as the possibility of a company experiencing changes in the level of its profit before interest as a result of changes in turnover or operating costs. For this reason it is also referred to as operating risk. Business risk relates to the nature of the business operations undertaken by a company. For example, we would expect profit before interest to be more volatile for a luxury goods manufacturer than for a food retailer, since sales of luxury goods will be more closely linked to varying economic activity than sales of a necessity good such as food.

The nature of business operations influences the proportion of fixed costs to total costs. Capital intensive business operations, for example, will have a high proportion of fixed costs to total costs. From this perspective, operational gearing is a measure of business risk. As operational gearing increases, a business becomes more sensitive to changes in turnover and the general level of economic activity, and profit before interest becomes more volatile. A rise in operational gearing may therefore lead to a business experiencing difficulty in meeting interest payments. Managers of businesses with high operational risk will therefore be keen to keep fixed costs under control.

Financial risk in the context of this question can be described as the possibility of a company experiencing changes in the level of its distributable earnings as a result of the need to make interest payments on debt finance. The earnings volatility of companies in the same business will therefore depend not only on business risk, but also on the proportion of debt finance each company has in its capital structure. Since the relative amount of debt finance employed by a company is measured by gearing, financial risk is also referred to as gearing risk.

As financial gearing increases, the burden of interest payments increases and earnings become more volatile. Since interest payments must be met, shareholders may be faced with a reduction in dividends; at very high levels of gearing, a company may cease to pay dividends altogether as it struggles to find the cash to meet interest payments.

The pressure to meet interest payments at high levels of gearing can lead to a liquidity crisis, where the company experiences difficulty in meeting operating liabilities as they fall due. In severe cases, liquidation may occur.

The focus on meeting interest payments at high levels of financial gearing can cause managers to lose sight of the primary objective of maximizing shareholder wealth. Their main objective becomes survival and their decisions become focused on this, rather than on the longer-term prosperity of the company. Necessary investment in fixed asset renewal may be deferred or neglected.

A further danger of high financial gearing is that a company may move into a loss-making position as a result of high interest payments. It will therefore become difficult to raise additional finance, whether debt or equity, and the company may need to undertake a capital reconstruction.

It is likely that a business with high operational gearing will have low financial gearing, and a business with high financial gearing will have low operational gearing.

This is because managers will be concerned to avoid excessive levels of total risk, i.e. the sum of business risk and financial risk. A business with a combination of high operational gearing and high financial gearing clearly runs an increased risk of experiencing liquidity problems, making losses and becoming insolvent.

ACCA marking scheme

		Marks
(a)	Sales and administration cost	1
	Cost of sales	1
	Interest	1
	Profit after tax	1
	Retained earnings	1
		5
(b)	Revised share capital and reserves	1
	Financial gearing	2
	Operational gearing	2
	Interest cover	2
	Earnings per share	2
	Calculation of current values	1
	Discussion	2
		12
(c)	Explanation of business risk	1
	Explanation of financial risk	1
	Up to 2 marks for each danger of high gearing	6
		8
Total		25

15 JERONIMO PLC

Key answer tips

In part (a) note there are three parts to this requirement - (1) the difference between the two types of issue, (2) why companies make rights issues and (3) the effect on private investors. Marks are allocated for each part - don't throw them away by overlooking any of them.

Part (b)(i) hinges around the computation of the theoretical ex-rights price, a fairly standard formula with which you should be familiar. The price at which the investor will sell the rights should be that which leaves him no worse off than if he had taken them up. Taking them up will give him a share worth £1.55, at a cost of £1.30, a net gain of £0.25. This is therefore the compensation he needs for selling the rights instead.

Part (c) – the dividend growth model is central to equity value theory, and you must be confident in using it. Here, growth is estimated from past dividends, and applied to the current dividend to estimate next year's.

Part (d) really tests your understanding of the *implications* of market efficiency, rather than simply the ability to regurgitate definitions.

(a) A **rights issue** is a way of raising finance via the issue of shares to existing equity shareholders. In order to make such an issue, a company must have an authorised share capital which exceeds the share capital that would be in issue after the rights issue. (The shareholders could be asked to vote for an increase in the authorised share capital if necessary.) Companies choose to make rights issues because they need to raise long-term finance, and choose to do so by raising new equity finance. A rights issue might well be the most cost effective or desirable method of raising finance. The finance raised may be used to fund any type of long-term investment such as an acquisition, expansion of production facilities, or overseas investment.

A **scrip issue** (also called a bonus issue or capitalisation issue) is an issue of shares to existing shareholders, in proportion to their existing shareholdings, for which no charge is made. In other words, the shares are issued free to existing shareholders.

The advantage of a rights issue to existing shareholders, as opposed to an issue via public subscription, is that existing shareholders are assumed to have some level of commitment to the company already. As such, it may prove relatively easy to persuade them to buy new shares, and certainly easier and less costly than making a public offering. It is, however, important for the company to explain the reason behind the share issue – what it is going to do with the cash raised. If an investor is to be persuaded to pay cash for additional shares, then it must be demonstrated that their newly-invested cash will be used to earn returns at least equal to those they are currently receiving from their investment. If the return on capital is expected to decline in the company after the rights issue, then the issue is unlikely to be successful. As with any new share issue, it is common practice for a rights issue to be underwritten.

In the UK, it is a legal requirement that, unless existing shareholders have voted to waive their pre-emption rights, a new issue of shares for cash must be in the form of a rights issue.

The individual investor in a company which is making a rights issue will be invited to take up or sell his/her rights. If the rights are taken up, then the investor will have to make a payment to the company equal to the price of the rights purchased. Alternatively, the investor may choose not to increase his investment, and instead can sell the rights on the open market. In an efficient market, the investor is no better nor no worse off by choosing to sell his/her rights.

Scrip issues are often justified on the basis that there is a need to increase the number of shares in issue in order to bring down the price per share. It is often argued that the market 'dislikes' shares which individually have a very high price, and by increasing the number of shares in issue, the unit share price can be diluted. This can be beneficial to shareholders, because research evidence suggests that the drop in the unit share price is not as great as the proportionate change in the number of shares in issue. For example, if 10 million shares are in issue, and the current market price is £10 each, the market value of the equity is £100 million. If 10 million shares are now distributed via a scrip issue, one would expect the share price to drop to £5, leaving the overall equity value at £100 million. In practice, the lowering of the share price may make the shares more marketable, such that the post issue price settles at, say, £6. This results in an increase in the value of individual shareholdings, together with a rise in the total value of the equity. Individual investors may therefore experience some capital gain from a scrip issue.

When making a scrip issue, a company is converting some of the reserves into share capital, and the number of shares (fully paid up) to which an investor is entitled, will be expressed in relation to the current holding, e.g. a 2 for 5 issue means that two new shares will be given to shareholders for every five shares they currently hold. As already suggested, although the private investor gains no theoretical advantage from this conversion of reserves, there may be a benefit in practice, because the shares are now likely to be more marketable.

(b) (i) **Theoretical ex-rights price/value**

$$\frac{(\text{No. shares in issue} \times \text{market value}) + (\text{No. rights shares} \times \text{rights share price})}{\text{Total shares in issue post rights}}$$

$$= \frac{(5\text{m} \times £1.60) + (1\text{m} \times £1.30)}{6\text{m}}$$

$= £1.55$ per share

After taking up the rights issue, James Brown will hold 10,000 + (0.2 × 10,000) = 12,000 shares. The theoretical value of the holding, at £1.55 per share is thus £18,600.

Alternative method of calculation

	£
Current value of 5 existing shares (× £1.60)	8.00
Value of 1 new share in rights issue	1.30
Theoretical value of 6 shares	9.30

Theoretical ex-rights price per share = £9.30/6 = £1.55 per share.

(ii) **The value of the rights per share**

= Theoretical ex-rights price – Cost of taking up the rights

The value of the rights per share = £1.55 – £1.30

The value of the rights per share = £0.25 per share

If James Brown sells all of his rights to 2,000 shares, he can expect to receive: 2,000 × £0.25 = £500.

Alternative method of calculation

	£
Current value of shares	1.60
Theoretical ex-rights price	1.55
Theoretical value of rights per existing share	0.05

Theoretical value of each new share that can be purchased = 5 × 5p =£0.25. The value of the rights per share is therefore £0.25.

(c) **Using the dividend growth formula:**

$$R = \left(\frac{D_1}{MV} + g\right) \times 100$$

Where:

D_1 = Next year's dividend

g = Dividend growth rate

MV = Market price of share

R = Percentage required return

It is assumed that the average growth rate in dividends between 20X5 and 20X9 will be a reliable guide to the future annual growth rate in dividends. Between 20X5 and 20X9 (4 years) dividends per share have grown by a factor of 12/8 = 1.5 times. The average annual growth rate over this period is calculated as the fourth root of 1.5, minus 1.

$$g = \sqrt[4]{\frac{12}{8}} - 1$$

$$= 0.1067 \text{ or } 11\%$$

$$D1 = 1.11 \times 12 \text{ pence}$$

$$= 13.32 \text{ pence, say 13 pence.}$$

$$R = \left(\frac{13}{160} + 0.11\right) \times 100$$

$$R = 19.125\%$$

(d) In a strongly efficient market, finance directors will be alert to the fact that market prices are an accurate reflection of their company's financial prospects, and that if they behave in a manner which results in bad financial decisions, the share price will quickly fall to compensate for the worsening prospects.

This means that the effect of an efficient market on financial management is that it keeps managers alert to the consequences of their decisions. In an inefficient world, prices may take a while to adjust to reflect poor planning or control, but in a semi-strong or strong market environment this will not be true. It can thus be said that a strong-form efficient market encourages higher quality financial management. In a similar vein, it also serves to discourage the artificial manipulation of accounting information, as the truth will quickly be realised, and prices adjusted accordingly.

16 TECHFOOLS

(a) **Why convertibles might be an attractive source of finance for companies**

(i) Convertibles can provide immediate finance at lower cost since the conversion option effectively reduces the interest rates payable.

(ii) They represent attractive investments to investors since they are effectively debt risks for future equity benefits. Hence, finance is relatively easily raised.

(iii) Should the company's assumption regarding the likelihood of conversion prove true then there is no problem of establishing a large sinking fund for the redemption of the debentures.

(iv) Convertibles allow for higher gearing levels than would otherwise be the case with straight debt (interest costs are potentially lower with convertibles).

Tutorial note

This solution assumes that a company has sufficient creditworthiness to be able to issue convertibles in the bond market. By no means all companies can do this.

(b) (i)

Calculate **PV of cash flows per £100 (nominal value) of debentures** (assuming conversion at end of year 5)

Year	*Cash flow*	*Discount factor at 15%*	*PV at 15%*
1 (Annual interest at 8%)	8	0.870	6.96
2 (Annual interest at 8%)	8	0.756	6.05
3 (Annual interest at 8%)	8	0.658	5.26
4 (Annual interest at 8%)	8	0.572	4.58
5 (Annual interest at 8%)	8	0.497	3.98
5 (Conversion): $= 4 \times 45$	180	0.497	89.46
Estimated market value per £100 of debentures			116.29

The value of 45 shares in 5 years' time is expected to be £4 × 45 = £180. The value of debenture redemption will be £110. Hence **it is likely that conversion will take place**, because the conversion value of the bonds will be higher than their redemption value.

(ii) Arguably, the most important reservation concerns the future value of the share since it is likely to be the most uncertain aspect of the calculation. Other factors that may be relevant, but which are less uncertain, are issue price, and the cost of capital used.

(c) The conversion premium for convertible bonds is the amount by which the value of the convertible as a bond exceeds the current market value of the shares into which they will be convertible in the future.

By maximising the conversion premium the greatest amount of funds are raised for the fewest number of new shares issued.

Companies can issue convertibles with a high conversion premium because, firstly, the calculation in part (a)(i) produces a positive NPV against issue costs and, secondly, because there is high growth potential in share value.

(d) Financial intermediation refers to the role of a bank or other financial institution that serves to bring together lenders and borrowers. Investors are seeking avenues to place surplus funds whilst companies are seeking sources of finance. Because of the disparate nature of both investors and companies it is difficult to match investors to a company where the requirements of the investor are met and the needs of the company are satisfied. Thus, banks (as an example) act as a conduit through which investors can place funds and companies can borrow funds. In return, investors obtain interest on their deposits and the banks obtain interest on their loans. Clearly, the interest charged by the bank to the company is higher than it pays out to investors.

The role that financial intermediaries perform is to pool together investor funds to facilitate easy access by companies. Without financial intermediaries, companies would almost certainly face capital shortages.

The **benefits of financial intermediation** are as follows:

Investors can pool their funds in a bank deposit account to facilitate access by companies to larger resources than would otherwise be the case. This enables companies to:

(i) Exploit investment opportunities that would otherwise be untapped.

(ii) Become larger than would otherwise be the case and thus take advantage of economies of scale.

(iii) Find capital readily and easily thus reducing the costs associated with raising funds.

(iv) Reduce the cost of finance since:

(1) Banks can, with their greater financial expertise, more accurately assess the risk of corporate investments.

(2) Banks can diversify their risk across many companies thus lowering their required rate of return, which in turn reduces the cost base on which interest charges to companies will be referenced.

(3) Banks can reduce interest costs because of their size. They are able to borrow on the wholesale market at rates that are not accessible to small banks or individual investors.

(v) Bridge the maturity gap. Banks can lend longer term than individual investors desire since banks will have access to a level of funds that is largely constant irrespective of a high turnover of constituent investors.

(vi) Access finance for high-risk projects that banks may find acceptable because of their capacity to diversify.

Investors benefit substantially from financial intermediation because:

(i) By investing in a market or bank, investors can get access to diversified portfolios which might otherwise be difficult. Since their funds are pooled, investors benefit from the banks' abilities to aggregate funds and allocate them efficiently.

(ii) Investors can access bank expertise in assessing corporate risk, thus obtaining the best return for a particular level of risk.

(iii) Investor risk is reduced because of the banks' diversifying activities. Minimised risk, subject to a required rate of return, is passed onto investors in a competitive banking market.

(iv) Legislation that provides for investor protection should a bank fail (in terms of either central bank support or investor guarantee schemes by other banks), further reduces the risk investors face.

(v) Investors can choose their exposure to a particular level of risk subject to depositing money in appropriate funds. For example, mutual funds offer a range of risk profiles from which the investor can choose.

ACCA marking scheme			
			Marks
(a)		Up to 2 marks for each detailed point on convertibles as a source of finance	4
(b)	(i)	Cash flows	2
		NPV calculation	1
		Assessment	2
	(ii)	Identification and justification of major reservation	2
(c)		Explanation of maximising conversion premium	2
		Explanation of ability to obtain high premium	2
(d)		2 marks for each detailed advantage for companies	up to 7
		2 marks for each detailed advantage for investors	up to 7
		Maximum marks available	10
Total			25

17 TIRWEN PLC

(a) Rights issue price = 4.00 × 0.85 = £3.40

(i) Theoretical ex rights price = ((5 × 4.00) + 3.40)/6 = £3.90

(ii) Value of rights per existing share = (3.90 – 3.40)/5 = 10p

(b) Value of 1,200 shares after rights issue = 1,200 × 3.90 =£4,680

Value of 1,000 shares before rights issue = 1,000 × 4.00 =£4,000

Value of 1,000 shares after rights issue = 1,000 × 3.90 = £3,900

Cash subscribed for new shares = 200 × 3.40 = £680

Cash raised from sale of rights = 1,000 × 0.1 = £100

The investor could do nothing, take up the offered rights, sell the rights into the rights market, or any combination of these actions. The effect of the rights issue on the wealth of the investor depends on which action is taken.

The rights issue has a neutral effect if the rights attached to the 1,000 shares are exercised to purchase an additional 200 shares, since the value of 1,200 shares after the rights issue (£4,680) is equal to the sum of the value of 1,000 shares before the rights issue (£4,000) and the cash subscribed for new shares (£680). Part of the investor's wealth has changed from cash into shares, but no wealth has been gained or lost. The theoretical ex rights per share therefore acts as a benchmark following the rights issue against which other ex rights share prices can be compared.

The rights issue also has a neutral effect on the wealth of the investor if the rights attached to existing shares are sold. The value of 1,000 shares after the rights issue (£3,900) plus the cash received from the sale of rights (£100) is equal to the value of

1,000 shares before the rights issue (£4,000). In this case, part of the investor's wealth has changed from share into cash.

If the investor neither subscribes for the new shares offered nor sells the rights attached to the shares already held, a loss of wealth of £100 will occur, due to the difference between the value of 1,000 shares before the rights issue (£4,000) and the value of 1,000 shares after the rights issue (£3,900).

The theoretical ex rights price is simply a weighted average of the cum rights price and the rights issue price, ignoring any use made of the funds raised. The actual ex rights price will depend on the use made of the funds raised by the rights issue, as well as the expectations of investors and the stock market.

(c) Current share price = £4.00

Earnings per share = 100 × (4.00/15.24) = 26.25p

Number of ordinary shares = 2m/0.5 = 4m shares

Earnings of Tirwen = 4m × 0.2625 = £1.05m

Funds raised from rights issue = 800,000 × £4.00 × 0.85 = £2,720,000

Funds raised less issue costs = 2,720,000 – 220,000 = £2,500,000

Debenture interest saved = 2,500,000 × 0.12 = £300,000

Profit before tax of Tirwen = 1,050,000/(1 – 0.3) = £1,500,000

Current debenture interest paid = 4,500,000 × 0.12 = £540,000

Current overdraft interest = 1,250,000 × 0.07 = £87,500

Total interest = 540,000 + 87,500 = £627,500

Current profit before interest and tax = 1,500,000 + 627,500 = £2,127,500

Revised total interest = 627,500 – 300,000 = £327,500

Revised profit after tax = (2,127,500 – 327,500) × 0.7 = £1,260,000

(Or revised profit after tax = 1,050,000 + (300,000 × 0.7) = £1,260,000)

New shares issued = 4m/5 = 800,000

Shares in issue = 4,000,000 + 800,000 = 4,800,000

Revised earnings per share = 100 × (1,260,000/4,800,000) = 26.25p

(d) As the price/earnings ratio is constant, the share price expected after redeeming part of the debentures will remain unchanged at £4.00 per share (26.25 × 15.24). Since this is greater than the theoretical ex rights share price of £3.90, using the funds raised by the rights issue to redeem part of the debentures results in a capital gain of 10p per share. The proposal to use the rights issue funds to redeem part of the debentures therefore results in an increase in shareholder wealth.

(e) A rights issue will be an attractive source of finance to Tirwen plc as it will reduce the gearing of the company. The current debt/equity ratio using book values is:

Debt/equity ratio = 100 × 4,500/3,500 = 129%

Including the overdraft, debt/equity ratio = 100 × 5,750/3,500 = 164%

Both values are above the sector average of 100% and issuing new debt will not be attractive in this situation. A substantial reduction in gearing will occur, however, if the rights issue is used to redeem £2.5m of debentures:

Debt/equity ratio = 100 × 2,000/6,000 = 33%

Including the overdraft, debt/equity ratio = 100 × 3,250/6,000 = 54%

If the rights issue is not used to redeem the debenture issue, the decrease in gearing is less dramatic:

Debt/equity ratio = 100 × 4,500/6,000 = 75%

Including the overdraft, debt/equity ratio = 100 × 5,750/6,000 = 96%

In both cases, the debt/equity ratio falls to less than the sector average, signalling a decrease in financial risk. The debt/equity ratio would fall further if increased retained profits were included in the calculation, but the absence of information on Tirwen's dividend policy makes retained profits uncertain.

If the rights issue is used to redeem £2.5m of debentures, there will be an improvement in interest cover from 3.4 times (2,127,500/627,500), which is below the sector average of 6 times, to 6.5 times (2,127,500/327,500), which is marginally better than the sector average. Interest cover might also increase if the funds raised are invested in profitable projects.

A rights issue will also be attractive to Tirwen plc since it will make it more likely that the company can raise further debt finance in the future, possibly at a lower interest rate due to its lower financial risk.

It should be noted that a decrease in gearing is likely to increase the average cost of the finance used by Tirwen plc, since a greater proportion of relatively more expensive equity finance will be used compared to relatively cheaper debt. This will increase the discount rate used by the company and decrease the net present value of any expected future cash flows.

ACCA marking scheme		
		Marks
(a)	Theoretical ex rights price per share	2
	Value of rights per existing share	1
		3
(b)	Effect on wealth of exercising rights	2
	Effect on wealth of sale of rights	2
	Discussion of right issue and shareholder wealth	2
		6
(c)	Current earnings per share	1
	Current earnings	1
	Funds raised via rights issue	1
	Interest saved by redeeming debentures	1
	Revised earnings	1
	Revised earnings per share	1
		6
(d)	Expected share price after redeeming debentures	1
	Comparison with theoretical ex rights price	1
	Discussion and conclusion	1
		3
(e)	Effect of rights issue on debt/equity ratio	2
	Effects of rights issue on interest cover	2
	Discussion and link to Tirwen plc	3
		7
Total		25

CAPITAL INVESTMENT APRAISAL

18 INVESTMENT APPRAISAL

(a) **Accounting rate of return (ARR)** is a measure of the return on an investment where the annual profit before interest and tax is expressed as a percentage of the capital sum invested. There are a number of alternative formulae which can be used to calculate ARR, which differ in the way in which they define capital cost. The more common alternative measures available are:

- average annual profit to initial capital invested, and
- average annual profit to average capital invested.

The method selected will affect the resulting ARR figure, and for this reason it is important to recognise that the measure might be subject to manipulation by managers seeking approval for their investment proposals. The value for average annual profit is calculated after allowances for depreciation, as shown in the example below:

Suppose ARR is defined as: $\dfrac{\text{Average profit (after depreciation)}}{\text{Initial capital invested}} \times 100$

A project costing £5 million, and yielding average profits of £1,250,000 per year after depreciation charges of £500,000 per year, would give an ARR of:

$1,250,000/5,000,000 \times 100 = 25\%$

If the depreciation charged were to be increased to £750,000 per year, for example as a result of technological changes reducing the expected life of an asset, the ARR becomes:

$1,000,000/5,000,000 \times 100 = 20\%$

The attraction of using ARR as a method of investment appraisal lies in its simplicity and the ease with which it can be used to specify the impact of a project on a company's profit and loss account. The measure is easily understood and can be directly linked to the use of ROCE as a performance measure. Nonetheless, ARR has been criticised for a number of major drawbacks, perhaps the most important of which is that it uses accounting profits after depreciation rather than cash flows in order to measure return. This means that the capital cost is over-stated in the calculation, via both the numerator and the denominator. In the numerator, the capital cost is taken into account via the depreciation charges used to derive accounting profit, but capital cost is also the denominator. The practical effect of this is to reduce the ARR and thus make projects appear less profitable. This might in turn result in some worthwhile projects being rejected. Note, however, that this problem does not arise where ARR is calculated as average annual profit as a percentage of average capital invested.

The most important criticism of ARR is that it takes no account of the time value of money. A second limitation of ARR, already suggested, is that its value is dependent on accounting policies and this can make comparison of ARR figures across different investments very difficult. A further difficulty with the use of ARR is that it does not give a clear decision rule. The ARR on any particular investment needs to be compared with the current returns being earned within a business, and so unlike NPV for example, it is impossible to say 'all investments with an ARR of X or below will always be rejected.

The **payback method** of investment appraisal is used widely in industry - generally in addition to other measures. Like ARR, it is easily calculated and understood. The payback approach simply measures the time required for cumulative cash flows from an investment to sum to the original capital invested.

Example

Original investment £100,000

Cash flow profile: Years 1–3 £25,000 p.a.

Years 4 – 5 £50,000 p.a.

Year 6 £5,000

The cumulative cash flows are therefore:

End Year 1	£25,000
End Year 2	£50,000
End Year 3	£75,000
End Year 4	£125,000
End Year 5	£175,000
End Year 6	£180,000

The original sum invested is returned via cash flows some time during the course of Year 4. If cash flows are assumed to be even throughout the year, the cumulative cash flow of £100,000 will have been earned halfway through year 4. The payback period for the investment is thus 3 years and 6 months.

The payback approach to investment appraisal is useful for companies which are seeking to claw back cash from investments as quickly as possible. At the same time, the concept is intuitively appealing as many businessmen will be concerned about how long they may have to wait to get their money back, because they believe that rapid repayment reduces risks. This means that the payback approach is commonly used for initial screening of investment alternatives.

The disadvantages of the payback approach are as follows:

(i) Payback ignores the overall profitability of a project by ignoring cash flows after payback is reached. In the example above, the cash flows between 3–5 years and the end of the project total £80,000. To ignore such substantial cash flows would be naïve. As a consequence, the payback method is biased in favour of fast-return investments. This can result in rejecting investments that generate cash flows more slowly in the early years, but which are overall more profitable.

(ii) As with ARR, the payback method ignores the time value of money.

(iii) The payback method, in the same way as ARR, offers no objective measure of what is the desirable return, as measured by the length of the payback period.

(b) (i) **Discounted cash flow analysis** is a technique whereby the value of future cash flows is discounted back to a present value, so that the monetary values of all cash flows are equivalent, regardless of their timing. The logic for discounting is that the value of money declines over time because of individual time preferences and the impact of inflation in eroding spending power. People value money received sooner rather than later because as soon as cash is received they can increase consumption, or re-invest the capital.

NPV uses discounting to calculate the present value of all cash flows associated with a project. The present value of cash outflows is then compared with the present value of cash inflows, to obtain a net present value (NPV). If the present value (PV) of cash outflows exceeds the PV of cash inflows, then the NPV will be negative. If the present value (PV) of cash inflows exceeds the PV of cash outflows, then the NPV will be positive. The size of the NPV is dependent on the cash flow pattern and the rate of discount that is applied. The general rule is that a company will discount the forecast cash flows at a rate equal to its cost of capital. The reason for this is that if a company has an overall cost of capital of, for example, 12%, it is essential that the rate of return exceeds 12% or the funding costs will not be covered. Hence if the cash flows are discounted at the cost of capital and the project yields a positive NPV, this implies that the return exceeds the cost of capital. When using NPV for investment appraisal then a simple rule is applied: invest if NPV is positive, and do not invest if it is negative.

IRR uses discounting in a slightly different way to determine the profitability of an investment. The Internal Rate of Return is defined as the discount rate at which the net present value equals zero. For example, an investment may yield a forecast NPV of £15,000 when the cash flows are discounted at 10%. If the rate of discount is increased, the net present value will fall, and the IRR represents the effective, break-even discount rate for the investment. Suppose, for example, that the IRR is 15%, this figure can then be used to establish a decision rule for investments. An IRR of 15% means that if the cost of capital exceeds 15% then the investment would generate a negative NPV. If the company is currently having to pay 12% on its investment funds, then it knows that it can afford to see its cost of capital rise by 3% before the investment will become financially non-viable. As long as the IRR exceeds the cost of capital, then the company should invest and so, as a general rule, the higher the IRR the better.

NPV and IRR measures may sometimes contradict one another when used in relation to **mutually exclusive investments**. An example of the ambiguity which can occur when choosing between mutually exclusive decisions is when one of the investments has a higher NPV than the other, and so is preferable on that basis, but at the same time it has a lower IRR. When IRR and NPV give conflicting results, the preferred alternative is the project with the highest NPV

In conclusion, although both NPV and IRR use discounted cash flows as a method of arriving at an investment decision, the results that they generate need to be interpreted with care, and they do not always yield the same investment decisions. NPV is the preferred criterion for selecting between two or more mutually exclusive investments, where the two approaches give differing recommendations.

(ii) If the laptops are replaced every year:

NPV of one year replacement cycle

Year	*Cash flow*	*Discount factor at 14%*	*PV*
	£		£
0	(2,400)	1.000	(2,400.0)
1	1,200	0.877	1,052.4
			(1,347.6)

Equivalent annual cost = PV of cost of one replacement cycle/Cumulative discount factor

= £1,347.6/0.877

= **£1,536.6**

NPV of two-year replacement cycle

Year	*Cash flow*	*Discount factor at 14%*	*PV*
	£		£
0	(2,400)	1.000	(2,400.0)
1	(75)	0.877	(65.8)
2	800	0.769	615.2
			(1,850.6)

Equivalent annual cost = PV of cost of one replacement cycle/Cumulative discount factor

= £1,850.6/1.647

= **£1,123.6**

NPV of three-year replacement cycle

Year	*Cash flow*	*Discount factor at 14%*	*PV*
	£		£
0	(2,400)	1.000	(2,400.0)
1	(75)	0.877	(65.8)
2	(150)	0.769	(115.4)
3	300	0.675	202.5
			(2,378.7)

Equivalent annual cost = PV of cost of one replacement cycle/Cumulative discount factor

= £2,378.7/2.322

= **£1,024.4**

Conclusion

The **optimal cycle for replacement is every three years**, because this has the lowest equivalent annual cost. Other factors which need to be taken into account are the non-financial aspects of the alternative cycle choices. For example, computer technology and the associated software is changing very rapidly and this could mean that failure to replace annually would leave the salesmen unable to utilise the most up to date systems for recording, monitoring and implementing their sales. This could have an impact on the company's competitive position. The company needs to consider also the compatibility of the software used by the laptops with that used by the in-house computers and mainframe. If system upgrades are made within the main business which render the two computers incompatible, then rapid replacement of the laptops to regain compatibility is essential.

19 BREAD PRODUCTS LTD

Tutorial note

This question tests your ability to carry out a DCF asset replacement analysis. The solution below demonstrates both the lowest common multiple technique and the equivalent annual cost technique.

(a) There are a number of methods to answering this question and two are presented. The first problem is in deciding which broad approach to use. The broad approach which seems best is to inflate the cash flows at their different inflation rates and to discount them at the money discount rate.

1 **Lowest common multiple method**

The lowest common multiple is 2 × 3 = 6 years. Hence the cash flows for each of the alternatives will be presented in these terms.

Two-year cycle for replacement: (Cash flows are inflated according to their individual inflation rates, original cost and resale values at 5% each year and maintenance costs at 10%.)

Year	*0*	*1*	*2*	*3*	*4*	*5*	*6*
Original cost	24,500		27,011		29,780		
Maintenance		550	968	666	1,170	805	1,417
Resale values			(17,199)		(18,962)		(20,905)
Total net cost	24,500	550	10,780	666	11,989	805	(19,488)
Discount factor at 15%	1.000	0.870	0.756	0.658	0.572	0.497	0.432
Present values	24,500	479	8,150	438	6,858	400	(8,419)
NPV of cost	**32,406**						

Three-year cycle for replacement: (Cash flows are inflated according to their individual inflation rates)

Year	*0*	*1*	*2*	*3*	*4*	*5*	*6*
Original cost	24,500			28,362			
Maintenance		550	968	1,997	732	1,288	2,657
Resale values				(12,965)			(15,009)
Total net cost	24,500	550	968	17,394	732	1,288	(12,352)
Discount factor at 15%	1.000	0.870	0.756	0.658	0.572	0.497	0.432
Present values	24,500	478	732	11,445	419	640	(5,336)
NPV of cost	**32,878**						

Hence, a **two-year replacement cycle is preferable** since it represents (slightly) the lower cost over a six-year cycle.

2 **Equivalent annual cost method**

Alternatively, an equivalent annual cost approach could be used:

Two-year cycle for replacement: (Cash flows are inflated according to their individual inflation rates)

	0	*1*	*2*
Original cost	24,500		
Maintenance		550	968
Resale values			(17,199)
Net total cost	24,500	550	(16,231)
Discount factor	1.000	0.870	0.756
Present values	24,500	479	(12,271)
Net present value of costs	**12,708**		

Equivalent annual cost = 12,708/(annuity factor at 15% for two years) = 12,708/1.626 = **7,815**.

Three-year cycle for replacement: (Cash flows are inflated according to their individual inflation rates)

	0	*1*	*2*	*3*
Original cost	24,500			
Maintenance		550	968	1,997
Resale values				(12,965)
Net total cost	24,500	550	968	(10,968)
Discount factor at 15%	1.000	0.870	0.756	0.658
Present values	24,500	479	732	(7,217)
Net present value of costs	**18,494**			

Equivalent annual cost = 18,494/(annuity factor at 15% for three years) = 18,494/2.283 = **8,101**.

Again, the conclusion is that a two-year replacement cycle is preferable.

(b) **General limitations of Net Present Value when applied to investment appraisal**

NPV is a commonly used technique employed in investment appraisal, but it is subject to a number of restrictive assumptions and limitations which call into question its general relevance. Nonetheless, if the assumptions and limitations are understood then its application is less likely to be undertaken in error.

Some of the difficulties with NPV are listed below:

(i) NPV assumes that firms pursue an objective of maximising the wealth of their shareholders. This is questionable given the wider range of stakeholders who might have conflicting interests to those of the shareholders.

(ii) NPV is largely redundant if organisations are not wealth maximising. For example, public sector organisations may wish to invest in capital assets but will use non-profit objectives as part of their assessment.

(iii) NPV is potentially a difficult method to apply in the context of having to estimate what is the correct discount rate to use. This is particularly so when questions arise as to the incorporation of risk premia in the discount rate, since an evaluation of the riskiness of the business, or of the project in particular, will have to be made but may be difficult to discern. Alternative approaches to risk analysis, such as sensitivity and decision trees are, themselves, subject to fairly severe limitations.

(iv) NPV assumes that cash surpluses can be reinvested at the discount rate. This is subject to other projects being available which produce at least a zero NPV at the chosen discount rate.

(v) NPV can most easily cope with cash flows arising at period ends and is not a technique that is used easily when complicated, mid-period cash flows are present.

(vi) NPV is not universally employed, especially in a small business environment. The available evidence suggests that businesses assess projects in a variety of ways (payback, IRR, accounting rate of return). The fact that such methods are used which are theoretically inferior to NPV calls into question the practical benefits of NPV, and therefore hints at certain practical limitations.

(vii) The conclusion from NPV analysis is the present value of the surplus cash generated from a project. If reported profits are important to businesses, then it is possible that there may be a conflict between undertaking a positive NPV project and potentially adverse consequences on reported profits. This will particularly be the case for projects with long time horizons, large initial investment and very delayed cash inflows. In such circumstances, businesses may prefer to use accounting measures of investment appraisal.

(viii) Managerial incentive schemes may not be consistent with NPV, particularly when long time horizons are involved. Thus managers may be rewarded on the basis of accounting profits in the short term and may be incentivised to act in accordance with these objectives, and thus ignore positive NPV projects. This may be a problem of the incentive schemes and not of NPV; nonetheless, a potential conflict exists and represents a difficulty for NPV.

(ix) NPV treats all time periods equally, with the exception of discounting far cash flows more than near cash flows. In other words, NPV only accounts for the time value of money. To many businesses, distant horizons are less important than near horizons, if only because that is the environment in which they work. Other factors besides applying higher discount rates may work to reduce the impact of distant years. For example, in the long term, nearly all aspects of the business may change and hence a too-narrow focus on discounting means that NPV is of limited value and more so the further the time horizon considered.

(x) NPV is of limited use in the face of non-quantifiable benefits or costs. NPV does not take account of non-financial information which may even be relevant to shareholders who want their wealth maximised. For example, issues of strategic benefit may arise against which it is difficult to immediately quantify the benefits but for which there are immediate costs. NPV would treat such a situation as an additional cost since it could not incorporate the indiscernible benefit.

ACCA marking scheme			
		Marks	
(a)	Identification of appropriate cash flows for each alternative	4	
	Identification of appropriate cash flows for each alternative	2	
	Calculation of discounted cash flows	2	
	Calculation of optimal policies	4	
			12
(b)	Up to 2 marks for each detailed limitations of NPV		
	(1 mark each for limited responses). Up to a maximum of:		13
Total			25

20 HOWDEN PLC

Key answer tips

In part (a) the answer implies that it is possible to determine a 'real' rate of return which can then be adjusted in the light of estimated future rates of inflation. The most likely method of calculating a company's required rate of return will actually produce a 'money cost of capital'. To produce a 'real' cost of capital requires some tinkering with this initial calculation.

In part (b) a clear lay out will greatly assist both you and the marker. With projects of short time span, up to, say, five years, a horizontal tabulation is generally best. Where various annuities in real terms are inflating at different rates the best approach is to split them into single year flows and inflate each separately.

Note that in (c), the consideration is not limited to investment decisions – take care to read the requirements carefully.

(a) Investors invest capital in companies expecting a reward for both the delay in waiting for their returns (time value of money) and also for the risks to which they expose their capital (risk premium). In addition, if prices in general are rising, shareholders require compensation for the erosion due to inflation in the real value of their capital.

For example, suppose that in the absence of inflation, shareholders require a company to offer a return of 10%. The need to cover price inflation of, say, 5% will raise the overall required return to about 15%. If people in general expect a particular rate of inflation, the structure of interest rates in the capital market will adjust to incorporate these inflationary expectations. This is known as the **'Fisher effect'**.

More precisely, the relationship between the **real required return (r)** and the nominal or **money rate of return (m)**, i.e. the rate which includes an allowance for inflation, is given by:

$(1 + r) \times (1 + p) = (1 + m)$, where p is the expected rate of price inflation.

It is essential when evaluating an investment project under inflation that future expected price level changes are treated in a consistent way. Companies may correctly allow for inflation in two ways each of which computes the real value of an investment project:

(i) Inflate the future expected cash flows at the expected rate of inflation (allowing for inflation rates specific to the project), and discount these cash flows at a discount rate of at m. This is the fully-inflated rate or 'money terms' approach.

(ii) Strip out the inflation element from the market-determined rate and apply the resulting real rate of return, r, to the stream of project cash flows expressed in today's or constant prices. This is the 'real terms' approach.

(b) First, the **relevant set-up cost** needs identification. The **offer of £2m for the building**, if rejected, represents an opportunity lost, although this appears to be compensated by its predicted eventual resale value of £3m.

The **cost of the market research study** has to be met irrespective of the decision to proceed with the project or not and is thus **not relevant**.

Secondly, **incremental costs and revenues** are identified. All other items are avoidable except the element of apportioned overhead, leaving the incremental overhead alone to include in the evaluation.

Thirdly, all items of incremental cash flow, including this additional overhead, must be **adjusted for their respective rates of inflation**. Because (with the exception of labour and variable overhead) the inflation rates differ, a disaggregated approach is required.

The appropriate discount rate is given by:

$(1 + p) \times (1 + r) - 1 = m$

$= (1.06) \times (1.085) - 1$

$= 15\%$

Assuming that the inflated costs and prices apply from and including the first year of operation, the cash-flow profile is as follows.

Cash flow profile				*Year*		
Item	*0*	*1*	*2*	*3*	*4*	*5*
	£m	£m	£m	£m	£m	£m
Equipment	(10.50)					2.00
Forgone sale of buildings	(2.00)					
Residual value of building						3.00
Working capital*	(0.50)					0.50
Revenue		5.04	5.29	5.56	5.83	6.13
Materials		(0.62)	(0.64)	(0.66)	(0.68)	(0.70)
Labour and variable overhead		(0.43)	(0.46)	(0.49)	(0.52)	(0.56)
Relevant fixed overhead	-	(0.53)	(0.55)	(0.58)	(0.61)	(0.64)
Net cash flows	(13.00)	3.46	3.64	3.83	4.02	9.73
Discount factor at 15%	1.000	0.870	0.756	0.658	0.572	0.497
Present value	(13.00)	3.01	2.75	2.52	2.30	4.84

NPV = +£2.42m

NPV = +£2.42m, i.e. positive, therefore, the project appears to be acceptable.

However, the financial viability of the project depends quite heavily on the estimate of the residual value of the building and equipment.

****Note:*** The working capital cash recovery towards the end of the project is approximately equal to the initial investment in stocks, because the rate of material cost inflation tends to cancel out the JIT-induced reduction in volume, leading to roughly constant stock-holding in value terms throughout most of the project life-span.

(c) Inflation adds an extra element of uncertainty into forecasting future cash flows, because it becomes more difficult to estimate what future prices and costs will be. This extra uncertainty means that financial evaluations will be less reliable.

In addition to the problems offered for investment appraisal such as forecasting the various rates of inflation relevant to the project, inflation poses a wider range of difficulties in a variety of business decision areas.

Inflation may pose a problem for businesses if it distorts the signals transmitted by the market. In the absence of inflation, the price system should translate the shifting patterns of consumer demand into price signals to which producers respond in order to plan current and future output levels. If demand for a product rises, the higher price indicates the desirability of switching existing production capacity to producing the goods or of laying down new capacity.

Under inflation, however, the producer may lose confidence that the correct signals are being transmitted, especially if the prices of goods and services inflate at different rates. He may thus be inclined to delay undertaking new investment. This applies particularly if price rises are unexpected and erratic.

Equally, it becomes more difficult to evaluate the performance of whole businesses and individual segments when prices are inflating. A poor operating performance may be masked by price inflation, especially if the price of the product sold is increasing at a rate faster than prices in general or if operating costs are inflating more slowly. The rate of return on capital achieved by a business is most usefully expressed in real terms by removing the effect on profits of generally rising prices (or better still, the effect of company-specific inflation). The capital base of the company should also be expressed in meaningful terms. A poor profit result may translate into a high ROI if the capital base is measured in historic terms. Unless these sorts of adjustment are made, inflation hinders the attempt to measure company performance on a consistent basis and thus can cloud the judgement of providers of capital in seeking out the most profitable areas for investment.

21 FILTREX PLC

Key answer tips

The first parts of (a) are textbook definitions, leading into a discussion as to the circumstances under which soft capital rationing may arise. To get maximum marks, clearly split your response to this into separate points (reasons).

The sentence that dictates the approach to (b)(i) is 'Project A and C are mutually exclusive and no project can be sub-divided.' This rules out the pure NPV/£ invested key factor analysis approach, and some trial and error is needed. Take care not to overrun here – even if you don't arrive at the actual optimal solution, a well-argued, logical approach will gain most of the marks.

Part (c) requires some imaginative thinking; whilst raising further finance is an obvious possibility (and you should be specific about the various methods to get good marks) the examiner will reward any alternatives solutions, such as that given in the answer.

(a) **Hard capital rationing** applies when a firm is restricted, due to a shortage of capital, from undertaking all apparently worthwhile investment opportunities, and the reasons for the capital shortage are factors external to the company, over which it has no control. These factors might include government monetary restrictions and the general economic and financial climate, for example, a depressed stock market, precluding a rights issue of ordinary shares.

Soft capital rationing applies when a company decides to limit the amount of capital expenditure that it is prepared to authorise. The capital budget becomes a control variable, which the company may relax if it chooses. Segments of divisionalised companies often have their capital budgets imposed on them by the main board of directors, and have to make their investment decisions within this imposed capital constraint.

A company may purposely curtail its capital expenditure for a number of reasons:

(i) It may consider that it has **insufficient depth of management expertise** to exploit all available opportunities without jeopardising the success of both new and ongoing operations.

(ii) It may be deliberate board policy to restrict the capital budget, **to concentrate managerial attention** on generating the very best and most carefully thought out and analysed proposals. In this regard, self-imposed capital rationing may be an exercise in quality control.

(iii) Many companies adopt the policy of **restricting capital expenditure to the amounts which can be generated by internal resources,** i.e. retained earnings and depreciation provisions (or in reality, internally-generated cash flow). This reluctance to use the external capital markets may be due to a risk-averse attitude to financial gearing, possibly because of the operating characteristics of the industry e.g. high operating gearing in a cyclical industry. Alternatively, it may be due to reluctance to issue equity in the form of a rights issue, for fear of diluting earnings, or in the case of an unlisted company, reluctance to seek a quotation owing to the time and expense involved and the dilution of ownership.

(b) (i) Assuming Filtrex wishes to maximise the wealth of its shareholders, it will seek the set of investment projects with the highest combined NPVs.

As a first approximation, it may examine the projects ranked according to their estimated NPVs, and select the projects with the highest NPVs, consistent with the budget limitation. However, this approach would confine the programme to project E alone, which apart from losing any benefits of diversification, is a solution which can be improved upon. This is because it overlooks the relationship between the NPV itself and the amount of capital required to yield the estimated NPV. Under capital rationing, it is often considered desirable to examine the productivity of each pound of scarce capital invested in the various projects. This information is given by the **profitability index (PI)**, which is the ratio of the NPV to the capital outplay in the year of capital rationing. The ranking of the five projects according to their PIs is:

A	65/150	=	0.43
B	50/120	=	0.42
C	80/200	=	0.40
D	30/80	=	0.38
E	120/400	=	0.30

Moving down the ranking, Filtrex would select projects A and B, but then, due to the **indivisibility problem**, and also the fact that projects A and C are mutually exclusive, it would have to depart from the rankings and move down as far as D, where after the remaining project E is too demanding of capital. The selected programme of ABD would require an outlay of £350,000 and generate an NPV of £145,000. £50,000 of scarce capital would remain unspent and according to the stated policy, would be invested in short-term assets. Although of low risk, these offer a return less than the 18% required by shareholders. Consequently, it might be preferable to return this unspent capital to shareholders in the form of a dividend or share repurchase, if shareholders are able to invest for higher returns in alternative activities. Perhaps, closer liaison with major shareholders is required to determine their preferences.

It is possible to improve on both of the previous selections by **trial and error**, in an attempt to utilise the whole of the capital budget. The optimal selection is BCD which offers a joint NPV of £160,000. However, even this result is suspect, as it relies on evaluating the projects at the rate of return required in the absence of rationing, in this case, 18% post-tax. This neglects the impact of capital rationing on the cost of capital – if apparently worthwhile projects are rejected, there is an opportunity cost in the form of the returns otherwise obtainable on the rejected projects. Projects should be evaluated at the discount rate reflecting the rate of return on the best of the rejected projects. Unfortunately, until the evaluation and selection is made, this remains an unknown! Unless project indivisibility is a problem, ranking and selection using the internal rate of return (IRR) will yield the same solution – it would therefore be helpful to find the IRR for each project.

(ii) In addition to IRRs, other information which may aid the decision-maker might include the following.

(1) Whether the rationing is likely to apply **over the long-term**, in which case its cost of capital (i.e. its opportunity cost of capital) should be raised.

(2) The degree of **postponability of projects** should be more closely assessed, i.e. whether a project can be postponed and what would be the impact of postponement on its profitability. If projects can be postponed, it may be desirable for Filtrex to select projects in the base period offering a rapid return flow of cash in order to provide funds to enable investment to be made in the postponed projects in the next time period. In other words, it would be helpful to examine the cash flow profiles of these projects and hence their **speed of payback**.

(3) The **respective degrees of risk** of these projects. It is implied in the analysis above that all projects have a similar degree of risk, but this is unlikely in practice, especially for the types of new product development planned by Filtrex. A capital-constrained company may use its limited access to finance to justify rejecting a high risk activity, especially if it is reliant on subsequent cash flows to finance postponed projects.

(4) The likelihood of obtaining marginal supplies of finance and on what terms.

(c) There are two basic ways in which a company in Filtrex's position might still manage to exploit more projects. On one hand, it can involve other parties in the project, and on the other, it can resolve to seek outside capital.

Sharing the projects

(i) To the extent that some part of the project(s) still require further development, for example design and market research, some of this work can be sub-contracted to specialist agencies. These might be able to perform the work at lower cost, and might even agree to take a deferred payment out of the project cash flows.

(ii) The production and/or sale of the products can be **licensed or franchised** to another party, with Filtrex arranging to receive a royalty or a percentage of sales. This is particularly appropriate for overseas activities.

(iii) A **joint venture** could be mounted with a competitor, although for commercial reasons, it is often safer to arrange such alliances with companies outside the industry, or with overseas companies wishing to penetrate the UK market. Clearly, such an agreement would have to be carefully negotiated.

(iv) The **patent rights to one or more products could be sold** and the purchaser allowed to develop the projects.

Raising external finance

(i) A certain amount of marginal finance could be squeezed out of more intensive use of working capital, although this could be counter-productive, for example reducing credit periods for customers may lose sales.

(ii) Some equipment could be leased, reducing the requirement for investment capital to buy assets.

(iii) If Filtrex has assets of sufficient quality, it may be possible to raise a mortgage or issue debentures secured on these assets.

(iv) Alternatively, good quality property assets could be sold to a financial institution and their continued use secured via a leaseback arrangement.

(v) Filtrex might approach official sources of aid such as a regional development agency, if relevant, or perhaps the European Investment Bank.

(vi) Filtrex might approach a venture capitalist which specialises in extending development capital to small-to-medium-sized firms. However, the venture capitalist will probably require a substantial equity stake, and possibly insist on placing an appointee on the Board to monitor their interests.

(vii) Filtrex may decide to seek a Stock Exchange quotation, either on the main London market or AIM. However, this would be time-consuming and costly, and involve releasing a substantial part of the equity (less for AIM) to a wider body of shareholders.

22 ARMCLIFF LTD

Key answer tips

In part (a) the first part of the data in the question relates to current operations - try to think why the examiner has given you this. The requirement is to determine whether the proposed project is attractive to *Armcliff* - not the parent company. Presumably what will make a project attractive to a division's management is one that will improve their current performance measure. Thus it is useful to know what the current level of ARR being achieved. This can then be compared with the project ARR.

Remember that the ARR is a financial accounting based measure - returns are in terms of accounting profits, and investments valued at balance sheet amounts - you must try to put all 'relevant cost' principles to the back of your mind. Whilst there are various possible definitions of the ARR (a point that can be raised in (b)) here you are given precise directions, so make sure you follow them. Both average profits and average investment need to be ascertained.
Don't forget to conclude by comparison with both current and required rates of return.

In part (b) the question requires you to show both theoretical and practical knowledge about investment appraisal methods. Your points must be made in sufficient depth to convince the examiner you actually understand the relevance of what you are saying. *Why* is the use of accounting profits potentially a problem?

In part (c), even though this is a examining a general area of credit management, try wherever you can to relate your points to the business in the question - it is stated that Armcliff intends to extend its credit to improve sales. Again make sure that you explain points enough to get the marks available, whilst still offering sufficient variety. Note that it is not enough simply to say that the advantages of APR is its simplicity. With spreadsheets, this is hardly going to be a consideration. Show instead that you appreciate that mangers are influenced by the methods used for their performance measurement - both internally and externally.

(a) **Current return on capital employed**

= Operating profit/capital employed

= £20m/(£75m + £25m)

= £20m/£100m = 20%.

Analysis of the project

Project capital requirements are £14 million fixed capital plus £0.5 million stocks. The annual depreciation charge (straight line) is:

(£14m – expected residual value of £2m)/4 = £3 million per annum.

Profit profile (£m)

Year	*1*	*2*	*3*	*4*
Sales	(5.00 × 2m) = 10.00	(4.50 × 1.8m) = 8.10	(4.00 × 1.6m) = 6.40	(3.50 × 1.6m) = 5.60
Operating costs	(2.00)	(1.80)	(1.60)	(1.60)
Fixed costs	(1.50)	(1.35)	(1.20)	(1.20)
Depreciation	(3.00)	(3.00)	(3.00)	(3.00)
Profit	3.50	1.95	0.60	(0.20)

Total profit over four years = £5.85 million.

Capital employed (start-of-year):

Fixed	14.00	11.00	8.00	5.00
Stocks	0.50	0.50	0.50	0.50
Total capital employed	14.50	11.50	8.50	5.50

Average capital employed = (14.50 + 11.50 +8.50 + 5.50)/4 = £10 million.

$$\text{Average rate of return} = \frac{\text{Average profit}}{\text{Average capital employed}} = \frac{£5.85\text{m}/4}{£10.0\text{m}} = \frac{£1.46\text{m}}{£10.0\text{m}}$$

= 14.6%

Note: If debtors were to be included in the definition of capital employed, this would reduce the calculated rate of return, while the inclusion of creditors would have an offsetting effect. However, using the ARR criterion as defined, the proposal has an expected return above the minimum stipulated by Shevin plc. It is unlikely that the managers of Armcliff will propose projects which offer a rate of return below the present 20% even where the expected return exceeds the minimum of 10%. To undertake projects with returns in this range will depress the overall divisional return and cast managerial performance in a weaker light.

However, it is unlikely that the senior managers of the Armcliff subsidiary would want to undertake the project.

(b) (i) The **ARR can be expressed in a variety of ways**, and is therefore susceptible to manipulation. Although the question specifies average profit to average capital employed, many other variants are possible, such as average profit to initial capital, which would raise the computed rate of return.

It is also **susceptible to variation in accounting policy** by the same firm over time, or as between different firms at a point in time. For example, different methods of depreciation produce different profit figures and hence different rates of return.

Perhaps, most fundamentally, it is **based on accounting profits expressed net of deduction for depreciation provisions, rather than cash flows**. This effectively results in double-counting for the initial outlay i.e. the capital cost is allowed for twice over, both in the numerator of the ARR calculation and also in the denominator. This is likely to depress the measured profitability of a project and result in rejection of some worthwhile investment.

Finally, because it simply averages the profits, it **makes no allowance for the timing of the returns** from the project.

(ii) The continuing use of the ARR method can by explained largely by its utilisation of balance sheet and profit-and-loss-account magnitudes familiar to managers, namely 'profit' and 'capital employed'. In addition, the impact of the project on a company's financial statements can also be specified. Return on capital employed is still the commonest way in which business unit performance is measured and evaluated, and is certainly the most visible to shareholders. It is thus not surprising that some managers may be happiest in expressing project attractiveness in the same terms in which their performance will be reported to shareholders, and according to which they will be evaluated and rewarded.

(c) Armcliff intends to achieve a sales increase by extending its debtor collection period. This policy carries several dangers. It implies that credit will be extended to customers for whom credit is an important determinant of supplier selection, hinting at financial instability on their part. Consequently, the risk of later than expected, or even no payment, is likely to increase. Although losses due to default are limited to the incremental costs of making these sales rather than the invoiced value, Armcliff should recognise that there is an opportunity cost involved in tying up capital for lengthy periods. In addition, companies which are slow payers often attempt to claim discounts to which they are not entitled. Armcliff may then face the difficult choice between acquiescence to such demands versus rejection, in which case, it may lose repeat sales.

The **creditworthiness of customers can be assessed** in several ways as follows.

Analysis of accounting statements

In the case of companies which publish their annual accounts, or file them at Companies House, key financial ratios can be examined to assess their financial stability. However, these almost certainly will be provided in arrears and may not give a true indication of the companies' current situation. Some customers may be prepared to supply more up-to-date accounts directly to the seller, although these are unlikely to have been audited.

Analysis of credit reports

It may be possible to obtain detailed assessment of the creditworthiness of customers from other sources, such as their bankers, specialist credit assessment agencies such as Dun & Bradstreet, and from trade sources such as other companies who supply them. These assessments are likely to be more up-to-date than company accounts, but will inevitably be more subjective.

Previous experience

If the firm has supplied the customer in the past, its previous payment record will be available.

Cash-only trial period

If accounting and other data is sparse, and there is no previous trading record with the customer, the seller may offer a trial period over which cash is required, but if the payment record is acceptable (e.g. if the customer's cheques always clear quickly), further transactions may be conducted on credit.

Background information

General background information on the industry in which the customer operates will generate insights into the financial health of companies in that sector, and by implication, that of the customer. Many agencies supply such information, although it should only be used as a back-up to other assessments.

23 SLUDGEWATER PLC

(a) The expected present value of the fines is equal to:

EV = (0.3 × £1.0m) + (0.5 × £1.8m) + (0.2 × £2.6m)

= £0.3m + £0.9m + £0.52m

= £1.72 million.

Calculation of the net present value of the investment requires computation of the capital cost plus incremental production costs as set out in the following table:

Year	0	1	2	3	4
	£m	£m	£m	£m	£m
Equipment purchase	(4.0)				
European Union grant (25% of cost)		1.000			
Increased production costs		(0.315)	(0.331)	(0.347)	
Tax saving at 30%			0.095	0.099	0.104
Tax saving on WDA (see note 3 below)		0.300	0.225	0.169	0.506
Net cash flow	(4.0)	0.985	(0.011)	(0.079)	0.610
Discount factor at 10%	1.000	0.909	0.826	0.751	0.683
Present value of cash flow	(4.0)	0.895	(0.009)	(0.059)	0.417

Net Present Value = (£2.756m)

Notes:

1 The consultant's charge has already been incurred and (as a committed cost) is therefore irrelevant to the current decision. The consultant's charge has already been incurred, and as a committed or sunk cost, it is not relevant to the current decision.

2 *Increased production costs*

Year	*Sales*	*Extra production costs (2%)*
	£m	£m
1	15.750	0.315
2	16.538	0.331
3	17.364	0.347

3 *Writing down allowances*:

Year	*Written down value*	*Writing down allowance (25%)*	*Tax saved (one year in arrears, at 30%)*
0	4.00	1.000	0.300
1	3.00	0.750	0.225
2	2.25	0.563	0.169
3	1.687 (balance)		0.506

The negative NPV on the investment in spray painting equipment exceeds the present value of the fines which Sludgewater might expect to pay. It therefore seems that the project is not viable in financial terms, and it would be cheaper to risk payment of the fines. However, the company must accept that to do so might risk incurring the wrath of both shareholders and the environmental lobby.

(b) **MEMORANDUM**

To: Sludgewater Board

From: Accountant

Subject: **Air pollution**

On purely non-financial criteria, it can be argued that our company has a moral and community responsibility to install anti-pollution equipment as long as the cost of installation does not jeopardise the long-term survival of the company.

However, the figures attached suggest that **the project is not wealth-creating** for Sludgewater's shareholders, because the value of the expected saving in fines (£1.72 million) is below the expected cost of the project (£2.756 million). The difficulty is that this conclusion is dependent on the current size of the fines payable, and if they were to rise substantially, then the optimal choice (in financial terms) might change. The difference between the expected value of the fines and the cost of the project is currently just over £1 million. This means that the fines would need to rise by nearly 60% (1/1.72 x 100) before the project becomes financially worthwhile. Changes in the size of the fines would be very difficult to predict as it is a political issue. However, since the company is a persistent offender, and the green lobby is becoming more influential, it is not unreasonable to anticipate that the fines will rise in the future as a result of political pressure.

It would be advisable, from a **public relations perspective**, for the Board to consider alternative and perhaps less expensive anti-pollution measures. It is also possible that the market for this company's products might increase if it is perceived to be more environmentally friendly, and if customers are sensitive to this. It is even possible that the company's share price might benefit from managers of 'ethical' investment funds deciding to include Sludgewater shares in their portfolio.

In addition, the company needs to think about its **long-term strategic objectives**, and its stance on anti-pollution systems in relation to these objectives. The market positioning of the company over the longer term is likely to be affected by decisions made in the short term, and so even if not investing in the project makes short-term financial sense, it may be more attractive from a long-term viewpoint. It is also possible that technological and legal circumstances will change over time, and such changes need to be anticipated in current decisions.

ACCA marking scheme

		Marks
(a)	Omission of consultants fee	1
	EV fines	2
	Production costs	1
	Tax saving on higher costs	1
	Writing down allowance	1
	Tax on WDA	1
	Net cash flow	1
	Discount factor	1
	Net present value	1
	Discussion	2
		12

(b) Memo format	1
Community responsibility	2
Significance of fine size	2
Possible changes in fines	1
Market effect of pollution avoidance	2
	8
Total	20

24 LEAMINGER PLC

(a) **Purchase outright**

	20X2	*20X3*	*20X4*	*20X5*	*20X6*	*20X7*
	£	£	£	£	£	£
Outlay/residual value	(360,000)				20,000	
Maintenance		(15,000)	(15,000)	(15,000)	(15,000)	
Resulting reduction in tax			4,500	4,500	4,500	4,500
Tax effect of WDAs (W1)		27,000	20,250	15,188	11,391	
Tax effect of balancing allowance (W2)						28,172
Cash flow	(360,000)	12,000	9,750	4,688	20,891	32,672
Discount factor at 10%	1.000	0.909	0.826	0.751	0.683	0.621
Present value	(360,000)	10,908	8,054	3,251	14,269	20,289

NPV of cost = £(302,959)

(W1) *Writing down allowances*

Year	*Tax written down value b/d*	*Writing down allowance (WDA) 25%*	*Tax effect at 30% - tax reduction*
	£	£	£
20X2	360,000	90,000	27,000
20X3	270,000	67,500	20,250
20X4	202,500	50,625	15,188
20X5	151,875	37,969	11,391
20X6	113,906		

The tax effect is one year in arrears, so the reduction relating to 20X2 affects cash flows in 20X3, and so on.

(W2) *Balancing allowance/charge and its tax effect*

	£
Tax written down value at start of year of sale	113,906
Sale proceeds	20,000
Balancing allowance	93,906
Effect on tax: reduction in tax at 30%	£28,172

The cash flow effect is one year in arrears.

Finance lease

	£
Annual lease rental	135,000
Maintenance	15,000
Annual expenditure	150,000

The tax saving on this annual cash flow is 30% × £150,000 = £45,000, one year in arrears.

Discount factor at 10%, years 1 - 5	3.791
Discount factor at 10%, year 1	0.909
Discount factor at 10%, years 2 - 5	2.882

Years		*Cash flow*	*Discount factor at 10%*	*Present value*
		£		£
1 – 4	Annual expenditure	(150,000)	3.170	(475,500)
2 - 5	Annual reduction in tax	45,000	2.882	129,690
	Net PV of cost			**(345,810)**

Operating lease

The present value of cost is calculated on the assumption that the agreement will last for four years, with annual renewals.

The tax saving on the annual rental cost is 30% × £140,000 = £42,000, one year in arrears.

Years		*Cash flow*	*Discount factor at 10%*	*Present value*
		£		£
0 - 3	Annual expenditure	(140,000)	3.487	(475,500)
1 - 4	Annual reduction in tax	42,000	3.170	129,690
	Net PV of cost			**(345,810)**

On the basis of net present value, purchasing outright appears to be the least cost method.

(b) Each £1 of outlay before 31 December 20X3 would mean a loss in NPV on the alternative project of £0.20. There is thus an opportunity cost of using funds in 20X2.

Purchasing

	£
Net present value of cost	(302,959)
Opportunity cost (0.2 × 360,000)	(72,000)
Net PV of cost	**(374,959)**

Finance lease

Net present cost = £(345,818)

There is no cash flow before 31 December 20X3 in this case, and thus no opportunity cost.

Operating lease

	£
Net present value of cost	(355,040)
Opportunity cost (0.2 × 140,000)	(28,000)
Net PV of cost	**(383,040)**

Thus the finance lease is now the lowest cost option.

All the above assume that the alternative project cannot be delayed.

(c) **REPORT**

To: The Directors of Leaminger plc

From: A business advisor

Date: xx/xx/xx

Subject: Acquiring the turbine machine

Introduction

In financial terms, and without capital rationing, outright purchase is the preferred method of financing as it has the lowest NPV of cost. With capital rationing, a finance lease arrangement becomes the least-cost method. There are, however, a number of other factors to be considered before a final decision is taken.

(1) If capital rationing persists into further periods, the value of cash used in leasing becomes more significant and so purchasing would become relatively more attractive.

(2) Even without capital rationing, leasing has a short-term cash flow advantage over purchasing, which may be significant for liquidity.

(3) The use of a 10% cost of capital may be inappropriate as these are financing issues and are unlikely to be subject to the average business risk. Also they may alter the capital structure and thus the financial risk of the business and thus the cost of capital itself. This may alter the optimal decision in the face of capital rationing.

(4) The actual cash inflows generated by the turbine are constant for all options, except that under an operating lease the lessor may refuse to lease the turbine at the end of any annual contract thus making it unavailable from this particular source. On top of capital rationing, we need to consider the continuing availability of finance under the operating lease.

(5) Conversely, however, with the operating lease Leaminger plc can cancel if business conditions change (e.g. a technologically improved asset may become available). This is not the case with the other financing options. On the other hand, if the market is buoyant then the lessor may raise lease rentals, whereas the cost is fixed under the other options and hence capital rationing might be more severe.

(6) On the issue of maintenance costs of £15,000 per annum, this is included in the operating lease if the machine becomes unreliable, but there is greater risk beyond any warranty period under the other two options.

(7) It is worth investigating if some interim measure can be put in place which would assist in lengthening the turbine's life such as sub-contracting work outside or overhauling the machine.

ACCA marking scheme		
		Marks
(a)	**Purchase**	
	Capital allowances	3
	Maintenance	1
	Taxation	1
	NPV	1
	Finance lease	
	PV outflows	1
	PV tax relief	1
	NPV	1

	Operating lease	
	PV outflows	1
	PV tax relief	1
	NPV	1
	Recommendation	1
(b)	Opportunity cost	1
	Revised NPV for each option (1 mark each)	3
	Evaluation	1
(c)	2 marks for each explained point	8
Total		25

25 CAPITAL RATIONING

Key answer points

You need to start your answer in part (a) by calculating the NPV of each project. Having calculated the NPVs, you can (1) work out an NPV per unit of limiting factor (per £1 invested) to answer the question assuming that projects are divisible, and (2) compare the feasible combinations of projects if they are not divisible, within the constraints imposed by limited capital to invest.

Unless you are aware of 'hard' and 'soft' capital rationing, you might struggle to provide a complete answer to part (c).

It is worth noting that although parts (b) and (d) should be straightforward, you need to make your points clearly and briefly.

(a) (i)

Analysis of projects assuming they are divisible

	Discount factor at 12%	*Project 1* *Cash flow*	*PV*	*Project 3* *Cash flow*	*PV*
		£	£	£	£
Initial investment	1.000	(300,000)	(300,000)	(400,000)	(400,000)
Year 1	0.893	85,000	75,905	124,320	111,018
Year 2	0.797	90,000	71,730	128,795	102,650
Year 3	0.712	95,000	67,640	133,432	95,004
Year 4	0.636	100,000	63,600	138,236	87,918
Year 5	0.567	95,000	53,865	143,212	81,201
PV of savings			332,740		477,791
NPV			32,740		77,791
Profitability index			332,740/300,000 = 1.11		477,791/400,000 = 1.19

	Discount factor at 12%	*Project 2* *Cash flow*	*PV*
		£	£
Initial investment	1.000	(450,000)	(450,000)
Annual cash flows, years 1 - 5	3.605	140,800	507,584
Net present value			57,584
Profitability index	507,584/450,000		= 1.13

Order of preference (in order of profitability index) = Project 3 then Project 2 then Project 1.

Project	*Profitability index*	*Ranking*	*Investment*	*NPV*	
			£	£	
3	1.19	1st	400,000	77,791	
2	1.13	2nd	400,000	51,186	(= 57,584 × 400/450)
			800,000	128,977	

(ii) **Analysis of projects assuming they are indivisible**

If the projects are assumed to be indivisible, the total NPV of combinations of projects must be considered.

Projects	*Investment*	*NPV*	
	£	£	
1 and 2	750,000	90,324	£(32,740 + 57,584)
1 and 3	700,000	110,531	£(32,740 + 77,791)
2 and 3	850,000	not feasible, too much investment	

The optimum combination is now projects 1 and 3.

(b) The NPV decision rule requires that a company invest in all projects that have a positive net present value. This assumes that sufficient funds are available for all incremental projects, which is only true in a perfect capital market. When insufficient funds are available, that is when capital is rationed, projects cannot be selected by ranking by absolute NPV. Choosing a project with a large NPV may mean not choosing smaller projects that, in combination, give a higher NPV. Instead, if projects are divisible, they can be ranked using the profitability index in order make the optimum selection. If projects are not divisible, different combinations of available projects must be evaluated to select the combination with the highest NPV.

(c) The NPV decision rule, to accept all projects with a positive net present value, requires the existence of a perfect capital market where access to funds for capital investment is not restricted. In practice, companies are likely to find that funds available for capital investment are restricted or rationed.

Hard capital rationing is the term applied when the restrictions on raising funds are due to causes external to the company. For example, potential providers of debt finance may refuse to provide further funding because they regard a company as too risky. This may be in terms of financial risk, for example if the company's gearing is too high or its interest cover is too low, or in terms of business risk if they see the company's business prospects as poor or its operating cash flows as too variable. In practice, large established companies seeking long-term finance for capital investment are usually able to find it, but small and medium-sized enterprises will find raising such funds more difficult.

Soft capital rationing refers to restrictions on the availability of funds that arise within a company and are imposed by managers. There are several reasons why managers might restrict available funds for capital investment. Managers may prefer slower organic growth to a sudden increase in size arising from accepting several large investment projects. This reason might apply in a family-owned business that wishes to avoid hiring new managers. Managers may wish to avoid raising further equity finance if this will dilute the control of existing shareholders. Managers may wish to avoid issuing new debt if their expectations of future economic conditions are such as to suggest that an increased commitment to fixed interest payments would be unwise.

One of the main reasons suggested for soft capital rationing is that managers wish to create an internal market for investment funds. It is suggested that requiring investment projects to compete for funds means that weaker or marginal projects, with only a small chance of success, are avoided. This allows a company to focus on more robust investment projects where the chance of success is higher (*Tutorial note*: Watson, D. and Head, A. (2001) *Corporate Finance: Principles and Practice*, 2nd edition, FT Prentice Hall, p.73.) This cause of soft capital rationing can be seen as a way of reducing the risk and uncertainty associated with investment projects, as it leads to accepting projects with greater margins of safety.

(d) When undertaking the appraisal of an investment project, it is essential that **only relevant cash flows** are included in the analysis. If non-relevant cash flows are included, the result of the appraisal will be misleading and incorrect decisions will be made. A relevant cash flow is a differential (incremental) cash flow, one that changes as a direct result of an investment decision.

If current fixed production overheads are expected to increase, for example, the additional fixed production overheads are a relevant cost and should be included in the investment appraisal. Existing fixed production overheads should not be included.

A new cash flow arising as the result of an investment decision is a relevant cash flow. For example, the purchase of raw materials for a new production process and the net cash flows arising from the production process are both relevant cash flows.

The incremental tax effects arising from an investment decision are also relevant cash flows, providing that a company is in a tax-paying position. Direct labour costs, for example, are an allowable deduction in calculating taxable profit and so give rise to tax benefits: tax liabilities arising on incremental taxable profits are also a relevant cash flow.

One area where caution is required is interest payments on new debt used to finance an investment project. They are a differential cash flow and hence relevant, but the effect of the cost of the debt is incorporated into the discount rate used to determine the net present value. Interest payments should not therefore be included as a cash flow in an investment appraisal.

Market research undertaken to determine whether a new product will sell is often undertaken prior to the investment decision on whether to proceed with production of the new product. This is an example of a **sunk cost**. These are costs already incurred as a result of past decisions, and so are not relevant cash flows.

ACCA marking scheme

			Marks
(a)	(i)	NPV of project 1	1
		NPV of project 2	1
		NPV of project 3	2
		Calculation of profitability indices	2
		Optimum investment schedule	2
	(ii)	Selection of optimum combination	2
			10
(b)		NPV decision rule	1
		Link to perfect capital markets	1
		Explanation of ranking problem and solution	1
			3
(c)		Hard capital rationing	3
		Soft capital rationing	4
			7
(d)		Explanation of relevant cash flows	2
		Examples of relevant cash flows	3
			5
Total			25

26 UMUNAT PLC

(a) The investment appraisal process is concerned with assessing the value of future cash flows compared to the cost of investment.

Since future cash flows cannot be predicted with certainty, managers must consider how much confidence can be placed in the results of the investment appraisal process. They must therefore be concerned with the risk and uncertainty of a project. Uncertainty refers to the situation where probabilities cannot be assigned to future cash flows. Uncertainty cannot therefore be quantified and increases with project life: it is usually true to say that the more distant is a cash flow, the more uncertain is its value. Risk refers to the situation where probabilities can be assigned to future cash flows, for example as a result of managerial experience and judgement or scenario analysis. Where such probabilities can be assigned, it is possible to quantify the risk associated with project variables and hence of the project as a whole.

If risk and uncertainty were not considered in the investment appraisal process, managers might make the mistake of placing too much confidence in the results of investment appraisal, or they may fail to monitor investment projects in order to ensure that expected results are in fact being achieved. Assessment of project risk can also indicate projects that might be rejected as being too risky compared with existing business operations, or projects that might be worthy of reconsideration if ways of reducing project risk could be found in order to make project outcomes more acceptable.

(b) Contribution per unit = 3.00 – 1.65 = £1.35 per unit

Total annual contribution = 20,000 × 1.35 = £27,000 per year

Annual cash flow after fixed costs = 27,000 – 10,000 = £17,000 per year

Payback period = 50,000/17,000 = 2.9 years

(assuming that cash flows occur evenly throughout the year)

The payback period calculated is greater than the maximum payback period used by Umunat plc of two years and on this basis should be rejected. Use of payback period as an investment appraisal method cannot be recommended, however, because payback period does not consider all the cash flows arising from an investment project, as it ignores cash flows outside of the payback period. Furthermore, payback period ignores the time value of money.

The fact that the payback period is 2.9 years should not therefore be a reason for rejecting the project. The project should be assessed using a discounted cash flow method such as net present value or internal rate of return, since the project as a whole may generate an acceptable return on investment.

(c) Calculation of project net present value

Annual cash flow = ((20,000 × (3 – 1.65)) – 10,000 = £17,000 per year

Net present value = (17,000 × 3.605) – 50,000 = 61,285 – 50,000 = £11,285

Alternatively:	PV (£)
Sales revenue: 20,000 × 3.00 × 3.605 =	216,300
Variable costs: 20,000 × 1.65 × 3.605 =	(118,965)
Contribution	97,335
Initial investment	(50,000)
Fixed costs: 10,000 × 3.605 =	(36,050)
Net present value:	11,285

Sensitivity of NPV to sales volume

Sales volume giving zero NPV = ((50,000/3.605) + 10,000)/1.35 = 17,681 units

This is a decrease of 2,319 units or 11.6%

Alternatively, sales volume decrease = 100 × 11,285/97,335= 11.6%

Sensitivity of NPV to sales price

Sales price for zero NPV = (((50,000/3.605) + 10,000)/20,000) + 1.65 = £2.843

This is a decrease of 15.7p or 5.2%

Alternatively, sales price decrease = 100 × 11,285/216,300 = 5.2%

Sensitivity of NPV to variable cost

Variable cost must increase by 15.7p or 9.5% to make the NPV zero.

Alternatively, variable cost increase = 100 × 11,285/118,965 = 9.5%

Sensitivity analysis evaluates the effect on project net present value of changes in project variables. The objective is to determine the key or critical project variables, which are those where the smallest change produces the biggest change in project NPV. It is limited in that only one project variable at a time may be changed, whereas in reality several project variables may change simultaneously. For example, an increase in inflation could result in increases in sales price, variable costs and fixed costs. Sensitivity analysis is not a way of evaluating project risk, since although it may identify the key or critical variables, it cannot assess the likelihood of a change in these variables. In other words, sensitivity analysis does not assign probabilities to project variables. Where sensitivity analysis is useful is in drawing the attention of management to project variables that need careful monitoring if a particular investment project is to meet expectations. Sensitivity analysis can also highlight the need to check the assumptions underlying the key or critical variables.

(d) Expected value of sales volume:

(17,500 × 0.3) + (20,000 × 0.6) + (22,500 × 0.1) = 19,500 units

Expected NPV = (((19,500 × 1.35) – 10,000) × 3.605) – 50,000 = £8,852

Since the expected net present value is positive, the project appears to be acceptable. From earlier analysis we know that the NPV is positive at 20,000 per year, and the NPV will therefore also be positive at 22,500 units per year. The NPV of the worst case is:

(((17,500 × 1.35) – 10,000) × 3.605) – 50,000 = (£882)

The NPV of the best case is:

(((22,500 × 1.35) – 10,000) × 3.605) – 50,000 = £23,452

There is thus a 30% chance that the project will produce a negative NPV, a fact not revealed by considering the expected net present value alone.

The expected net present value is not a value that is likely to occur in practice: it is perhaps more useful to know that there is a 30% chance that the project will produce a negative NPV (or a 70% chance of a positive NPV), since this may represent an unacceptable level of risk as far as the managers of Umunat plc are concerned. It can therefore be argued that assigning probabilities to expected economic states or sales volumes has produced useful information that can help the managers of Umunat to make better investment decisions. The difficulty with this approach is that probability estimates of project variables or future economic states are likely to carry a high degree of uncertainty and subjectivity.

ACCA marking scheme

		Marks
(a)	Discussion of risk	2
	Discussion of uncertainty	1
	Value of considering risk and uncertainty	2
		5
(b)	Calculation of payback period	2
	Discussion of payback period	2
		4
(c)	Calculation net present value	2
	Sensitivity of NPV to sales volume	2
	Sensitivity of NPV to sales price	2
	Sensitivity of NPV to variable cost	1
	Discussion of sensitivity analysis	3
		10
(d)	Calculation of expected value of sales	1
	Calculation of expected net present value	1
	Discussion of expected net present value	4
		3
Total		25

27 AGD CO

Key answer tips

Part (a): To evaluate lease v buy the examiner's preferred approach is to perform two separate calculations. A combined approach will also gain credit but be careful of the signs of cash flows. Particular care is needed regarding the tax flows; they are delayed in this question and the asset would be bought on the first day of a new accounting period. Likewise the lease payments are in advance.

In part (b) ensure you both explain and discuss the differences. This requires you to describe the differences and look at the implications of them.

In part (c) the key is to recognise that there will be ten payments with an interest rate of 5% per six months.

(a) Evaluation of purchase versus leasing compares the net cost of each financing alternative using the after-tax cost of borrowing.

Borrowing to buy evaluation

	Year 0	*Year 1*	*Year 2*	*Year 3*	*Year 4*
	£000	£000	£000	£000	£000
Purchase and sale	(320)			50	
Capital allowance tax benefits			24	18	39
Maintenance costs		(25)	(25)	(25)	
Maintenance cost tax benefits			8	8	8
Net cash flow	(320)	(25)	7	51	47
Discount factors (7%)	1.000	0.935	0.873	0.816	0.763
Present values	(320)	(23)	6	42	36

PV of borrowing to buy = –£259,000

Workings: Capital allowance tax benefits

Year	*Capital allowance*		*Tax benefit*	*Taken in year*
1	320,000 × 0.25 =	80,000	80,000 × 0.3 = 24,000	2
2	80,000 × 0.75 =	60,000	60,000 × 0.3 = 18,000	3
3	Balancing allowance =	130,000	130,000 × 0.3 = 39,000	4

Balancing allowance = (320,000 – 50,000) – (80,000 + 60,000) = £130,000

Leasing evaluation

	Year 0	*Year 1*	*Year 2*	*Year 3*	*Year 4*
	£000	£000	£000	£000	£000
Lease rentals	(120)	(120)	(120)		
Lease rental tax benefits			36	36	36
Net cash flow	(120)	(120)	(84)	36	36
Discount factors (7%)	1.000	0.935	0.873	0.816	0.763
Present values	(120)	(112)	(73)	29	27

PV of leasing = –£249,000

On financial grounds, leasing is to be preferred as it is cheaper by £10,000. Note that the first lease rental is taken as being paid at year 0 as it is paid in the first month of the first year of operation.

An alternative form of evaluation combines the cash flows of the above two evaluations. Because this evaluation is more

complex, it is more likely to lead to computational errors.

Combined evaluation

	Year 0	*Year 1*	*Year 2*	*Year 3*	*Year 4*
	£000	£000	£000	£000	£000
Purchase and sale	(320)			50	
Capital allowance tax benefits			24	18	39
Maintenance costs		(25)	(25)	(25)	
Maintenance cost tax benefits			8	8	8
Lease rentals saved	120	120	120		
Lease rental tax benefits lost			(36)	(36)	(36)
Net cash flow	(200)	95	91	15	11
Discount factors (7%)	1.000	0.935	0.873	0.816	0.763
Present values	(200)	89	79	12	8

The PV of –£12,000 indicates that leasing would be £12,000 cheaper than borrowing. The difference between this and the previous evaluation is due to rounding.

(b) A finance lease exists when the substance of the lease is that the lessee enjoys substantially all of the risks and rewards of ownership, even though legal title to the leased asset does not pass from lessor to lessee. A finance lease is therefore characterised by one lessee for most, if not all, of its useful economic life, with the lessee meeting maintenance and similar regular costs. A finance lease cannot be cancelled, once entered into, without incurring severe financial penalties. A finance lease therefore acts as a kind of medium- to long-term source of debt finance which, in substance, allows the lessee to purchase the desired asset. This ownership dimension is recognised in the balance sheet, where a finance-leased asset must be capitalised (as a fixed asset), together with the amount of the obligations to make lease payments in future periods (as a liability).

In contrast, an operating lease is a rental agreement where several lessees are expected to use the leased asset and so the lease period is much shorter than the asset's useful economic life. Maintenance and similar costs are borne by the lessor, with this cost being reflected in the lease rentals charged. An operating lease can usually be cancelled without penalty at short notice. This allows the lessee to ensure that only up-to-date assets are leased for use in business operations, avoiding the obsolescence problem associated with the rapid pace of technological change in assets such as personal computers and photocopiers. Because the substance of an operating lease is that of a short-term rental agreement, operating leases do not require to be capitalised in the balance sheet, allowing companies to take advantage of this form of 'off-balance sheet financing'[3].

(c) (i) The offer of 10% per year with interest payable every six months means that the bank will require 5% every six months. This is equivalent to an annual percentage rate of 10.25% ($100 \times (1.05^2 - 1)$) before tax.

OR

$1 + \text{annual rate} = (1 + \text{six monthly rate})^2 = 1.05^2 = 1.1025$

(ii) To calculate the repayment schedule use:

PV of repayments = PV of amount borrowed

Here we have a simple annuity, so

Instalment (A) × annuity factor = 320,000

where we want an annuity discount factor for ten payments and a rate of 5%.

Using annuity tables:

A = 320,000/7.722 = £41,440

An alternative solution can be found using the formula for the present value of an annuity given in the formula sheet, a six-monthly interest rate of 5% and 10 periods of six months over the 5-year period of the loan:

320,000 = (A/r) × (1 – 1/(1 + r)n) = (A/0.05) × (1 – 1/1.0510)

Hence the amount to be paid at the end of each six-month period = A = £41,441

The difference between the two values is due to rounding in the annuity tables.

ACCA marking scheme		
		Marks
(a)	Purchase price	1
	Sale proceeds	1
	Capital allowances	1
	Balancing allowance	1
	Capital allowance tax benefits	1
	Maintenance costs	1
	Maintenance cost tax benefits	1
	NPV of borrowing to buy	1
	Lease rentals	1
	Lease rental tax benefits	1
	NPV of leasing	1
	Selection of cheapest option	1
		12

(b)	Explanation and discussion	
	Finance lease	4–5
	Operating lease	4–5
	Maximum	8
(c)	Annual percentage rate	2
	Amount of equal instalments	3
		5
Total		25

COSTING SYSTEMS AND TECHNIQUES

28 BUD PLC

(a) **Preliminary workings:**

Budgeted sales (units and value)

Product	*Units*	*Price*	*Value (£)*
F1	34,000	£50.00	1,700,000
F2	58,000	£30.00	1,740,000
			3,440,000

Budgeted production (units)

Product	*Sales units*	*Stock increment units*	*Production units*
F1	34,000	1,000	35,000
F2	58,000	2,000	60,000

(i) **Component purchase and usage budget (units and value)**

Product		*Component C3 units*		*Component C4 units*	*Total*
F1	(35,000 × 8)	280,000	(35,000 × 4)	140,000	
F2	(60,000 × 4)	240,000	(60,000 × 3)	180,000	
		520,000		320,000	
		£		£	
Value	(× £1.25)	650,000	(× £1.80)	576,000	£1,226,000

(ii) **Direct labour budget (hours and value)**

Product		*Assembly hours*		*Finishing hours*	*Total*
F1	(35,000 × 30 mins)	17,500	(35,000 × 12 mins)	7,000	
F2	(60,000 × 15 mins)	15,000	(60,000 × 10 mins)	10,000	
		32,500		17,000	
		£		£	
Value	(× £5)	162,500	(× £6)	102,000	£264,500

(iii) **Departmental manufacturing overhead recovery rates**

	Assembly	*Finishing*
Total overhead cost per month	£617,500	£204,000
Total direct labour hours	32,500	17,000
Overhead recovery rate (per direct labour hour)	£19.00	£12.00

(iv) **Selling overhead recovery rate**

Total overhead cost per month	£344,000
Total sales value (Month 9)	£3,440,000
Selling overhead recovery rate	10%

Unit manufacturing costs			*F1*		*F2*
			£		£
Materials	C3	8 × £1.25	10.00	4 × £1.25	5.00
	C4	4 × £1.80	7.20	3 × £1.80	5.40
Labour	Assembly	30/60 × £5	2.50	15/60 × £5	1.25
	Finishing	12/60 × £6	1.20	10/60 × £6	1.00
M'fg. overhead	Assembly	30/60 × £19	9.50	15/60 × £19	4.75
	Finishing	12/60 × £12	2.40	10/60 × £12	2.00
Manufacturing cost			32.80		19.40

(v) **Closing stock budget**

Product	*Units*	*Cost £*	*Value £*
F1	1,000	32.80	32,800
F2	2,000	19.40	38,800
			7,1600

(b) **Standard unit cost (Month 9)**

		F1	*F2*
		£/unit	£/unit
Material	C3	10.00	5.00
	C4	7.20	5.40
Labour	Assembly	2.50	1.25
	Finishing	1.20	1.00
M'fg. overhead	Assembly	9.50	4.75
	Finishing	2.40	2.00
Manufacturing cost		32.80	19.40
Selling overhead (10% of price)		5.00	3.00
Total cost		37.80	22.40
Selling price		50.00	30.00
Profit		12.20	7.60

(c) **Budgeted profit and loss account (Month 9)**

Cost element	£
Direct materials (see note)	1,226,000
Direct labour (see note)	264,500
Manufacturing overhead (617,500 + 204,000)	821,500
	2,312,000
Less closing stock	71,600
Manufacturing cost of sales	2,240,400
Selling overhead	344,000
Total cost of sales	2,584,400
Sales	3,440,000
Net profit	855,600

Note: *Direct materials cost*

(35,000 × £17.20) + (60,000 × £10.40) = £1,226,000.

Direct labour cost

(35,000 × £3.70) + (60,000 × £2.25) = £264,500

(d) Under a system of absorption costing, an overhead rate is used to apply overheads to each unit produced. At present, the company applies manufacturing overhead to products based on the budgeted labour hours and the budgeted expenditure in each month. Such figures are used to establish a **separate predetermined rate for each month**. As a result, **unit overhead costs fluctuate** from one month to the next if production levels fluctuate, because any fixed element of overheads is spread over the fluctuating volumes.

It can be disconcerting and misleading for production and sales staff to be dealing with product costs which fluctuate on a monthly basis. This is especially so when the fluctuation has not been caused by changes in production efficiency and it bears no relation to changes in the general market price.

One way to overcome this is to compute an overhead rate based on a longer time period, for example quarterly or a predetermined annual rate as mentioned in the question. This enables large fluctuations in, and extreme values of, product costs to be avoided. This would mean that management would be able to monitor the business volume and overhead costs on which the calculations were based, to ensure that over the longer term the average product costs which were predicted are in fact achieved.

29 ABC

(a) Activity Based Costing (ABC) has been implemented across a range of organisations to enhance management information systems. The introduction of ABC changed the focus of cost accumulation from processes to activities. In this way, decision-relevant costs could be identified since management could, in principle, alter the activities undertaken. Traditional methods of product costing were often volume related (e.g. hours of labour used) but this did not develop with the growth in activities that had no relation to volume, or in multi-product businesses where there are complex production processes.

There are general conditions under which ABC are most likely to operate and these relate to the following factors:

(i) Where there is a requirement to apportion costs (e.g. in a multi-product business).

(ii) Where there are significant overheads to apportion.

(iii) Where the availability of sophisticated information retrieval systems allows management to track product costs as they pass through a production system.

Multi-product businesses

The main issue is that there have to be at least two products in the business otherwise there are no costs to apportion between products. For a single product company, all the costs of the business are identifiable with the product.

However, ABC might still be useful in single product businesses when management decisions are required to determine the level of production. In such cases, optimum levels of output can be defined once costs can be split between fixed and variable elements. ABC will help identify variable costs as those that vary with the level of activities that incur costs. In principle, fixed costs are then those costs that do not vary with activity, and hence it becomes possible to undertake profitability analysis in relation to activity levels.

Other advantages of ABC in multiproduct business relate to the accurate valuation of stock and facilitating the effective management of stock levels with multiple products. There is also reduced cross-subsidisation of products: with costs accurately identified with products, it becomes easier for management to distinguish which products are profitable from those that are not.

The significance of overheads and the ABC method of charging costs

Since ABC is a cost apportionment system then it is principally beneficial when there is a high proportion of overhead costs to apportion to products. If a business incurs only direct costs, there is no issue for ABC to resolve.

ABC is based on the premise that activities lead to costs being incurred and that costs should therefore be apportioned on the basis of the activities that different products consume. In this way, management can better understand the behaviour of overheads as they relate to decisions.

ABC apportions costs by first identifying the activities that generate costs. Cost drivers are then chosen that reflect the events that create costs when the activities are undertaken. The costs associated with each activity are then collected into cost pools where there are common cost drivers. Finally, costs are allocated to products on the basis of the activities they use. In sum, if product overheads can be seen in terms of activities, and activities have costs associated with them, then the use of activities by a product can be costed.

Retrieval systems

A basic requirement for any cost allocation system is information availability. This is particularly so for ABC systems which rely heavily on activity information. Moreover, production systems are far more complex than in the days when traditional absorption costing was most effective. For example, manufacturing processes rely far more on quality control monitoring, inspection and set-up processes than they ever did and are not necessarily related to the volume of activity. With many products, and variants on products, the monitoring of costs itself becomes a large and complex process. With complexity inevitably follows greater support services, of which a major category would be computer support services.

In addition, ABC requires the monitoring of activities that have not involved monitoring previously. This raises issues of information capture and it is in new technology that answers to this are most likely to be found.

(b) One of the key problems in assessing manager performance is in ensuring that costs on which managers' performance is judged are **controllable** and **hence traceable to manager decisions.** Manager performance will be unfairly assessed if non-controllable costs are incorrectly taken into account, and the manager is made accountable for them. ABC is often claimed to rest on a more accurate information base than absorption costing, and hence the impact of management decisions is potentially more easily seen under ABC than it is under traditional volume-related absorption methods. Thus, it becomes possible to more closely align management decisions with their consequences and improve performance appraisal.

For example, in allocating and apportioning overheads, the re-apportionment of service department costs is reduced or eliminated under ABC. This is because ABC establishes separate cost pools for support activities and the costs of these activities are assigned to products directly on the basis of the appropriate driver. The accuracy of ABC in this context rests on the accurate identification of cost pools and cost drivers.

Also, ABC absorbs costs into products in a wider variety of ways than traditional absorption methods, which rely mostly on labour and/or machine hours. In extending the range of absorption bases, ABC is able to more closely track costs to the causes of the costs which then links to management decisions.

The foregoing does not rule out accurate costing using traditional absorption methods, especially when a business has most of its costs varying with production volume. However, when overheads do not vary with output, other means of determining absorption rates are preferable, such as those based on cost drivers. Thus, the scope for arbitrariness in manager performance appraisal is reduced.

ACCA marking scheme			
		Marks	
(a)	Comments on general conditions for ABC	1	
	2 marks each for detailed comments on overheads and the methods ABC uses to allocate costs. Up to a maximum of:	7	
	Comments on the impact of ABC for multi-product businesses	3	
	Comments on information retrieval systems	4	
	Quality and presentation of report	2	
			17
(b)	General comments on performance evaluation	2	
	2 marks each for detailed comments on ABC and absorption costing. Up to a maximum of:	6	
			8
Total			25

30 ABKABER PLC

(a) (i) **Absorption costing using labour hour absorption rate**

Total overhead cost	=	£2,400,000 + £6,000,000 + £3,600,000
	=	£12,000,000
Total labour hours	=	200,000 + 220,000 + 80,000
	=	500,000
Overhead absorption rate/labour hour	=	£12,000,000/500,000 = £24

	Sunshine	*Roadster*	*Fireball*
Units of production and sale	2,000	1,600	400
Direct labour hours	200,000	220,000	80,000

	£	£	£
Direct labour (£5/hour)	1,000,000	1,100,000	400,000
Materials (at £400/600/900)	800,000	960,000	360,000
Overheads (£24/direct labour hour)	4,800,000	5,280,000	1,920,000
Total costs	6,600,000	7,340,000	2,680,000
	£	£	£
Cost per unit	3,300	4,587.5	6,700
Selling price	4,000	6,000.0	8,000
Profit/(loss) per unit	700	1,412.5	1,300
Total profit/(loss) per product	£1,400,000	£2,260,000	£520,000

Total profit = £4,180,000

(ii) **Activity Based Costing**

Number of deliveries to retailers	100 + 80 + 70	=	250
Charge rate for deliveries	£2,400,000/250	=	£9,600
Number of set-ups	35 + 40 + 25	=	100
Charge rate for set-ups	£6,000,000/100	=	£60,000
Number of purchase orders	400 + 300 + 100	=	800
Charge rate for deliveries inwards	£3,600,000/800	=	£4,500

	Sunshine	*Roadster*	*Fireball*
Units of production and sale	2,000	1,600	400
	£	£	£
Direct labour (as above)	1,000,000	1,100,000	400,000
Materials (as above)	800,000	960,000	360,000
Overheads:			
Deliveries at £9,600 (100:80:70)	960,000	768,000	672,000
Set-ups at £60,000 (35:40:25)	2,100,000	2,400,000	1,500,000
Purchase orders at £4,500 (400:300:100)	1,800,000	1,350,000	450,000
Total costs	6,660,000	6,578,000	3,382,000
	£	£	£
Cost per unit	3,330	4,111.25	8,455
Selling price	4,000	6,000.00	8,000
Profit/(loss) per unit	670	1,888.75	(455)
Total profit/(loss) per product	£1,340,000	£3,022,000	£(182,000)

Total profit = £4,180,000

(b) **REPORT – ABKABER PLC**

To: Directors of Abkaber plc

From: Management Accountant

Date: xx/xx/xx

Subject: **The Introduction of Activity Based Costing**

(i) **Direct costs**

The direct costs of labour and materials are unaffected by the use of ABC as they are directly attributable to units of output.

Notwithstanding the fact that labour is a relatively minor cost, however, the use of labour hours to allocate overheads magnifies its importance.

The labour hours allocation basis

As labour appears to be paid at a constant rate, an allocation using labour cost or labour hours gives the same result.

The central concern is, however, whether there is a cause and effect relationship between overheads and labour hours. Moreover for this allocation base to be correct overheads would need to be directly variable with labour hours. This seems unlikely on the basis of the information available.

ABC and labour hours cost allocation

ABC attempts to allocate overheads using a number of cost drivers rather than just one (such as direct labour hours). It therefore attempts to identify a series of cause-and-effect relationships. Moreover, those in favour of ABC argue that it is activities that generate costs, not direct labour hours – at least in the longer term if not the shorter term.

While costs are likely to be caused by multiple factors, the accuracy of any ABC system will depend on both the number of factors selected and the appropriateness of each of these activities as a driver for costs. Each cost driver should be appropriate to the pool of overheads to which it relates. As noted already, there should ideally be a direct cause-and-effect relationship between the cost driver and the relevant overhead cost pool (whereby costs increase proportionately with the number of activities operated).

The contrast between the labour hours costing system and ABC can be seen in requirement (a). These differences can be brought out by reviewing the comments of the directors.

(ii) **The Finance Director**

Using the labour hours method of allocation, the Fireball makes an overall profit of £520,000 but using ABC it makes a loss of £182,000. There is a significant difference in the levels of cost allocated, and so in profitability, between the two methods.

The major reason for the difference appears to be that while labour hours are not all that significant for Fireball production, the low volumes of Fireball sales cause a relatively high amount of set-ups, deliveries and purchase processes, and this is recognised by ABC.

If the Fireball model is to continue, a review of the assembly and distribution systems may be needed in order to reduce costs.

There may, however, be other non-financial reasons to maintain the Fireball, e.g. maintaining a wide product range and raising the reputation of the motorcycles, which may increase sales of other models.

The Marketing Director

The marketing director suggests that ABC may have a number of problems and its conclusions should not be believed unquestioningly. These problems include:

(1) For decisions such as the closure of Fireball production or the pricing of the new motorbike rental contract, what is really needed is the incremental cost to determine a break-even position. While ABC may be closer to this concept than a labour hours allocation basis, its accuracy depends upon identifying appropriate cost drivers.

(2) The use of ABC for one-off decisions can be distinguished from its use in normal, ongoing costing procedures. It is perfectly possible that while

labour hours may have been used for normal costing, an incremental costing analysis would be undertaken for important one-off decisions such as the closure of Fireball production or the pricing of the new motorbike rental contract. In these circumstances, the introduction of ABC in normal costing procedures may have restricted benefits.

(3) There may be interdependencies between both costs and revenues that ABC is unlikely to capture. Where costs are truly common to more than one product then this may be difficult to capture by any given single activity.

(4) As with labour hours allocations it is the future that matters. Any relationship between costs and activities based upon historic experience and observation may be unreliable as a guide to the future.

The Managing Director

(1) ABC normally assumes that the cost per activity is constant as the number of times the activity is repeated increases. In practice there may be a learning curve, such that costs per activity are non-linear. As a result, the marginal cost of increasing the number of activities is not the same as the average.

(2) Also in this case, fixed costs are included which would also mean that the marginal cost does not equal the average cost.

(3) The MD is correct in stating that some costs do not vary with either labour hours or any cost driver, and thus do not fall easily under ABC as a method of cost attribution as there is no cause and effect relationship. Depreciation on the factory building might be one example.

The Chairman

From a narrow perspective of reporting profit, it is true that the two methods give the same overall profit of £4,180,000, as is illustrated in answer (a). There are, however, a number of qualifications to this statement:

(1) If the company carried stock then the method of cost allocation would, in the short term at least, affect stock values and thus would influence profit.

(2) If the ABC information can be relied on as a method of identifying overhead costs that vary with activity, a decision might be taken to cease Fireball production, as it generates a negative profit of £182,000. This 'loss' was not apparent using traditional absorption costing and a direct labour hour absorption rate. Although we do not know the extent to which overheads would be reduced by ceasing production of fireball, ABC suggests that there is a possibility that closure would improve profitability, by up to £182,000 each year.

Further issues

The following should also be considered in evaluating ABC:

- The need to develop new data capture systems, and the relevant costs of doing so
- Increased and on-going analysis work
- Continued evaluation of cause and effect relationships between cost drivers and cost pools.

ACCA marking scheme		
		Marks
(a)	**Absorption costing using labour hours**	
	Overhead per labour hour	1
	Labour costs for each product	1
	Materials	1
	Total profit	1
	ABC	
	Costs per activity	3
	Labour	1
	Materials	1
	Overheads	3
	Total profit	1
(b)	Report format	1
	2 marks for each detailed point	12
Total		25

31 ADMER

Key answer tips

Part (a) of the question might seem straightforward, but you must beware of writing an over-simplified answer. Activity-based costing should be based on a close analysis of activities, the costs of activities and the drivers of those costs. The question does not provide this depth of analysis, and part (a) of the question expects you to recognise this. If your answer explains how useful ABC can be for management, you have missed much of the point of the question, because it is very doubtful whether ABC can be applied here usefully with the information available. The risk is that ABC becomes nothing more than an alternative approach to absorption costing, which would be of little information value to management.

Part (b) of the question asks for an ABC analysis, but leaves it to you to decide what the cost drivers might be. This is not necessarily clear, and your answer should state the assumptions that you make. Part (c) requires you to compare the original profit figures with ABC profit figures, and to discuss a possible decision to close the bathrooms department. It is essential to remember that for decision-making purposes, relevant costs and benefits should be considered - not absorption costing information. In part (c), you should also consider the many other factors that will influence a decision about whether to shut the department or not. There are a lot of points that can be made!

Part (d) of the question is challenging because it takes the basic issue of the usefulness of activity-based costing, and asks you to apply it to a specific case study – here, a chain of home furnishing stores. Your answer should refer specifically to the case study.

(a) Activity-based costing is based on identifying the activities that give rise to costs. This identification process does not seem to have been undertaken in this case. Simply collecting information on different activities is not enough. A detailed analysis of business operations is needed in order to identify relationships between costs and cost drivers. There should ideally be a one-to-one relationship between cost and cost driver. To the extent that this is not so, activity-based costing provides less useful information on product costs and for the purpose of cost control.

The management accountant believes that he can use the information provided to review the store's performance from an activity-based costing perspective. However, the relationship between 'other costs' for the three-month period and the proposed cost drivers (number of items sold, purchase orders, etc) is unclear.

If sales staff, warehouse staff, consultation staff and administration staff are on fixed salaries, their wage costs will not be linked to items sold, purchase orders or consultations. If wage costs are apportioned to product costs using the proposed cost drivers, it is likely that better product cost information will arise, simply because the apportionment bases being used are likely to be more appropriate to retailing than floor area. However at what point does a more sophisticated absorption costing system become an activity-based costing system?

The information provided can be used in an activity-based costing analysis if wage costs do depend to some extent on the proposed cost drivers, for example if sales staff wages include a commission for each purchase order raised. The management accountant needs to eliminate confusion by undertaking an investigation to establish and clarify the links between costs and activities if he wishes to use activity-based costing.

(b) **Proposed cost drivers:**

Total number of items sold = 1,000 + 1,500 + 4,000 = 6,500

Total number of purchase orders = 1,000 + 900 + 2,500 = 4,400

Total floor area = 16,000 + 10,000 + 14,000 = 40,000

Total number of consultations = 798 + 200 + 250 = 1,248

Sales staff wages

Are sales staff wages linked to items sold or to purchase orders?

(1) If sales staff wages are linked to items sold:

Sales staff wages recovery rate = £64,800/6,500 = £9.97/item sold

(2) If sales staff wages are linked to purchase orders:

Sales staff wages recovery rate = £64,800/4,400 = £14.727/purchase order

Consultation staff wages

It seems reasonable to link consultation staff wages to the number of consultations:
Consultation staff wages recovery rate = £24,960/1,248 = £20.00/consultation

Warehouse staff wages

Warehouse staff wages could be linked to either purchase orders fulfilled or to items sold:

(1) If each item needs to be handled, items sold might be preferred;

Warehouse staff wages recovery rate = £30,240/6,500 = £4.652/ item sold

(2) If warehouse staff wages are linked to purchase orders fulfilled:

Warehouse staff wages recovery rate = £30,240/4,400 = £6.873/purchase order

Administration staff wages

Administration staff process purchase orders and organise consultations, but no indication is given as to whether these tasks are equally weighted. If they are, the total number of tasks = 4,400 + 1,248 = 5,648 and:

Administration staff wages recovery rate = £30,624/5,648 = £5.422/task

General overheads

General overheads appear to be related to floor space, but there will be other overheads that are not space costs; these will need to be apportioned on a different basis, or even not apportioned at all. Using the information provided:

General overheads absorption rate = £175,000/40,000 = £4.375/square metre

Possible activity-based costing profit statement:

Department	*Kitchens*	*Bathrooms*	*Dining Rooms*	*Total*
	£	£	£	£
Sales	210,000	112,500	440,000	762,500
Cost of goods sold	(63,000)	(37,500)	(176,000)	(276,500)
Variable contribution	147,000	75,000	264,000	486,000
Sales staff wages	(14,727)	(13,255)	(36,818)	(64,800)
Consultation staff wages	(15,960)	(4,000)	(5,000)	(24,960)
Warehouse staff wages	(4,652)	(6,978)	(18,610)	(30,240)
Admin staff wages	(9,749)	(5,964)	(14,911)	(30,624)
General overheads	(70,000)	(43,750)	(61,250)	(175,000)
Profit	31,912	1,053	127,411	160,376

Notes:

1 Sales staff wages are apportioned using purchase orders.

2 Warehouse staff wages are apportioned using items sold.

Other choices are possible.

(c) The absorption costing system currently used by the company indicates that the bathrooms department makes a loss.

From an activity-based costing perspective, however, the bathrooms department might make a small profit. The department makes a contribution towards other costs and overheads of £75,000 and a profit before general overheads of £44,803. Therefore financial grounds for closure do not appear to be compelling, although there may be a need to investigate the department with a view to improving profitability.

A more detailed profitability analysis of bathroom sales might lead to a greater understanding of which products were relatively profitable, which products were slow-moving and which products might be removed from sale without adversely affecting sales of other lines. Less drastic alternatives than closure might be suggested by such an analysis.

If the department were closed, it could be argued that general overheads would still need to be met and so overall profit would fall by about £45,000 in each three-month period. Overall profit could fall by more than this if some of the other costs allocated to the bathroom department remained after the closure. For example, the number of staff laid off would not correspond exactly to allocated wage costs.

However, it is unlikely the space vacated by the bathrooms department would remain unused. The remaining departments might be expanded to fill it, or it might be used for a new venture (selling carpets, for example). The key question is whether a better use exists for the space. If an alternative use is found, staff redundancies might be reduced or eliminated entirely.

A further problem is that closure of the bathrooms department could affect sales of the other departments. The store might be seen as no longer offering an adequate range of products and potential customers might prefer other stores with a greater range of home furnishings. The potential for satisfied customers to return with further business would also be reduced if the store offered a more limited range of products.

It is also unlikely that the closure decision would be made at the level of an individual store, since it carries consequences for the company as a whole. The image of the company might suffer if it were seen to be changing its product range, or if it were seen as being unable to compete with other stores selling bathrooms.

(d) Activity-based costing could help Admer understand more clearly the factors that 'drive' its costs. The nature of Admer's business means that only a small number of cost drivers is likely to exist, but even given the limited information provided, the revised profit statement is likely to be more useful than treating all overhead costs as being related to floor area.

Activity-based costing can help Admer to control costs by highlighting the activities that generate them. For example, consultation staff wages are high compared to sales staff wages in the kitchen department in this store. Perhaps sales staff could be trained to provide in-store consultations and the number of home visits reduced; this could lower administration costs and reduce the cost of consultations.

It is clear that general overheads are the most significant cost other than cost of sales and existing information does not suggest ways of reducing these. However, a more detailed analysis of overheads might reveal activity-based costs that are currently aggregated. Once disaggregated, they become more amenable to understanding and control.

It is argued that activity-based costing leads to more accurate product costs, and in order to achieve this Admer needs a more detailed analysis of sales revenue and cost, based on the nature of the products sold. For example, the company might be able to classify kitchens as basic, intermediate and deluxe, and collect sales and cost data accordingly.

A key advantage claimed for activity-based costing is that it can provide better information to aid decision-making. In this case, it could provide more appropriate information to aid managers in reaching a decision on whether to close the bathrooms department. With better or more detailed information on product cost, managers are likely to make better decisions in key areas such as product pricing and cost control.

Even after introducing activity-based costing, however, Admer will still face the problem that some arbitrary apportionment of costs may still be required when pooling costs. The general overheads of light, heat and rates, for example, are likely to need to be treated in this way, along with the wages of administration staff. A related problem is that not all costs are generated by activities that can be measured in quantitative terms.

The management accountant of Admer should also be aware that the costs of introducing and maintaining an activity-based costing system may exceed the benefits that such a costing system may provide. Appropriate cost drivers will need to be determined and the required information may not be available. The existing management accounting information system may therefore need to be modified to generate the required information, and perhaps new accounting software purchased or developed.

ACCA marking scheme		
		Marks
(a)	Costs and cost drivers	2
	Limitations of information provided	2
		4
(b)	Analysis and discussion	4
	Activity-based profit statement	5
		8
(c)	Evaluation and discussion of closure proposal	6
(d)	Up to 2 marks for each detailed advantage	6
	Up to 2 marks for each detailed disadvantage	4
Total		25

32 BML

(a) **Existing costing system:**

Calculation of overhead recovery rate:

Labour cost = (£4 × 7,500) + (£8 × 12,500) + (£6.40 × 4,000)

= £155,600

$$\text{Overhead rate} = \frac{\text{Overhead cost}}{\text{Labour cost}} \times 100\%$$

$$= \frac{£718,688}{£155,600} \times 100\%$$

= 462% of labour cost.

	P1	*P2*	*P3*
	£	£	£
Direct materials	18.00	25.00	16.00
Direct labour cost	4.00	8.00	6.40
Overhead cost (462% of labour)	18.48	36.96	29.57
Unit cost	40.48	69.96	51.97

(b) **Activity-based costing**

ABC workings:

Receiving and handling materials cost

Total cost = £150,000

Cost driver = Number of materials movements

Number of materials movements = 4 + 25 + 50 = 79 movements

Cost per material movement = £150,000/79 = £1,898.73.

Cost per unit of P1 = (£1,898.73 × 4)/7,500 = £1.01 per product unit

Cost per unit of P2 = (£1,898.73 × 25)/12,500 = £3.80 per product unit

Cost per unit of P3 = (£1,898.73 × 50)/4,000 = £23.73 per product unit.

Maintenance and depreciation cost

Total cost = £390,000

Cost driver = Number of machine hours

Number of machine hours = (0.5 × 7,500) + (0.5 × 12,500) + (0.2 × 4.000) = 10,800

Cost per machine hour = £390,000/10,800 = £36.11 per machine hour

Cost per unit of P1 = £36.11 × 0.5 = £18.06 per product unit

Cost per unit of P2 = £36.11 × 0.5 = £18.06 per product unit

Cost per unit of P3 = £36.11 × 0.2 = £7.22 per product unit.

Set-up labour cost

Total cost = £18,688

Cost driver = Number of set-ups

Number of set-ups 1 + 5 + 10 = 16

Cost per set-up = 18,688/16= £1,168 per set-up

Cost per unit of P1 = (£1,168 × 1)/7,500 = £0.16 per product unit

Cost per unit of P2 = (£1,168 × 5)/12,500 = £0.47 per product unit

Cost per unit of P3 = £(1,168 × 10)/4,000 = £2.92 per product unit.

Engineering cost

Total cost = £100,000

Cost driver: Based on proportion of engineering work.

Cost per unit of P1 = (£100,000 × 30%)/7,500 = £4.00 per product unit

Cost per unit of P2 = (£100,000 × 20%)/12,500 = £1.60 per product unit

Cost per unit of P3 = (£100,000 × 50%)/4,000 = £12.50 per product unit.

Packing cost

Total cost = £60,000

Cost driver = Number of orders packed

Number of orders packed = 1 + 7 + 22 = 30

Cost per order = £60,000/30 = £2,000

Cost per unit of P1 = (£2,000 × 1)/7,500 = £0.27 per product unit

Cost per unit of P2 = (£2,000 × 7)/12,500 = £1.12 per product unit

Cost per unit of P3 = £(2,000 × 22)/4,000 = £11.00 per product unit

Unit costs	*P1*	*P2*	*P3*
	£	£	£
Direct materials	18.00	25.00	16.00
Direct labour	4.00	8.00	6.40
Overhead costs:			
Receiving/materials handling	1.01	3.80	23.73
Maintenance and depreciation	18.06	18.06	7.22
Set-up labour	0.16	0.47	2.92
Engineering	4.00	1.60	12.50
Packing	0.27	1.12	11.00
Sub total overhead costs	23.50	25.05	57.37
Total unit cost	45.50	58.05	79.77

Examiner's note

An alternative approach to the ABC calculations would be to allocate the total overhead costs to each product line using the cost drivers identified above, finally dividing by the number of units to arrive at the unit cost, as follows:

	Total	*P1*	*P2*	*P3*
	£	£	£	£
Receiving and handling	150,000	7,595	47,468	94,937
Maintenance/depreciation	390,000	135,417	225,694	28,889
Set-up labour	18,688	1,168	5,840	11,680
Engineering	100,000	30,000	20,000	50,000
Packing	60,000	2,000	14,000	44,000
Sub-total overhead costs	718,688	176,180	313,002	229,506
Number of units		7,500	12,500	4,000
Unit overhead cost (£)		£23.49	£25.04	£57.38

Any difference between the figures for unit overhead costs derived by the two methods is due to rounding differences.

(c) P1 is shown to have lower unit costs under the original ('traditional') absorption costing system than on the ABC basis. This is caused by its relatively higher machine hour usage and smaller proportion of labour cost, compared to the other products, and the effect this has on the overhead cost allocation. Using ABC, P1 has a very small profit margin. This must therefore raise questions about its viability at its current selling price of £47.

It is a relatively simple product to make. For example, it seems to consist of just one production run and one packing order for the whole output, which means it does not use much of these supporting resources. However it does use a considerable proportion of machine hours, which is what gives rise to much of its allocated overhead cost.

In comparison to P1, Product P3 seems to be a complex product to administer, made in small batches with small orders. In the original system, P3 was being under-costed, being subsidised by P2. It appears to offer a good margin based on its original cost, but the ABC analysis shows that at a selling price of £68, it does not manage to cover all of the direct and overhead costs assigned to it.

There is therefore little surprise that this new product line is attracting additional business, because it is priced below the cost of making it if all of the activities the company undertakes are needed. The company cannot afford to continue business at this price and needs to find some way of managing up the price of this product to make it viable in the future. An alternative may be to re-examine the way it is manufactured, and the ABC system may offer some help in this by assisting with an analysis of what is involved in its manufacture. Presently, it is the high proportion of overhead costs for material movement, engineering and packing which make it expensive. If it is seen to have a future, BML may need to re-engineer their manufacturing methods in relation to this product which makes quite modest use of machining resources.

P2 has the highest volume of the three products, though we are told it is suffering a loss of market share. It is the most labour intensive product and this resulted in serious over-costing under the original system, because overhead was apportioned on a labour cost basis. To put it another way, the ABC cost is lower because the product makes less use of engineering machine hours etc, than the other products. It would seem competitors discovered that they could manufacture this and sell it for a lower price and still make a profit. BML should realise that its major cost is in the use of machinery, and for the volume produced it makes little use of other support costs. It is therefore quite economical to make, though the original system does not reveal this. BML still make a good volume of this product and although we do not know much about the market for it a lower price might stimulate demand, and offer higher sales volumes recovering some of the market share.

Examiner's note

The above comments are based on the information as presented in the question. We know nothing about any other overhead costs relating, for example, to administration and selling. No information about the market for the three products is supplied, e.g. market shares or competitors' prices. Such information as this would place the company in a better position to judge the adequacy of the results of its costing system.

33 ABC PLC

Key answer tips

For Part (a), (i) the computations will only account for 1-2 marks, so don't waste time by repeating detail from the question - start with the operating profit figures given, and deduct the allocated overhead costs as a total figure for each store. Explanation of the term 'cost driver' should be reasonably straightforward from a rudimentary knowledge of ABC; for what is required for 'volume' and 'complexity' in both explanation and comment, you must focus on the area of cost allocation and think how these issues can affect it.

Part (a), (ii) the apportionment of individual overhead costs between cost centres on different bases is a procedure that should be familiar to you. The relevant bases are fairly obvious from the cost driver information given in the question, with the exception of warehouse costs (depreciation and part of HO costs). Don't waste time worrying about the 'right' basis to use, make a rational decision, jot it down, and carry on. Again, the computations account for a minority of the allocated marks - ensure you allow enough time to consider what the figures show. Try not to be too categorical – 'this method now produces the correct allocation of costs and shows that store C is unprofitable and must be closed' - as any method of allocating true central shared costs between units will have some arbitrary element and needs to be used with care in decision making. Remember fixed costs are fixed whatever fancy methods are used to split them.

In the computations, time could be saved by working in £000s and using a total column.

In part (b), do not waste any of the few marks allocated to this part by explaining the mechanics of the techniques themselves; think how they can be applied in this particular context. Discuss both regression and correlation

(a) (i) **Report**

To: Group management

From: Accountant

Date: xx/xx/xx

Subject: Reporting store's profits

This report presents the budgeted profits for 20X8 of stores A, B and C based on the method of sharing central costs that was originally employed by the group - sales value. As a result of discussions with management at various levels, alternative 'drivers' of these costs have been revealed. This is explained and then applied to the results budgeted for 20X8, finally drawing some conclusions.

	A	*B*	*C*
	£	£	£
Operating profit	840,000	370,000	290,000
Central costs (apportion 5:4:3)	416,667	333,333	250,000
Net profit	423,333	36,667	40,000

Cost drivers are events or activities which result in costs being incurred. They are commonly used to allocate costs to cost objectives, or reported and 'managed' in order to 'manage' the costs they influence. It is argued that in many traditional costing systems, the cost drivers or allocation bases which were used have 'volume' implications, for example the number of units produced or sold, the machine hours worked or, in our case, sales value. It is clear that there are many other factors which give rise to costs being incurred or resources consumed. It is not only the volume of business but the way that business is done which causes costs. Dealing with a small volume of business in a **complex product** or for a **difficult customer** is sometimes more costly than a large volume in a familiar situation. It is important that cost reports reveal this issue of complexity, so that management can take steps to deal with any business issues which arise. In the original allocation it is implied that store A, which makes the most sales, consumes the greatest proportion of the central resources. This need not be the case, because it depends on what and how it sells and how it is served by the central resource.

Our company has used sales value to allocate all central costs. It is unlikely that this accurately reflects the way central resources have been consumed by the three stores. The basis seems to be one which is conveniently available and one which is related more to what each store can 'bear' of the central costs, rather than any cost causality. It has a tendency to penalise a store if its sales are high, and this can be seen in the case of store A. It is therefore a discouragement to a better-performing store. Additionally, it may influence the accuracy of the budgets, in that stores might deliberately under-state their budgets in order to attract a lower overhead charge.

(ii) A revised profit for each store is shown below which uses the information obtained from recent discussions with staff at all locations.

	Total	*Warehouse operations*	*Store A*	*Store B*	*Store C*
Head office	£	£	£	£	£
Salaries	200,000	20,000	60,000	60,000	60,000
Advertising (5:4:3)	80,000	-	33,333	26,667	20,000
Establishment (10:30:30:30)	120,000	12,000	36,000	36,000	36,000
		32,000			
Warehouse					
Depreciation (40:30:30) *(note 1)*	100,000		40,000	30,000	30,000
Storage (40:30:30) *(note 1)*	80,000		32,000	24,000	24,000
Operating and despatch	120,000 + 32,000	*(note 2)*	55,000	45,000	52,000
Delivery *(note 3)*	300,000		100,000	71,429	128,571
Store costs			356,333	293,096	350,571
Operating profit			840,000	370,000	290,000
Net profit/(loss)			483,667	76,904	(60,571)

Notes:

1 Apportion on the basis of storage space occupied.

2 Apportion on the basis of the number of despatches (550:450:520).

3 Apportion on the basis of delivery distances (70:50:90).

The revised calculations show that the costs identified with store C exceed the current level of operating profit, and an overall loss is disclosed. Stores A and B show improved results based on these allocations. The bases selected are believed to bear a closer relationship to how the resources are consumed in providing service to the three stores. The allocation reflects the benefit they receive rather than their 'ability to bear' the cost. There are, however, still some costs which will always prove difficult to identify, and these inevitably result in an arbitrary allocation (if management requires them to be allocated). Advertising costs are one such example. It is useful for management to be aware of this analysis, though they should use it with care, since it does not directly make decisions for them. It does not give any information about the efficiency with which store C is managed, nor does it indicate that the company would make more profit by closing store C.

It would be useful to see a trend of this information over a period of years. It would also be important to know the extent of competition in the area and the market being served.

In the current situation, it may be uneconomic to service store C at its present volume. Having made this point, store C has the smallest gross margin percentage (37%), compared with store A (44%). It has a different sales mix or different pricing structure. From the further statistics, it is also a difficult store to support. It requires proportionately more despatches and greater delivery distances to be travelled. This information suggests there is scope to rationalise delivery to reduce costs, consider direct delivery from some suppliers, examine vehicle routing schedules, and so on.

Further investigation and discussion is required before taking any firm decisions but the information presented above has highlighted issues which would not have been disclosed by the allocation method previously adopted.

(b) **Regression analysis** and the use of r^2 would demonstrate the association between some of the central costs and allocation bases proposed. In the case of delivery miles, it would be necessary to accumulate cost of delivery for a number of periods, say quarterly for three years, and set these against the miles travelled. The value would require adjusting for accruals and inflation over the three year periods. A **regression equation** would identify the variable and fixed elements of the cost. The **coefficient of determination** (r^2) would express the degree of association between the variable cost and the delivery miles. A close association between these would produce a value for r^2 of close to 1.

34 PARSER LTD

(a) Opportunity costs represent the value of the loss or sacrifice when choosing between scarce alternatives. It is the benefit forgone by choosing one course of action instead of the next most profitable option. Lack of scarcity implies zero opportunity cost.

(b) Revised costs for special order = **relevant costs**:

	Notes	£
Sub-contractor costs	1	31,300
Supervisor costs	2	1,000
General overheads	3	1,000
Machine maintenance	4	500
Machine overheads	5	22,000
Materials	6	31,500
Interest costs	7	900
Total relevant costs		88,200

Notes

1 The choice lies between the two alternative sub-contractors that have to be employed because of the shortage of existing labour. The relevant cost is the least-cost alternative, which is to employ the subcontractor who is skilled in the special process.

2 Only the difference between the bonus and the incentive payment represents an additional cost that arises due to the special order. Fixed salary costs do not change. The relevant cost is the extra bonus payable (£3,500) minus the normal incentive payments that will be saved (£2,500).

3 Only incremental costs are relevant. Apportioned fixed overhead costs are not an incremental cost and so are not relevant.

4 Depreciation is both a period fixed cost, not related to the special order, and also a non-cash item of expenditure. It is therefore not relevant. Additional

maintenance costs, however, are relevant because they represent extra cash spending.

5 The relevant costs are the extra variable overheads (£3 × 6,000 hours) that will be incurred, plus the displacement costs (loss of contribution) of £2 × 2,000 hours making a total of £22,000.

6 Since the materials are no longer used, the replacement cost is irrelevant (because if the existing stock is used, it will not be replaced). The historical cost of £34,000 is a sunk cost (past cost) and so is also irrelevant. The relevant cost is the lost sale value if the stock used in the special order. This is 7,500 kg × £4.20 per kg = £31,500.

7 Full opportunity costing will also allow for imputed interest costs on the incremental loan. The correct interest rate is the overdraft rate since this represents the incremental cost (i.e. the actual cash payment) the company will pay. Simple interest charged for three months is therefore: 3/12 × £20,000 × 18% = £900.

(c) **Introduction**

SMEs contribute in a significant way to many economies in the world. Besides generating income, in often large proportions in relation to GNP across the world, they are frequently major employers and the sector which is most identified with new ideas and entrepreneurial spirit. It is these latter factors that help sustain and support growth rates in many economies.

Despite this background of potential, SMEs often experience difficulties in accessing appropriate sources of finance. There are three main issues involved: uncertainty concerning the business, lack of assets available to offer as collateral or security, and the sources of finance for business start-ups or very new businesses.

Uncertainty concerning the business

It has been recognised in various studies that the problem of adequately financing SMEs is a problem of uncertainty. A defining characteristic of SMEs is the uncertainty surrounding their activities. However much owners or managers inform their banks of what they are doing, there is always an element of uncertainly remaining that is not a feature of larger businesses. Larger businesses have grown from smaller businesses and have a track record – especially in terms of a long-term relationship with their bankers. Bankers can observe over a period of time that the business is well-run, and that managers can manage its affairs and can therefore be trusted with handling bank loans in a proper way. New businesses, typically SMEs, obviously don't have this track record. The problem is even broader. Large businesses conduct most of their activities in public (e.g. subject to more external scrutiny) than do SMEs. Thus, if information is public, there is less uncertainty. For example, a larger business might be quoted on a stock exchange and therefore be subject to press scrutiny, the stock exchange rules regarding the certain of its activities, and would have to publish audited accounts. Many SMEs do not have to have audits, certainly don't publish their accounts to a wide audience and the press are not really interested in them.

Lack of assets available to offer as collateral security

If SMEs wish to access bank finance, for example, then banks will wish to address the information problem referred to above. First, banks will screen loan applications to assess the underlying product or service, the management team, the market addressed and, importantly, any collateral or security that can be offered. It is this last point which is of interest here. Besides investigating business plans, banks will look to see what security is available for any loan provided. This phase is likely to involve an audit of the firm's assets and detailed explanation of any personal security offered by the directors and owner managers. Collateral is important because it can reduce the level of credit risk a bank is exposed to in granting a loan to a new business. In assessing a business plan and security, a bank would make assessment of the risk of the business and any loan interest rate will reflect that risk. A key feature for accessing bank finance is therefore in the assessment of risk from the information gathered and the security offered.

Potential sources of finance for very new businesses

Initial owner finance is nearly always the first source of finance for a business, whether from the owner or from family connections. At this stage, many of the assets may be intangible and thus external financing is an unrealistic prospect at this stage or at least has been in the past. This is often referred to as the equity gap.

With no organised market for 'Business Angel' finance, there are only limited means by which SMEs can find equity investors. Trade credit finance is important at this stage too, although it is nearly always very expensive if viewed in terms of lost early payment discounts. Also, it is inevitably very short-term and very limited in duration (except that always taking 60 days to pay a creditor will obviously roll-over and become medium term financing. 'Business Angel' financing might be important. This refers to 'high net worth' individuals or groups of individuals who invest directly in small businesses. It is possible, when a new business or its owner can offer adequate security, that a bank loan may be arranged. Another form of security that may underpin a bank loan is in the form of a guarantee from a reliable individual or other business with a banking track record.

ACCA marking scheme

		Marks	
(a)	Definition of opportunity cost, up to		2
(b)	Subcontractor costs	2	
	Supervisor costs	1	
	General overheads	1	
	Machine depreciation	1	
	Machine variable overheads	2	
	Materials	2	
	Interest costs	2	
			11
(c)	Up to 2 marks each for detailed points relating to uncertainty	5	
	Up to 2 marks each for detailed points relating to collateral	5	
	Up to 2 marks each for detailed points relating sources of finance	5	
	Presentation and quality of argument	2	
	Maximum available	17	
	Maximum awarded		12
Total			25

35 ALBION PLC

(a) The optimum production schedule is found using **limiting factor analysis**.

		AR2		*GL3*		*HT4*
		£		£		£
Material R2 (£2.50/kg)	*2kg*	5.00	*3kg*	7.50	*3kg*	7.50
Material R3 (£2/kg)	*2kg*	4.00	*2.2kg*	4.40	*1.6kg*	3.20
Labour (£4/hour)	*0.6hrs*	2.40	*1.2hrs*	4.80	*1.5hrs*	6.00
Variable o/hd (£/unit)		1.10		1.30		1.10
Variable cost/unit		12.50		18.00		17.80
Selling price (£/unit)		21.00		28.50		27.30
Contribution (£/unit)		8.50		10.50		9.50

	AR2	*GL3*	*HT4*
	£	£	£
Material R2 (kg/unit)	2	3	3
Contribution/kg of R2 (£)	4.25	3.50	3.17
Ranking	1st	2nd	3rd

Product	*Demand*	*R2 used*	*Production*		*Contribution*
	units	kg	units		£
AR2	950	1,900	950	(× £8.50)	8,075
GL3	1,000	3,000	1,000	(× £10.50)	10,500
		4,900			
HT4	900	600	200	(× £9.50)	1,900
		5,500			20,475

The optimum production schedule is 950 units of Product AR2, 1,000 units of GL3 and 200 units of HT4, giving a total contribution of £20,475. The fixed production overheads are ignored in this analysis because they are assumed not to vary with changes in the level of production.

(b) Further supplies of Material R2 will be used to produce additional units of Product HT4. The contribution per kg of Material R2 of Product HT4 is £3.17. The normal price of R2 is £2.50/kg, and so if Albion pays £3.17 + £2.50 = £5.67 per kg for Material R2, the additional units of Product HT4 produced will make a zero contribution towards fixed costs. Therefore **£5.67 is the maximum price** that the company should be prepared to pay.

(c) The variable cost of Product XY5:

	£/unit
Material R3: 3kg x £2	6.00
Labour: 1.7 hours x £4	6.80
Variable overhead	1.40
	14.20

The substitute offered by Folam gives a saving of £4 per unit. However, Albion plc would also pay an annual fee of £50,000 for the right to use the substitute. The company would need to manufacture more than 50,000/4 = 12,500 units per year of Product XY5, or 1,042 units per month, in order for the offered substitute to be financially acceptable. If it needed less than 12,500 units of Product XY5 per year, it would be cheaper to manufacture the product in-house.

This evaluation is from a short-term perspective: in the longer term, buying in may lead to fixed cost savings and lower investment, increasing the benefits of buying in and lowering the break-even point.

Albion plc would also need to assure itself that the **quality of the substitute** was acceptable and that this quality could be maintained: the lower price offered by Folam might be associated with poorer quality than that deemed necessary by Albion plc. Orders for the substitute product would also **need to be delivered promptly** in order to avoid production hold-ups. Albion plc could also become **dependent on Folam Limited for supplies** of the substitute product and might be vulnerable to future price increases by the supplier. Such price increases might reduce or even eliminate the cost saving of buying in.

(d) Marginal costing (variable costing) treats fixed costs as a period cost, on the assumption that fixed costs do not change in the short term. The difference between selling price and variable costs is the variable contribution made by units sold towards meeting fixed costs and generating profit.

Marginal costing has traditionally been used for short-term decisions such as whether to cease production of a product, whether to make a product or buy it from a supplier, and how to allocate scarce resources in order to maximise contribution.

A major limitation with using marginal costing as the basis for making short-term decisions is the assumption that fixed costs are irrelevant to short-term decisions. In the longer term, fixed costs will change: for example, rent is usually regarded as a fixed cost and in the longer term rent might be expected to increase due to inflation. However, a change in fixed costs may be the result of a short-term decision: for example, if a product is discontinued and as a result the work of the marketing department decreases, in the longer term marketing costs would be expected to decrease.

This points to the danger of relying on a simplistic analysis of costs into fixed costs and variable costs, and of assuming that only variable costs are relevant for decision-making purposes. It is possible for a fixed cost to be a relevant cost. It is also possible for a variable cost to be irrelevant, for example in the case where a variable cost is common to two decision alternatives. If fuel costs are incurred whether a machine is leased or bought, for example, these costs are not relevant to the decision on whether to lease or buy.

Reliance on marginal costing as a basis for making short-term decisions may therefore lead to sub-optimal decisions overall for a company, as the analysis may fail to consider all relevant costs. A **relevant cost** is an incremental or differential cost at the whole company level. If a cost changes or is incurred, now or in the future, as a result of a decision, it is a relevant cost and should be considered when making a decision. When making short-term decisions, therefore, it is essential to adopt a whole company perspective in determining relevant costs.

When making short-term decisions, a **detailed analysis of cost behaviour** is therefore needed in order to determine not only variable costs and fixed costs, but all other relevant costs as well.

ACCA marking scheme		
		Marks
(a)	Calculation of contribution per unit	2
	Calculation of contribution per kg of R2	2
	Optimum production schedule	4
		8
(b)	Calculation of maximum price	1
	Discussion	2
		3
(c)	Calculation of cost saving	1
	Calculation of breakeven point	1
	Discussion of relevant issues	5
		7
(d)	Up to 2 marks for each detailed point made	7
Total		25

36 THROUGHPUT

(a) Identification of the bottleneck resource.

Machine X: Maximum output per week

= 180 frame panels/4 panels per TRL

= 45 TRLs/week

On average 17.5 hours per month or 4.375 hours per week can be lost, reducing the maximum capacity by 10.9375% $\left(\frac{4.375}{40}\times100\%\right)$. This reduces Machine X's capacity to 40 TRLs, on average, per week (45 × (1 - 0.109375)).

Machine Y: Maximum output = 52 TRLs/week

Machine Z: Maximum output = 30 TRLs/week

***Machine Z* is therefore the key, or bottleneck resource.**

Calculation of return per factory hour

Time on key resource (machine Z) $= \frac{40 \text{ hours}}{30 \text{ TRLs}} = 1.3333$ hours/TRL

Sale price – material cost = £2,000 - £600

= £1,400

∴ Return per factory hour $= \frac{£1,400}{1.3333} =$ £1050/hour

Calculation of cost per factory hour

Fixed costs are £450,000/48 = £9,375/week.

Cost per factory hour $= \frac{£5,500 + £8,000 + £9,375}{40} =$ £571.875/hour

Throughput accounting ratio $= \frac{£1,050}{£571.875}$

= **1.836**

(b) Throughput accounting is an approach advocated as a means of applying the 'Theory of Constraints' first developed by Goldratt and Cox in the early 1980s. The basic concept of throughput accounting is the notion of throughput itself. This can be defined as:

'The rate of production of a defined process over a stated period of time'

CIMA Official Terminology

Throughput is calculated as sales revenue minus the cost of materials, which is regarded as the only variable cost in the short term.

Underpinning this basic concept are three further concepts, which can be stated as follows:

(1) In the short-term all manufacturing costs, with the exception of material costs, are largely pre-determined and can, therefore, be regarded as fixed. 'Contribution' is therefore sales minus material costs.

(2) Holding and producing inventory is not a value-added activity. Profitability is seen as being inversely proportional to the time taken for production to respond to demand, i.e. throughput time. In other words, the longer it takes to produce output, the lower the profitability. Since holding inventory lengthens throughput time, profitability can be seen as being inversely proportional to the level of inventory in the system. This supports the advocacy of a 'Just-in-Time' system of inventory management.

(3) Overall product profitability is determined by two factors:

(i) The rate at which it contributes money – this is a measure of the product's *relative* profitability, and

(ii) The rate at which the factory spends money.

Comparing the rate at which a product contributes money to the rate at which the factory spends it determines absolute profitability.

The objective is to maximise the 'throughput' in any given time period and this automatically focuses attention on any bottleneck resource(s). If profit is to be maximised (in the short-term) then the optimal utilisation of any bottleneck resources needs to be determined and, if possible, the bottleneck resource removed.

(c) The throughput accounting ratio, as defined, measures the rate at which the business generates money compared with the rate at which the business spends money. This ratio needs to exceed one if the business is to maintain itself as a going concern. The definition of throughput, explained in part (a), is similar to the existing concept of 'value added'.

In effect, MN Ltd needs to add value to the business at a greater rate than it is expending conversion costs to add that value. The ratio implies that only products with a throughput accounting ratio greater than one should be produced and that these products can be ranked in terms of profitability by their throughput accounting ratio. To maximise this throughput in the short-term, the product(s) with the highest throughput accounting ratio should be produced.

However, this short-term approach may conflict with longer-term measures of profitability. For instance, MN Ltd is proposing to replace machine Z with machine G and possibly overhaul machine X. This proposal may cause the throughput accounting ratio for the TRLs to decline in the short-term.

(d) Whilst throughput accounting and marginal costing have many similarities, the main difference arises from the definition of contribution or, more specifically, what can be regarded as a variable cost. The traditional marginal costing approach assumes that direct labour is a variable cost. Whilst this may have been true 30 or 40 years ago when labour was typically paid a piece rate, this is no longer the case – in the short-term, throughput accounting treats labour as a fixed cost. Marginal costing also tends to emphasise cost behaviour, especially overheads, and usually attempts to separate these into fixed and variable components. As with labour costs, throughput accounting treats all production overhead costs as fixed in the short-term and aggregates these with labour into what is referred to as 'total factory cost'. Consequently, in throughput accounting the only cost that is treated as variable in the short-term is the direct material cost.

Furthermore, marginal costing does not provide a direct disincentive to produce for, or carry stock. Throughput accounting discourages this by using the *total* cost of direct materials *purchased* in the period in the calculation of throughput, rather than the cost of material actually used, as is the case with marginal costing.

(e) If machine G is purchased and machine X is overhauled, then the capacity of each machine will be as follows:

Machine X = 45 TRLs per week

Machine G = 45 TRLs per week

Machine Y = 52 TRLs per week

This means that both machine X and machine G will become potential bottleneck resources. However, demand is not forecast to exceed 45 TRLs per month until July so the emphasis, initially, will be on ensuring that the new machine is installed and machine X is overhauled by the end of June at the latest, and preferably by the end of May. Once these machines are fully operational they will both need to be monitored to ensure they are fully utilised, especially in periods where demand exceeds maximum available capacity. Calculation of the return per factory hour for each machine and the associated throughput accounting ratio will assist this process, as will monitoring the level of reworks and rejects that use the bottleneck resources.

37 SPRING PLC

(a) Activity-based costing is based on the insight that activities create costs, while products consume activities. It is claimed that activity-based costing attaches overheads to product cost in a more meaningful way than traditional absorption costing.

A key feature of activity-based costing is that overhead costs are collected in cost pools, which correspond to a particular activity or group of activities that generate costs. A classic example of a cost pool is set-up costs for a production line. The cost of each set-up is included in the cost pool reflecting the recognition that it is set-ups that incur costs, rather than the volume of production on the production line. Set-up costs are an example of an indirect cost, and both traditional absorption costing and activity-based costing are concerned with the allocation of indirect costs onto product cost. Traditional absorption costing assigns indirect costs or overheads to production departments and service departments and then reallocates service department overheads to production centres. Activity-based costing is likely to use, or has the potential to use, considerably more cost pools than traditional absorption costing uses production centres. In activity-based costing, the link between cost pools and product cost is called a cost driver. A cost driver represents the extent to which a particular activity has been used by a particular product in its production. Continuing our example, an appropriate cost driver would be number of set-ups. A product which is produced in frequent short production runs would therefore incur a greater share of set-up costs than a product produced in a single production run. In traditional absorption costing, overheads are linked to product cost through overhead absorption rates such as cost per machine hour or cost per labour hour. Activity-based costing is likely to use considerably more cost drivers than traditional absorption costing uses overhead absorption rates.

The key steps in introducing an activity-based costing system are as follows:

1 Identify the main activities that generate costs through activity analysis

2 Assign costs to cost pools

3 Select appropriate cost drivers for assigning cost pool costs to products

4 Calculate activity-based charge rates to assign the cost of activities to products

The following benefits have been claimed for an activity-based costing:

1 Product costs are more accurate due to the more sophisticated analysis and assignment of overhead costs. Overhead costs are assigned on a cause-and-effect basis rather than on an ad hoc or subjective basis.

2 Cost behaviour is better understood due to the analysis of activities.

3 Cost control is facilitated through the identification and management of cost-generating activities. For example, in order to reduce set-up costs, production planning could be used to eliminate short production runs and hence reduce the number of set-ups.

4 Poor decisions due to inadequate cost information are less likely to occur.

As for disadvantages, identifying the main activities that generate costs in an organisation is expensive. Careful thought must also be given to the ability of existing management accounting information systems to provide the detailed activity and cost information required by an activity-based costing system: upgrading or replacement may be needed. A further expense is the cost of training staff to use the new costing system. Once introduced, an activity-based costing system can be significantly more expensive than a traditional absorption costing system. It is possible, therefore, that in some organisations the cost of introducing and maintaining an activity-based costing system may exceed the benefits gained.

Activity-based costing may be most appropriate in an organisation where indirect costs are a significant proportion of total cost, or where a wide product range is maintained with a variety of different activity consumption patterns. Spring plc should consider the significance of indirect costs to its product costs and undertake a cost-benefit analysis before making a decision to implement an activity-based costing system. Spring plc should also consider that further developments can flow from the introduction of an activity-based costing system, for example in budgeting (activity-based budgeting) and management philosophy (activity-based management).

(b) Managerial performance and organisational performance are inextricably linked, since managers are the key decision makers in an organisation and their decisions therefore determine organisational performance.

Managerial and organisational performance needs to be measured as part of the control process within an organisation. The three elements of the control process are recording or measuring actual performance or output, comparing performance with planned performance or some benchmark, and taking action to correct or modify continuing performance in order to achieve planned performance. Managerial and organisational performance can be measured in a wide variety of ways, depending on which aspect of performance, financial or non-financial, is the object of interest.

A wide variety of financial (or money) performance measures can be used to assess managerial and organisational performance. Financial performance is of interest to internal and external stakeholders who are concerned to monitor the progress and risk of their investment, the security of their employment, and so on. Examples of financial performance measures include:

Profit

Profit before interest and tax or profit after tax are usually expected to increase on an annual basis and the financial media often refer to profit when discussing managerial and organisational performance. Managers are expected to deliver increasing profits and organisations are expected to produce profit increases equal to or greater than their competitors.

Earnings per share

Earnings per share is a profit measure of interest to shareholders and the financial market, since it represents the maximum dividend per share that a company could pay. Managerial rewards could be linked in part to meeting performance targets based on earnings per share.

Cash flow

Because profit may be affected by arbitrary adjustments linked to accounting policies and because profit does not measure directly the ability to generate returns for investors, many shareholders and providers of debt finance prefer to concentrate on changes in cash flow as a means of assessing managerial and organisational performance.

Costs

A focus on managerial and organisational performance in terms of cost control or cost reduction may be especially appropriate for organisations in the public sector. Here, profitability is an inappropriate performance measure and a key objective is value for money, in terms of the drive for economy, efficiency and effectiveness.

Share price

Since one of the ways in which shareholders receive a return from their investment in a company is through capital growth, they will be interested in assessing managerial and organisational performance in terms of share price growth. If managers invest in projects with a positive net present value then, theoretically, the share price should increase to reflect the rise in corporate net present value. Conversely, organisations in which managers are believed to be poor performers will experience a share price decrease.

Measuring financial performance alone is not sufficient, since financial performance results from a range of organisational activities which must also therefore be monitored. Non-financial performance measures may be quantitative or qualitative. An example of a quantitative performance measure is the number of complaints received from customers. An example of a qualitative performance measure is feedback from a sales representative to the effect that most customers are very happy with the after-sales service provided by the organisation.

An attempt is usually made to replace qualitative performance measures with a substitute measure that can be quantified. For example, the number of customer complaints can be used as a substitute measure of product quality or customer satisfaction. Similarly, the number of warranty claims can be used as a substitute measure of product reliability.

Modern organisations compete in terms of product quality, flexibility and reliability, customer satisfaction, and product dimensions such as after-sales care and customer loyalty. These features are captured by non-financial indicators such as number of customer complaints, number of warranty claims, and quality ratings (such as the star ratings of hotels or restaurants, or the position of an organisation in a league table).

A more balanced assessment of organisational and managerial performance will consider both financial and non-financial performance. For example, Kaplan and Norton's Balanced Scorecard considers the customer perspective, the innovation perspective, the internal process perspective and the financial perspective, and requires the identification of quantitative and non-quantitative goals and performance measures.

ACCA marking scheme		
		Marks
(a)	Key features of activity-based costing	5-6
	Advantages of activity-based costing	5-6
	Disadvantages of activity-based costing	4-5
		14
(b)	Need for measurement of performance	3-4
	Examples of financial performance measures	4-5
	Examples of non-financial performance measures	4-5
		11
Total		25

38 LINEACRE CO

Key answer tips

Part (a) is a routine calculation of ABC recovery rates.

In applying these rates in part (b) it is simplest to calculate the total costs for the product before converting to a cost per unit. Care must be taken to distinguish between customer orders and component orders.

Part (c) asks for a discussion of ABC in a modern manufacturing environment and should be familiar ground for most students.

(a) Activity-based recovery rates are found by dividing the expected cost in each cost pool by the number of cost driver transactions expected during the coming year.

Cost Pool	*Cost*	*Number of Drivers*	*ABC Recovery Rate*
Production set-ups	£105,000	300 set-ups	£350.00 per set-up
Product testing	£300,000	1,500 tests	£200.00 per test
Component supply/storage	£25,000	500 component orders	£50.00 per order
Customer orders/delivery	£112,500	1,000 customer orders	£112.50 per order

(b) Production of product ZT3 = (100 × 60) + (60 × 50) = 9,000 units per year

Number of production runs = number of set-ups = 9,000/900 = 10 set-ups

Number of product tests = 10 × 4 = 40 tests

Number of component orders = number of production runs = 10 orders

Number of customer orders = 100 + 60 = 160 orders

General overheads absorption rate = 900,000/300,000 = £3.00 per direct labour hour

Annual direct labour hours for Product ZT3 = 9,000 × 10/60 = 1,500 hours

Activity	*ABC recovery rate*	*Number of Drivers*	*Annual cost* (£)
Setting up	£350.00 per set-up	10 set-ups	3,500
Product testing	£200.00 per test	40 tests	8,000
Component supply	£50.00 per order	10 orders	500
Customer supply	£112.50 per order	160 orders	18,000
			30,000
General overheads = 1,500 × £3.00 per hour =			4,500
Total annual overhead cost			34,500

Total unit cost	£
Components	1.00
Direct labour = 7.80 × 10/60 =	1.30
Overheads = 34,500/9,000 =	3.83
	6.13
Profit mark up	2.45
Selling price	8.58

(c) Traditional absorption costing allocates a proportion of fixed overheads (indirect costs) to product cost through an overhead absorption rate, usually based on labour hours, machine hours, or some other volume-related measure of activity. These overhead absorption rates may be factory-wide absorption rates (blanket rates) or, for increased accuracy in determining product cost, departmental absorption rates. In the traditional manufacturing environment, indirect costs constituted a relatively small proportion of total product cost compared to direct costs such as direct material cost, direct labour cost and direct expenses (collectively referred to as prime cost).

The modern manufacturing environment

In the modern manufacturing environment, indirect costs constitute a relatively high proportion of total product cost. There are several reasons for this.

Modern manufacturing is characterised by shorter and more frequent production runs rather than continuous or high volume production runs. This increases the frequency of production line set-ups and therefore the total cost arising from set-up activity.

Widespread use of computer control and automation has decreased the importance and use of direct labour. Direct labour cost as a proportion of total cost has therefore declined. This decline has been accelerated by the use of salaried employees rather than staff whose wages depend on production output, transferring labour costs from a direct cost to an indirect cost.

Increased use of just-in-time production methods and customer-led manufacture has led to quality control costs and production planning costs forming a higher proportion of total cost. These costs relate to particular production runs rather than to manufacture as a whole.

Activities and costs

Traditional absorption costing, by employing volume-related overhead absorption rates, failed to take account of the relationship between costs, activities and products. The insight at the heart of activity-based costing is that it is activities that incur costs and products that consume activities. Analysis of the way in which products consume activities allows the overhead costs incurred by those activities to be related to product cost using cost drivers derived from those activities rather than using production volume-related overhead absorption rates.

For example, set-up costs under traditional absorption costing could have been allocated to product cost using an overhead absorption rate based on machine hours. This would transfer a disproportionate amount of set-up costs to high volume products, which in fact gave rise to fewer set-ups because of their longer production runs. If set-up costs were transferred using number of set-ups as the cost driver, a fairer allocation of set-up costs would be achieved and products with longer production runs would not be penalised with a disproportionate share of their indirect costs.

Improved cost control

Activity-based costing can lead to more detailed product cost information because a larger number of ABC cost drivers are likely to be identified in a given manufacturing organisation. An average of fifteen ABC cost drivers tends to be used, compared with one or two overhead absorption rates in traditional absorption costing. This more detailed product cost information can lead to improved cost control, since managers can seek to control costs by controlling the activities that cause the costs to be incurred. Production scheduling, for example, can optimise the number of production runs in order to minimise set-up costs.

Better information on product profitability

Since product cost information is more accurate, managers have more accurate information on the relative profitability of individual products. This can lead to better decisions on product promotion and pricing, since managers can promote higher margin products while seeking to improve margins on products where margins are lower.

Activity-based budgeting

Budget planning and formulation can use an activity-based approach to determining the required level of support activities, rather than an incremental approach based on prior year figures. With activity-based budgeting, the required level of production is used to determine the required number of cost driver transactions (e.g. number of set-ups), which in turn are used to determine the level of support activity that must be budgeted for (e.g. number of set-up engineers). In this way managers can seek to identify and eliminate any unnecessary slack in support activities, thereby improving efficiency and profitability.

ACCA marking scheme		
		Marks
(a)	ABC recovery rates	4
(b)	Cost drivers for Product ZT3	2
	ABC overheads for Product ZT3	2
	General overheads for Product ZT3	1
	Total overhead per unit	1
	Direct labour cost	1
	Standard total unit cost	1
	Standard selling price	1
		9
(c)	Discussion of relevant issues	12
Total		25

STANDARD COSTING AND VARIANCE ANALYSIS

39 STANDARD COSTING

(a) Standard costing has been employed for many years in situations where there is a **significant degree of repetition** in the production process or the service supplied. Repetition is a condition, since standards presuppose that averages, as expected values, are accurate to a fair degree.

The main uses of standard costing relate to:

1 **Valuation of stocks** and costs of production for reporting purposes, either internally or for statutory reasons.

2 Providing an excellent device which enables costs to be monitored, reviewed and controlled by management.

3 Enabling **exception reporting** through the use of variance analysis. Exception reporting allows management to exercise control with a lower degree of effort and less time than otherwise would be the case.

4 Assisting in the **budgeting** process. Standards, once established in a business, become the common language by which performance is discussed and measured.

5 **Evaluating managerial performance.**

6 **Motivation** of staff by setting standards at levels to which staff feel able to respond. In this respect, standards have been characterised as 'ideal', 'attainable', 'current' and 'basic' as a way of categorising the different ways standards may be viewed in terms of their motivational impact.

7 **Improving efficiency.** Standard setting is often viewed as a way of understanding the detail of a process through monitoring its important components. If standards are an accurate reflection of a process, then they can be used to highlight ways of improving efficiency and act as signals when the process becomes inefficient.

Once standards have been set, they cannot be assumed to be accurate over long periods of time. **Standards have to be reviewed** to enable the benefits of standard costing to continue. In this respect, standards must change with the changing practices of an organisation. For example, in environments which continuously seek greater efficiency and reduced costs of production, standards have to change to reflect such improvements. In fact, under such circumstances, standards can very quickly become out of date. In order to review standards, they must be continually assessed to ensure that the basis of their calculation still applies. Moreover, other purposes of standards are undermined, if they are not continually reviewed. Thus, for example:

1 The motivational impact of standards may no longer be effective if standards are out of date.

2 Assessment of managerial performance becomes inaccurate.

3 Reporting procedures are undermined.

4 The credibility of standards in their role in assisting with the budget setting process is called into question.

5 The fate of standard costing as a management tool is put at risk if management do not trust the standards. Alternative mechanisms for management control inevitably emerge which may be undesirable, untested and lack organisational approval.

(b) Financial statements of any sort are only an expression of organisational activities that can be measured. Many of the activities of an organisation cannot be easily measured, nor can its relations with various stakeholder groups who may have a non-financial interest in the organisation.

Non-finance objectives that may be difficult to measure or express in financial terms include:

1 Welfare of employees and management
- Health
- Safety
- Leisure and other services

2 Welfare in the broader community
- Minimisation of intrusion into the community (e.g. traffic)

3 The provision of a service for which no charge is made, for example:
- Public hospitals
- Local or regional government services
- Housing
- Education

4 The effective supply of goods or services (in addition to costs/efficiency issued) such as:
- Product or service quality
- Ensuring product or service supply (e.g. vital services)

- Timeliness
- After-sales support
- Customer/user satisfaction

5 Fulfilment of product or services responsibilities: this is a very broad area and would cover many of the core activities of a business such as:

- Leadership in research and development
- Product development
- Maintenance of standards in goods or service provision
- Maintenance of good business and community relationships
- Employee training and support.

6 Support for community activities

7 Minimisation of externalities (e.g. pollution and other socially responsible objectives)

8 Fulfilment of statutory or regulatory responsibilities

Whilst it may be argued that many of the objectives expressed have an impact on profitability or costs, they only do so in an indirect manner. Moreover, as with most organisational activities, non-financial objectives crystallises into financial issues given enough time. Thus, for example, poor service provision will ultimately lead to loss of customers in a competitive environment.

The range of stakeholders that may have an interest in an organisation's activities are wide and, because organisations have to respond to stakeholder interests, the non-financial responsibilities and hence range of objectives, is extended. In this respect, stakeholders create for organisations a range of non-financial issues that have to be addressed. If organisations are responsive then these issues become part of the culture of an organisation and hence part of its broader purposes. Interest in the organisation's activities from a non-financial perspective can arise even if the stake holder has a financial relationship with the organisation. Thus, the stakeholders who may have an interest might include the following:

1 shareholders

2 suppliers and trade creditors

3 debt holders

4 customers

5 employees

6 pensioners and ex-employees

7 competitors

8 local community

9 broader national and international interests

10 government

11 regulatory authorities

12 tax authorities

13 special interest groups concerned with pollution, for example

Moreover, many of the stakeholders have common interests and hence stakeholders groupings can emerge.

ACCA marking scheme			
		Marks	
(a)	1 mark for each item referring to the use of standard costing	8	
	2 marks for each detailed item on why standards need reviewing	8	
	Maximum available	16	
	Maximum awarded		13
(b)	Up to 2 marks for each detailed item on describing non-financial objectives	12	
	Up to 2 marks on role of stakeholders in shaping objectives	2	
	1 mark for identification of stakeholder	1	
	Maximum available	15	
	Maximum awarded		12
Total			25

40 MATERIAL VARIANCES

(a) **Standard cost per tonne of input**

			£
Material X:	60%	at £30 per tonne	18
Material Y:	40%	at £45 per tonne	18
	100%		36
Standard loss	10%		
Standard yield	90%		

Standard cost per standard tonne of output = £36/90% = £40.

Material price variance

	January £	*February* £	*March* £
Material Y:			
Actual price of £45 = standard price. So material price variance =	Nil	Nil	Nil
Material X:			
Total cost of all materials	32,400	31,560	38,600
Less cost of material Y (360 × £45)	16,200	16,200	16,200
Actual cost of material X	16,200	15,360	22,400
Standard price of material X used			
January: 540 tonnes should cost (× £30)	16,200		
February: 480 tonnes should cost (× £30)		14,400	
March: 700 tonnes should cost (× £30)			21,000
Material X price variance	Nil	960 (A)	1,400 (A)

Mix variances

January	*Actual mix* tonnes		*Standard mix* tonnes	*Mix variance* tonnes
Material X	540	(60%)	540	0
Material Y	360	(40%)	360	0
	900		900	0

February	*Actual mix* tonnes		*Standard mix* tonnes	*Mix variance* tonnes	*Standard price* £	*Mix variance* £
Material X	480	(60%)	504	24 (F)	30	720 (F)
Material Y	360	(40%)	336	24 (A)	45	1,080 (A)
	840		840			360 (A)

March	*Actual mix* tonnes		*Standard mix* tonnes	*Mix variance* tonnes	*Standard price* £	*Mix variance* £
Material X	700	(60%)	636	64 (A)	30	1,920 (A)
Material Y	360	(40%)	424	64 (F)	45	2,880 (F)
	1,060		1,060			960 (F)

Yield variances

January

810 tonnes of output	should use (× 10/9)	900	tonnes
	did use (540 + 360)	900	tonnes
Yield variance		0	tonnes

February

765 tonnes of output	should use (× 10/9)	850	tonnes
	did use (480 + 360)	840	tonnes
Yield variance		10	tonnes (F)
Standard price per tonne of input		£36	
Yield variance in £		£360 (F)	

March

900 tonnes of output	should use (× 10/9)	1,000	tonnes
	did use (700 + 360)	1,060	tonnes
Yield variance		60	tonnes (A)
Standard price per tonne of input		£36	
Yield variance in £		£2,160 (A)	

Summary

	January £	£	*February* £	£	*March* £	£
Material price variance						
Material X		0		960 (A)		1,400 (A)
Material Y		0		0		0
Materials mix variance	0		360 (A)		960 (F)	
Materials yield variance	0		360 (F)		2,160 (A)	
Materials usage variance		0		0		1,200 (A)
Total materials variances		0		960 (A)		2,600 (A)

Tutorial note: In the time available, it should be permissible to calculate the usage variance as the sum of the mix and yield variances. If you wanted to calculate the usage variances from first principles, you could use the following method.

January		*Material X* *tonnes*		*Material Y* *tonnes*
810 units of output:				
should use	(60% of 900)	540	(40% of 900)	360
did use		540		360
Usage variance in tonnes		0		0

February		*Material X* *tonnes*		*Material Y* *tonnes*
765 units of output:				
should use	(60% of 850)	510	(40% of 850)	340
did use		480		360
Usage variance in tonnes		30 (F)		20 (A)
Standard price per tonne		£30		£45
Usage variance in £		£900 (F)		£900 (A)

Total usage variance = £0

March		*Material X* *tonnes*		*Material Y* *tonnes*
900 units:				
should use	(60% of 1,000)	600	(40% of 1,000)	400
did use		700		360
Usage variance in tonnes		100 (A)		40 (F)
Standard price per tonne		£30		£45
Usage variance in £		£3,000 (A)		£1,800 (F)

Total usage variance = £1,200 (A)

(b) Production in January is exactly according to standard. The price of Y has remained at standard for the whole period. The price of X is £2 (£960/480) in excess of standard in February and £2 (£1,400/700) in excess of standard in March. If this continues, the standard price of X will need to be increased. The proportion of X in the mix changed to 57% (480/840) and 66% (700/1,060) in February and March respectively. The cost increase in February, shown as an adverse mix variance of £360, is caused by dearer Y being used instead of cheaper X. There is an improvement in yield in February. The increased yield could be viewed as an abnormal gain of 9 tonnes [(840 × 90% – 765)] with a standard value of (× £40 =) £360. There is also a reduction in volume produced in February.

In March, the significant increase in the usage proportion of X (which is cheaper) has caused a favourable mix variance but may also have contributed to the large adverse yield variance. Production in March is considerably higher than for January and February - this may be a reason for the adverse yield variance.

Overall, there appears to be a link between mix and yield. If the proportion of Y is increased, causing an adverse mix variance since Y is more expensive, the yield is improved - as occurred in February. The opposite took place in March.

There could also be a link between yield and the volume of production - in February production is low and yield is high, whereas in March production is high and yield is low.

(c) This information helps to explain the increased proportion of Y used in February. If not used. Y would be wasted, and this could involve disposal costs. It could therefore be argued that the adverse mix variance on Y of £1,080 in February is a sunk cost, i.e. using a greater proportion of Y has not increased the purchase quantity. Using more of Y has improved yield.

In March, the restriction on Y has resulted in adverse yield arising from the increased proportion of X needed to increase production volume. This has resulted in an overall adverse usage variance of £1,200. This excess cost should be included in the evaluation of decisions to try to obtain more of Y by, for example, paying a premium price.

It would be necessary to ascertain whether and how the quality of the final product is affected by changes in mix, and whether the quality is then acceptable to customers.

41 PERSEUS CO LTD

Key answer tips

This is a straightforward variances question, and provided you are well-prepared on this topic is quite manageable in the time allowed. Note in the answer to (a), the two statements have been combined in columnar form, which saves time. Whilst the answer interprets "standard costing profit statement" as a flexed budget, it would be equally acceptable to base this statement on the budgeted activity level.

Whether you include a sales volume variance in part (b) depends upon the approach taken in (a); note that mix and yield variances are not generally required unless specifically requested or the working of the question indicates they would be useful/relevant.

(a) ***Workings***

Standard variable cost per unit

		£
Materials:		
007	6 kilos at £12.25 per kilo	73.50
XL90	3 kilos at £3.20 per kilo	9.60
		83.10
Labour	4.5 hours at £8.40 per hour	37.80
		120.90

Standard usages and time:

Material 007	15,400 units should use (× 6)	92,400 kilos
Material XL90	15,400 units should use (× 3)	46,200 kilos
Labour	15,400 units should take (× 4.5)	69,300 hours

15,400 units of production and sale

	Actual		Standard	
	£	£	£	£
Sales	(at £138.25)	2,129,050	(at £140)	2,156,000
Costs				
Materials				
007		1,256,640	(15,400 × £73.50)	1,131,900
XL90		132,979	(15,400 × £9.60)	147,840
Labour		612,766	(15,400 × £37.80)	582,120
Fixed overheads		96,840		86,400
Total costs		2,099,225		1,948,260
Profit		29,825		207,740

(b) **Reconciliation**

Workings

Sales price	£	
15,400 units should sell for	2,156,000	
They did sell for	2,129,050	
Sales price variance	26,950	(A)

Materials 007	*kg*	
15,400 units should use	92,400	
They did use	98,560	
Material 007 usage variance (kg)	6,160	(A)
Standard price/kg	£12.25	
Usage variance in £	£75,460	(A)

Materials 007	£	
98,560 kg should cost (× £12.25)	1,207,360	
They did cost	1,256,640	
Material price variance	49,280	(A)

Materials XL90	*kg*	
15,400 units should use	46,200	
They did use	42,350	
Material 007 usage variance (kg)	3,850	(F)
Standard price/kg	£3.20	
Usage variance in £	£12,320	(F)

Materials XL90	£	
42,350 kg should cost (× £3.20)	135,520	
They did cost	132,979	
Material price variance	2,541	(F)

$$\text{Actual hours worked} = \frac{£612,766}{£8.65} = 70,840 \text{ hours}$$

Labour efficiency	*Hours*	
15,400 units should take	69,300	
They did take	70,840	
Labour efficiency variance (hrs)	1,540	(A)
Standard rate/hour	£8.40	
Efficiency variance in £	£12,396	(A)

Labour rate	£	
70,840 hours should cost (× £8.40)	595,056	
They did cost	612,766	
Material price variance	17,710	(A)

Fixed overhead expenditure	£	
Budgeted fixed overhead costs	86,400	
Actual fixed overhead costs	96,840	
Expenditure variance	10,440	(A)

Reconciliation

			£
Standard profit on 15,400 units of sale, on previous page			207,740
	Fav	*Adverse*	
	£	£	£
Variances:			
Sales price		26,950	
Materials 007 usage		75,460	
Materials XL90 usage	12,320		
Materials 007 price		49,280	
Materials XL90 price	2,541		
Labour efficiency		12,936	
Labour rate		17,710	
Fixed overhead expenditure variance		10,440	
	14,861	192,776	
Total variances			177,915 A
Actual profit			29,825

(c) The causes of variances might be inter-related, and the reason why one variance is favourable could also help explain why another variance is adverse.

Using poor quality materials could result in a favourable price variance because of paying a lower price. The poor quality material could be the cause of both an adverse material usage variance and an adverse labour efficiency variance, because cheaper materials might be more difficult to work with, resulting in more rejects/spoilt work, or more waste.

If a higher grade of labour was used, compared with that which was planned, there would most certainly be an adverse labour rate variance. The higher skill level employed could well be the reason for a favourable labour efficiency variance and a favourable material usage variance, for example due to a lower number of rejects and less waste of materials.

42 WOODEEZER LTD

(a) ***Workings***

	Units	
Budgeted sales	4,000	
Actual sales	3,200	
Sales volume variance	800	(A)
Standard profit/unit	£28	
Sales volume profit variance	£22,400	(A)

	£	
3,200 units of sales should sell for (× £220)	704,000	
but did sell for	720,000	
Sales price variance	16,000	(F)

	£	
80,000 kg of wood should cost (× £3.20)	256,000	
but did cost	280,000	
Materials price variance	24,000	(A)

	kg	
3,600 units produced should use (× 25 kg)	90,000	
but did use	80,000	
Materials usage variance in kg	10,000	(F)
Standard price/kg of wood	£3.20	
Sales volume profit variance	£32,000	(F)

Labour rate	£	
16,000 hours should cost (× £8)	128,000	
but did cost	112,000	
Labour rate variance	16,000	(F)

	Hours	
3,600 units produced should take (× 4 hrs)	14,400	
but did take	16,000	
Efficiency variance in hours	1,600	(A)
Standard rate/hour for labour	£8	
Labour efficiency variance	£12,800	(A)
Standard rate/hour for variable overhead	£4	
Variable overhead efficiency variance	£6,400	(A)
Standard rate/hour for fixed overhead	£16	
Fixed overhead efficiency variance	£25,600	(A)

Variable overhead expenditure	£	
16,000 hours should cost (× £4)	64,000	
but did cost	60,000	
Variable overhead expenditure variance	4,000	(F)

Fixed overhead expenditure	£	
Budgeted fixed costs (4,000 units × £64)	256,000	
Actual fixed costs	196,000	
Fixed overhead expenditure variance	60,000	(F)

	Hours
Budgeted hours of work (4,000 × 4 hrs)	16,000
Actual hours of work	16,000
Capacity variance in hours (and £)	0

Operating statement	£	
Budgeted profit (4,000 × £28)	112,000	
Sales volume profit variance	(22,400)	(A)
Standard profit on actual sales	89,600	
Sales price variance	16,000	(F)
	105,600	

Cost variances	*Fav*	*Adv*		
	£	£		
Material price		24,000		
Material usage	32,000			
Labour rate	16,000			
Labour efficiency		12,800		
Variable overhead expenditure	4,000			
Variable overhead efficiency		6,400		
Fixed overhead expenditure	60,000			
Fixed overhead efficiency		25,600		
	112,000	68,800	43,200	(F)
Actual profit			148,800	

(b) **Motivation and budget setting**

Absorption costing profit has increased by £53,600, from £95,200 (28 × 3,400) to £148,800.

It would apear that in the past an expectations budget has been set whereby the target output was set at the level that employees were expected to achieve.

Mr Beech appears to have considered the evidence that suggests that the best budget for motivating employees to maximize achievement (in this case output) is one which is difficult but credible (an aspirations budget). In maximising actual performance, however, it is normally expected that production will fall short of the budget target. This means that there is an expectation of adverse planning variances.

Explanations of variances

The sales volume variance and the sales price variance may be inter-related as an increase in price is likely to reduce demand, thus an adverse sales volume variance is consistent with a favourable sales price variance given the price increase.

Better quality materials are being purchased by Mr Beech and, given this was not foreseen at the time of the budget, then it may explain a higher price resulting in an adverse materials price variance. Conversely, however, with better materials there may be less waste and thus it may have contributed to the favourable materials usage variance.

The lower skilled labour may account for the favourable labour rate variance but may also account for the adverse labour efficiency variance as less skilled labour may take longer to complete a given task. Also if new labour is introduced there may be an initial learning effect.

The impact of the efficiency variance is magnified by the variable and fixed overhead efficiency variances as they are directly related to the labour efficiency variance. The meaning of the fixed overhead efficiency variance is questionable however. By definition fixed overheads do not vary with labour hours and this variance merely ‘balances the books’ in an absorption costing system.

The fixed overhead expenditure variance is significant and requires further consideration. This is particularly the case if it involves discretionary expenditure which has been reduced but which may have a long-term impact on the business.

(c) **Marginal costing**

Standard contribution/unit = £(220 – 80 – 32 – 16) = £92.

Marginal cost statement (this could be in summarised form)

	Fav	Adv		
			£	
Budgeted contribution (4,000 × £92)			368,000	
Sales volume contribution variance (800 units × £92)			73,600	(A)
Standard contribution on actual sales			294,400	
Sales price variance			16,000	(F)
			310,400	
Cost variances	Fav	Adv		
	£	£		
Material price		24,000		
Material usage	32,000			
Labour rate	16,000			
Labour efficiency		12,800		
Variable overhead expenditure	4,000			
Variable overhead efficiency		6,400		
	52,000	43,200	8,800	(F)
Actual contribution			319,200	
Budgeted fixed overhead		256,000		
Fixed overhead expenditure variance (favourable)		60,000		
Actual fixed overheads			196,000	
Actual profit			123,200	

Reconciliation	£
Absorption costing profit	148,800
Fixed costs in additional closing stocks (400 units × £64)	(25,600)
Marginal costing profit	123,200

Tutorial note

The absorption costing profit is higher than the marginal costing profit because closing stocks are higher than opening stocks of finished goods. Consequently, with absorption some fixed overhead costs are carried forward in the stock value whereas in marginal costing all fixed overhead costs are charged against profit in the current period.

Thus some of the 'success' of Mr. Beech in increasing profit arises from the fact that fixed overheads of £25,600 are not being written off in the current month but are being carried forward as part of closing stock, notwithstanding that they are period costs and are thus sunk costs. Unless sales can be increased this position is unsustainable.

Nevertheless, some improvement has been made as the previous contribution was £312,800 [3,400 × (£220 – 128)], taking the budget as the historic norm. This is lower than the £319,200 achieved by Mr. Beech. The difference is, however, much lower than would be implied by the absorption costing statement.

ACCA marking scheme		
		Marks
(a)	1 mark for each variance (including Fixed overhead capacity nil variance) Budgeted profit Standard profit Reconciliation to actual profit	14
(b)	Effect on profitability Comments on motivation (1 mark for each explained profit) Comments on explaining variances (1 mark for each explained point)	6
(c)	1 mark for each of correct calculations relating to budgeted contribution, standard contribution on actual sales, actual contribution, appropriate inclusion of fixed overheads (maximum 3) Reconciliation Comments on marginal costing (2 marks for each explained point)	5
Total		25

43 BICYCLES

(a) (i)

$$\text{Break-even point} = \frac{\text{Fixed costs}}{\text{Contribution per unit}}$$

Fixed costs = £1,200,000 + £340,000 = £1,540,000

Variable costs per unit (from Table 1) = (£45 + £15 + £15) = £75.

Contribution per unit = £190 - £75 = £115.

$$\text{Break-even point} = \frac{£1{,}540{,}000}{£115 \text{ per unit}} = 13{,}391 \text{ units}$$

(ii) It is assumed that the Sales Manager, given his interest in break even, will calculate the profit using marginal costing principles.

		£000
Sales	11,800 units × £190	2,242
Variable costs	11,800 units × £75	885
Contribution		1,357
Fixed costs		1,540
Loss		(183)

(b) (i)

Manufacturing fixed overhead volume variance:

Budgeted production volume	20,000 units	
Actual production volume	16,800 units	
Volume variance in units	3,200 units	(A)

Manufacturing fixed overhead recovery rate (from Table 1)

$$\frac{£1{,}200{,}000}{20{,}000} \frac{£1{,}200{,}000}{} = £60 \text{ per unit}$$

Volume variance in £ = 3,200 units (A) × £60 = **£192,000 (A).**

The volume variance is caused by the actual production level for the period falling below the production volume that was used to compute the fixed overhead recovery rate, in this case the budgeted volume. It is an under-recovery of fixed overhead, which the company must charge against the profits for the period. It occurs because a standard absorption costing system charges fixed overhead costs to products on a unit rate. It does not specifically represent an extra cost or a 'real' loss to the company, as these fixed costs would be incurred anyway. However, since fixed overheads incurred have not been fully recovered, because of the shortfall in production volume, the un-recovered amount is written off against profits for the period.

(ii) ***Tutorial note***: It is most unusual to absorb fixed sales overhead into the cost of sales. It is much more usual to treat fixed sales and administration overheads as period costs, and write them off against profits in the period they arise. The only variances are therefore expenditure variances.

Variable selling overhead:	£000	
11,800 units of sale		
Overhead expenditure should be (11,800 × £15 per unit)	177	
Actual variable selling overhead expenditure	138	
Variable selling overhead expenditure variance	39	(F)

Fixed selling overhead:	£000	
Budgeted expenditure	340	
Actual expenditure	376	
Fixed selling overhead expenditure variance	36	(A)

Tutorial note: Should you wish to calculate a fixed sales overhead volume variance, it would be the difference between actual and budgeted sales volume (= 20,000 – 11,800 units) multiplied by the budgeted fixed sales overhead cost per unit (= 340/20 = £17). The fixed sales overhead volume variance would then be 8,200 units (A) × £17 = £139,400 (A). However, it must be stressed that this would be an unusual variance to come across in practice.

(c) ***Tutorial note:*** The reconciliation must allow for the fact that the profit of £72,000 is based on absorption costing principles, and the loss of £183,000 is based on marginal costing principles. The absorption costing profit is higher because some fixed overheads are carried forward in closing stock values, and are not charged against the profit of the current period.

			£000	
Predicted loss, Sales Manager			(183)	
Expenditure variances:				
Manufacturing	48	(A)		
Variable sales	39	(F)		
Fixed sales	36	(A)		
			45	(A)
			(228)	
Fixed overhead carried forward in closing stock value (5,000 units at £60)			300	(F)
Actual profit recorded, absorption costing			72	

An explanation of why an actual profit is revealed when a loss was anticipated by the sales manager is contained within the reconciliation above. The reconciliation is achieved when all the differences between the two statements are accounted for. This involves expenditure variances, which were not in the sales manager's budgeted statement but which are in the actual profit statement.

Finally, and most significantly, a variable costing statement applies only variable manufacturing costs to stock values. An absorption costing statement, which the company uses for reporting actual results, values stock at full manufacturing costs. The production and sales levels for the period imply 5,000 units were added to stock, therefore a difference between the two stock values accounts for a difference in profit. The absorption costing statement is adjusted (relieved of cost) by fixed overhead carried forward in the increased stock value. That is 5,000 units at £60 per unit fixed overhead rate, £300,000. Thus the loss anticipated by the sales manager becomes a profit in the actual results reported.

ACCA marking scheme			
			Marks
(a)	(i)	Break even point calculation	2
	(ii)	Budgeted loss	2
			4
(b)	(i)	Variance calculation	2
		Explanation	3
	(ii)	1 mark for each variance, including mention or calculation of sales overhead volume variance	3
			8
(c)		Expenditure variances	2
		Overheads in stock	2
		Achieving correct reconciliation	2
		Explanation	2
			8
Total			20

44 PAN-OCEAN CHEMICALS

(a) (i) **Direct materials mix variance:**

Method 1 of calculation

Standard cost per batch:			£
S1:	8 kg × £0.3	=	2.4
S2:	5 kg × £0.5	=	2.5
S3:	3 kg × £0.4	=	1.2
	16 kg:		6.1

	Actual usage	*Standard price*	*Actual usage at standard price*
	kg	£	£
S1	8,284	0.3	2,485.2
S2	7,535	0.5	3,767.5
S3	3,334	0.4	1,333.6
	19,153		7,586.3

Actual usage in standard mix:

	Actual usage	*Standard mix*	*Actual usage in standard mix*
			kg
S1		(8)	9,576.5
S2		(5)	5,985.3
S3		(3)	3,591.3
Total	19,153		19,153.0

Standard cost of input per kg: £6.1/16 kg = £0.38125

Input in standard mix = 19,153 kg × £0.31825 = £7,302.1

	£	
Actual usage/mix at standard price	7,586.3	
Standard mix at standard price	7,302.1	
Mix variance	284.2	(A)

Method 2 of calculation

	Actual usage		*Actual usage in standard mix*	*Mix variance*	*Standard cost per kg*	*Mix variance*
	kg		kg	kg	£	£
S1	8,284	(8)	9,576.5	1,292.5 F	0.30	387.8 F
S2	7,535	(5)	5,985.3	1,549.7 A	0.50	774.9 A
S3	3,334	(3)	3,591.2	257.2 F	0.40	102.9 F
Total	19,153		19,153.0			284.2 A

Direct materials yield variance:

Standard cost of input per kg 6.1/16 = £0.38125.

15,408 kg of output	should use (× 10/9)	17,120	of input materials (kg)
	did use	19,153	of input materials (kg)
Yield variance (in kg)		2,033	(A) of input materials (kg)
Standard price per kg		£0.38125	
Yield variance (in £)		£775.1	(A)

Materials usage variance:

Usage variance = Yield variance + Mix variance

= 775.1 A + 284.2 (A)

= £1,059.3A

Tutorial note: Proof of usage variance

Actual production of 15,408kgs required input of (10/9) × 15,408 = 17,120 kgs. This can be divided into standard usage for each material.

		Standard usage	*Actual usage*	*Usage variance*	*Standard price per kg*	*Usage variance*
		kg	kg	kg	£	£
S1	(8)	8,560	8,284	276 (F)	0.30	82.8 (F)
S2	(5)	5,350	7,535	2,185 (A)	0.50	1,092.5 (A)
S3	(3)	3,210	3,334	124 (A)	0.40	49.6 (A)
		17,120	19,153			1,059.3 (A)

(ii) **Labour cost variances**

Standard labour cost for 1 kg of output = £5/(90% of 16) = £5/14.4

= £0.3472 per kg

Rate variance: 6,916 – (1,235 × 5) = £741A

Efficiency variance (1,235 × 5) – (15,408 × 0.3472) = £825A

Total variance = 6,916 – (15,408 × 0.3472) = 825A + 741A = £1,566A.

Tutorial note: Alternative methods of calculation

		£	
1,235 hours	should cost (× £5)	6,175	
	did cost	6,916	
Rate variance		741	(A)

15,408 units of output	should take (/14.4)	1,069.72	hours
	did take	1,235.00	hours
Efficiency variance (in hours)		165.28	hours (A)
Standard rate per hour		£5	
Efficiency variance (in £)		£826.4	(A)

This is the same amount as calculated by the other method, except with a small rounding difference.

(b) The total mix variance measured in quantity is zero since the expected mix is based on the total quantity actually used and hence the difference between total expected and total actual is nil.

(c) **Analysis of variance for Pan-Ocean Chemicals**

Circulation: Pan-Ocean Chemicals: Senior Management

Author:

Date: xx/xx/xx

Subject: **Variances**

General

The appendix to this report (results in part (a)) details mix, yield and usage variances for materials and rate and efficiency variances for labour over the last seven days. The purpose of this report is to explain what is meant by the analysis undertaken and to interpret the results derived.

Materials variances

Materials variances can be categorised in four ways: usage, mix, yield and price. We are concerned only with mix and yield for the purposes of this report.

The three types of material used to produce Synthon (S1, S2 and S3) are not always used in the same proportions. Whilst it is the intention of the production team to use a constant or standard mix, this is not always achieved. In practice, the proportions of input chemicals used can vary for many reasons, mostly associated with the physical properties of the chemicals (which need not concern us here). To the extent that the standard mix is not used in the production of Synthon, then mix variances arise which simply record to what extent the standard mix has not been followed.

Materials yield variances record the differences arising in what inputs should have been used for the output achieved against what inputs have actually been used. Essentially, yield variances are a description of how efficiently inputs have been used.

The adverse yield variance should give rise to some concern since such results indicate an inefficient use of inputs against what was expected. The adverse variance may have arisen, for example, because of a batch of poor quality input chemicals or because of inefficient working practices which have led to a significant degree of spoilage.

Labour variances

The labour rate variance has a simple interpretation, in that it reflects changes in the hourly rate paid to workers during the year that are not reflected in the standard cost details. In the case of Pan Ocean, a wage increase from £5 per hour to £5.60 per hour took place. It is possible that the standard rate reflects an average of a variety of rates and that the variance arose because of an unexpected change of higher paid workers undertaking the tasks of lower paid workers. No information is given on the possible mix of rates of pay used.

The labour efficiency variance reflects an assessment of the difference from the standard allocation in the time that was booked to a batch by the workers involved. In other words, the work undertaken on a batch over a weekly period was longer (because the variance was adverse) than that expected in the standard. This may have arisen because of inferior quality of input materials being used, or the introduction of new equipment or procedures.

Final comments

Variances of any type should be a signal for some sort of investigative action by management. This can involve either looking to see how the variances have arisen or re-assessing the suitability of the standards that have been set. It might have to be accepted that the standard by which materials and labour performance is being measured might not be an accurate one.

Recognition should also be given to the fact that new employees might have been deployed, in which case there will be some inefficiency as they go through the learning curve period. This would also arise in a situation where new chemicals are being used, or new processes to be learnt, such that – again – employees would not be fully familiar with their tasks.

ACCA marking scheme			
Marking guide		*Marks*	
(a)	Materials usage variance	1	
	Materials mix variance	3	
	Materials yield variance	3	
	Labour rate variance	2	
	Labour efficiency variance	2	
			11
(b)	Explanation of equivalence of total mix variances		3
(c)	Explanation of mix and yield variances	5	
	Up to 2 marks each for identification of possible reasons for the variances calculated in part (a)	6	
			11
Total			25

45 CARAT

Key answer tips

This question is largely a straightforward test of your ability to calculate variances, including materials mix and yield variances, and labour variances when idle time is recorded. However, do not overlook part (d) of the question: there are 7 marks available for a description of the different types of standard cost. The answer here describes a basic, current, attainable and ideal standard. It would also be relevant to answer the question by discussing 'ex post' and 'ex ante' standards, as a means of separating planning and operational variances.

(a) Standard cost and standard contribution

	£	£
Standard sales price		12.00
Material A: (2.5 × £1.70)	4.25	
Material B: (1.5 × £1.20)	1.80	
Labour: (0.45 × £6.00)	2.70	
		8.75
Standard contribution		3.25

Calculation of variances

(i) *Sales variances*

	£	
48,000 units should sell for (× £12)	576,000	
They did sell for	580,800	
Sales price variance	**4,800**	**(F)**

	Units	
Budgeted sales volume	50,000	
Actual sales volume	48,000	
Sales volume variance	2,000	(A)
Standard contribution/unit	£3.25	
Sales volume contribution variance	**£6,500**	**(A)**

(ii) *Materials variances*

Material A price variance	£	
121,951 kg should cost (× £1.70)	207,317	
They did cost	200,000	
Material A price variance	**7,317**	**(F)**

Material B price variance	£	
67,200 kg should cost (× £1.20)	80,640	
They did cost	84,000	
Material A price variance	**3,360**	**(A)**

Mix variance

The standard mix is 2.5kg of A for each 1.5kg of B, i.e. 62.5% Material A and 37.5% Material B.

	Actual quantities used		*Actual quantities in standard mix*	*Mix variance*	*Standard price*	*Mix variance*
	kg		kg	kg	£	£
Material A	121,951	(62.5%)	118,219	3,732 (A)	1.70	6,344 (A)
Material B	67,200	(37.5%)	70,932	3,732 (F)	1.20	4,478 (F)
	189,151		189,151			1,866 (A)

		48,000 units should use	*Actual quantities in standard mix*	*Yield variance*	*Standard price*	*Yield variance*
		kg	kg	kg	£	£
Material A	(× 2.5 kg)	120,000	118,219	1,781 (F)	1.70	3,027 (F)
Material B	(× 1.5 kg)	72,000	70,932	1,068 (F)	1.20	1,282 (F)
						4,309 (F)

Tutorial note: It is unusual to be required to separate the yield variance into an amount for each of the materials individually, but this is what the question asks for. The yield variance would normally be calculated as a single total figure, as follows.

The standard cost per kg of material for A and B together is:

(£4.25 + £1.80)/(2.5kg + 1.5kg) = £6.05/4kg = £1.5125 per kg.

	kg	
48,000 units of ZP should use (× 4kg)	192,000	
They did use	189,151	
Total yield variance	2,849	(F)
Standard cost per kg	£1.5125	
Material yield variance	**£4,309**	**(F)**

(iii) *Labour variances*

	£	
19,200 hours should cost (× £6.00)	115,200	
They did cost	117,120	
Material A price variance	**1,920**	**(A)**

Idle time variance = (19,200 – 18,900) hours = 300 hours (A).

At the standard rate per hour, the idle time variance = 300 hours (A) × £6.00 = **£1,800 (A).**

Labour efficiency variance	*Hours*	
48,000 units of ZP should take (× 0.45 hours)	21,600	
They did use	18,900	
Total yield variance	2,700	(F)
Standard rate/hour	£6	
Labour efficiency variance	**£16,200**	**(F)**

(b) Budgeted contribution = 50,000 units × £3.25 = £162,500.

Budgeted gross profit = £162,500 - £62,500 = £100,000.

	£	£	£	
Budgeted gross profit			100,000	
Budgeted fixed production overhead			62,500	
Budgeted contribution			162,500	
Sales volume contribution variance		6,500 (A)		
Sales price variance		4,800 (F)		
			1,700	(A)
Actual sales less standard variable cost of sales			160,800	
Variable cost variances:	(F)	(A)		
Material A price	7,317			
Material B price		3,360		
Material B mix		6,344		
Material A mix	4,478			
Material A yield	3,027			
Material B yield	1,282			
Labour rate		1,920		
Labour idle time		1,800		
Labour efficiency	16,200			
	32,304	13,424	18,880	(F)

	£	£	£
Actual contribution			179,680
Budgeted fixed production overhead		62,500	
Fixed production overhead expenditure variance		1,500 (A)	
Actual fixed production overhead			64,000
Actual gross profit			115,680

(c) The **favourable material A price variance** indicates that the actual price per kilogram was less than standard. Possible explanations include buying lower quality material, buying larger quantities of material A and thereby gaining bulk purchase discounts, a change of supplier, and using an out-of-date standard.

The **adverse material A mix variance** indicates that more of this material was used in the actual input than indicated by the standard mix. The favourable material price variance suggests this may be due to the use of poorer quality material (hence more was needed than in the standard mix), or it might be that more material A was used because it was cheaper than expected.

The **favourable material A yield variance** indicates that more output was produced from the quantity of material used than expected by the standard. This increase in yield is unlikely to be due to the use of poorer quality material: it is more likely to be the result of employing more skilled labour, or introducing more efficient working practices.

It is only appropriate to calculate and interpret material mix and yield variances if quantities in the standard mix can be varied.

It has also been argued that calculating yield variances for each material is not useful, as yield is related to output overall rather than to particular materials in the input mix. A further complication is that mix variances for individual materials are inter-related and so an explanation of the increased use of one material cannot be separated from an explanation of the decreased use of another.

The **unfavourable labour rate variance** indicates that the actual hourly rate paid was higher than standard. Possible explanations for this include hiring staff with more experience and paying them more (this is consistent with the favourable overall direct material variance), or implementing an unexpected pay increase. The **favourable labour efficiency variance** shows that fewer hours were worked than standard. Possible explanations include the effect of staff training, the use of better quality material (possibly on Material B rather than on Material A), employees gaining experience of the production process, and introducing more efficient production methods. The **adverse idle time variance** may be due to machine breakdowns; or a higher rate of production arising from more efficient working (assuming employees are paid a fixed number of hours per week).

(d) The **theory of motivation** suggests that having a clearly defined target results in better performance than having no target at all, that targets need to be accepted by the staff involved, and that more demanding targets increase motivation provided they remain accepted. It is against this background that basic, ideal, current and attainable standards can be discussed.

A **basic standard** is one that remains unchanged for several years and is used to show trends over time. Basic standards may become increasingly easy to achieve as time passes and hence, being undemanding, may have a negative impact on motivation. Standards that are easy to achieve will give employees little to aim at.

Ideal standards represent the outcome that can be achieved under perfect operating conditions, with no wastage, inefficiency or machine breakdowns. Since perfect operating conditions are unlikely to occur for any significant period, ideal standards will be very demanding and are unlikely to be accepted as targets by the staff involved as they are unlikely to be achieved. Using ideal standards as targets is therefore likely to have a negative effect on employee motivation.

Current standards are based on current operating conditions and incorporate current levels of wastage, inefficiency and machine breakdown. If used as targets, current standards will not improve performance beyond its current level and their impact on motivation will be a neutral one.

Attainable standards are those that can be achieved if operating conditions conform to the best that can be practically achieved in terms of material use, efficiency and machine performance. Attainable standards are likely to be more demanding than current standards and so will have a positive effect on employee motivation, provided that employees accept them as achievable.

ACCA marking scheme

		Marks
(a)	Sales volume contribution variance	1
	Sales price variance	1
	Material price variances	1
	Material mix variances	2
	Material yield variances	2
	Labour rate and efficiency variances	1
	Idle time variance	1
	Marks available	9
	Maximum awarded	8
(b)	Budgeted gross profit	1
	Budgeted contribution	1
	Fixed production overhead expenditure variance	1
	Actual gross profit	1
	Format of operating statement	1
		5
(c)	Material price, mix and yield variances	3
	Labour rate and efficiency variances	2
		5
(d)	Basic standard	1
	Ideal standard	2
	Current standard	2
	Attainable standard	2
		7
Total		25

46 FOOD MANUFACTURER

Key answer tips

You are given an original budget, followed by some post-budget planning changes, and then actual figures. This should lead you into thinking along the lines of planning and operational variances. However, four things point towards these being required as part of the discussion in (c) rather than as an explicit part of the variance analysis in (b):

- the question states that the original budget is to be used as a reference point
- there is no detail about the changes to the methods of working
- there is no mention of planning and operational variances in requirement (b)
- the budget prepared in (a) is based upon the original figures.

So parts (a) and (b) are standard budget/variance analysis computations. Whilst the examiner has incorporated some of his workings in the discussion in (c), you are best advised to set these out clearly following your answer to (b).

It is in part (c) that you should make use of the information regarding post-budget planning changes. Start with an overall summary of the picture painted by the analysis in (b), then look at individual variances, tying them in to the changes where possible. You must also address the specific areas required by the question, interrelationships and overheads.

(a) Actual sales were £1,080,000, but the sale price was (× 4.50/5.00) of the budgeted price. The actual sales at the budgeted price were therefore £1,080,000 × (5.00/4.50) = £1,200,000.

	Flexed budget		*Actual*		*Variance*
Units	240,000		240,000		
	£000	£000	£000	£000	£000
Sales		1,200		1,080	120 A
Ingredients (40%)	480		520		40 A
Labour and energy (10%)	120		110		10 F
		600		630	
Contribution		600		450	
Fixed overheads		300		340	40 A
Profit		300		110	190 A

Note: The answer only specifically required the flexible budget (flexed budget).

(b) ***Workings***

Budgeted ingredients cost	£400,000
Price per kg	£0.40
Budgeted kg (400,000/0.40)	1,000,000
Kg of ingredients in each pack	5
Budgeted number of packs (1,000,000/5)	200,000
Actual sales by volume	Sales = £1,080,000a £4.50/pack = 240,000 packs

Actual ingredients used £520,000/£0.375 per kg = 1,386,667 kg.

	kg
240,000 packs should use (× 5)	1,200,000
but did use	1,386,667
Usage variance	186,667 kg (A)
Standard price per kg	£0.40
Usage variance in £	£74,667 (A)

	£
1,386,667 kg should cost (× £0.40)	554,667
but did cost	520,000
Ingredient price variance	34,667 F

An overall reconciliation of profit is as follows:

	£000	£000
Budget profit		200.0
Sales volume contribution variance		100.0 F
Budget profit for actual sales		300.0
Sales price variance	120.0 A	
Ingredient usage variance	74.7 A	
Ingredient price variance	34.7 F	
Labour and energy variance	10.0 F	
Overhead expenditure variance	40.0 A	
		190.0 A
Actual profit		110.0

(c) **Commentary**

The budgeted **sales volume** was 200,000 packs, whereas 240,000 packs were actually sold, a volume increase of 20%. The material, labour and energy costs are dealt with as totally variable costs. This results in the contribution margin (using the original budget) being £2.50 per pack (£1,000,000–£400,000–£100,000)/200,000. It can be seen that the increased volume earned £100,000 extra standard contribution (40,000 × £2.50) compared to the original budget. The **price reduction** of 50p per pack, however, resulted in lower sales revenue - and lower profits by £120,000. It would be useful to examine the sales price and volume variances together because of the interrelationship between them. The price reduction will have had an impact on the volume sold and this, which was probably anticipated, should be noted by the management. This marketing tactic of trading off price and volume (moving along the demand curve) does not appear to have been entirely successful, but we have no information about the experiences of other manufacturers of similar products. There could have been an unexpected downturn of the whole market. For example, the position could have been worse if the company had not decided to reduce the price. To investigate further they should, perhaps, look outside the organisation for more market intelligence.

The actual total **cost of material** exceeded that which was planned by £40,000. It is possible to analyse this difference further from the information supplied. The price reduction obtained was worth £34,667, a favourable variance. A substantial adverse usage variance of £74,667 occurred. The purchasing department would appear to have succeeded in making purchases of ingredients at favourable prices. If, however, after further investigation the ingredient usage variance is found to be due to waste caused by poorer quality purchases, this has been a false economy. This is a further example of possible interrelationships among variances and should be noted to inform future decisions on ingredient sourcing. It is not appropriate from current information to jump to conclusions about poor quality ingredients; theft or an error in the figures collected could be the cause. If, however, the ingredients are of a poorer quality then there may also be long-term repercussions in subsequent sales of these or other products, another example of interrelationships between the variances which should be borne in mind.

The labour and energy costs show a small favourable variance so the changed method of working has made a difference, providing these are completely variable costs. The actual costs incurred were more than the original budget, but less than the budget when it is flexed for the increased volume. From the information given, it is not possible to isolate labour and energy variances separately. Nor is it possible to identify rate and efficiency variances for these variable costs.

The actual **fixed overheads** were greater than the budget by £40,000. The detailed expenses should be consulted to identify any reasons for cost differences, to judge whether the costs are controllable and what action is needed, or whether the budget should be revised. Reduction of fixed overheads in the short-term may be particularly problematic. Scope to 'manage' the fixed costs (see expenditure variance) may occur when there is some potential to renegotiate prices or use resources more efficiently, perhaps resulting in some resources being disposed of (including staffing economies). However, some of the fixed costs may be uncontrollable in the short-term, for example, the rates applied to premises cannot change unless some premises are vacated. Such changes cannot be made immediately, and there may therefore be a lag in any economies in this area. The company is attempting to increase market share through increased sales, and although this should result in a greater total contribution to overall costs, this in itself does not reduce costs.

47 LINSIL

Key answer tips

It is easy to get confused by part (a) of this question. Planning variances should compare the original standard cost (the 'ex ante' standard) with the revised standard cost (the 'ex post' standard). Operational variances should compare actual costs with the revised standard cost. In this question, the variances have not been calculated in this way, and we would take the view that they are incorrectly calculated. However, the question asks you to show how the variances *have been* calculated, not how they *should* be calculated.

If you can work out the solution to part (a), the rest of the question is more straightforward. Part (b) asks for traditional variance calculations, part (b) asks about the reasons for separating planning and operational variances, and part (d) asks about the factors to consider in deciding whether or not to investigate a variance – all basic study text topics.

(a) **Revised standard costs**

After 3% price increase:	direct material price	2.30 × 1.03 =	£2.369/kg
After savings of 5%:	direct material usage	3.00 × 0.95 =	2.85 kg/unit
Adding 4% wage increase:	direct labour rate	12.00 × 1.04 =	£12.48/hour
Adding back 10% decrease:	direct labour hours	1.25/0.90 =	1.3889 hrs/unit

Planning variances

Direct materials

Actual usage = 122,000 units × 2.80 kg = 341,600 kg.

Actual direct materials costs = 341,600 kg × £2.46/kg = £840,336.

Direct materials price	£	
Original standard: 341,600 kg should cost (× 2.30)	785,680	
Revised (ex post) standard: 341,600 kg should cost (× 2.369)	809,250	
Direct materials price planning variance	23,570	(A)

Direct materials usage	kg	
Original standard: 122,000 units should use (× 3.00)	366,000	
Revised (ex post) standard: 122,000 units should use (× 2.85)	347,700	
Direct materials usage planning variance in kg	18,300	(F)
Standard rate per kilogram (balancing figure)	£2.30	
Direct materials usage planning variance in £	£42,090	(F)

The standard rate per kilogram used to calculate the usage planning variance is the original (ex ante) standard price of £2.30. This is unusual, but has been used in this case.

Direct labour

Actual hours worked = 122,000 units × 1.30 hours /unit = 158,600 hours.

Actual direct labour costs = 158,600 hours × £12.60/hour = £1,998,360.

Direct labour rate	£	
Original standard: 158,600 hours should cost (× 12)	1,903,200	
Revised standard: 158,600 hours should cost (× 12.48)	1,979,328	
Direct labour rate planning variance	76,128	(A)

Direct labour efficiency	hours	
Original standard: 122,000 units should take (× 1.25)	152,500	
Revised standard: 122,000 units should take (× 1.3889)	169,446	
Direct labour efficiency planning variance in hours	16,946	(A)
Standard rate per hour (balancing figure)	£12	
Direct labour efficiency planning variance in £	£203,333	(A)

The standard rate per hour used to calculate the efficiency planning variance is the original (ex ante) standard rate of £12.00. This is unusual, but has been used in this case.

Operational variances

Direct materials

Direct materials price	£	
341,600 kg should cost (× 2.369)	809,250	
They did cost	840,336	
Direct materials price operational variance	31,086	(A)

Direct materials usage	kg	
122,000 units should use (× 2.85)	347,700	
They did use	341,600	
Direct materials usage operational variance in kg	6,100	(F)
Standard rate per kilogram (balancing figure)	£2.30	
Direct materials usage operational variance in £	£14,030	(F)

The standard rate per kilogram used to calculate the usage operational variance is the original (ex ante) standard price of £2.30. This is most unusual, but has clearly been used in this case.

Direct labour

Direct labour rate	£	
158,600 hours should cost (× 12.48)	1,979,328	
They did cost	1,998,360	
Direct labour rate operational variance	19,032	(A)

Direct labour efficiency	hours	
122,000 units should take (× 1.3889)	169,446	
They did take	158,600	
Direct labour efficiency operational variance in hours	10,846	(F)
Standard rate per hour (balancing figure)	£12	
Direct labour efficiency operational variance in £	£130,133	(F)

The standard rate per hour used to calculate the efficiency operational variance is the original (ex ante) standard rate of £12.00. This is most unusual, but has clearly been used in this case.

(b) The direct material and direct cost variances based on the standard cost data applied during the three-month period can be found by adding the relevant planning and operational variances.

Direct material price variance = £23,570 (A) + £31,086 (A) = £54,656 (A)

Direct material usage variance = £42,090 (F) + £14,030 (F) = 56,120 (F)

Direct labour rate variance = £76,128 (A) + £19,032 (A) = £95,160 (A)

Direct labour efficiency variance = £203,333 (A) + £130,133 (F) = £73,200 (A).

Alternative calculations:

Direct materials price	£	
341,600 kg should cost (× 2.30)	785,680	
They did cost	840,336	
Direct materials price variance	54,656	(A)

Direct materials usage	kg	
122,000 units should use (× 3)	366,000	
They did use	341,600	
Direct materials usage variance in kg	24,400	(F)
Standard rate per kilogram	£2.30	
Direct materials usage variance in £	£56,120	(F)

Direct labour

Direct labour rate	£	
158,600 hours should cost (× 12)	1,903,200	
They did cost	1,998,360	
Direct labour rate variance	95,160	(A)

Direct labour efficiency	hours	
122,000 units should take (× 1.25)	152,500	
They did take	158,600	
Direct labour efficiency variance in hours	6,100	(A)
Standard rate per hour	£12	
Direct labour efficiency variance in £	£73,200	(A)

(c) If an operating statement had been prepared which did not take into account the changes that were needed to keep the standard cost data relevant, it would have reported the direct material and direct labour variances calculated in part (b). These variances contain both controllable and uncontrollable elements. For the variances to be more useful, these elements can be reported separately.

Each variance was separated into a planning variance and an operational variance. As a general rule, planning variances are not controllable, whereas operational variances could be controllable. Managers cannot be held responsible for variances over which they have no control and so their attention is focused on operational variances. For example, the operating statement shows that the labour efficiency variance consists of an adverse planning variance of £203,333 but a favourable operational variance of £130,133. If the controllable and uncontrollable elements had not been separated, an adverse variance of £73,200 would have been reported.

The planning variances indicate where investigation may result in an improvement in the planning and budgeting process. For example, if it could reasonably have been expected that a wage increase would be agreed at the start of the budget period, the anticipated increase should have been incorporated. The reason for the omission of the 3% increase in direct material price should be investigated: was it a case of forgetfulness or were budget figures not checked before the budgets were sent for approval?

(d) The following factors might be considered in deciding whether to investigate a variance.

Size

Larger cost savings are likely to arise from taking action to correct large variances and a policy could be established of investigating all variances above a given size. Size can be linked to the underlying variable in percentage terms as a test of significance: for example, a policy could be established to investigate all variances of 5% or more.

Adverse or favourable

It is natural to concentrate on adverse variances in order to bring business operations back in line with budget. However, whether a variance is adverse or favourable should not influence the decision to investigate. The reasons for favourable variances should also be sought, since they may indicate the presence of budgetary slack or suggest ways in which the budgeting process could be improved. Favourable variances may also indicate areas where the budget is easy to achieve, suggesting that the motivational effect of a budget could be improved by introducing more demanding targets.

Cost versus benefits

If the expected cost of investigating a variance is likely to exceed any benefits expected to arise from its correction, it may be decided not to investigate.

Historical pattern of variances

A variance which is unusual when compared to historical patterns of variances may be considered worthy of investigation. Statistical tests of significance may be used to highlight such variances.

Reliability and quality of data

If data is aggregated or if the quality of the measuring and recording system is not as high as would be liked, there may be uncertainty about the benefits to arise from investigation of variances.

Cumulative variances over time

A variance might be investigated if the cumulative variances over time suggest that there is a continuing trend of averse (or favourable variances). The size of the variance in each period might not on its own be sufficient to justify investigation, but the continuing trend might indicate an underlying cause for the variances that should be investigated.

ACCA marking scheme		
		Marks
(a)	Revised standard costs	3
	Calculation of planning variances	4
	Calculation of operational variances	4
		11
(b)	Direct material price variance	1
	Direct material usage variance	1
	Direct labour rate variance	1
	Direct labour efficiency variance	1
		4
(c)	Controllable and uncontrollable variances	2
	Discussion of calculated variances	3
		5
(d)	Up to 2 marks for each factor discussed	5
Total		25

48 MERMUS PLC

(a) The flexed budget will be based on the actual activity level of 90,000 units.

	£	£
Sales: £950,000 × 90/95 =		900,000
Cost of sales		
Raw materials: 133,000 × 90/95 =	126,000	
Direct labour: 152,000 × 90/95 =	144,000	
Variable production overheads: 100,700 × 90/95	95,400	
Fixed production overheads	125,400	
		490,800
		409,200

(b) Raw materials cost total variance = 126,000 – 130,500 = £4,500 (Adverse)

Direct labour cost total variance = 144,000 – 153,000 = £9,000 (Adverse)

Fixed overhead absorption rate = 125,400/28,500 = £4.40 per machine hour

Standard machine hours for actual production = 28,500 × 90/95 = 27,000 hrs

Standard fixed overhead (actual production) = 27,000 × 4.4 = £118,800

Fixed overhead absorbed on actual hours = 27,200 × 4.4 = £119,680

Fixed overhead efficiency variance = 118,800 – 119,680 = 880 (Adverse)

Fixed overhead absorbed on actual hours = 27,200 × 4.4 = £119,680

Fixed overhead absorbed on budgeted hours = 28,500 × 4.4 = £125,400

Fixed overhead capacity variance = 119,680 – 125,400 = £5,720 (Adverse)

Budgeted overhead expenditure = £125,400

Actual overhead expenditure = £115,300

Fixed overhead expenditure variance = 125,400 – 115,300 = £10,100 (Favourable)

(c) **Raw materials cost variance**

The budgeted raw material cost for production of 95,000 units was £1.40 per unit (133,000/95,000) but the actual raw material cost for production of 90,000 units was £1.45 per unit (130,500/90,000). The raw material cost per unit may have increased either because more raw material per unit was used than budgeted, or because the price per unit of raw material was higher than budgeted. Calculation of the raw material price and usage sub-variances would indicate where further explanation should be sought.

Fixed overhead efficiency variance

The fixed overhead efficiency variance measures the extent to which more or less standard hours were used for the actual production than budgeted. In this case, a total of 27,200 machine hours were actually used, when only 27,000 standard machine hours should have been used. The difference may be due to poorer production planning than expected or to machine breakdowns.

Fixed overhead expenditure variance

The fixed overhead expenditure variance measures the extent to which budgeted fixed overhead differs from actual fixed overhead. Here, actual fixed overhead is £10,100 less than budgeted. This could be due to an error in forecasting fixed production overheads such as rent and power costs, or to a decrease in fixed production overheads, such as changing to a cheaper cleaning contractor.

(d) Key purposes of a budgeting system that could be discussed include planning, co-ordination, communication, control, motivation and performance evaluation. Students were required only to discuss three key purposes.

Planning

One of the key purposes of a budgeting system is to require planning to occur. Strategic planning covers several years but a budget represents a financial plan covering a shorter period, i.e. a budget is an operational plan. Planning helps an organisation to anticipate key changes in the business environment that could potentially impact on business activities and to prepare appropriate responses. Planning also ensures that the budgeted activities of the organisation will support the achievement of the organisation's objectives.

Co-ordination

Many organisations undertake a number of activities which need to be co-ordinated if the organisation is to meet its objectives. The budgeting system facilitates this co-ordination since organisational activities and the links between them are thoroughly investigated during budget preparation, and the overall coherence between the budgeted activities is reviewed before the master budget is agreed by senior managers. Without the framework of the budgeting system, individual managers may be tempted to make decisions that are not optimal in terms of achieving organisational objectives.

Communication

The budgeting system facilitates communication within the organisation both vertically (for example between senior and junior managers) and horizontally (for example between different organisational functions). Vertical communication enables senior managers to ensure that organisational objectives are understood by employees at all levels. Communication also occurs at all stages of the budgetary control process, for example during budget preparation and during investigation of end-of-period variances.

Control

One of the most important purposes of a budgeting system is to facilitate cost control through the comparison of budgeted costs and actual costs. Variances between budgeted and actual costs can be investigated in order to determine the reason why actual performance has differed from what was planned. Corrective action can be introduced if necessary in order to ensure that organisational objectives are achieved. A budgeting system also facilitates management by exception, whereby only significant differences between planned and actual activity are investigated.

Motivation

The budgeting system can influence the behaviour of managers and employees, and may motivate them to improve their performance if the target represented by the budget is set at an appropriate level. An inappropriate target has the potential to be demotivating, however, and a key factor here is the degree of participation in the budget-setting process. It has been shown that an appropriate degree of participation can have a positive motivational effect.

Performance evaluation

Managerial performance is often evaluated by the extent to which budgetary targets for which individual managers are responsible have been achieved. Managerial rewards such as bonuses or performance-related pay can also be linked to achievement of budgetary targets. Managers can also use the budget to evaluate their own performance and clarify how close they are to meeting agreed performance targets.

ACCA marking scheme

		Marks
(a)	Sales and raw materials	1
	Direct labour and variable overheads	1
	Fixed overheads	1
	Flexed budget	1
		4
(b)	Raw material total cost variance	1
	Direct labour total cost variance	1
	Fixed overhead absorption rate	1
	Fixed overhead efficiency variance	2
	Fixed overhead capacity variance	2
	Fixed overhead expenditure variance	1
		8

(c)	Raw material total cost variance	2
	Fixed overhead efficiency variance	2
	Fixed overhead expenditure variance	2
		6
(d)	Up to 3 marks per key function discussed	9
	Maximum	7
Total		25

49 BRK

(a) Calculation of standard profit

Budgeted machine hours = (10,000 × 0·3) + (13,000 × 0·6) + (9,000 × 0·8) = 18,000 hours

Overhead absorption rate = 81,000/18,000 = £4·50 per machine hour

Product	*B* (£)	*R* (£)	*K* (£)
Direct material	5.40 (3 × 1.80)	4.10 (1.25 × 3.28)	4.85 (1.94 × 2.50)
Direct labour	3.25 (0.5 × 6.50)	5.20 (0.8 × 6.50)	4.55 (0.7 × 6.50)
Fixed production overhead	1.35 (0.3 × 4.50)	2.70 (0.6 × 4.50)	3.60 (0.8 × 4.50)
Standard cost	10.00	12.00	13.00
Selling price	14.00	15.00	18.00
Standard profit	4.00	3.00	5.00

Budgeted sales quantity in standard mix at standard profit:

Product	*Quantity*	*Standard profit*	£
B	10,000	£4	40,000
R	13,000	£3	39,000
K	9,000	£5	45,000
	32,000		124,000

Average standard profit per unit = 124,000/32,000 = £3·875 per unit

Actual sales quantity in actual mix at actual selling price less standard cost:

Product	*Quantity*	*Actual selling price less standard cost*	£
B	9,500	(14.5 – 10.0)	42,750
R	13,500	(15.5 – 12.0)	47,250
K	8,500	(19.0 – 13.0)	51,000
	31,500		141,000

Actual sales quantity in actual mix at standard profit:

Product	*Quantity*	*Standard profit*	£
B	9,500	£4	38,000
R	13,500	£3	40,500
K	8,500	£5	42,500
	31,500		121,000

Actual sales quantity in standard mix at standard profit:

Using the average standard profit per unit calculated earlier: 31,500 x 3·875 = £122,062

Sales price variance = 141,000 – 121,000 = £20,000 (F)
Sales volume profit variance = 121,000 – 124,000 = £3,000 (A)
Sales mix profit variance = 121,000 – 122,062 = £1,062 (A)
Sales quantity profit variance = 122,062 – 124,000 = £1,938 (A)

Reconciliation	£	£	£
Budgeted sales at standard profit			124,000
Sales price variance		20,000 (F)	
Sales mix profit variance	1,062 (A)		
Sales quantity profit variance	1,938 (A)		
Sales volume profit variance		3,000 (A)	
			17,000 (F)
Actual sales at actual price less standard cost			141,000

(b) The sales mix profit variance explains how the change in sales mix contributed to the sales volume profit variance. It compares the actual sales quantity in the actual mix with the actual sales quantity in the standard mix, valued at the standard profit per unit.

The adverse variance calculated in part (a) using the average standard profit per unit was £1,062, indicating that the actual sales mix contained more lower-margin products and fewer higher-margin products. The changes in the sales mix can be shown in tabular form, as follows.

Product	*Standard mix*	*Actual mix*	*Difference*	*Standard profit*	£
B	9,844	9,500	(344)	£4	1,376 (A)
R	12,797	13,500	703	£3	2,109 (F)
K	8,859	8,500	(359)	£5	1,795 (A)
	31,500	31,500			1,062 (A)

The difference column shows that more of Product R, with the lowest standard profit of £3 per unit, was sold than was budgeted for. Less of Products B and K, with the higher standard profits per unit, were sold than budgeted for. Calculation of the individual mix variances for Products B, R and K does not offer information which is any more useful than that contained in the 'difference' column.

Sales mix profit variance has significance only when products are inter-related and these relationships are taken into account at the planning stage. If the products sold are not inter-related, the mix variance offers no useful information, since it incorrectly implies that a possible cause of the sales volume profit variance is a change in the mix1. In fact, only deviations from the planned volumes for individual products need to be investigated if products are not inter-related. In this case the products are substitutes and so are inter-related. The individual sales mix profit variances may therefore be useful.

(c) A standard costing system requires preparation of standard costs, comparison of standard costs with actual costs, investigation of variances and instigation of corrective action if needed, and review of standard costs on a regular basis. Standard costs are predetermined unit costs arising under efficient operating conditions. Standard costing can be applied to repetitive or common operations where the input to produce a required output can be clearly specified.

Preparation of standard costs

Standards are required for amount of materials, labour and services required to perform a particular operation, and cost standards are compiled from the standard costs of the individual operations needed to produce a given product. The quantities and costs needed for each standard can be derived using the engineering approach or through the analysis of historical records.

The engineering approach requires a detailed study of each operation so that the materials, labour and equipment used in the operation can be verified by observation, for example by using time and motion studies.

Analysis of historical records can be carried out using quantitative analysis, including the high-low method, scattergraphs and regression analysis. Standards are set by these methods by averaging historical data and so there is a danger that past inefficiencies may be perpetuated. This approach to standard setting is widely used in practice[2].

Variance analysis

Variances obtained by comparing standard costs with actual costs form the basis of cost control and support the use of responsibility accounting. A wide range of variances can be calculated, depending in part on the costing system employed. The causes of individual variances can be investigated if a variance is deemed to be significant, in order to inform the instigation of appropriate corrective action where necessary. Both favourable and adverse variances should be investigated, since useful information can be derived from both.

Review of standard costs

Standard costs must be reviewed and updated if they are to retain their relevance to an organisation. The review should consider changes in the prices of inputs such as labour and materials as well as changes in working practices and production methods. The exception to this is the basic standard, which is left unchanged for long periods of time so that trends over time can be established. However, basic standards are not commonly used. It is more usual to find ideal, current and attainable standards being used and these all need regular review.

ACCA marking scheme

		Marks	
(a)	Overhead absorption rate	1	
	Standard costs and standard profits	3	
	Sales price variance	2	
	Sales volume profit variance	2	
	Sales mix profit variance	2	
	Sales quantity profit variance	2	
	Profit reconciliation	1	
			13
(b)	Significance of sales mix profit variance	3	
	Comment on individual mix variances	1	
			4
(c)	Elements of a standard costing system	2-3	
	Preparation of standard costs	2-3	
	Variance analysis	2-3	
	Review of standards	2-3	
	Maximum		8
Total			25

BUDGETING, BUDGETARY CONTROL AND DECISION-MAKING

50 ALL PREMIER SERVICES PLC

(a) (i)

	X	*Y*	*Z*
Number of beds	60	40	45
Fee per bed per night £	225	200	170
Assumed occupancy %	65	80	100
Occupied beds	39	32	45
Number of nights per week	7	7	7

Budgeted profit and loss statement per week

	X	*Y*	*Z*	*Total*
Occupied beds	39	32	45	
	£	£	£	£
Income *(see working 1)*	61,425	44,800	53,550	159,775
Variable costs (*working 2*)	16,305	11,892	14,215	42,412
Fixed costs (60:40:45) – *working 3*	52,676	35,117	39,507	127,300
Total costs	68,981	47,009	53,772	169,712
Income less costs	(7,556)	(2,209)	(172)	(9,937)
Cost per occupied bed	1,769	1,469	1,194	

Workings

(W1) *Income*

X: 39 beds × £225/night × 7 nights = £61,425

Y: 32 beds × £200/night × 7 nights = £44,800

Z: 45 beds × £170/night × 7 nights = £53,550

(W2) *Variable costs*

Total variable costs = £42,412.

Total income = £159,775.

Variable costs are therefore 0.26544829 of income.

(W3) *Fixed costs*

Fixed costs = £127,300/145 beds = £877.931/bed.

(ii)

	X	*Y*	*Z*
Number of beds	60	40	75
Fee per bed per night £	225	200	170
Assumed occupancy %	80	95	100
Occupied beds	48	38	75
Number of night per week	7	7	7
Price per bed per night	£336	£266	£525

Budgeted profit and loss statement per week

	X	*Y*	*Z*	*Total*
Income *(working 4)*	75,600	53,200	89,250	218,050
Variable costs (*working 5*)	20,068	14,122	23,691	57,881
Fixed costs (*working 6*)	43,646	29,097	54,557	127,300
Total costs	63,714	43,219	78,248	185,181
Income less costs	11,886	9,982	11,002	32,869
Cost per occupied bed	1,327	1,137	1,043	

Workings

(W4) *Income*

X: 48 beds × £225/night × 7 nights = £75,600

Y: 38 beds × £200/night × 7 nights = £53,200

Z: 75 beds × £170/night × 7 nights = £89,250

(W5) *Variable costs*

Total variable costs = £57,881.

Total income = £218,050.

Variable costs are therefore 0.26544829 of income.

(W6) *Fixed costs*

Total number of beds = 60 + 40 + 75 = 175.

Fixed costs = £127,300/175 beds = £727.4286/bed.

(b) (i) **Ward Z patients from Wards X and Y**

The patients in Ward Z are existing patients and do not represent new admissions. For that reason, Ward Z only exists as a further outlet for Wards X and Y. This implies a degree of dependency in operations. Decisions concerning Ward Z cannot therefore be separated from the decisions concerning X and Y. It may well be the case that, given the hospital is private and presumably subject to competition, patients may choose All Premier Services because of the facilities offered in Ward Z that might be available elsewhere.

(ii) **The relevance of the allocation bases**

Given that fixed overheads must be incurred irrespective of occupancy, then the fact that costs are allocated to unoccupied beds, irrespective of occupancy, is probably the correct approach. On the other hand, variable overheads are allocated on a fee earned per bed basis. The incorporation of fees into the allocation of variable overheads might reflect the fact that wards X and Y deal with patients with different medical conditions and costs. The fees charged by the hospital reflect this fact. The adjustment for occupancy through the fees earned allocation base reflects the fact that variable overheads relate directly to the consumption of additional resources when beds are occupied. For this reason, it is probably an appropriate allocation base.

(c) The characteristics of a **responsibility accounting system** imply a well-organised system of budgetary control, such that individuals are personally accountable for their budget centres and there is a monitoring system which facilitates performance evaluation. The components of a well-organised system of control are:

1 A **hierarchy of budget centres** which mirror the lines of reporting within an organisation.

2 A **defined purpose to the budget centre** such that attached costs and revenues have an interpretation associated with the budget centre. Thus, if costs are

rising in catering services and this is a budget centre, then a course of action can be devised which outlines alternatives to the way current catering facilities are delivered.

3 **Cost and revenues** associated with a budget centre then become **the responsibility of the budget holder** to the extent that the budget holder can influence how the costs and revenues behave.

The **difficulties associated with non-profit organisations** are that the requirements for responsibility accounting are not easily met. For example:

1 Non-profit organisations often do not have clearly defined objectives or the objectives may be multiple. For example, local government offers a wide range of public services for which there are only fairly imprecise objectives. To the extent that objectives are unclear, then responsibility will be hard to define because there is no clear link between inputs and outputs (objectives).

2 Many non-profit making organisations do not charge for their services and hence budget centres are then left monitoring rather that controlling costs. For example, hospital resources are consumed according to clinical decisions, but budget holders are often not medical staff.

3 Value for money performance measures are sometimes used in the public sector that rely on measures relating to economy and efficiency. Whilst economy and efficiency may be measured in money terms, effectiveness may not be. Thus, non-financial objectives may be set off which may not be comparable between budget centres or to any overall objective.

4 Public services are often characterised by a high level of fixed costs over which there is little discretion or room to change. Hence, responsibility is harder to define because change is difficult to implement

ACCA marking scheme

			Marks	
(a)	(i)	calculation of costs incurred per bed in each ward	5	
	(ii)	calculation of costs incurred per bed in each ward	5	
				10
(b)	(i)	detailed comment that ward z is serviced from wards x and y	2	
	(ii)	detailed comment of relevance of allocation bases	3	
				5
(c)		Up to 2 marks each for detailed points on responsibility accounting.	6	
		Up to 2 marks each for detailed points on non-profit organisations	6	
		Presentation and quality of argument	2	
		Maximum marks available	14	
		Maximum marks awarded		10
Total				25

51 ACRED LIMITED

Key answer points

Part (a) of the question calls for a lot of calculations and a clear presentation of the budgeted figures. You need to be well-organised to complete the solution within the time available. Note that part (a) of the question is worth just 13 marks, only one half of the total marks for the question. You should therefore beware of spending too much time getting the figures right in part (a) leaving yourself insufficient time to answer part (b) – which should be reasonably straightforward to answer.

(a) (i) **Acred Ltd: Production budget for 6 months to end of December 20X4**

	July	*Aug*	*Sept*	*Oct*	*Nov*	*Dec*
	units	units	units	units	units	units
Sales	10,000	11,000	12,000	13,000	14,000	15,000
Stock increase	200	200	200	200	200	0
Production	10,200	11,200	12,200	13,200	14,200	15,000

(ii) **Acred Ltd: Cash budget for 6 months to end of December 20X4**

	July	*Aug*	*Sept*	*Oct*	*Nov*	*Dec*
	£	£	£	£	£	£
Receipts (W2)						
Cash sales	30,000	33,000	36,000	39,000	42,000	45,000
Credit sales	90,000	90,000	99,000	108,000	117,000	126,000
	120,000	123,000	135,000	147,000	159,000	171,000
Payments						
Materials (W3)	48,480	51,360	56,160	60,960	65,760	70,080
Labour (W4)	18,360	20,160	21,960	23,760	25,560	27,000
Direct expenses (W5)	12,240	13,440	14,640	15,840	17,040	18,000
Fixed o'hds (W6)	22,000	22,000	22,000	22,000	22,000	22,000
Advertising	-	95,000	-	-	-	-
Interest	-	-	30,000	-	-	-
	101,080	201,960	144,760	122,560	130,360	137,080
Receipts less payments	18,920	(78,960)	(9,760)	24,440	28,640	33,920
Opening cash	50,000	68,920	(10,040)	(19,800)	4,640	33,280
Closing cash	68,920	(10,040)	(19,800)	4,640	33,280	67,200

Workings

(W1) **Sales budget for 6 months to end of December 20X4**

	June	*July*	*Aug*	*Sept*	*Oct*	*Nov*	*Dec*
Sales (units)	10,000	10,000	11,000	12,000	13,000	14,000	15,000
Sales price	£12	£12	£12	£12	£12	£12	£12
Revenue (£)	120,000	120,000	132,000	144,000	156,000	168,000	180,000

(W2) **Sales receipts**

	June	*July*	*Aug*	*Sept*	*Oct*	*Nov*	*Dec*
Sales revenue	120,000	120,000	132,000	144,000	156,000	168,000	180,000
Cash sales (25%)	30,000	30,000	33,000	36,000	39,000	42,000	45,000
Credit sales (75%)	90,000	90,000	99,000	108,000	117,000	126,000	135,000

(W3) **Material purchases**

	June	*July*	*Aug*	*Sept*	*Oct*	*Nov*	*Dec*
Production (units)	10,000	10,200	11,200	12,200	13,200	14,200	15,000
Materials for production (kg)	20,000	20,400	22,400	24,400	26,400	28,400	30,000

	£	£	£	£	£	£	£
Materials for production	48,000	48,960	53,760	58,560	63,360	68,160	72,000
Half delivered in month	24,000	24,480	26,880	29,280	31,680	34,080	
Closing stock delivered	24,480	26,880	29,280	31,680	34,080	36,000	
Total purchases in month	48,480	51,360	56,160	60,960	65,760	70,080	
Payable in	July	Aug	Sept	Oct	Nov	Dec	

(W4) **Payments for labour**

Calculation of labour cost: production units × £1·80 per unit

(W5) **Payments for direct expenses**

Calculation of direct expenses: production units × £1·20 per unit

(W6) **Payments for fixed overheads**

Calculation of cash fixed overheads: £34,000 – £12,000 = £22,000 per month

Depreciation is excluded as a non-cash item.

(b) A **periodic budget** is one that is drawn up for a full budget period, such as one year. A new budget will not be introduced until the start of the next budget period, although the existing budget may be revised if circumstances deviate markedly from those assumed during the budget preparation period.

A **continuous or rolling budget** is one that is revised at regular intervals by adding a new budget period to the full budget as each budget period expires. A budget for one year, for example, could have a new quarter added to it as each quarter expires. In this way, the budget will continue to look one year forward. Cash budgets are often prepared on a continuous basis.

The advantages of periodic budgeting are that it involves less time, money and effort than continuous budgeting. For example, frequent revisions of standards could be avoided and the budget-setting process would require managerial attention only on an annual basis.

A major advantage of continuous budgeting is that the budget remains both relevant and up to date. As it takes account of significant changes in economic activity and other key elements of the organisation's environment, it will be a realistic budget and hence is likely to be more motivating to responsible staff. Another major advantage is that there will always be a budget available that shows the expected financial performance for several future budget periods.

It has been suggested that if a periodic budget is updated whenever significant change is expected, a continuous budget would not be necessary. Continuous budgeting could be used where regular change is expected, or where forward planning and control are essential, such as in a cash budget.

(c) **Budget bias (budgetary slack)** occurs when managers aim to give themselves easier budget targets by understating budgeted sales revenue or overstating budgeted costs.

Cost control using budgets is achieved by comparing actual costs for a budget period with budgeted or planned costs. Significant differences between planned and actual costs can then be investigated and corrective action taken where appropriate.

Budget bias will lead to more favourable results when actual and budgeted costs are compared. Corrective action may not be taken in cases where costs could have been reduced and in consequence inefficiency will be perpetuated and overall profitability reduced.

Managers may incur unnecessary expenditure in order to protect existing budget bias with the aim of making their jobs easier in future periods, since if the bias were detected and removed, future budget targets would be more difficult to achieve. Unnecessary costs will reduce the effectiveness of cost control in supporting the achievement of financial objectives such as value for money or profitability.

Where budget bias exists, managers will be less motivated to look for ways of reducing costs and inefficiency in those parts of the organisation for which they bear responsibility. The organisation's costs will consequently be higher than necessary for the level of performance being budgeted for.

ACCA marking scheme

			Marks
(a)	(i)	Sales budget	1
		Stock increase	1
		Production budget	1
	(ii)	Cash sales	1
		Credit sales	1
		Material costs	3
		Labour costs	1
		Direct expenses and overheads	1
		Marketing expenditure	1
		Interest payment	1
		Closing balance	1
			13
(b)		Discussion of periodic budgeting	3
		Discussion of continuous budgeting	4
			7
(c)		Meaning of budget bias	1
		Cost control	1
		Consequences of budget bias	3
			5
Total			25

52 PRIVATE HOSPITAL

(a) **For the year to 31 May 20X3:**

Actual patient days = £4.4 million/£200 per day = 22,000.

Bed occupancy = 22,000/(80 beds × 365 days) = 0.75 or 75%.

Profit/(Loss) statement	£	£	£
Total revenue			4,400,000
Variable costs			1,100,000
			3,300,000
Personnel:			
Supervisors	4 × £22,000 =	88,000	
Nurses	13 × £16,000 =	208,000	
Assistants	24 × £12,000 =	288,000	(584,000)
Fixed charges			(1,650,000)
Profit			1,066,000

In the statement above, the number of patient days exceeded 20,500, so personnel costs are as shown. If the number of patient days is less than 20,500, personnel costs would be:

(4 × £22,000) + (10 × £16,000) + (20 × £12,000) = £488,000.

$$\text{Break-even point(s)} = \frac{\text{Fixed costs}}{\text{Contribution per patient day}}$$

Fixed costs consist of fixed charges and personnel costs for the bands of patient days shown in the question. The **contribution per patient day is £150**, being the charge per day of £200 less the variable cost of £50 per day.

Given the stepped nature of the staffing costs there are three break-even levels which can be calculated.

Two are shown below.

(1) 14,254 patient days [= (£1,650,000 + £488,000)/£150], and

(2) 14,893 patient days [= (£1,650,000 + £584,000)/£150]

Examiner's note

Just two break-even points are shown above. The third, and highest, is shown below for reference, but since it is unlikely to apply for the year to May 20X3, it is not required as part of the answer to (a).

15,427 patient days [= (£1,650,000 + £664,000)/£150].

(b) The changes for the year to 31 May 20X4 are 20 extra beds occupied for 100 days. This has implications for bed capacity and for the patient days, and thus for the variable and fixed costs charged and the personnel employed.

Budget for year to 31 May 20X4:

Revised patient days = 22,000 + (100 × 20) = 24,000

Bed occupancy = 24,000/(100 beds × 365 days) = 0.66 or 66%.

It is assumed that since fixed costs are charged on bed capacity, the amount of apportioned fixed costs will now increase by a factor of × 100/80, from £1,650,000 to £2,062,500.

Revised Profit/(Loss) statement

		£	£
Total revenue			4,800,000
Variable costs			1,200,000
			3,600,000
Personnel			
Supervisors	4 × £24,200	96,800	
Nurses	15 × £17,600	264,000	
Assistants	28 × £13,200	369,600	
			(730,400)
Fixed charges	100/80 × £1,650,000		(2,062,500)
Profit			807,100

Required profit to achieve same profit as in (a) = £1,066,000.

Required contribution = (£1,066,000 + £730,400 + £2,062,500) = £3,858,900

Contribution per patient day = £150.

Required patient days = (£3,858,900/£150) = 25,726 days per year in 20X4 to achieve the same profit as in 20X3. This calculation uses the highest level of staffing costs.

(c) In the year to May 20X3, the bed occupancy for 100 days was 100% (i.e. 8,000 patient days) and for the remaining 265 days it was 66% (22,000-8,000)/(265 days × 80 beds). Attempting to deal with the 100 days extra demand with 20 extra beds would reduce the overall occupancy from 75% to 66%. To cater for the 2,000 patient days demanded, an extra number of potential patient days of 7,300 (365 × 20) were provided. This usage rate of 27% is a little unrealistic for this business. The extra fixed costs of bed capacity and extra costs of personnel (including the higher employment costs) exceed the extra contribution from patients by £258,900 which shows as a reduction in profit.

If the paediatric unit proceed to provide 2,000 extra patient days in this way, it will suffer a reduced profit of almost 25% after covering the increased employment costs and fixed overhead apportionment. It would have to achieve another 1,726 patient days per year, above the level anticipated for the year to May 20X4, to attain the profit level reported in May 20X3. It could accept the profit reduction in the interests of meeting its other objectives of patient and social welfare, but for a private sector company this seems unlikely. It would require a significant increase in patient occupancy to regain the profit position, assuming no further changes to costs.

A possible alternative course of action would be to account for bed occupancy differently, being more flexible and charging for part of a year. That may involve having beds available to move to areas of high demand as the occasion arises. Alternatively, the hospital could decide to de-emphasise the net profit measure because of the influence of fixed costs, and **focus on contribution rather than profit**. Achieving the 2,000 extra patient days would increase the contribution after personnel costs of £153,600. But this would have the disadvantage of not highlighting the efficient occupation of beds in this unit or, no doubt throughout the whole hospital, which could have adverse repercussions on overall profitability.

Attention to improved planning of bed occupancy could offer improvements in terms of increasing overall occupancy. One option, if not already undertaken, would be to prioritise demand for the paediatric unit when it has no empty beds available. This would involve treating the most urgent cases first, rather than first come first served, leaving less urgent cases until demand has fallen away during the remaining 265 days. This would not alter the fact that people were waiting for admission (or the size of the waiting list), though to the extent it was not adopted before, arguably it would improve the overall welfare of society.

(d) Any business will have a variety of objectives. Some of these will be orientated towards **financial aspects**, for example, achieving sufficient profitability to enable an adequate return to shareholders or staying within a financial budget allocation of revenue. **Social objectives** involve provision of an adequate level of public health and welfare, safety and security education opportunities, and so on.

For many businesses, there is likely to be a conflict between financial and social aspects. In other words, greater financial return can be achieved only at the expense of poorer social provision of the reduced change of meeting social objectives. Alternatively, improved social provision is possible, but the chance of achieving financial objectives may be compromised. This is where management judgement is often needed in balancing the trade-off between these objectives in any given situation.

In the provision of health care, improved quality of care or shorter waiting lists can be achieved if more public sector funding is provided or, in the private sector business, if a smaller profit is earned or higher prices are charged. In education likewise, more can always be spent on employing more teachers, reducing class sizes and improving education, but this will add considerably to the costs incurred. The private sector will generally make provision only where it will achieve adequate financial return. Some aspects of social provision can be perceived to be so important that they are provided by the government, because they are unlikely to be provided in entirety by a profit-seeking business.

ACCA marking scheme		
		Marks
(a)	Patient days	1
	Occupancy	1
	Profit/loss	2
	Break-even number(s)	2
		6
(b)	Patient days	1
	Occupancy	1
	Profit/loss	2
	Required patient days	1
		5
(c)	Each developed point 2 marks, up to a maximum of:	6
(d)	Objectives	1
	Conflict	1
	Example	1
		3
Total		20

53 PUBLIC SECTOR ORGANISATION

(a) **Budget preparation**

It would be in line with the principles of modern management if the department manager was encouraged to participate more in setting the budget. In this way, he would be more likely to show commitment to the organisational goals in general and the budget in particular. He is closer to the activity for which the budget is prepared, and so the relevance and accuracy of the budget should be improved. This involvement should extend also to discussion of the form and frequency of the reporting which is to take place for his/her department.

Activity volume

The volume of visits undertaken is 20% greater than that budgeted. It is inappropriate to compare the actual costs of visiting 12,000 clients with a budget for 10,000 clients. Costs such as wages, travel expenses and consumables would be expected to be higher than the fixed budget in these circumstances.

One way to deal with this is to adjust or flex the budget to acknowledge the cost implications of the higher number of visits, or to be aware of it when making any comparison. If a factor of 1.20 is applied to the overall wages budget for permanent and casual staff (i.e. on the assumption that it is a variable cost), the flexed budget £5,040 (£4,200 × 1.2) is greater than the actual cost of £4,900. Taking a similar approach to travel expenses and consumables expenses:

- actual travel expenses are exactly in line with the flexed budget (1,500 × 1.20), but
- the consumables costs seem to be highly overspent (4,000 × on it difficult to predict.

To circulate a report as originally constructed seems to highlight and publicise some invalid comparisons on which inappropriate conclusions may be drawn. It is recommended that for cost control purposes, a report is prepared which compares actual spending with a flexible budget based on the actual activity. This would require an estimate of the variable, fixed and semi-variable nature of the cost items.

Controllability

It is possible to question whether all the costs shown need to feature in the report. For example, the allocated administrative costs and equipment depreciation are book entries which do not directly affect the department and are not likely to be controllable by employees of the department. There are, therefore, adverse variances on the report contributing to the overall overspend which are not the responsibility of the departmental manager. The difference between actual and budgeted cost of administration serves no useful purpose in this report, because the manager can take no action to directly influence this. The only justification to include this is if the manager can bring about some pressure to reduce this spending by someone else.

It may be unwise to adopt the guide of a 5% deviation to judge variances. The key is whether a cost is out of control and can be corrected by managerial action. Also, 5% of some values can be significant whilst on others 5% of the total cost might be of little consequence.

Funding allocation

The Director is correct in pointing out that 'the department must live within its funding allocation'. It is not like a commercial organisation where more output can result in more revenue and hence more money to spend. Increased funding will only be achieved if this organisation and the department is allocated more funds as a result of national or local government decisions to support an increase in services.

It would be appropriate for the funding allocation to be compared with the flexible budget (based on actual activity) to encourage the managers to be aware of and live within the budget allocation. Ways can always be found to spend more money, and so authority structures must be in place to ensure that requests to spend have been budgeted and appropriately funded. Hence the organisational arrangements which authorised the increased visits would be examined.

The nature of the activity for which the budget is being developed should not be lost sight of. It is more complex to deal with budget decisions related to the welfare needs of society than those for a typical manufacturing firm. There are no clear input-output relationships in the former, and hence it is difficult to judge what is justifiable spending for the department compared with other departments and public sector organisations.

Other aspects

One possible outcome from discussion over the appropriate form of report would be the use of **non-financial measures**. The total staff hours worked, client satisfaction and size of the potential client population are all examples of extensions to the reporting procedure which would help to place the results in context.

The style of the approach adopted by the Director may show some lack of behavioural insight. The despatch of a memo to deal with a prototype report may result in lower staff morale and increased tension in the Homecare department. This may lead to inappropriate future decisions on spending and budget 'game playing' within the department. It may, of course, be a conscious decision of the Director to place the manager in the position of having to reduce spending to the allocated level.

Although this is the first month's report, in the future it may be helpful to use an additional column of the report to show the **year-to-date figures**. This would help to **identify trends** and assist discussion of whether costs are being controlled over the longer term. To show future results for only one month may be insufficient; for example, the repairs to equipment may not follow a regular pattern and this would be revealed if cumulative data existed.

(b) Traditional budgeting, sometimes called incremental budgeting, takes a current level of spending as a starting point. Discussion then takes place on any extra expenditure or what, of the current expenditure, to cut. **Zero Based Budgeting (ZBB)** is an approach which takes nothing for granted, and which requires justification of all expenditure. This technique would not suit expenditure planning in line departments of a manufacturing company because clear relationships of input and output will exist and be defined by standard values. In less clearly defined areas such as service departments or non-profit orientated businesses, ZBB might have some value if selectively applied.

ZBB would involve describing all of the organisation's activities in a series of **decision packages**, for example, visit frequency, level of eligibility for visit, type of support (medical care, food preparation, wash and clean, shopping needs etc). The **packages can then be evaluated and ranked**: what is essential, highly desirable, desirable and so on. The resources would be allocated according to the packages selected, discussion could also take place between other departments so that a wider allocation of funding is brought into the discussion. Once the budget is set the packages are adopted up to the spending level indicated, this is the cut-off point.

It is possible that economies and increased efficiency could result if departments were to justify all the expenditure, and not just incremental expenditure. It is argued that if expenditure were examined on a cost/benefit basis, a more rational allocation of resources would take place. Such an approach would force managers to make plans and **prioritise their activities** before committing themselves to the budget. It should achieve a more structured involvement of departmental management and should improve the quality of decisions and management information, enabling such questions as: Should this be done?, At what quality/quantity?, Should it be done this way?, What should it cost?

ZBB may not be simple and easy to install, could be expensive in time and effort to analyse all expenditure and difficult to establish priorities for the activities or decision packages. Managers are often reluctant to commit themselves to ZBB because they believe they already do it. Critics of ZBB have asserted that no real change in funding allocation takes place as a result of the exercise. However, any system which encourages managers to examine, and communicate about, their spending and performance levels must be useful providing it does not prevent individuals fulfilling their other duties and responsibilities.

54 ZERO BASED BUDGETING

Introduction

(a) Zero Based Budgeting (ZBB) is a method of budgeting that re-examines, at each budgeting exercise, whether the budgeted activity is to be funded at any level. Hence, the budgeting exercise begins at a **zero or nil cost base**. It is a device that is particularly useful when an organisation is unsure if its costs are at the most efficient levels. Most efficient costs are not the same as minimum levels, since very low costs might impinge on service or product quality. The purpose of ZBB is to overcome inefficient forms of budgeting that might lead to **slack practices**, which consume more resources than the most effective and efficient organisations face.

(b) There are a series of steps that would ordinarily be taken in order to implement an effective ZBB system.

The questioning of why expenditure needs to be incurred

The development of a questioning attitude to activities that incur costs is the first step to ensuring that costs are kept to most efficient levels. It is important to recall that ZBB, in the short term, can only change costs over which the organisation has short-term control. Longer-term, or period costs, can only be changed over a longer horizon. Taxes and other regulatory costs cannot be the focus of ZBB because they are difficult to influence.

Thus ZBB can be immediately effective where costs can be related to identifiable activities. The questions that might emerge in such situations are as follows:

Can costs associated with an activity be isolated? If costs cannot be identified to a particular activity to a degree that provides management with confidence that they can change the costs then there is little point in applying ZBB techniques to the cost.

An even more basic question is to ask how important the activity is to the business and what, if the costs can be identified, is the total cost saving that might result should the activity be stopped. In this respect, it is important to identify effects on costs elsewhere in the business. If the activity to be stopped absorbed fixed costs, then the fixed costs will have to be re-apportioned without absorption to the activity that is to be stopped. Moreover, there may be joint costs such that stopping one activity may have an uncertain effect on joint costs incurred with another activity.

Is the activity in question the cheapest way of providing the service or contribution to production? Thus, it is important not to ask simply if the costs relating to the activity are the most efficient, but are there alternatives that might reduce costs still further and still maintain a given level of service or production.

A more fundamental question about conducting ZBB processes is whether the benefits of employing ZBB outweigh the costs. It is important to appreciate that conducting a ZBB exercise is not a costless process if, as will inevitably be the case, management time is consumed.

How a decision is made as to which activities should be provided with a budget?

Budgeted activities should be capable of being monitored and controlled. If an activity is recognised as a budget centre, and is going to be subject to a ZBB process, then it is important that management undertake the task of monitoring costs in relation to activity and taking corrective action when appropriate. Thus, if an activity consumes resources and is capable of being monitored and controlled then it should be provided with a budget. This will then make the activity subject to ZBB processes.

'Decision packages' are sometimes referred to in the context of ZBB and activities. These relate to how activities can be described when thinking about how ZBB can be used to judge an activity. There are two types of decision activity:

1. **Mutually exclusive decisions**: When ZBB assessments are made of an activity, alternative courses of action are sometimes benchmarked against existing activities. A choice is then made over which activity might be the preferable course of action. The preferred choice will involve budgeted information, but may also involve other factors such as product quality and service level provision.

2. **Incremental decisions**: ZBB assessments are often related to the level of activity within a budget centre. Thus, there will be a minimum level of activity that provides the essential level of product or service. This is often referred to as the **'base' activity**. Further levels of activity are then incremental and, subject to correctly identifying and isolating the variable costs related to an activity, ZBB assessments can be made separately of both the base and the incremental activities. This division might then provide management with an understanding of the degree of flexibility the organisation has.

What questions should be asked when budgeted activities need to be ranked to allocate scarce resources?

The allocation of scarce resources is a key management task. Scarce resources will have to be allocated to the activities of a business in terms of providing appropriate labour and materials, along with any other costs related to an activity. Whilst ZBB is most often applied to support activities the technique can also be applied to a production process.

Some sorting of **ranking** will have to be applied in order to determine which activities are funded by a budget against those that are not. The key question for budgeting purposes relates to:

1 defining the appropriate decision package (as described above)

2 the importance of the activity in relation to the organisation in terms of:

   – support for the organisation's objective (for example, maximising shareholder wealth)

   – support for other service or product activities

3 how the ranking system is to be used:

   – are all activities to be funded above a certain rank, or

   – is there a scaling of funds allocated against funds requested as determined by the rank, or

   – is there a combination of methods?

Essentially, a judgement has to be made by management of the benefit of the activity to the organisation. Theoretically, this is best achieved by determining deprival value. In practice, deprival values are difficult tools and some level of arbitrary judgement has to take place in which non-financial factors might play a significant role.

(c) **Critical assessment of the use of Zero Based Budgeting as a tool that might be used to motivate employees**

The motivation of employees is one of the most difficult tasks facing management since the problems are complex and not always referable to financial performance indicators. To the extent that employees are not responsive to financial performance indicators then ZBB is going to be less effective as a device to motivate employees.

The problem of employee motivation is one of achieving goal congruence with the organisational objectives. ZBB can be useful in this respect as a method of tackling the problem of incentivising employees to achieve targeted performance when a clear understanding of the activities and their related decision packages is essential for the management tasks of monitoring and controlling an activity.

In this respect ZBB has the following advantages

1 It ensures that only forward looking objectives are addressed. This limits the potential for historical abuses in budget-setting to be established. Employees can be set targets that are consistent with the future objectives of the organisation.

2 Building 'budget slack' is minimised because, in principle, the entire costs of an activity are reviewed at each budget-setting stage. Employees are then set realistic targets that relate to activity levels that are the most efficient.

3 Managers are made to understand, as part of the ZBB process, the activity itself. This reduces tension between those who decide (management) and those who have to implement manager decisions. Claims that management do not really understand the nature of an activity are thus reduced.

4 ZBB encourages flexibility in employees since they know that, potentially, activities may be stopped. Flexibility induces goal consistency by enabling incentive schemes to reflect activity. In other words, employees are more likely to be responsive to management directives if they are aware and trust that the

budget setting process encourages and supports payments that are responsive to flexibility.

(d) **The advantages of encouraging employee participation in budget-setting**

Generally, participative budget-setting will result in:

1 An informed budget-setting process, such that management are aware of the detail of budgeted activities as provided by the people who work daily within the budgeted activity.

2 Avoiding the criticism that budgets are unrealistic.

3 Reducing the adverse effects of budget imposition when difficult management decisions have to be made (e.g. staff reduction).

4 Employees become aware and more involved in the management activities of the organisations. To the extent that they become more aware, then a greater understanding of the needs of the organisation as a whole is reached.

5 Co-ordination within an activity might be improved. If activities are jointly budgeted, or are part of the same process, then co-ordination between activities might be improved.

6 Budgetary slack may be reduced as management become more aware of the operational activities within an activity.

7 Achievable budgets are more likely to be set.

8 When budgets are not met management are more likely to have a deeper knowledge of the operational issues involved.

9 There is less risk that budgets will be undermined by subordinates.

ACCA marking scheme

			Marks
(a)	2 marks for references to budgetary slack/ efficient costs		4
(b)	2 marks for each point relating to framing questions	up to 3	
	2 for references to decision packages	up to 3	
	For reference to importance of activity to organisation	2	
	For reference to ranking	2	
	Available	10	
	Maximum awarded		8
(c)	Up to 2 marks for each detailed point on motivation		6
(d)	1 mark for each detailed point on advantages of ZBB	max	7
Total			25

55 ROLLING BUDGETS

Key answer tips

In part (a), even if you can't remember exactly what a rolling budget is, the question itself makes this fairly clear. Give a concise explanation of how such a budget is prepared, and then think about its advantages - again, even if you haven't specifically learnt these, you should be able to come up with some common sense ideas.

In part (b) in the introduction to the data in the question, it refers to 'the cost behaviour' of each cost item. This should alert you to the possibility that some will be fixed costs (which should be obvious), some will be purely variable (change proportionately with volume) and some will be semi-variable (change with volume, though not proportionately). You thus need to determine the fixed and variable elements of the costs from the Q1 to Q3 data, and apply these to Q4.

In part (c) this budget is prepared for three different production levels, using the Q4 unit and fixed costs computed in (b). Note that as the stock adjustment is at a standard cost, not necessarily matching that used in valuing Q4 production, you cannot simply use the sales volume to get cost of sales directly.

In part (d), given both the requirement to produce your answer in summary form only and the number of marks you have for this and comment, you need to think before launching into long repetitious revised budgets. Basically, if you produce the extra 8,000 units instead of using stock, the profit will be charged with the extra actual variable cost instead of the standard full factory cost for these units. The difference between these costs gives you most of the profit difference. You then need to recognise the impact of the bonus - which helps with the discussion part that follows.

(a) Accounting budgets are typically prepared for the year ahead, each year being divided into months or quarters. A company can then monitor its progress as the year passes. A variation and extension of the annual budget is to regularly add a further quarter to a budget as the immediate quarter passes, so that a full budget year is always in view. This approach is called a **rolling or continuous budget**. As Q1 progresses, Q2 is reviewed and revised in some detail, at the same time the budget for the other quarters are reviewed and updated.

Benefits of this approach are that management can always have in front of them plans for a full year. This will emphasise the longer term focus of the organisation. It also ensures that managers are constantly thinking about planning for the future and the validity of these plans. It keeps planning at the front of the manager's mind all of the year, not just at the annual budget round. As a result of this it is likely that the actual performance is being compared with a more realistic target than if the budget was prepared only once a year.

(b) The costs are variable, semi-variable or fixed. It is necessary to determine the cost behaviour from Q1–Q3, then adjust this for Q4.

	Q1 – Q3		*Q4*		
	Variable costs	*Fixed costs*	*Variable costs*		*Fixed costs*
	£	£	£		£
Material (W1)	2.5	-	2.75		-
Labour (W2)	5.0	80,000	5.00		80,000
Factory overhead (W3)	1.5	140,000	1.50	(+ 5%)	147,000
Admin overhead	-	30,000	-		30,000
Selling overhead (W4)	0.5	20,000	0.50	(+ 5%)	21,000

Workings:

(W1)

Material Q1= $\frac{£50,000}{20,000}$ = £2.5 per unit in Q1 – Q3 Material costs will be10% higher in Q4, i.e. £2.75.

(W2) *Labour*

Calculate variable cost per unit and fixed labour costs using the high-low method.

	£
Total labour cost of 40,000 units	280,000
Total labour cost of 20,000 units	180,000
Variable labour cost of 20,000 units	100,000
Variable labour cost/unit	£5

Substituting:

	£
Total labour cost of 40,000 units	280,000
Variable labour cost of 40,000 units (× £5)	200,000
Fixed labour costs	80,000

These costs will not change, since rate increases will be offset by productivity improvements.

(W3) *Factory overhead*

Calculate the variable cost per unit and fixed costs using the high-low method.

	£
Total cost of 40,000 units	200,000
Total cost of 20,000 units	170,000
Variable cost of 20,000 units	30,000
Variable cost/unit	£1.50

Substituting:

	£
Total cost of 40,000 units	200,000
Variable cost of 40,000 units (× £1.50)	60,000
Fixed costs	140,000

These fixed costs will increase by 5% in Quarter 4.

Selling overhead (based on sales)

Calculate variable cost per unit and fixed costs using the high-low method.

	£
Total cost of 34,000 units	37,000
Total cost of 30,000 units	35,000
Variable cost of 4,000 units	2,000
Variable cost/unit	£0.50

Substituting:

	£
Total cost of 30,000 units	35,000
Variable cost of 30,000 units (× £0.50)	15,000
Fixed costs	20,000

These fixed costs will increase by 5% in Quarter 4.

(c) Required reduction in stock in Quarter 4 = the amount by which production in Quarters 1 – 3 (90,000 units) exceeded sales (82,000 units). The reduction in stock levels will therefore be 8,000 units, and the production volume should be lower than the sales volume by this amount.

Flexible budget profit statements

	Low	*Most likely*	*High*
	000s	000s	000s
Sales	38	44	50
Production	30	36	42

	£000	£000	£000
Material (£2.75 per unit produced)	82.5	99.0	115.5
Labour (see working)	230.0	260.0	295.0
Factory overhead (£147,000 + £1.50 per unit produced)	192.0	201.0	210.0
Admin. overhead	30.0	30.0	30.0
Selling overhead (£21,000 + £0.50 per unit sold)	40.0	43.0	46.0
Costs	574.5	633.0	696.5
Add decrease in stock (8,000 × £13)	104.0	104.0	104.0
Cost of sales	678.5	737.0	800.5
Sales (at £18/unit)	684.0	792.0	900.0
Profit	5.5	55.0	99.5

Working: Labour costs

When production is 30,000 units: (30,000 × £5) + £80,000 = £230,000.

When production is 36,000 units: (36,000 × £5) + £80,000 = £260,000.

When production is 42,000 units: (42,000 × £5) + (2,000 × £2.50) + £80,000 = £295,000.

(d) The change in profit will be caused by the change in costs as a result of greater production, rendering the stock adjustment undertaken for the quarter (based on absorption costing principles) unnecessary. Change in costs = 8,000 units × variable production cost £9.25 = £74,000. (Variable production cost per unit, see above, = £2.75 + £5 + £1.50 = £9.25).

Production (000s units)	38	44	50
	£000	£000	£000
Extra variable production costs	74	74	74
Additional bonus (see note)	–	10	25
Extra costs:	74	84	99
Stock adjustment (Reduction in cost of sales)	104	104	104
Increase in profit	30	20	10

Note:

Bonus: At 44,000 = 4,000 × 50% of £5 per unit

Bonus: At 50,000 = 10,000 × 50% of £5 per unit.

Under the assumption of a simple linear relationship of variable costs to volume, the only extra costs for 8,000 units are the variable production costs which are £9.25 per unit. For any volume above 40,000 units there is also the bonus payment to incorporate. If the budgeted production volume is made equal to sales then the stock level at the start of quarter four will remain at the end. There is no need for a stock adjustment. Put another way, the adjustment made in part (c) above can be added back. The above table shows the profit increase which will occur for the three volume levels.

Under the original volume prediction (and absorption costing principles), quarter four was being charged with fixed overhead contained in the opening stock value in addition to the fixed overhead of the period. Such overhead being transferred to that quarter from earlier accounting periods where production exceeded sales. With the revised stocking policy, the production for quarter four is equal to the sales of the quarter, and this fixed overhead is, in effect, being passed into the following year.

Regarding **managerial motivation and production levels**, it is apparent that the reported profit levels, under absorption costing, respond to changes in the levels of production. We have seen that during a quarter, an increase in the production results in an increase in the reported profit. This presents the possibility of opportunistic behaviour by managers wishing to enhance the level of profit being reported in any one period. They may deliberately over-produce, compared to prevailing sales demand, this production would be held in stock to be sold later, and reported profits would increase. This action would occur if they were placed in a position of needing to achieve a target profit for their bonus or performance appraisal purposes. It may be storing up trouble for the future however, because future production may have to be cut back in order to allow stock levels to be reduced. It would really only be justified if, for example, future sales were expected to be so high that they could not be met by the existing production capacity.

56 STORRS PLC

(a) The centred moving averages can be compared with actual sales for each quarter in order to determine the seasonal variations.

Quarter	*Actual sales*	*Centred moving average*	*Seasonal variation*
	£000	£000	£000
20X1			
Quarter 3	3,400	3,200.0	200.0
Quarter 4	3,000	3,300.0	(300.0)
20X2			
Quarter 1	3,100	3,375.0	(275.0)
Quarter 2	3,900	3,450.0	450.0
Quarter 3	3,600	3,562.5	37.5
Quarter 4	3,400	3,687.5	(287.5)

The average seasonal variations and the residual error term can now be calculated (although with a limited amount of historical data).

	Quarter 1	*Quarter 2*	*Quarter 3*	*Quarter 4*	*Total*
	£000	£000	£000	£000	£000
20X1	-	-	200.00	(300.00)	
20X2	(275.0)	450.0	37.50	(287.50)	
Average	(275.0)	450.0	118.75	(293.75)	Nil

Since the residual error term is nil, there is no need to net this off against the average seasonal variations. The average trend of the centred moving averages is (3,687.5 – 3,200)/5 = £97,500. This means that in our model, it is assumed that there is an upward trend in sales, with the underlying trend in sales increasing by £97,500 each quarter.

The sales for Quarter 3 of 20X3 can now be forecast.

		£
Centred moving average, Q4 of 20X2		3,687,500
Trend growth for 3 quarters	= 3 × 97,500 =	292,500
Trend line sales, Q3 of 20X3		3,980,000
Seasonal variation		118,750
Forecast sales, Q3 of 20X3		**4,098,750**

The sales for Quarter 4 of 20X3 can also be forecast.

				£
Centred moving average, Q4 of 20X2				3,687,500
Trend growth for 4 quarters	=	4 × 97,500	=	390,000
Trend line sales, Q3 of 20X3				4,077,500
Seasonal variation				(293,750)
Forecast sales, Q4 of 20X3				**3,783,750**

Both forecasts are higher than those made by the Sales Director (7.0% more for the Quarter 3 forecast and 5.1% for the Quarter 4 forecast). This may be because the Sales Director built some slack into his forecasts, or because the forecasts were made using data prior to the current year (although applying the additive model to earlier sales data does not support this).

(b) The **additive model** assumes that the trend and seasonal variations are independent of each other, and that an increasing trend is not linked to increasing seasonal variations. There is no evidence of an increasing trend in the sales of Storrs plc, and in such circumstances use of the additive model may be acceptable.

The model assumes that the historical pattern of the trend and the seasonal variations will continue in the future. This may not happen for a number of reasons, for example because of unexpected events occurring or because of changes in consumer preferences. The forecast sales figures should be compared with the expectations and opinions of sales staff, who may have a more detailed knowledge of likely sales and market factors.

The reliability of the forecasting method is linked to the amount and accuracy of the data analysed. Since only two years of data has been considered, the forecast is unlikely to be reliable. The reliability of the forecast will also decrease as the forecasting period increases, but the forecast period here is only six months.

(c) With the **top-down approach to budget-setting** , budgets are imposed by senior management. This has the advantage that budgets are more likely to support the strategic objectives of the company, and the operations of different divisions are more likely to be co-ordinated. It may be an appropriate form of budget-setting in small organisations, where senior managers are likely to have a detailed knowledge of all aspects of the business, or in situations where close control of planned costs is called for, such as business start-up or difficult economic conditions. It also has the advantage of decreasing the amount of time taken, and the resources consumed, by budget preparation.

There are number of difficulties with the top-down approach, making it likely that it will not regularly be used in isolation.

- Staff may be demotivated if they have not been involved in the formulation of budgets that produce targets they are expected to achieve, especially if their rewards and incentives are linked to their performance against budget.
- This reduction in motivation could result in strategic objectives and organisational goals being less than fully supported at the operational level, with company performance and profitability suffering as a result.
- Initiative and innovation could also be lost as staff simply 'work to budget', rather than making creative suggestions for improving performance that they feel are unlikely to be rewarded, or form part of future plans.

The **bottom-up approach to budget-setting** implies that functional and other junior managers participate in the preparation of budgets. This approach is likely to lead to more realistic and more co-ordinated budgets than the top-down approach if these managers have a more detailed knowledge of the operations and markets of the organisation. It is also likely to be useful in large, established companies where the complexity of the budget-setting process calls for detailed input from lower levels of the organisation. This approach will also lead to higher levels of motivation and commitment, since managers will have contributed towards the targets against which their performance will be measured.

There are a number of difficulties with the bottom-up approach.

- It can be more time-consuming than the top-down approach because of the larger number of participants in the budget-setting process.
- Participants may become dissatisfied if their budget proposals are subsequently amended by senior managers.
- Managers may introduce an element of budgetary slack into their budget estimates, giving them a 'zone of comfort' in reaching budget targets. Any variances between planned and actual performance are then likely to be favourable ones.

The bottom-up approach also requires detailed planning and co-ordination of the budget-setting process, perhaps supported by a budget manual.

The top-down and bottom-up approaches represent two extremes of the budget-setting process. In practice, a compromise or **negotiated approach** is likely to be used, with senior management reviewing and amending the budget proposals of junior or operational managers in the light of the organisation's strategic plan, and junior or operational managers negotiating amendments to aspects of the budget they find unacceptable.

ACCA marking scheme

		Marks
(a)	Calculation of seasonal variances	2
	Calculation of average seasonal variations	1
	Consideration of residual error term	1
	Sales forecasts for quarter 3 and quarter 4	2
	Discussion and explanation	2
		8
(b)	Discussion of trend and seasonal variations	2
	Historical pattern may not be repeated	2
	Amount of data used in the analysis	1
		5
(c)	Discussion of top-down budgeting	6
	Discussion of bottom up budgeting	6
		12
Total		25

57 BUDGET BEHAVIOUR

Key answer tips

Part (a) should not present much difficulty, requiring a discussion of four purposes of budgeting, a list of at least six of which should be imprinted on your mind! However, you should not just reproduce the 'heading' in your list - expand it out with a couple of sentences.

Part (b) needs a bit of careful thought and planning to first of all decide exactly what it is you are being asked, and then how to answer it. The key word here is *behavioural* - do not discuss other problems of budgetary control, even if you do know a lot more about them! The best approach to a structured answer might be to think (1) what are the behavioural factors to take account of (target setting, motivation, participation etc) (2) how would they ideally be incorporated into the system and (3) what are the practical problems that may arise?

(a) An answer should cover four purposes from the six provided below.

Planning

The budget is a major short-term planning device placing the overall direction of the company into a quarterly, monthly and, perhaps, weekly focus. It ensures that managers have thought ahead about how they will utilise resources to achieve company policy in their area.

Control

Once a budget is formulated a regular reporting system can be established so that the extent to which plans are, or are not, being met can be established. Some form of management by exception can be established so that deviations from plans are identified and reactions to the deviation developed if desirable.

Co-ordination

As organisations grow the various departments benefit from the co-ordination effect of the budget. In this role budgets ensure that no one department is out of line with the action of others. They may also hold in check anyone who is inclined to pursue his or her own desires rather than corporate objectives.

Communication

The construction of the budget can be a powerful aid to defining or clarifying the lines of horizontal or vertical communication within the enterprise. Managers should have a clearer idea of what their responsibilities are, what is expected of them, and are likely to work better with others to achieve it.

Performance evaluation

When budgets are 'tailored' to a department or manager they become useful tools for evaluating how the manager or department is performing. If sales targets are met or satisfactory service provided within reasonable spending limits then bonus or promotion prospects are enhanced.

Motivation

The value of a budget is enhanced still further if it not only states expectations but motivates managers to strive towards those expectations. This is more likely achieved if a manager has had some involvement in the budget construction, understands its implications and agrees it is fair and controllable by him/her.

(b) If budgetary control is to be successful, attention must be paid to behavioural aspects, i.e. the effect of the system on people in the organisation and vice versa. The following are some of the points which should be borne in mind:

Budget difficulty

It is generally agreed that the existence of some form of target or expected outcome is a greater motivation than no target at all. The establishment of a target, however, raises the question of the degree of difficulty or challenge of the target. If the performance standard is set too high or too low then sub-optimal performance could be the result. The degree of budget difficulty is not easy to establish. It is influenced by the nature of the task, the organisational culture and personality factors. Some people respond positively to a difficult target others, if challenged, tend to withdraw their commitment.

Budgets and performance evaluation

The emphasis on achievement of budget targets can be increased, but also the potential for dysfunctional behaviour, if the budget is subsequently used to evaluate performance. This evaluation is frequently associated with specific rewards such as remuneration increases or improved promotion prospects. In such cases it is likely that individuals will concentrate on those items which are measured and rewarded neglecting aspects on which no measurement exists. This may result in some aspects of the job receiving inadequate attention because they are not covered by goals or targets due to the complexity of the situation or the difficulty of measurement.

Managerial style

The use of budgets in evaluation and control is also influenced by the way they are used by the superior. Different management styles of budget use have been observed, for example:

Budget constrained	–	placing considerable emphasis on meeting budget targets
Profit conscious	–	where a balanced view is taken between budget targets, long-term goals and general effectiveness
Non-accounting	–	where accounting data is seen as relatively unimportant in the evaluation of subordinates.

The style is suggested to influence, in some cases, the superior/subordinate relationship, the degree of stress and tension involved and the likelihood of budget attainment. The style adopted and its implications are affected by the environment in which management is taking place. For example, the degree of interdependency between areas of responsibility, the uncertainty of the environment and the extent to which individuals feel they influence results are all factors to consider in relation to the management style adopted and its outcomes.

Participation

It is often suggested that participation in the budget process and discussion over how results are to be measured has benefits in terms of budget attitude and performance. Views on this point are varied however, and the personality of the individuals participating, the nature of the task (narrowly defined or flexible) and the organisation structure influence the success of participation. But a budget when carefully and appropriately established can extract a better performance from the budgetee than one in which these considerations are ignored.

Bias

Budgetees who are involved in the process from which the budget standards are set are more likely to accept them as legitimate. However, they may also be tempted to seize the opportunity to manipulate the desired performance standard in their favour. That is, they may make the performance easier to achieve and hence be able to satisfy personal goals rather than organisational goals. This is referred to as incorporating 'slack' into the budget. In this context there may be a relationship between the degree of emphasis placed on the budget and the tendency of the budgetee to bias the budget content or circumvent its control.

Any organisational planning and control system has multiple objectives but primary amongst these is encouraging staff to take organisationally desirable actions. It is never possible to predict with certainty the outcomes of all behavioural interaction however it is better to be aware of the various possible behavioural implications than to be ignorant of them.

58 NOT-FOR-PROFIT ORGANISATIONS

(a) Not-for-profit (NFP) organisations such as charities deliver services that are usually limited by the resources available to them. It may be possible neither to express their objectives in quantifiable or measurable terms, nor to measure their output in terms of the services they deliver. The financial focus in NFP organisations is therefore placed on the control of costs.

(i) **Selection of cost units**

A cost unit for a NFP organisation is a unit of service for which costs are ascertained. These cost units will be used to assess the efficiency and effectiveness of the organisation. The problem for a NFP organisation is that it may not have easily identifiable cost units, and it may not be possible to identify costs with specific outputs. Once appropriate cost units have been identified, however, they can be used to provide cost control information. Examples of costs units used by an NFP organisation are patients, wards, drug treatment programmes, bed-nights and operations, which are all used by a hospital.

(ii) **The use of performance measures to measure output and quality**

Where output for a NFP organisation can be quantified, targets can be set and performance against these targets can be measured. In a university, for example, targets could be set in terms of the number of students graduating with a first-class degree, the number of students in a tutorial group, and the percentage of students who complete a degree course having started it. Information could easily be gathered to enable an assessment of the University's performance compared to agreed, budgeted or imposed targets.

Measuring performance in terms of quality is not so easy. It may be possible to use a surrogate or substitute performance measure if a quality cannot be directly measured. For example, the efficiency of hospital outpatient treatment could be measured by the average length of the queue for treatment. The quality of a University course could be assessed by a composite weighting of responses to individual student questionnaires.

(iii) **Comparison of planned and actual performance**

It is likely that a NFP organisation will have a budget that details expected levels of income (for example from donations and investments) and expenditure (for example on staff wages, continuing programmes, fixed overheads and planned purchases). The use and application of costing principles and information here is no different than in a profit-making organisation. Planned performance can be compared to actual performance, income and cost variances calculated and investigated, and corrective action taken to remedy under-performance.

Where objectives cannot be specified in terms of quantifiable targets, costing information will serve no purpose and assessment of actual performance with planned performance will need to be undertaken from a more subjective perspective.

(b) Zero-based budgeting requires that activities be re-evaluated as part of the budget process so that each activity, and each level of activity, can justify its consumption of the economic resources available. This is in contrast to incremental budgeting, where the current budget is increased to allow for expected future conditions. Zero-based budgeting prevents the carrying forward of past inefficiencies that can be a feature of incremental budgeting and focuses on activities rather than departments or programmes. Each activity is treated as though it was being undertaken for the first time and is required to justify its inclusion in the budget in terms of the benefit expected to be derived from its adoption.

The first step in zero-based budgeting is the formulation of decision packages. These are documents which identify and describe a given activity or group of activities in detail. The base package represents the minimum level of activity that is consistent with the achievement of organisational objectives. Incremental packages describe higher levels of activity which may be delivered if they are acceptable from a cost-benefit perspective.

Following the formulation of decision packages, they are evaluated by senior management and ranked by decreasing benefit to the budgeting organisation. Resources should then be allocated, theoretically at least, to decision packages in order of decreasing marginal utility until all resources have been allocated.

Advantages claimed for zero-based budgeting are that it eliminates the inefficiencies that can arise with incremental budgeting, that it fosters a questioning attitude towards current activities and that it focuses attention on the need to obtain value for money from the consumption of organisational resources.

Value for money is important in not-for-profit (NFP) organisations, where the profit motive found in the private sector is replaced by the need to derive the maximum benefits from limited resources available. Providers of funds to NFP organisations expect to see their cash being used wisely, with as much as possible being devoted to the achievement of organisational aims. For this reason, NFP organisations emphasise cost control and the need for economy in the selection of resources, efficiency in the consumption of resources and effectiveness in the use of resources to achieve organisational objectives (i.e. value for money).

Zero-based budgeting can therefore be applied in a NFP organisation to analyse its activities and the services it provides into decision packages, with a view to ranking them on a cost-benefit basis relative to organisational aims and objectives. In has been noted that zero-based budgeting can be applied more effectively in service-based rather than manufacturing organisations and so it may be ideally suited to a NFP organisation such as a charity.

(c) Activity-based budgeting (ABB) would need a detailed analysis of costs and cost drivers so as to determine which cost drivers and cost pools were to be used in the activity-based costing system. However, whereas activity-based costing uses activity-based recovery rates to assign costs to cost objects, ABB begins with budgeted cost-objects and works back to the resources needed to achieve the budget.

Once the budgeted activity levels have been determined, the demand for resource-consuming activities is assessed from an organisational perspective. The resources needed to provide for these activities are then assessed and action taken to ensure that these resources are available when needed in the budget period.

The budgeted activity levels are determined in the same way as for conventional budgeting in that a sales budget and a production budget are drawn up. ABB then determines the quantity of activity cost drivers (e.g. number of purchase orders, number of set-ups) needed to support the planned sales and production. Standard cost data would be compiled that included details of the activity cost drivers required to produce a product or number of products.

The resources needed to support the budgeted quantity of activity cost drivers would then be determined (e.g. number of labour hours to process purchase orders, number of maintenance hours needed to complete set-ups). This resource need would then be matched against the available capacity (i.e. number of purchase clerks to process purchase orders) to see whether any capacity adjustment were needed.

One advantage suggested for ABB is that organisational resources are allocated more efficiently due to the detailed cost and activity information obtained by implementing an ABB system. Another advantage of ABB is that it avoids the pitfalls of incremental budgeting due to its detailed assessment of the activities and resources needed to support planned sales and production. In ABB the costs of support activities are not seen as fixed costs to be increased by annual increments, but as depending to a large extent on the planned level of activity.

ACCA marking scheme			
		Marks	
(a)	Features of a not-for-profit organisation	1	
	Selection of cost units	3-4	
	Use of performance measures	3-4	
	Comparison of planned and actual performance	3-4	
	Maximum		10
(b)	Zero-based budgeting and incremental budgeting	1	
	Decision packages	2	
	Ranking decision packages	2	
	Allocating resources	1	
	Zero-based budgeting and NFP organisations	2	
			8
(c)	Explanation of activity-based budgeting	2	
	Need for detailed analysis of costs and activities	1	
	Stages in activity-based budgeting	2-3	
	Advantages of activity-based budgeting	2-3	
	Maximum		7
Total			25

59 THORNE CO

Key answer tips

In part (a) the key to success is to have clear, logical workings, even if you feel that this slows you down.

In part (b) you should apply your comments to the scenario where possible, bringing in issues such as seasonality, the amount of cash available and likely risk aversion, for example.

Part (c) asks for a more routine discussion of overdraft finance but again your answer should relate to the specific circumstances in the question.

In part (d) the key is to examine the assumptions underlying the Baumol model and see whether they apply to Thorne Co.

(a) **Cash Budget for Thorne Co:**

	January	*February*	*March*	*April*
Receipts	£	£	£	£
Cash fees	18,000	27,000	45,000	54,000
Credit fees	36,000	36,000	54,000	90,000
Sale of assets				20,000
Total receipts	54,000	63,000	99,000	164,000
Payments				
Salaries	26,250	26,250	26,250	26,250
Bonus			6,300	12,600
Expenses	9,000	13,500	22,500	27,000
Fixed overheads	4,300	4,300	4,300	4,300
Taxation				95,800
Interest			3,000	
Total payments	39,550	44,050	62,350	165,950
Net cash flow	14,450	18,950	36,650	(1,950)
Opening balance	(40,000)	(25,550)	(6,600)	30,050
Closing balance	(25,550)	(6,600)	30,050	28,100

Workings

Month	*December*	*January*	*February*	*March*	*April*
Units sold	10	10	15	25	30
Sales value (£000)	1,800	1,800	2,700	4,500	5,400
Cash fees at 1% (£)	18,000	18,000	27,000	45,000	54,000
Credit fees at 2% (£)	36,000	36,000	54,000	90,000	108,000
Variable costs at 0.5% (£)		9,000	13,500	22,500	27,000

Monthly salary cost = (35,000 × 9)/12 = £26,250

Bonus for March = (25 – 20) × 140 × 9 = £6,300

Bonus for April = (30 – 20) × 140 × 9 = £12,600

(b) The number of properties sold each month indicates that Thorne Co experiences seasonal trends in its business. There is an indication that property sales are at a low level in winter and increase as spring approaches. A proportion of any cash surplus is therefore likely to be short-term in nature, since some cash will be required when sales are at a low level. Even though net cash flow is forecast to be positive in the January, the month with the lowest level of property sales, the negative opening cash balance indicates that there may be months prior to December when sales are even lower.

Short-term cash surpluses should be invested with no risk of capital loss. This limitation means that appropriate investments include treasury bills, short-dated gilts, public authority bonds, certificates of deposit and bank deposits. When choosing between these instruments Thorne Co will consider the length of time the surplus is available for, the size of the surplus (some instruments have minimum investment levels), the yield offered, the risk associated with each instrument, and any penalties for early withdrawal4. A small company like Thorne Co, with an annual turnover slightly in excess of £1m per year, is likely to find bank deposits the most convenient method for investing short-term cash surpluses.

Since the company appears to generate a cash surplus of approximately £250,000 per year, the company must also consider how to invest this longer-term surplus. As a new company Thorne Co is likely to want to invest surplus funds in expanding its business, but as a small company it is likely to find few sources of funds other than bank debt and retained earnings. There is therefore a need to guard against capital loss when investing cash that is intended to fund expansion at a later date. As the retail property market is highly competitive, investment opportunities must be selected with care and retained earnings must be invested on a short- to medium-term basis until an appropriate investment opportunity can be found.

(c) In two of the four months of the cash budget Thorne Co has a cash deficit, with the highest cash deficit being the opening balance of £40,000. This cash deficit, which has occurred even though the company has a loan of £200,000, is likely to be financed by an overdraft. An advantage of an overdraft is that it is a flexible source of finance, since it can be used as and when required, provided that the overdraft limit is not exceeded. In addition, Thorne Co will only have to pay interest on the amount of the overdraft facility used, with the interest being charged at a variable rate linked to bank base rate. In contrast, interest is paid on the full £200,000 of the company's bank loan whether the money is used or not. The interest rate on the overdraft is likely to be lower than that on long-term debt.

A disadvantage of an overdraft is that it is repayable on demand, although in practice notice is given of the intention to withdraw the facility. The interest payment may also increase, since the company is exposed to the risk of an interest rates increase. Banks usually ask for some form of security, such as a floating charge on the company's assets or a personal guarantee from a company's owners, in order to reduce the risk associated with their lending.

(d) The Baumol model is derived from the EOQ model and can be applied in situations where there is a constant demand for cash or cash disbursements. Regular transfers are made from interest-bearing short-term investments or cash deposits into a current account. The Baumol model considers the annual demand for cash (D), the cost of each cash transfer (C), and the interest difference between the rate paid on short-term investments (r1) and the rate paid on a current account (r2), in order to calculate the optimum amount of funds to transfer (F). The model is as follows.

$F = ((2 \times D \times C)/(r1 - r2))0.5$

By optimising the amount of funds to transfer, the Baumol model minimises the opportunity cost of holding cash in the current account, thereby reducing the costs of cash management.

However, the Baumol model is unlikely to be of assistance to Thorne Co because of the assumptions underlying its formulation. Constant annual demand for cash is assumed, whereas its cash budget suggests that Thorne Co has a varying need for cash. The model assumes that each interest rate and the cost of each cash transfer are constant and known with certainty. In reality interest rates and transactions costs are not constant and interest rates, in particular, can change frequently. A cash management model which can accommodate a variable demand for cash, such as the Miller-Orr model, may be more suited to the needs of the company.

ACCA marking scheme

		Marks
(a)	Credit sales	2
	Cash sales	1
	Proceeds from asset disposal	1
	Salaries	1
	Bonus	1
	Expenses	1
	Fixed overheads	1
	Taxation and interest	1
	Closing balances	1
		10
(b)	Discussion of factors	5
(c)	Discussion of advantages and disadvantages	5
(d)	Discussion of Baumol model	2–3
	Discussion of applicability in this case	2–3
	Maximum	5
Total		25

PERFORMANCE MEASUREMENT

60 PERFORMANCE APPRAISAL

Key answer tips

A very straightforward discussion of divisional performance appraisal. Be careful in part (a) to link measures to the different types of centres. In part (b) you need to focus on appraising the manager, not the business unit.

(a) A responsibility centre is part of an organisation for whose activities a manager is deemed to be responsible. The type of responsibility centre depends on the type of activities for which responsibility is carried.

Cost Centre

A cost centre or expense centre can be defined as a responsibility centre where a manager is accountable only for costs which are under his control. It is a production or service location for which costs can be identified or accumulated prior to allocation to cost units. Cost centres may be either standard cost centres, where output can be measured and the input needed for a given output can be specified, or discretionary cost centres, where output cannot be measured easily and the relationship between inputs and outputs cannot be specified1. An example of a standard cost centre is a production unit within a factory, while an example of a discretionary cost centre is a health and safety department within a university. A cost centre manager is responsible for the cost of inputs to the organisation. The performance of the manager of a cost centre can be assessed by comparing actual performance with budgeted targets for price, usage and efficiency.

Revenue Centre

A revenue centre is a responsibility centre where a manager is accountable solely for the revenue generation that is under his control. An example would be a sales team with a target geographical area which is under the control of a sales manager. The manager would have no responsibility for the production cost of the items his team is selling, but has responsibility for meeting sales targets in terms of sales volume, sales revenue or market share. A revenue centre manager has responsibility for the revenue generated by outputs from the organisation. The performance of the manager of a revenue centre can be assessed by comparing actual performance with budgeted targets for price, mix and volume.

Profit Centre

A profit centre is a combination of a cost centre and a revenue centre where a manager has responsibility for both production costs and revenue generation. The degree of responsibility carried by a manager can be higher with a profit centre than with a cost centre or a revenue centre, and the manager may be responsible for purchasing, production planning, product mix and pricing decisions. The performance of the manager of a profit centre is unlikely to be assessed on the fine detail of cost and revenue data but by the extent to which agreed targets for overall cost, revenue and profit have been achieved.

Investment Centre

With an investment centre, the manager of a profit centre is given additional responsibility for investment decisions regarding working capital and the purchase and replacement of fixed assets. The manager of an investment centre is likely to be assessed with an aggregate measure that links periodic profit to the assets employed in the period to generate that profit. An example of such an aggregate measure is return on capital employed.

Controllable and Non-controllable Factors

It is a cardinal principle of responsibility accounting that managers can only be assessed on the cash flows that are under their control. If a manager has no control over a cash flow he cannot influence its size or timing and so cannot be held responsible if either of these values changes. The performance of the manager of a cost centre can thus only be assessed on the controllable costs over which he exercises control. In the case of a production cost centre, the manager may be able to control material usage but could have no influence over the price at which materials are bought by the purchasing department. For the production cost centre manager, material usage is a controllable factor whereas material purchase price is not.

With a revenue centre, a sales manager can be held responsible for generating revenue against agreed sales volume targets but may have no control over the selling price of his products as this is determined by market conditions. In this case sales volume is a controllable factor whereas selling price is not.

The manager of a profit centre will have control of operating costs but will not be able to influence the financing costs arising from investment decisions. The manager may thus have responsibility for operating profit but his performance should not be assessed on profit before tax since interest charges are outside of his control.

The manager of an investment centre could have his performance assessed on profit before tax, but the profit on which he is assessed should exclude non-controllable elements such as overhead costs that he cannot influence, for example allocated head office charges.

(b) While it is possible to assess the performance of an investment centre such as a division within a company on the basis of the profit it generates, considering profit alone and taking no account of the assets used to generate the profit will provide an incomplete picture of performance. Comparing profit between profit centres is also misleading if assets employed are ignored. Assessment of the performance of an investment centre will usually therefore include a performance measure that relates profit to assets employed. Two such measures are return on investment (ROI) and residual income (RI).

Return on investment expresses controllable profit as a percentage of capital employed. It is thus a relative, rather than an absolute, performance measure and is both widely used and understood. Controllable profit means that non-controllable factors are excluded as far as possible from the profit used in calculating ROI since these will diminish the usefulness of the calculated measure in assessing managerial performance.

Because ROI is a relative measure, it can be used to compare performance between investment centres. ROI also offers a way of assessing the past investment decisions made by an investment centre, since it is measured after these investment decisions have been made. It can thus be used to check that the performance predicted by investment appraisal decisions is in fact being achieved post implementation.

Since ROI assesses investment centre managerial performance on the basis of controllable profit generated, managers will be keen to maximise this as far as possible. The desire to maximise controllable profit can be assisted by the use of performance related pay and similar incentive schemes. But if performance is assessed using ROI, investment centre managers will be as keen to minimise capital employed as they will be to maximise controllable profit. While this can encourage managers to dispose of obsolete equipment and minimise working capital, it can also lead to sub-optimal decisions for the company as a whole.

If managers are assessed using ROI, there will be a disincentive to invest in projects with a ROI that is less than the current ROI of the investment centre. However, these projects should be accepted if the project ROI is greater than the company's cost of capital. In this case, the decision not to invest will not be consistent with the overall objective of maximizing shareholder wealth.

A similar problem arises with asset disposal decisions. Here, a manager assessed using ROI may choose to retain assets with a low written down value since these assets will generate a higher ROI than new, more expensive assets that could be more economical and efficient. This problem highlights the way in which short-term concerns can outweigh longer-term interests when ROI is used to assess managerial performance. It should be noted that ROI can simply increase due to ageing assets rather than from the actions of managers charged with increasing it.

Residual income has been suggested as a way of overcoming some of the perceived shortcomings of ROI as a managerial performance measure. Residual income (RI) is defined as controllable profit less a cost of capital charge on controllable investment. RI is therefore an absolute, rather than a relative, performance measure, which means that comparisons between investment centres cannot be made directly.

The advantage of RI as a performance measure is that the cost of capital charge (or imputed interest charge) is made by reference to the company's cost of capital, so that a positive residual income arises if an existing or proposed investment generates a return greater than the required minimum. Investment centre managers assessed on the basis of RI will therefore choose to accept all projects with a positive RI, increasing the company's overall return. Sub-optimal investment decisions should therefore be reduced or eliminated using RI. Investment centre managers will also be discouraged from retaining ageing and inefficient assets, since replacing such assets by more efficient ones is likely to lead to an increase in residual income.

Overall, it is felt that return on investment is an unsatisfactory way of assessing managerial performance as far as an investment centre is concerned, and that residual income should be used instead. Despite this, ROI appears in practice to be preferred to RI2.

ACCA marking scheme		
		Marks
(a)	Responsibility centres	5–6
	Performance measurement	4–5
	Controllable and non-controllable factors	2–3
	Maximum	12
(b)	Return on capital employed	7–8
	Residual income	5–6
	Conclusion	1
	Maximum	13
Total		25

61 WINDERMERE

Key answer tips

This is a standard type of divisional assessment question: ROCE used as the performance measure, bonuses for meeting target ROCE, schemes to improve ROCE - some actually profitable but showing poor results, some short term manipulation to improve reported results but not in the long term interests of the company. There is one useful note in the question - there is central control of cash - it is always useful to assume this otherwise an investment will have no effect on a division's net assets (fixed assets rise, bank balance falls). You will need to make an assumption about what is meant by 'cost savings' in (i), pre or post depreciation, but state your assumption. The requirement of (a) provides you with a useful structure for your answer, although some initial general comments on the use of ROCE might help. Don't anticipate (b) in your answer to (a).

(a) **Assessment of four year-end proposals**

Two general comments are of relevance to all four proposals:

- With ROCE based on NBV of assets employed there is an incentive to under-invest, to improve ROCE by 'reducing the bottom line' rather than 'increasing the top line' in the ratio.
- When ROCE-based assessment is linked to a bonus scheme there is a greater incentive to make ROCE appear satisfactory irrespective of the true commercial merit of an operation of project.

(i) **The works manager - new equipment**

An investment at the end of the year will increase capital employed without providing the opportunity to earn any of the savings forecast. ROCE is likely to fall from 14.6% to:

$$\frac{£120,000}{£820,000 + £100,000} \times 100 = 13.0\%$$

Without knowing the depreciation policy, it is not possible to state the effect of this proposal on 19X2 ROCE.

The project itself may well be viable. If 15% can be taken as the division's cost of capital and the £18,000 are net annual cash inflows, the NPV is:

$£18,000 \times 5.847 - £100,000 = £5,246.$

The project has a positive NPV and should be accepted.

Under the same assumptions and assuming straight line depreciation of £6,667 p.a. the ROCE at the end of the first year would be:

$$\frac{18,000 - £6,667}{£100,000 - £6,667} \times 100 = 12.1\%$$

This is less than the target, but that is a failure of the ROCE method and the method of depreciation used. (In the final year the project's ROCE would be $£11,333 \div £0$ = infinity).

There are no ethical issues at stake, but a number of management issues as introduced above and discussed in (b).

(ii) **The chief accountant - delay payments to creditors**

The effect of non-payment of creditors at the year end is to decrease assets by £42,000 and reduce profit by £1,000. ROCE will move from 14.6% to:

$$\frac{£120,000 - £1,000}{£820,000 - £42,000} \times 100 = 15.3\%$$

The required target has been achieved.

This proposal will have no effect on 20X2 ROCE.

The longer term effect is that the company has lost £1,000 and saved one month's interest on £42,000. The cost of this proposal is therefore 1/42 = 0.024 per month, or:

$[(1.024)^{12} - 1] \times 100 = 32.6\%$ per year.

This makes the scheme appear rather costly.

The company do not want to get a reputation for being poor payers, suppliers may withhold goods and it may become difficult to obtain further credit.

The ethics of deferring payment of debt, which is commercially non-viable, in order to earn a bonus, needs questioning.

(iii) **The sales manager - bring forward completion of order**

The effect of this transaction would be to increase profit by either £6,000. As work in progress changes to debtors in the accounting records, capital employed would increase by £6,000 (since debtors includes profit, but work in progress includes cost only). ROCE would change from 14.6% to:

(£120,000 + £6,000)/(£820,000 + £6,000)

= £126,000/£826,000

= 0.153 or 15.3%.

This proposal achieves the desired ROCE.

This proposal will reduce 20X2 profit by £6,000, because it has the effect of bringing profit forward from 20X2 to 20X1.

Looking at the transaction without regard to year-end performance, £1,500 has been spent with no benefit to cash inflows, although the balance sheet will look more impressive.

This is another example of dysfunctional decisions based on a form of assessment and related remuneration scheme that encourages manipulation of year end accounts.

As with the previous proposal, the ethics of taking a commercially unsound decision, in order to secure a bonus, should be challenged.

(iv) **The head of internal audit - closing a regional plant**

This proposal would have a dramatic effect on capital employed, immediately reducing it by £90,000. The effect on profit would be a fall of £50,000 through redundancy and a rise of £30,000 profit on sale of assets. However, none of these would be included in trading profit (since they are presumably non-recurring) and so ROCE would increase to:

$$\frac{£120{,}000}{£820{,}000 - £90{,}000} \times 100 = 16.4\%$$

This easily achieves the required standard.

Without knowing the depreciation policy, or the life of the assets, the effect of this proposal on 20X2 ROCE cannot be determined.

The loss of £12,600 p.a. for 15 years comes from a net disinvestment of £120,000 – £50,000 = £70,000. The PV of the lost profit (ignoring the possibility of 'profit' of £12,600 being increased by depreciation of £90,000 ÷ 15 = £6,000 to £18,600) for 15 years at 15% is

£12,600 × 5.847 = £73,672.

This suggests that the plant should be retained in order to earn these profits. (ROCE appraisal has been ignored.)

Sacking people to improve ROCE despite the move being against the long-term benefit of the business is unethical. The analysis has also excluded any possible loss of business in other parts of the division from customers inconvenienced by this particular closure.

(b) **Remedial action by company finance director**

Many of the problems above come from the use of return on capital employed (ROCE) based on year end figures which encourages under-investment and manipulation. Possible solutions include:

- Change to Residual Income (RI) when divisions will be rewarded for making wise long-term investment decisions.
- Use DCF methods for assessing capital projects. This overcomes the short-term view taken by using ROCE. Performance can then be assessed by seeing whether the cash flow projections used to assess a project are achieved in reality.
- If there is an insistence on the use of ROCE, it can be improved by:
  - using average capital employed figures rather than year-end ones;
  - using gross book values rather than net-book values;
  - changing depreciation methods to ensure that ROCE does not improve just by retaining assets whose book value steadily falls.
- Ensure central approval of investment (and disinvestment) budgets and controls to check that commitments are met.
- Central control of payments to creditors and collection of debtors.
- If the above is too 'interventionist' lay down guidelines for payments and collection periods.
- The Divisional Manager deserves a reprimand for 'window dressing' although he is trying to make his accounts look better in a way that will not only boost his bonus but will also appeal to outside analysts.
- The importance of ethical considerations in decision-making should be emphasised to Divisional management.
- Change the bonus scheme and pay each manager a fair day's salary for doing a fair day's work without the troublesome complication of a bonus scheme.

62 KDS LTD

(a) **Divisional administrator's proposal**

Effect on 20X5 ROCE

It will have been assumed in arriving at the 31/12/X5 net assets that the trade creditor will have been paid. Reversing this assumption has the effect of increasing liabilities and has no effect on assets, as cash is excluded. Thus net assets will be reduced by £90,000 (to £4,310,000).

Whether the £2,000 late payment penalty is accounted for in 20X5 or 20X6 will depend to some extent on the company's accounting policy. The accruals concept would, however, lean towards it being accounted for in 20X5. Thus operating profits would be reduced by £2,000 (to £647,000).

The new ROCE would thus be $\frac{£647,000}{£4,310,000} \times 100 = 15.01\%$

Thus the target will have been achieved and bonuses paid. This is, of course, no indication of improved performance, but simply an arithmetical anomaly arising as a result of one side of the transaction being ignored in the calculation. In fact, the finance cost of the late payment is extremely high:

Pay £2,000 to delay payment of £90,000 by 12 days: cost = $\frac{£2,000}{£90,000} \times 100 = 2.22\%$

Converting this 12 day cost to an equivalent annual cost gives $(1.0222)^{365/12} - 1 = 95\%$

Longer term effects

There would be no quantifiable long term effects, although relationships with the creditor may be adversely affected by the late payment.

The works manager's proposal

Effect on 20X5 ROCE

Assuming no depreciation charge in 20X5, net assets would be increased by the cost of the new assets, £320,000 (to £4,720,000), and operating profits would be unaffected.

The new ROCE would thus be $\frac{£649,000}{£4,720,000} \times 100 = 13.75\%$

This represents a reduction of ROCE in the short term.

Longer term effects

In 20X6 and beyond, the full impact of the cost savings and depreciation charge would be felt - operating profits would be increased by a net £(76,000 - 40,000) = £36,000. Net assets value will be increased, but the increase will be smaller each year as the asset is depreciated.

In 20X6, the equipment's own ROCE would be $\frac{£36,000}{£(320,000 - 40,000)} \times 100 = 12.86\%$

This will still not help the division to achieve its target of 15%, although it does exceed the company's cost of capital and thus may be desirable overall.

However, by the end of 20X7, the equipment WDV will be £(320,000 - 80,000) = £240,000, giving a ROCE of 15%, exactly on target. As it increases above this level it will help the division to achieve its overall target.

This illustrates one of the major problems with using book values for assets in performance measures - as the assets get older, they appear to give better performance. This can have the effect of deterring managers from replacing assets even though this may be of benefit in the long term through cost savings (as above), increased productivity etc.

(b) Residual income (RI) is an absolute measure of performance, and is arrived at by deducting a notional interest charge at the company's cost of capital on the net assets. Appraising the two divisions' performance forecasts under this method would have the following results:

	20X5 operating profit	*Interest charge (12% net assets)*	*Residual income*
	£	£	£
Division K	649,000	528,000	121,000
Division D	120,000	57,600	62,400

The performance rankings of the two divisions are now apparently reversed. However, the RIs of the two divisions are not directly comparable - whilst Division K has produced nearly twice the level of RI than that of Division D, the net asset base required to do this is over nine times as large. RI cannot be meaningfully used to compare investments of differing sizes, as ROCE can.

One could also question the use of the company's average cost of money in computing the notional interest charge. The two divisions have been set a target well above this - this may be because they are considered riskier than average. If 15% had been used in the computation, Division K would have negative RI, whilst Division D has positive RI- reflecting the same information as the ROCE, that K is not achieving its target return.

The RI uses the same principles for establishing profit and asset values as the ROCE, and thus shares the same problems. As assets get older and their WDV falls, the imputed interest falls and RI rises.

However, RI can be of greater benefit than ROCE in management decision making. Management may only feel inclined to undertake new investment if doing so improves their performance measure. For example, Division D currently enjoys a ROCE of 25% and its manager may only consider new projects that give a return at least as good as this (although this may depend upon the particular structure of the bonus scheme - a fixed bonus provided the target of 15% is reached may not provoke such an attitude).

However, the RI measure will improve with new investment, ie increase, provided the investment's returns are at least covering the rate used in computing the notional interest (12% or 15%). This will ensure that projects that are worthwhile from the company's point of view will also be seen as such by the divisional manager (goal congruence).

In summary, RI has advantages and disadvantages over ROCE as a performance measure, and both suffer from common valuation problems. One of these can be used as part of a package of performance indicators - market share, productivity, employee satisfaction, technological advancement etc - but neither is perfect in isolation.

(c) **Non-financial performance measures**

As mentioned above, financial measures taken in isolation are unlikely to tell the whole story of a division's or company's performance. They must be put into context, taking account of the circumstances in which they were achieved - new products being introduced, market changes, technological changes, competitors moves, availability of resources etc.

For example, one might question why the two divisions in KDS are apparently performing at such different levels. Whilst quality of management may well be a contributory factor, it is unlikely to explain a difference of over 10 percentage points in ROCE.

The age profile of assets used should be considered, as discussed above. Division K may have recently invested in new machinery, possibly in response to technological advances. Not to do so would put them at a disadvantage over their competitors, and thus is for long term benefit. The industry of the much smaller Division D may be more static, requiring less asset changes.

Performance relative to the market and competitors should be considered (market share, product leadership etc) and the degree of innovation achieved. Level of complaints received may also be monitored.

Finally, employee measures are relevant when assessing the effectiveness of a manager - labour turnover, staff morale, manager's relationships with both subordinates and superiors. The level of job satisfaction felt by employees at all levels is an important consideration in the plan for achievement of company objectives.

63 PROPOSALS FOR DIVISION X

(a) The calculations of manager's bonus are shown in the following table.

Year 1	*Year 2*	*Year 3*	*Total*	
Original draft	£15,625	£13,500	Nil	£29,125
Project (i) - W1	£15,625	£13,250	£20,375	£49,250
Project (ii) -W2	Nil	Nil	£25,000	£25,000
Project (iii) - W3	£12,500	£16,000	£16,875	£45,375

Workings

For each 1% by which ROCE exceeds 10%, the bonus is increased by 2.5% of £50,000, i.e. by £1,250.

(W1) **Project (i)**

	Year 1	*Year 2*	*Year 3*
PBIT	£3.0m	£2.7m	£4.4m
Asset base	£24m	£25.5m	£27m
ROI	12.5%	10.6%	16.3%
	£	£	£
Basic bonus @ 25% of salary	12,500	12,500	12,500
Additional bonus	3,125	750	7,875
Total bonus	15,625	13,250	20,375

Note

Additional bonus Year 1 = 2.5 × £1,250 = £3,125

Additional bonus Year 2 = 0.6 × £1,250 = £750

Additional bonus Year 3 = 6.3 × £1,250 = £7,875

(W2) **Project (ii)**

	Year 1	*Year 2*	*Year 3*
PBIT	£2.0m	£1.7m	£6.4m
Asset base	£24m	£25m	£26m
ROI	8.3%	6.8%	24.6%
	£	£	£
Basic bonus @ 25% of salary	0	0	12,500
Additional bonus	0	0	12,500
Total bonus	0	0	25,000

Note:

Additional bonus Year 3 = (ignoring the bonus cap) 14.6 × £1,250 = £18,250, but total bonus capped at 50% of £50,000 = £25,000.

(W3) **Project (iii)**

	Year 1	*Year 2*	*Year 3*
PBIT	£2.4m	£3.2m	£3.5m
Asset base	£24m	£25m	£26m
ROI	10.0%	12.8%	13.5%
	£	£	£
Basic bonus @ 25% of salary	12,500	12,500	12,500
Additional bonus	0	3,500	4,375
Total bonus	12,500	16,000	16,875

Note:

Additional bonus Year 2 = 2.8 × £1,250 = £3,500

Additional bonus Year 3 = 3.5 × £1,250 = £4,375

The manager is likely to be influenced in his choice of projects by the personal rewards he can expect from them. In this case, he would favour Project (i) with total bonuses of £49,250, and Project (iii) with total bonuses of £45,375 over the three-year period. Both the first draft plan and adoption of Project (ii) are less attractive from this perspective. Moreover, this view is reinforced by the fact that most weight is likely to be given to bonuses achievable in the short term: on this basis Project (ii) is easily the least attractive, since no bonuses will arise until Year 3.

These considerations illustrate a common problem of bonus systems, namely that they may not achieve goal congruence. In the present case, Project (ii) is the most attractive from the organisation's point of view because its NPV is higher than the alternatives. However, because of its impact on the manager's own bonus Project (ii) is unlikely to be favoured. Indeed, from the manager's point of view it is the project with the lowest NPV that appears most attractive.

(b) (i) The calculations of the manager's bonuses are shown in the following table.

	Year 1	*Year 2*	*Year 3*	*Total*
Original draft (W1)	£12,000	£4,000	Nil	£16,000
Project (i)	£12,000	£3,000	£25,000	£40,000
Project (ii) - W2	Nil	Nil	£25,000	£25,000
Project (iii) - W3	Nil	£14,000	£18,000	£32,000

Workings

(W1) **Original draft**

	Year 1	*Year 2*	*Year 3*
PBIT	£3.0m	£2.7m	£2.4m
Interest at 10% on asset base	£2.4m	£2.5m	£2.6m
Residual income	£0.6m	£0.2m	Nil
Bonus at 2%	£12,000	£4,000	Nil

(W2) **Project (ii)**

	Year 1	*Year 2*	*Year 3*
PBIT	£2.0m	£1.7m	£6.4m
Interest at 10% on asset base	£2.4m	£2.5m	£2.6m
Residual income	Nil	Nil	£3.8m
Bonus at 2% (limited to £25,000)	Nil	Nil	£25,000

(W3) **Project (iii)**

	Year 1	*Year 2*	*Year 3*
PBIT	£2.4m	£3.2m	£3.5m
Interest at 10% on asset base	£2.4m	£2.5m	£2.6m
Residual income	Nil	£0.7m	£0.9m
Bonus at 2%	Nil	£14,000	£18,000

(ii) Overall, the bonuses work out less generously under this scheme. However, the manager's preference is unaffected: he still benefits most from Project (i), followed by Project (iii). Once again, Project (ii) is the least attractive from his point of view.

It is noticeable that a different result would have been achieved if the 'cap' were removed from the manager's bonus. In this case, the large returns eventually arising from Project (ii) might well influence him to select this as his first preference. It would lead to a potential bonus of £76,000 in Year 3. However, the fact that this potential is to be realised only in Year 3, with no bonuses at all in Years 1 and 2, might still be a deterrent.

(c) The calculations and comments already made illustrate the basic conflict between the goals of the manager and the goals of the organisation. Under either version of the bonus scheme the manager does better by selecting the projects which are least attractive to the organisation. The conflict arises because the organisation wishes to maximise NPV, whereas the manager wishes to maximise ROI or RI.

The obvious approach to solving this problem is to base the manager's bonus on a measure which benefits the organisation, in other words to align the bonus with NPV rather than with ROI or RI. The basis of this change would be to focus on cash flows (the determinant of NPV) rather than on accounting measures (the determinant of ROI or RI).

Further, the bonus scheme should also encourage a long-term perspective by being based on cash flows over the life of the projects selected.

Section 4

ANSWERS TO SCENARIO-BASED QUESTIONS

64 FRANTIC LTD

(a) (i) **Creditor policy**

Tutorial note

By paying creditors after one month instead of after two months, the company will earn a discount of 1.5%. This means that by 'investing' 98.50 one month earlier in the payment of creditors, it will 'earn' 1.50, by not having to pay 100 one month later. The question is asking what the 'return on investment' would be from earning 1.50 by investing 98.50 for one month, expressed as an annualised yield.

The establishment of creditor payment policy involves a comparison of interest rates with the number of days credit in relation to the cash discount available.

Taking the discount yields a return of:

$$\frac{\text{Discount \%}}{(100 - \text{Discount \%})} \times \frac{365}{(\text{Final date} - \text{Discount date})}$$

$$\frac{1.5}{98.5} \times \frac{365 \text{ days}}{(60 \text{ days} - 30 \text{ days})}$$

= 0.1853 or 18.53%. This is more than the discount rate the company uses (i.e. the company's cost of capital). A one-month payment policy should therefore be preferred.

Alternative method of calculation:

	No discount £	*With discount* £
Payment to supplier (per engine)	1,300.0	1,280.5
Loss of interest on investing £1,280.5 for (60 – 30) = 30 days: = 1,280.5 × (30/365) × 15%	–	15.8
Total cost	1,300.0	1,296.3

Taking the discount costs less.

Examiner's note

This can be checked as: [(1,300 – 1,280.5) × (365/30)]/1,280.5 = 18.52%.

(ii) **Stock evaluation without early settlement discounting**

Annual production (demand) = 800 cars = 800 engines.

Cost of ordering = cost of delivery = £1,200.

Annual stock holding cost = 22% × £1,300 = £286.

EOQ ignoring volume discounts =

$$\sqrt{\frac{2 \times \text{delivery cost} \times \text{annual demand}}{\text{annual holding cost per unit}}}$$

$$\sqrt{\frac{2 \times 1{,}200 \times 800}{286}}$$

= 81.93 or 82 whole units.

At this batch ordering level, a quantity discount of 2% would apply. The annual holding cost would therefore be 22% × 98% x £1,300 = £280.28. Re-working the previous calculation with the quantity discount gives:

$$\sqrt{\frac{2 \times 1{,}200 \times 800}{280.28}}$$

= 82.77 or 83 whole units.

Hence the choice facing Frantic Ltd is between ordering 83 units and getting a 2% discount, or 250 units, which is the minimum purchase quantity needed to get a 3% discount.

Evaluation for an order quantity of 83:

		£
Total purchase costs:	£1,300 × 98% × 800 =	1,019,200
Holding costs:	83/2 × £280.28 =	11,632
Order costs:	(800/83) × £1,200 =	11,566
Total annual costs:		1,042,398

Evaluation for an order quantity of 250:

		£
Total purchase costs:	£1,300 × 97% × 800 =	1,008,800
Holding costs:	250/2 × 22% × 97% × £1,300 =	34,678
Order costs:	(800/250) × £1,200 =	3,840
Total annual costs:		1,047,318

Difference in costs: Buying in quantities of 250 is cheaper by £4,920 each year.

The optimal policy is to order in quantities that minimises total costs, which in this case is to **order in batches of 83 engines.**

Examiner's note

An alternative answer takes an incremental cost approach, and compares the incremental costs or savings from ordering in batches of 250 compared to ordering in batches of 83. The initial assumption is that the company orders in batches of 83. This approach is shown below.

	£	£
Saving in purchase price by buying 250: (800 × 1% × £1,300)		10,400
Saving in ordering costs by buying in batches of 250: [(800 × 1,200)/83] – [(800 × 1,200)/250]		7,726
Total cost savings		18,126
Holding costs with order quantity of 250 (above)	34,677	
Holding costs with order quantity of 83 (above)	11,631	
Additional holding costs from ordering in batches of 250		23,046
Increased costs arising from ordering 250 units		4,920

The same conclusion is reached as above. The optimal policy is to order 83 engines at a time.

(iii) **Debtors**

Tutorial note

This part of the question is similar to (a)(i), except here the question is whether to offer an early settlement discount, whereas in (a)(i) the question was whether to accept an early settlement discount.

Offering the discount implies an interest cost of:

$$\frac{\text{Discount \%}}{(100 - \text{Discount \%})} \times \frac{365}{(\text{Final date} - \text{Discount date})}$$

$$\frac{2}{98} \times \frac{365 \text{ days}}{(60 \text{ days} - 30 \text{ days})}$$

= 24.8%

This is more than the discount rate the company uses (i.e. more than the company's cost of capital). It is therefore **not worthwhile**.

Alternative method of solution

For every £100 worth of debtors:

	No discount £	*With discount* £
Receipt from debtor	100.0	98.0
Interest on investing £98 for (60 – 30) = 30 days:		
= 98 × (30/365) × 15%	–	1.2
Total income	100.0	99.2

Hence, it is not worthwhile to offer the discount.

(b) As stated in solution (a)(ii), the optimal policy is to order 83 engines at a time. This involves ordering 800/83 = 9.64 times per year. A production schedule can be drawn-up to assess when the orders would be made. If this is undertaken the following ordering schedule would result:

Month	*1*	*2*	*3*	*4*	*5*	*6*	*7*	*8*	*9*	*10*	*11*	*12*
Car production[1]	66.7	66.7	66.7	66.7	66.7	66.7	66.7	66.7	66.7	66.7	66.7	66.7
Orders placed	83	83	83	83	83		83	83	83	83		83
Stock at month-end	16	32	48	64	80	13	29	45	61	77	10	26

[1] Fractional production allowed and reflected in work in progress

Thus, no orders are placed in the sixth month. This does not have any implications for the six month cash flow since creditors will be paid with one month delay (as determined by the answer to part (a)(i)).

Cash flow for first six months:

Month	*1*	*2*	*3*	*4*	5	6
Receipts						
Cash sales (note 1)	1,416,667	1,416,667	1,416,667	1,416,667	1,416,667	1,416,667
Credit sales (note 1)	1,062,500	1,062,500	1,416,667	1,416,667	1,416,667	1,416,667
Total income	2,479,167	2,479,167	2,833,334	2,833,334	2,833,334	2,833,334
Payments						
Capital costs			3,200,000			
Engine costs (note 2)	97,500	104,156	104,156	104,156	104,156	104,156
Other expenses (note 3)	1,841,667	1,841,667	1,841,667	1,841,667	1,841,667	1,841,667
Fixed costs	18,000	18,000	18,000	22,000	22,000	22,000
Costs net of overdraft	1,957,167	1,963,823	5,163,823	1,967,823	1,967,823	1,967,823
Receipts less payments	522,000	515,344	(2,330,489)	865,511	865,511	865,511
Opening bank balance	(25,000)	496,687	1,012,031	(1,318,458)	(469,428)	390,215
Overdraft interest (note 4)	(313)	-	-	(16,481)	(5,868)	-
Closing bank balance	496,687	1,012,031	(1,318,458)	(469,428)	390,215	1,255,726

Notes:

(1) Monthly sales = 800/12 units. Cash sales are 50% of 800/12 × £42,500 = £1,416,667. Credit sales are the same in each month, but customers take two months' credit. Receipts from credit sales in months 1 and 2 are as stated in the question.

(2) Engine cost payments. Month 1 payment is given in the question. The company will take a bulk purchase discount of 2% and an early settlement discount of 1.5%. Cash paid in subsequent months = quantity purchased in previous month × 98.5% of 98% of £1,300 = £104,156 per month.

(3) Other expenses are 65% × monthly sales = 65% × (800/12) × £42,500 = £1,841,667.

(4) Assumption = Overdraft costs are calculated as (1/12) × 15% × opening bank balance. (Other bases of calculation are acceptable such as interest calculated on average balances.)

(c) **Report**

To: Managing Director and Senior Management Team

From:

Date: xx/xx/xx

Subject: Cash budgeting

Introduction

This report addresses a number of key issues concerning Frantic's cash flow position and has four elements which are of immediate concern to Frantic.

How cash flow problems arise

It is important first to **distinguish between profitability and cash availability**. The key idea relates to insolvency since even profitable companies can face insolvency if cash positions are not properly managed.

Thus cash positions require management to avoid the difficulties associated with cash shortages. Cash shortages are likely to arise in a number of situations. The following is not an exhaustive list, but is likely to represent the most common. Cash flow problems can arise due to:

(i) Sustained losses in the business such that cash resources have been drawn-down

(ii) Difficulties in dealing with inflating costs combined with an inability to raise sales prices proportionately

(iii) Overtrading and inadequate financing of growth. This is very common with new businesses which are not able to finance working capital requirements sufficiently. Generally, such problems are associated with under-capitalised businesses and a lack of recognition that working capital requirements require a large base of long-term capital funding

(iv) Seasonal trading against ongoing costs. This situation arises where income from sales is variable according to the time of year but fairly even monthly outgoings have to be met;

(v) Unplanned one-off large items of expenditure. This may arise, for example, as a result of a break down of a large piece of machinery, and

(vi) Poor credit management.

The importance and impact of each item will depend on a number of factors.

Thus, losses may be sustained for a period without a liquidity problem, depending on how large cash resources are, whether in the form of positive bank balances or the availability of overdraft facilities.

Suffering cost inflation at a higher rate than prices can be raised is not sustainable in the long-run. The importance of this may depend on the capability of the business to implement cost savings, or to diversify markets where prices could be increased.

Overtrading is a problem of forecasting and planning for adequate long-term capital. The idea is that growth should be within available resources.

Seasonal trading requires careful cash management and the extent to which cash resources can be smoothed over the year.

Unplanned major items of expenditure may be important if alternative sources of finance are not available, such as leasing.

Methods of easing cash shortages

There are several techniques for offsetting the short-term effects of cash shortages. In the long-term, however, the adequacy of cash has to be addressed. Thus, for example, cash shortages may be alleviated by the following.

(i) **Postponement of expenditure** where feasible. This would not be feasible in the payment of staff wages, but might be in relation to replacing an old piece of equipment that is still working.

(ii) **Accelerating cash inflows**. For example, by more effective use of credit collection, better credit control, improved early payment incentives, or even the factoring of debt.

(iii) **Sale of redundant assets** either before or after any necessary re-organisation. This may involve the sale of a building where accommodation can be centralised. Other assets may be sold on a sale and lease-back basis, although careful consideration will have to be given to the net benefits arising from this.

(iv) **Re-negotiation of supplier terms or overdraft arrangements**. In particular, bank debt may be mortgaged or secured to access lower rates. Suppliers may agree to lower prices or longer terms if negotiated agreements can be formalised such that a certain level of purchases are made over a period of time.

The importance of each item will depend on the degree of flexibility that Frantic has in its financial structure and agreements. The room for manoeuvre may be limited, but a thorough review of all possibilities is likely to yield at least a number of options. Furthermore, the impact of each potential response depends on how efficient Frantic has been in arranging its affairs in the first place. Finally, none of the items listed will have a sustained impact if the core problem is not identified and dealt-with.

Managing cash resources

A variety of methods might be of use in managing resources. The particular tool chosen will depend on its reliability and appropriateness. Appropriateness, in turn, will be governed by the underlying assumptions of the technique employed. Some of the methods that may be used to managed cash resources are listed below:

(i) **Inventory approach to cash management**. This method views cash in the same way as engine stock such that EOQ models may be employed. In such circumstances, cash is viewed as an asset with costs associated with it that should be minimised so as to determine what level of cash balances should be held. Thus, decreases or increases in cash balances can be determined according to planned growth, the time value of money and the costs of obtaining new funds.

(ii) The **Miller-Orr model** recognises that cash balance requirements are likely to fluctuate and that active management is required in responding to these fluctuations. In particular, attention is paid to the variability (or variance) of cash flows, interest rates and the transaction costs of adjusting cash balances. It is the variability of cash balances that is crucial to understanding cash management since this will depend directly on understanding how Frantic's operations (fundamentally, sales and production) vary. For a volatile business, it is likely that large cash balances will need to be kept. Miller-Orr suggest a simple formula to estimate this although the formula itself is limited by the assumptions on which it rests.

(iii) **Probability approaches** recognise a degree of uncertainty in predicting cash balances and allow for a range of outcomes to occur. If the assessment of such probabilities is accurate then cash resources can be put in place in readiness for the predicted events. The method is not wholly reliable in situations where the number of potential outcomes is small, since unfeasible expected outcomes may be predicted by using a probability approach.

(iv) Cash management is also about **managing surplus cash**. The response of management should depend on whether the surplus is large and how long it is likely to exist. If the balance is large and is likely to remain, then management have a duty to look for appropriate investment opportunities or else refund the investors with a special dividend, for example. Smaller cash balances can be actively managed via short term deposits.

A centralised treasury function

Treasury departments are normally a feature of larger companies than Frantic, although it is perhaps beneficial to consider the benefits of such departments to assess what practices might reasonably be adopted. Essentially, treasury centralisation is an issue concerned with economies of scale. The benefits of treasury departments are numerous and include the following.

(i) Consolidating bank accounts to create either a single account through which all cash resources are managed or a virtual single account with automatic offset between different accounts. Such an approach maximises deposit interest, which is typically higher on larger cash balances for positive balances whilst minimising overdraft costs for negative balances.

(ii) Borrowings can be arranged in bulk thus accessing lower rates.

(iii) Foreign exchange management is improved. In the same way that cash balances are effectively consolidated, foreign currency payments and receipts of all the divisions in the company can be amalgamated, and cash inflows and outflows in each currency set off against each other. This can reduce the need for expensive hedging agreements. Foreign exchange risk consolidation is common in practice.

(iv) Treasury expertise can be developed within a single department, thus enhancing the quality of resource management generally.

(v) Precautionary cash balances, when centralised, are likely to be lower than when considered on an individual account basis.

ACCA marking scheme				
			Marks	
(a)	(i)	Calculation of discount rate implied in the early settlement	2	
		Decision on payment period	1	
				3
	(ii)	Calculation of basic EOQ (ignoring discounts)	1	
		Evaluation of purchase costs with discounts	4	
		Decision on optimal policy	1	
				6
	(iii)	Calculation of discount rate implied in the early settlement	2	
		Decision on payment period	1	
				3
(b)		Defining frequency of orders	1	
		Consideration of scheduling of orders	4	
		Preparation of cash budget in accordance with answer to part (a)	9	
		Identification of overdraft costs	4	
				18
(c)		2 marks each for identification and elaborated examples of how cash problems arise. Up to a maximum of:	4	
		2 marks each for identification and elaborated examples of easing cash shortages. Up to a maximum of:	4	
		2 marks each for identification and elaborated examples of how cash resources may be managed. Up to a maximum of:	4	
		2 marks each for identification and elaborated examples of the benefits of a treasury function. Up to a maximum of:	6	
		Quality of presentation of report	2	
				20
Total				50

65 JACK GEEP

(a)

	High demand	*Medium demand*	*Low demand*	*Expected demand*
	£	£	£	£
February	22,000 × 0.05	20,000 × 0.85	19,000 × 0.1	20,000
March	26,000 × 0.05	24,000 × 0.85	23,000 × 0.1	24,000
April	30,000 × 0.05	28,000 × 0.85	27,000 × 0.1	28,000
May	29,000 × 0.05	27,000 × 0.85	26,000 × 0.1	27,000
June	35,000 × 0.05	33,000 × 0.85	32,000 × 0.1	33,000

	January £	*February* £	*March* £	*April* £	*May* £	*June* £
Receipts						
Capital	150,000					
Cash sales (W1)		2,000	2,400	2,800	2,700	3,300
Credit sales (W1)			8,775	10,530	12,285	11,846
				9,000	10,800	12,600
	150,000	2,000	11,175	22,330	25,785	27,746
Payments						
Fixed assets		200,000		50,000		
Labour (W3)	6,300	7,560	8,820	8,505	10,395	10,395
Materials (W3)		4,200	5,040	5,880	5,670	6,930
Overheads (W3)			2,100	2,520	2,940	2,835
Fixed costs	7,000	7,000	7,000	7,000	7,000	7,000
Consultant		12,000				
	13,300	230,760	22,960	73,905	26,005	27,160
Net cash flow	136,700	(228,760)	(11,785)	(51,575)	(220)	586
Opening balance	0	136,700	(92,060)	(103,845)	(155,420)	(155,640)
Closing balance	136,700	(92,060)	(103,845)	(155,420)	(155,640)	(155,054)

Workings

(W1) **Cash from sales**

	January £	*February* £	*March* £	*April* £	*May* £	*June* £
Cash sales (10%)		2,000	2,400	2,800	2,700	3,300
Credit sales:						
(90% × 0.5 × 0.975)			8,775	10,530	12,285	11,846
(90% × 0.5)				9,000	10,800	12,600

(W2) **Variable production costs** (£600 per £1,000 of sales)

	January £	*February* £	*March* £	*April* £	*May* £	*June* £
Cost of sales	12,000	14,400	16,800	16,200	19,800	19,800
Defects (5%)	600	720	840	810	990	990
Total	12,600	15,120	17,640	17,010	20,790	20,790

(W3) **Production cash flows** (see (W2))

	January £	*February* £	*March* £	*April* £	*May* £	*June* £
Labour (3/6 of total)	6,300	7,560	8,820	8,505	10,395	10,395
Materials (2/6 of total)		4,200	5,040	5,880	5,670	6,930
Overheads (1/6)			2,100	2,520	2,940	2,835

Tutorial note: Materials paid one month in arrears and variable overheads two months in arrears.

(b) ***Note:*** **Only the cash flows for sales and labour are required. The remainder of the cash budget is provided to prove the figures supplied in the question.**

The basic point is that high demand cannot be satisfied with a just-in-time stock management system.

	Medium demand	*Low demand*	*Expected sales*
	£	£	£
February	20,000 × 0.9	19,000 × 0.1	19,900
March	24,000 × 0.9	23,000 × 0.1	23,900
April	28,000 × 0.9	27,000 × 0.1	27,900
May	27,000 × 0.9	26,000 × 0.1	26,900
June	33,000 × 0.9	32,000 × 0.1	32,900

	January	*February*	*March*	*April*	*May*	*June*
	£	£	£	£	£	£
Receipts						
Capital	150,000					
Cash sales (W4)		1,990	2,390	2,790	2,690	3,290
Credit sales (W4)			8,731	10,486	12,241	11,802
				8,955	10,755	12,555
	150,000	1,990	11,121	22,231	25,686	27,647
Payments						
Fixed assets		200,000		50,000		
Labour (W6)		6,269	7,529	8,789	8,474	10,364
Materials (W6)			4,179	5,019	5,859	5,649
Overheads (W6)				2,090	2,510	2,930
Fixed costs	7,000	7,000	7,000	7,000	7,000	7,000
Consultant		12,000				
	7,000	225,269	18,708	72,898	23,843	25,943
Net cash flow	143,000	(223,279)	(7,587)	(50,667)	1,843	1,704
Opening balance	0	143,000	(80,279)	(87,866)	(138,533)	(136,690)
Closing balance	143,000	(80,279)	(87,866)	(138,533)	(136,690)	(134,986)

Workings

(W4) **Cash from sales**

	February	*March*	*April*	*May*	*June*
	£	£	£	£	£
Cash sales (10%)	1,990	2,390	2,790	2,690	3,290
Credit sales:					
(90% × 0.5 × 0.975)		8,731	10,486	12,241	11,802
(90% × 0.5)			8,955	10,755	12,555

(W5) **Variable production costs** (£600 per £1,000 of sales)

	February	*March*	*April*	*May*	*June*
	£	£	£	£	£
Cost of sales	11,940	14,340	16,740	16,140	19,740
Defects (5%)	597	717	837	807	987
Total	12,537	15,057	17,577	16,947	20,727

(W6) **Production cash flows** (see (W5))

	February	*March*	*April*	*May*	*June*
	£	£	£	£	£
Labour (3/6 of total)	6,269	7,529	8,789	8,474	10,364
Materials (2/6 of total)		4,179	5,019	5,859	5,649
Overheads (1/6)			2,090	2,510	2,930

Tutorial note: Materials paid one month in arrears and variable overheads two months in arrears.

Tutorial note: A quicker method is merely to deduct 63 from each of the totals in requirement (a) as the loss of sales is constant.

(c) The introduction of just-in-time stock management for finished goods has a number of benefits:

(1) It significantly improves the short-term liquidity of the business with a maximum financing requirement of £138,533 rather than £155,640. There is also a more rapidly improving deficit thereafter, with the balance falling to £134,986 by the end of June. In the longer term, however, there is continued loss of profitability due to lost sales when demand is high.

The primary reason for this is the reduced investment in stock that is tying up cash. Under the original proposal there is surplus stock amounting to the next month's sales which means production is necessary at an earlier stage thereby using up cash resources.

(2) Interest costs and stock holding costs are saved by reduced stock levels, thereby adding to profit.

(3) There already appears to be a just-in-time stock management policy with respect to raw materials and work in progress and such a policy for finished goods would be consistent with this.

There are, however, a number of problems with just-in-time stock management in these circumstances:

(1) When demand is higher than expected, the additional sales are lost as there is insufficient production to accommodate demand above the mean expected level. This is because no stock is carried. This, however, amounts to only £100 per month of sales on average, which may be a price worth paying in return for improved liquidity in terms of a reduced cash deficit.

(2) In addition to losing contribution there may be a loss of goodwill and reputation if customers cannot be supplied. They may go elsewhere not just for the current sale but also for future sales if Mr Geep is seen as an unreliable supplier. This results from the fact that customers demand immediate delivery of orders.

(3) Just-in-time management of stock relies upon not just reliable timing and quantities but also reliable quality. The number of defects can be planned if it is constant, but if they occur irregularly this presents an additional problem.

(4) If production in each month is to supply demand in the same month, this relies on the fact that demand parallels production within the month. If the majority of demand is at the beginning of each month this would cause problems without a level of safety stock, given that prompt delivery is expected by customers.

A number of compromises between the two positions would be possible:

(1) Stock could be held sufficient to accommodate demand when it was high. This amounts to only an extra £2,000 at selling values thus an extra £1,200 at variable cost. This is significantly lower than a whole month's production but would accommodate peak demand.

(2) Liquidity is very important initially as the business attempts to become established. Therefore minimal stocks could be held in the early months, with perhaps slightly increased stocks once the business and its cash flows become established.

(d) **REPORT**

To: Mr J Geep

From: An Accountant

Date: xx/xx/xx

Subject: Liquidity and financing

(i) **The extent of financing required**

Sales are uncertain with high, low and medium estimates of demand. This of itself gives some uncertainty but the reliability and probability of these estimates will need to be established by appropriate market research. If sales are lower than expected then any bank finance will take longer to repay, thus increasing the amount of finance needed and the proportion of longer-term finance.

If just-in-time stock management is not implemented, the maximum finance requirement is £155,640.

After July 20X3 the expected net cash inflow will be constant (ignoring any further purchases of fixed assets) as follows:

	£		£
Sales			33,000
Discounts: (33,000 × 0.9 × 0.025)			(742)
Labour	(9,900)		
Material	(6,600)		
Variable overheads	(3,300)		
Allowance for defects	(19,800)	× 1.05	(20,790)
Fixed costs			(7,000)
Net cash inflow			4,468

Thus, to pay off a loan of £155,054 it would mean payments over 35 months (155,054/4,468) would have to take place, ignoring interest charges. Any variation in these estimates would, however, affect the amount of the financing needed.

In addition to uncertain trading results affecting the amount of future financing, there will be a requirement to finance future capital investment as the business expands. This is likely to be a major financing need, depending on the rate of expansion.

The levels of the drawings, taxation and interest charges will also extend the amount of finance needed, as these items were not included in the cash budget presented.

(ii) **Short- and long-term financing mix**

In forming a new business, there is no business history to present to the bank. Consequently, there is additional uncertainty, which will need to be considered before any finance is likely to be forthcoming, either of a short-term or a long-term nature.

If there is a good relationship with the bank, an overdraft might be possible for the entire financing requirement, but an overdraft facility from a bank is uncommitted. There is a risk of it being payable immediately on demand. If planned cash flows did not turn out as expected, the bank may get nervous and possibly withdraw credit facilities.

A medium-term loan would also be possible to meet the entire financing requirement. This has the advantage of security in that it cannot be recalled unless there is a breach in the terms (breach of covenant). Most likely such funding would come from a bank, the issue of debentures being entirely out of the question on the grounds of size. Other considerations would be the term of the loan, security required, the interest rate, and covenants.

Another possible form of finance include leasing which can be regarded as a quasi-loan if entering into a long-term contract. However, other considerations may apply such as variability of rental terms, transfer of risk, residual value of asset, cancellation rights, amount of rentals, and the period of the lease agreement.

A further option would be for Mr. Geep to put in more ownership capital, perhaps secured on the equity in his house.

A mixture of these various forms of finance would be most likely.

The precise mix will depend upon a number of factors (although some of these may also influence the total amount of finance needed):

(1) The ability and willingness of Mr. Geep to supply funds initially and additionally if plans do not turn out as expected.

(2) A loan would require some security. The company has few assets to use as security as there does not appear to be any property, the machinery has a low net realisable value and there is little stock (which is normally poor security anyway). An overdraft may also require security, but may place increased emphasis on the cash-generating potential of the business to make appropriate repayments. Ultimately, however, this is an unlimited business and Mr. Geep's personal assets, and particularly the equity in his house, will act as security.

(3) Other costs are necessary including the drawings of the owner Mr. Geep and interest charges. These will reduce the ability of the business to repay any loan and thus extend the period of repayments in excess of the above estimate of 35 months.

(4) There may be more restrictive covenants in a loan agreement than an overdraft, because an overdraft is repayable on demand, and thus the bank needs less protection from other clauses in the contact. The documentation for an overdraft, unlike a longer-term loan, is fairly short and simple.

(5) Overdraft interest is only payable on the balance outstanding, thus if major inflows occur this will reduce interest costs.

(6) The difference between short- and long-term interest rates may influence the relative charges on an overdraft or a medium-term loan.

(7) The purpose of the finance is also likely to affect the form of finance. For example, if funds are required to finance fixed assets then it might be appropriate to use long-term finance to match the long-term usage of the **asset.**

(iii) **Working capital management**

It has already been seen (in answer (b)) that a reduction in stock due to the introduction of just-in-time stock management can improve liquidity and reduce any cash deficit. The same principle can be applied to reductions in other elements of working capital.

Some of the same arguments also apply, however, in that while liquidity may be improved there could be offsetting disadvantages in terms of lost profitability or increased risk.

Debtors

Giving two months' credit creates a significant level of debtors that need financing.

If sales are £33,000 per month, the cash flow needed to fund the debtors will be:

	£
Sales with one month's credit (£33,000 × 90% × 50% × 0.975)	14,479
Sales with two month's credit (£33,000 × 90% × 50% × 2m)	29,700
Total	44,179

This is a significant proportion of the maximum financing requirement.

Whether the credit terms themselves can be changed may depend on the credit terms of competitors when set alongside the other conditions of sale. If the business is out of line with competitors, lost sales may result. A balance may therefore need to be struck between liquidity and profitability.

In terms of debt collection, it would appear that all debtors are expected to pay on time so there is little that can be done in this area given the current credit terms.

Accelerated payment could be encouraged by a higher cash discount but this is expensive, particularly as customers who would pay within one month anyway would also receive a greater reduction in price without any benefit to the business.

Invoice discounting and debt factoring may be alternative sources of financing, but these can be expensive and in the particular circumstances of the business, where there are expected to be no late payers or bad debts, it might seem inappropriate to use outside assistance.

Creditors

It may be possible to delay payment to creditors in respect of materials and variable overheads. This may, however, damage relationships with suppliers and this might be significant for a new business.

ACCA marking scheme		
		Marks
(a)	Demand forecasts	2
	Production cash flows	5
	Sales cash flows	4
	Fixed cost cash flows	1
	Consultant cost cash flows	1
	Capital investment cash flows	1
	Fixed asset cash flows	1
	Bank balances	2
(b)	Sales	4
	Labour	2
(c)	2 marks for each explained point	6
(d)	Up to 2 marks for each explained point	18
	Report format	2
Total		50

66 DOE LIMITED

Key answer tips

For part (a) of the question, remember to present the answer in a report format. To provide an answer, you need to make it clear that you understand what overtrading is (trying to carry on too much business with insufficient long-term finance) and what the symptoms of overtrading might be (raid increase in sales, increases in current assets financed largely or entirely by current liabilities, growing bank overdraft, deteriorating current ratio and acid test ratio). These symptoms are evident in the figures for Doe Limited.

Part (b) tests your ability to evaluate the costs of using a factor to collect debts and provide factor finance. However, although the factor will provide a without recourse (non-recourse) service, no information is provided about the benefits that might arise from savings in bad debts. This should be mentioned in your answer. Part (c) calls for a broader consideration of debt collection policies and procedures.

Parts (d) and (e) are a good test of your understanding of DCF techniques, and you should check how long it takes you to write an answer. The two parts of the question together are only worth 15 marks, and you need to work quickly to complete the question within the time allowed.

(a) **REPORT**

To: The Board of Doe Limited

From: Accountant

Date: xx/xx/xx

Subject: **Is the company overtrading?**

1 **Introduction**

This report presents my findings regarding the suggestion made at the last board meeting that our company is overtrading. Overtrading is also known as under capitalisation, and occurs when the volume of trade is not supported by an adequate supply of capital. Overtrading can lead to liquidity problems that can cause serious difficulties if they are not dealt with promptly.

2 **Signs of overtrading**

There are a number of generally recognised signs that a company may be overtrading. These are considered, together with relevant financial data from Appendix 1, in the following paragraphs.

Rapid increase in turnover

The forecast financial statements for 20X3 show that our turnover is expected to increase by 25% during the year.

Rapid increase in current assets

Current assets are expected to rise by 27%, slightly more than the increase in turnover.

Increase in stock days and debtor days

Debtor days are expected to increase from 110 to 121 days, with a 38% increase in total debtors, but stock days are not expected to increase, but to fall from 265 days to 238 days. Nevertheless, a 19% increase in stocks is anticipated.

Increased reliance on short-term finance

Reserves are expected to increase by £100,000 whereas total assets are expected to increase by £1,400,000. The expansion of our business activity is therefore based primarily on an expansion of short-term finance (trade creditors and overdraft). Creditor days will increase from 177 to 190 days, while in relative terms creditors will increase by 42% – more than the expected rise in turnover (25%) and in our overdraft (20%).

Decrease in current ratio and quick ratio

The current ratio is expected to fall very slightly from 1·04 to 1·03, but the quick ratio is not expected to fall, but to increase from 0.44 to 0.47.

However, any interpretation of these ratios should reflect the fact that different industries have different working capital needs. Sector average data can be useful here.

3 **Comparison with sector averages**

Any conclusion about the signs of overtrading needs to be put in the context of the normal values of accounting ratios for other companies in the industry, as indicated by the sector averages. However, it should be recognised that averages exist because no two companies are identical, even when in the same business sector, and the following discussion should be read with this in mind.

The increasing trend of debtor days away from the sector average of 100 days is clearly a cause for concern. If our level of debtors was brought into line with the sector average our financing need would fall by £477,000 (£2.75m × 21/121), which is equivalent to 17% of our forecast overdraft. The decrease in stock days is encouraging, although forecast stock days remain 13% higher than the sector average, indicating the possibility of further improvement.

There is clear evidence of an increased reliance on short-term finance. The trend of creditor days is increasing away from the sector average of 120 days and the forecast of 190 days is a very worrying 58% more than the average. This represents £940,000 (£2.55m × 70/190) more in trade finance that our company is carrying compared to a similar company in our business sector. On this evidence, it is likely that our suppliers will begin to press for earlier settlement in the near future and this will add to the pressure already being exerted by our bank.

The quick ratio is expected to increase but will still be 15% below the sector average, while the current ratio is expected to be 25% lower than the average. The low current and quick ratios reflect the increased reliance of our company in comparative terms on short-term sources of finance.

4 **Conclusion on overtrading**

Most of the evidence suggests that our company is moving into an overtrading situation, although the evidence is not conclusive. Current pressure from our bank to reduce our overdraft serves to highlight the fact that our company needs to reduce its reliance on short-term finance, whether trade finance or overdraft finance. Improved working capital management could reduce the level of investment in debtors, and to a lesser extent perhaps in stocks, which would ease our financial difficulties. However, more drastic measures than this will be needed to deal with our reliance on short-term finance. Although the size of the reduction in the overdraft required by the bank is not known at present, simply reducing trade credit to an average level would need £1m of additional finance. Factoring of debtors has been suggested as a source of working capital finance and it is certainly true that this would produce an immediate injection of cash that could decrease our overdraft and lower our average trade credit period. A further consideration is that our company has no long-term debt and given our continuing growth, this source of finance also deserves serious consideration.

Appendix 1: Financial analysis

Growth in turnover	=	(8,300 – 6,638)/6,638 = 0.25 or 25%
Growth in current assets	=	(5,950 – 4,700)/4,700 = 0.27 or 27%
Increase in overdraft	=	(2,750 – 2,300)/2,300 = 0.20 or 20%
Increase in trade creditors	=	(2,550 – 1,800)/1,800 = 00.42 or 42%

		20X3		*20X2*
Stock turnover (days)	365 × 3,200/4,900	238 days	365 × 2,700/3,720	265 days
Debtor days	365 × 2,750/8,300	121 days	365 × 2,000/6,638	110 days
Creditor days	365 × 2,550/4,900	190 days	365 × 1,800/3,720	177 days
Current ratio	5,950/5,800	1.03	4,700/4,500	1.04
Quick ratio	2,750/5,800	0.47	2,000/4,500	0.44

(b) (i) **Evaluation of factor's offer using overdraft interest rate of 6%**

	£
Cost of financing with the factor	
80% of £8.3 million × 90/365 × 8%	130,981
20% of £8.3 million × 90/365 × 6%	24,559
	155,540
Current cost of financing debtors	
£2,750,000 × 6%	165,000
Saving in finance costs with factor	9,460
Saving in administration costs	15,000
	24,460
Factor's fee (£8.3 million × 1%)	(83,000)
Net cost of factoring	(58,540)

On this analysis, the factor's offer is not financially acceptable. The offer was on a non-recourse basis, however, and the information given does not refer to any reduction in bad debts. If bad debts are currently more than 0.7% of turnover (£58,540/£8.3m), the factor's offer might become financially attractive.

Evaluation of factor's offer using medium-term bank loan rate of 10%

As the overdraft must be reduced anyway, the 10% interest cost of the medium-term bank loan could be seen as the opportunity cost of not accepting the factor's offer. An alternative evaluation of the factor's offer could be as follows:

	£
Cost of financing with the factor	
80% of £8.3 million × 90/365 × 8%	130,981
20% of £8.3 million × 90/365 × 10%	40,932
	171,913

Current cost of financing debtors	
£2,750,000 × 10%	275,000
Saving in finance costs with factor	103,087
Saving in administration costs	15,000
	118,087
Factor's fee (£8.3 million × 1%)	(83,000)
Net benefit from factoring	35,087

On this analysis, in view of the high interest rate on the bank loan, the factor's offer is financially acceptable, even before considering any reduction in bad debts.

(ii) The following benefits of factoring are commonly identified.

Factor finance

The factoring company will advance up to 80% of the face value of invoices raised. This would create a one-off improvement in cash flow and allow Doe Ltd to pay its trade creditors promptly and perhaps take advantage of any early payment discounts available. It would also allow Doe Ltd to finance its growth from sales rather than by seeking external finance.

Reduces administration costs

The factor would take over the administration of Doe Ltd's sales ledger, allowing a reduction in administration costs in the longer term.

Factor expertise

In the areas of credit analysis and debtor collection, the expertise of the factor is likely to be higher than Doe Ltd's, leading to lower bad debts and more efficient collection of amounts owed by debtors.

Credit protection

If the factoring is with recourse, Doe Ltd will be effectively insured against the possibility of bad debts, although this will be included in the factor's fee.

(c) No information has been provided on the current methods used by Doe Ltd to manage its debtors and so this answer is in general terms.

Credit analysis: granting credit

Potential credit customers should be carefully screened using such methods as trade references, bank references, credit reports from credit reference agencies, and analysis of financial statements. The extent of the credit analysis should depend on the size of the initial order as well as the potential for repeat business. Credit analysis can improve debtor management by reducing the incidence of bad debts, slow payers and troublesome customers.

Terms of trade

Doe Ltd should negotiate agreed terms of trade with its customers in order to encourage prompter payment. These terms of trade may offer discounts for early payment, which apart from cash flow benefits will reduce the likelihood of late payments and bad debts.

Credit control

Once credit has been extended it is important to ensure that customers abide by agreed terms of trade. Regular checks on customer accounts, for example using an aged debtor analysis, can direct attention to overdue accounts or those close to their credit limit. Statements of account should be mailed to debtors on a regular basis in order to remind them of their outstanding debts. Late payers should be contacted by telephone to enquire after the reason for the delay in settling their accounts. A policy of charging interest on overdue accounts might be considered in order to encourage prompt payment.

Debt collection

The company should have an agreed policy or procedure for dealing with accounts in default. This policy should be included in the terms of trade so that customers are aware of the steps the company is likely to take if payment is not made on time. The company could decide, for example, to take legal action to recover debts more than one month old. However, the benefit of such action must always exceed the cost incurred.

Factoring and invoice discounting

The cash flow and other benefits of factoring were discussed earlier. Invoice discounting also offers cash flow advantages. With invoice discounting, selected invoices of good quality are sold in exchange for an advance of up to 80% of face value. The balance, less a fee charged by the invoice discounter, is received when the invoices are settled.

(d) It is appropriate to use the after-tax cost of borrowing as the discount rate since Doe Ltd is clearly in a tax-paying situation and hence is in a position to claim the tax benefits of lease payments and capital allowances.

Care must be taken when determining the timing of cash flows, since financial evaluation models seek to represent the real world. As lease payments are made on the first day of Doe Ltd's accounting period, it is appropriate to treat them for discounting purposes as though they occur at the end of the previous accounting period. However, the tax benefits of lease payments will occur in the accounting period following that in which payment is made. Similarly, it is appropriate to treat the purchase cost on 1 January of the first year of use as being made at year 0 for discounting purposes, even though the tax benefit from the first capital allowance will arise in year 2, i.e. in the accounting period following the one in which payment is made.

Capital allowances and associated tax benefits:

Start of Year	*Written down value of asset*	*Capital allowance (25%)*	*Tax benefit (30%)*	*Tax benefit cash flow in Year*
	£	£	£	
1	365,000	91,250	27,375	2
2	273,750	68,437	20,531	3
3	205,313	51,328	15,398	4
4	153,985	38,496	11,549	5
5	115,489		34,647	6

Evaluation of borrowing to buy:

Year		*Cash flow*	*Discount factor at 7%*	*Present value*
		£		£
0	Capital expenditure	(365,000)	1.000	(365,000)
2	Tax savings	27,375	0.873	23,898

Year		*Cash flow*	*Discount factor at 7%*	*Present value*
		£		£
3	Tax savings	20,531	0.816	16,753
4	Tax savings	15,398	0.763	11,749
5	Tax savings	11,549	0.713	8,234
6	Tax savings	34,647	0.666	23,075
	Net present value			(281,291)

The cost of borrowing to buy the machine is £281,291.

Evaluation of leasing

Years		*Cash flow*	*Discount factor at 7%*	*Present value*
		£		£
0 – 4	Lease rentals	(77,250)	4.387	(338,896)
2 – 6	Savings in tax payments	23,175	3.832	88,807
	Net present value			(250,089)

Notes:

Discount factor, years 0 – 4 = 1.000 + 3.387 = 4.387

Discount factor, years 2 – 6 = 4.767 – 0.935 = 3.832.

The cost of leasing is £250.089.

Leasing has the lower cost by £31,202 and is therefore preferred to borrowing.

(e) The optimum price will be the one that maximizes total contribution over the five-year life of the new machine. (Taxation and the time value of money are ignored, as required by the question.)

Sales price of £70 per unit

Contribution per unit = £70 – £42 = £28 per unit.

Sales growth is 20% per annum.

Year	1	2	3	4	5
Sales volume (units)	10,000	12,000	14,400	17,280	20,000
Contribution (£/unit)	28	28	28	28	28
Total contribution (£)	280,000	336,000	403,200	483,840	560,000

Year 5 sales volume is limited to the maximum capacity of the new machine.

Total contribution over the five years is £2,063,400

Sales price of £67 per unit

Contribution per unit = 67 – 42 = £25 per unit.

Sales growth is 23% per annum.

Year	1	2	3	4	5
Sales volume (units)	11,000	13,530	16,640	20,000	20,000
Contribution (£/unit)	25	25	25	25	25
Total contribution (£)	275,000	338,250	416,050	500,000	500,000

Sales volume is restricted in years 4 and 5.

Total contribution over the five years is £2,029,300.

Conclusion

The sales price of £70 per unit appears to be marginally preferable on the basis of total contribution. The incremental fixed production overheads will be the same irrespective of which sales price is selected and so may be omitted from the analysis.

ACCA marking scheme			
			Marks
(a)		Explanation of overtrading	1
		Symptoms of overtrading	2
		Calculation of relevant ratios	4
		Discussion of evidence for overtrading	3
		Conclusion and format	2
			12
(b)	(i)	Change in level of debtors	1
		Reduction in cost of financing	1
		Cost of advance by factor	1
		Administration savings	1
		Factor's fee	1
		Net cost of factor's offer	1
		Discussion	1
			7
	(ii)	Up to 2 marks for each detailed advantage	8
(c)		Up to 3 marks for each way discussed	8
(d)		Capital allowances	2
		Tax effects of capital allowances	1
		Evaluation of cost of borrowing to buy	2
		Lease payments	1
		Tax effects of lease payments	1
		Evaluation of cost of leasing	1
		Evaluation of leasing versus borrowing to buy	1
			9
(e)		Sales volumes	2
		Annual contributions	2
		Total contributions	1
		Conclusion	1
			6
Total			50

67 NESPA

Key answer tips

Parts (a) to (c) of the question should be straightforward, although cash flows must be adjusted for inflation, and in part (b) the effect of capital allowances on cash flows must also be calculated. The difficulty with these sections of the question is completing all the calculations accurately within the time available. When answering part (d), don't overlook the second part of the question, about Nespa's views of investment appraisal methods.

For part (e), there are several methods commonly considered to assess project risk and uncertainty, such as sensitivity analysis, probability analysis, risk-adjusted discount rates, certainty equivalents and range estimates. The question asks for a discussion of just two methods, although three methods are discussed in this solution.

Part (f) should be straightforward, but it is important to refer to the question scenario in your answer, rather than writing in general terms about alternative sources of finance.

(a) *Assumption*: It is assumed that the inflation rate of 3% in prices and variables costs applies from Year 1 onwards.

Strategy 1

Year	*1*	*2*	*3*	*4*	*5*
Demand (units)	100,000	105,000	110,250	115,762	121,551
Selling price (£/unit)	8.00	8.00	8.00	8.00	8.00
Variable cost (£/unit)	3.00	3.00	2.95	2.95	2.90
Contribution (£/unit)	5.00	5.00	5.05	5.05	5.10
Inflation factor at 3% per year	1.03	1.0609	1.0927	1.1255	1.1593
Inflated contribution (£/unit)	5.15	5.30	5.52	5.68	5.91
Total contribution (£)	515,000	556,500	608,580	657,528	718,366
10% discount factors	0.909	0.826	0.751	0.683	0.621
PV of contribution (£)	468,135	459,669	457,044	449,092	446,105

Total PV of strategy 1 contributions = £2,280,045 or approximately £2,280,000.

Strategy 2

Year	*1*	*2*	*3*	*4*	*5*
Demand (units)	110,000	126,500	145,475	167,296	192,391
Selling price (£/unit)	7.00	7.00	7.00	7.00	7.00
Variable cost (£/unit)	2.95	2.90	2.80	2.70	2.55
Contribution (£/unit)	4.05	4.10	4.20	4.30	4.45
Inflation factor at 3% per year	1.03	1.0609	1.0927	1.1255	1.1597
Inflated contribution (£/unit)	4.17	4.35	4.59	4.84	5.16
Total contribution (£)	458,700	550,275	667,730	809,713	992,738
10% discount factors	0.909	0.826	0.751	0.683	0.621
PV of contribution (£)	416,958	454,527	501,465	553,034	616,490

Total PV of strategy 2 contributions = £2,542,474 or approximately £2,542,000.

Strategy 2 is preferred as it has the higher present value of contributions.

(b) Evaluating the investment in the new machine using internal rate of return:

Year	*0*	*1*	*2*	*3*	*4*	*5*
	£	£	£	£	£	£
Contribution		458,700	550,275	667,730	809,713	992,738
Fixed costs		(114,400)	(118,976)	(123,735)	(128,684)	(133,832)
Taxable profit		344,300	431,299	543,995	681,029	858,906
Taxation at 30%		(103,290)	(129,390)	(163,199)	(204,309)	(257,672)
		241,010	301,909	380,796	476,720	601,234
Capital allowance tax benefits (see note)		112,500	84,375	63,281	47,461	142,383
Profit after tax		353,510	386,284	444,077	524,181	743,617

Note: capital allowances and tax benefits

Year		£
1	25% × £1,500,000 × 30% tax rate	112,500
2	75% of Year 1 amount	84,375
3	75% of Year 2 amount	63,281
4	75% of Year 3 amount	47,461
		307,617
5	Balancing amount	142,383
Total	£1,500,000 × 30% tax rate	450,000

Cash flows	(1,500,000)	353,510	386,284	444,077	524,181	743,617
10% discount factors	1.000	0.909	0.826	0.751	0.683	0.621
Present values	(1,500,000)	321,341	319,071	333,502	358,016	461,786

NPV at 10% = £293,716

Cash flows	(1,500,000)	353,510	386,284	444,077	524,181	743,617
20% discount factors	1.000	0.833	0.694	0.579	0.482	0.402
Present values	(1,500,000)	294,474	268,081	257,121	252,655	298,934

NPV at 20% = (£128,735)

IRR = 10% + [293,716 / (293,716 + 128,735)] × (20 – 10)% = 17%.

Since the internal rate of return is greater than the company's cost of capital of 10%, the investment is financially acceptable.

(c) Evaluating the investment using return on capital employed:

Annual depreciation charge = £1,500,000/5 = £300,000

Year	*1*	*2*	*3*	*4*	*5*
	£	£	£	£	£
Contribution	458,700	550,275	667,730	809,713	992,738
Fixed costs	(114,400)	(118,976)	(123,735)	(128,684)	(133,832)
Depreciation	(300,000)	(300,000)	(300,000)	(300,000)	(300,000)
Annual PBIT	44,300	131,299	243,995	381,029	558,906

Total profit before interest and tax (PBIT) over five years = £1,359,529.

Average investment = £1,500,000/2 = £750,000

Average annual accounting profit = £1,359,529/5 = £271,906

Return on capital employed = (£271,906/ £750,000) × 100% = 36%.

Since the return on capital employed is greater than the hurdle rate of 20%, the investment is financially acceptable.

(d) Internal rate of return (IRR) is a discounted cash flow investment appraisal method that calculates the discount rate which causes the net present value of an investment to become zero. An investment project is acceptable if it has an IRR greater than the cost of capital of the investing company. It uses cash flows rather than accounting profits in the evaluation of an investment project. It also takes account of the time value of money, the concept that the value of a given sum of money decreases over time due to the opportunity cost of selecting one investment rather than the best available alternative. IRR considers all cash flows over the life of an investment project and always gives correct advice, provided that investment projects being compared are not mutually exclusive.

Return on capital employed (ROCE) is also called accounting rate of return. Unlike IRR, ROCE uses average annual accounting profit before interest and tax in the evaluation of investment projects, expressing this as a percentage of the amount of capital invested. The decision as to whether a project is acceptable is made by comparing project ROCE with a target ROCE, such as a company's current ROCE.

The problem with using accounting profit rather than cash flow is that only cash flow (and not profit) is linked directly to an increase in company value. ROCE also ignores the time value of money. Because it averages accounting profit over the life of the project, the amount of profit in a given year is irrelevant; ROCE therefore ignores the timing of accounting profits.

ROCE also suffers from definition problems as there are several definitions in common use and so care must be taken to ensure comparisons are made using identical definitions. Capital invested can be defined as initial capital invested or average capital invested, but other definitions are met in practice.

Both IRR and ROCE offer a relative measure of return in percentage terms, a feature that is seen as attractive to managers who may have difficulty in interpreting the absolute measure of value offered by net present value. A relative measure of return ignores the size of the initial investment, however, and so should not be relied on as a sole measure of investment worth.

Academically, IRR is preferred to ROCE because it takes account of the time value of money, uses cash flows, and compares the return on investment projects with the cost of capital of a company.

Nespa's use of several investment appraisal methods is, however, common in practice as few companies rely on a single investment appraisal method.

The company is correct in its belief that NPV measures the potential increase in company value of an investment project, since theoretically the stock market value of a company increases by the total NPV of projects undertaken. This is correct as long as the capital market is efficient and information about new investment projects is made available to it.

It is possible that a high IRR offers a margin of safety for risky projects and it can be interpreted in this way. However, calculation of IRR is not a substitute for an assessment of project risk.

Nespa's decision rule for ROCE is flawed, in that if used continually it could eventually run out of investment projects that meet its hurdle rate (its existing before-tax ROCE). This hurdle rate could increase with each successive project accepted, causing the company to reject projects that would have been acceptable in a previous period. However, it is important to recognise that not all costs associated with the capital budgeting process are included in investment appraisal and that such costs will reduce the existing ROCE. The sunk cost of Nespa's market research is one example, and another would be infrastructure costs that increase on a stepped basis as a result of cumulative project investment. The existence of such costs offers a partial justification for Nespa's ROCE decision rule.

(e) In assessing project risk it is important to be clear about the meaning of risk. From an academic perspective, risk refers to a set of circumstances regarding a given decision to which probabilities can be assigned. This distinguishes risk from uncertainty, which implies that it is not possible to assign probabilities to future events. In practice, the two terms are often used interchangeably, but the distinction is a useful one for the purposes of analysis and discussion.

(***Note***: Three methods of analysis are described here. Only two are required for a solution. A discussion of (1) certainty equivalents and (2) range estimates would be equally acceptable.)

Sensitivity analysis

This method measures the change in project NPV arising from a fixed change in each project variable, or measures the change in each project variable required to make the NPV zero. Only one project variable is changed at a time. The key or critical project variables are the ones to which the NPV is most sensitive, or the ones where the smallest change results in a zero NPV.

Knowledge of the key project variables allows managers to confirm the strength of their underlying assumptions, thereby increasing their confidence that the forecast NPV will be achieved. It also allows managers to monitor these variables closely when the project is implemented as a way of ensuring success. However, sensitivity analysis does not indicate the likelihood of a change occurring in a given project variable and so, strictly speaking, does not assess project risk at all.

Probability analysis

This involves the assessment of the probabilities of future events linked to an investment project. If these events are general circumstances, the technique is called scenario analysis. For example, an assessment might be made of the outcome of an investment project under poor, moderate and good economic conditions, and the probability of each economic state arising assessed.

An alternative approach is to assess the likelihood of particular values of project variables occurring, so that a probability distribution for each variable can be determined. This leads to the technique called simulation or the Monte Carlo method, which results in a probability distribution for the project NPV.

With both approaches it is therefore possible to determine the expected net present value (ENPV) based on all possible outcomes, and the probability of a negative or zero NPV. The problem with probability analysis is that in practice it is difficult to determine the probabilities to be attached to future events. An inescapable element of subjectivity is likely to exist in probability estimates.

Risk-adjusted discount rates

One technique under this heading is the assignment of investment projects to one of a set of risk classes, and each risk class has a different discount rate. The assessment of risk depends here on the classification of the project: for example, asset replacements projects are considered to be low risk, while new product launches may be placed in a high risk category. The discount rate applied increases with the risk class to which a project is assigned. One problem with this technique is that there may be no academic justification for the discount rate assigned to each risk class, so that there is no explicit link between risk and required rate of return.

An alternative approach is to increase the discount rate by an amount that reflects the perceived risk of an investment project, i.e. to add a risk premium reflecting project risk. While this can be done on a rule of thumb basis, so that a different discount rate is used for each project, it would be preferable to use a technique that assesses project risk and derives a required rate of return based on that assessment. (*Note*: Such techniques are outside the syllabus.)

(f) Since Nespa has been listed on a stock exchange for some time, it will be able to access the capital market for new finance if it wishes. It can therefore consider issuing debt securities, such as debentures or loan stock, issuing shares to existing shareholders via a rights issue, issuing shares to new investors, a bank loan, and leasing. However, Nespa is a medium-sized company, and it is therefore doubtful whether the company would be able to access the domestic or international bond markets to issue debt securities. Equity finance, bank loans or lease finance seem the most practical alternatives.

Nespa should consider the following factors.

Amount of finance needed

Although the director suggests that equity finance is appropriate given the amount of finance needed, the amount alone does not rule out other financing methods. It would be sensible to review the effect of the new finance on the company's capital structure and cost of capital, to consider the relative issue costs of different sources of finance, and to assess the effect on the company of any change in financial risk.

Cost of capital

If Nespa can reduce its average cost of capital, this will increase its overall value. The information that its interest cover is higher than similar companies points to its competitors having proportionately more debt in their capital structures, a view supported by Nespa's return on capital employed being close to the sector average.

It is also worth noting that, since Nespa's average cost of capital (and hence its cost of equity) is 10%, and since equity is more expensive than debt, the cost of debt finance is certain to be less than 10%. The tax efficiency of debt will reduce the effective cost to Nespa even further, implying that debt finance at a cost of 6% or less is available; the cost will be even lower for secured debt. From this discussion it may be concluded that an issue of debt may well be in the best interests of Nespa's shareholders.

Security

Nespa appears to have an adequate supply of fixed assets to offer as security for an issue of new debt.

Interest cover and earnings

Nespa should also consider the volatility of its profit before interest and tax. Debt finance would not be as attractive if this volatility is high. This is because with gearing in the capital structure, profits after tax (= earnings) are even more volatile than profits before interest and tax.

The existence of similar companies with lower interest cover indicates that competitors may be comfortable with higher levels of debt than Nespa.

Maturity

Nespa should match the maturity of the finance with the life of the purchased asset, although no indication of the useful economic life of the new machine is provided.

Leasing

Clear advice cannot be given because we lack detailed financial information on the company. It may be worth considering leasing as an alternative to outright purchase, but this decision would depend on an assessment of relevant costs and benefits. For example, under an operating lease the lessor would be responsible for maintenance and servicing, but the cost of this would be reflected in the annual lease payments.

The least likely alternative in the circumstances described appears to be equity finance. While this financing choice keeps financial risk low, it does not appear to offer any other advantages to shareholders.

ACCA marking scheme		
		Marks
(a)	Variable costs	2
	Contribution	2
	Inflated contribution	2
	Present value of overall contribution	2
	Selection of contribution-maximising strategy	1
		9

(b)	Inflated fixed costs	1
	Taxable profit	1
	Tax liabilities	1
	Capital allowance tax benefits	3
	Net present values	2
	Calculation of internal rate of return	2
	Omission of cost of market research	1
	Recommendation	1
		12
(c)	Annual depreciation	1
	Average accounting profit	1
	Average investment	1
	Return on capital employed	1
	Recommendation	1
		5
(d)	Discussion of IRR	3
	Discussion of ROCE	3
	Discussion of company's views	2
		8
(e)	Discussion of risk and uncertainty	1
	Discussion of risk assessment methods	7
		8
(f)	Effect of listed company status	1
	Discussion of debt finance	4
	Discussion of other forms of finance	3
		8
Total		50

68 SPENDER CONSTRUCTION PLC

(a) (i) **Operational gearing** may be defined as a measure of the impact of a change in sales on Earnings Before Interest and Taxation (EBIT). The following formula can be used to calculate the level of operational gearing for a unit output level of Q:

$$\text{Level of operational gearing at point Q} = \frac{Q(P - VC)}{Q(P - VC) - FC}$$

Q = Units of output

P = Selling price per unit

VC = Variable cost per unit

FC = Total fixed costs

The numerator in the formula represents total contribution. The denominator represents EBIT (total earnings before interest and taxation).

Hence, for any given level of output the **level of operational gearing** =

Contribution/EBIT.

A company's level of operational gearing is dependent on the ratio of fixed to variable costs and the current level of profit. If a company has a high level of fixed costs, then beyond the break-even point, an increase in the volume of sales will lead to a high percentage increase in profit. However, the percentage increase declines as the size of the profit continues to grow. Applying the formula shown above to the 20X0 financial statements for Spender plc, we can compute the current level of operational gearing within the company:

$$\text{Operational gearing} = \frac{\text{Contribution}}{\text{EBIT}}$$

For 20X0:

Variable selling and distribution costs	= £348,000 - £100,000
	= £0.248 million.
Variable administration costs	= £8.250 m - £7 m (fixed)
	= £1.250 million
Contribution	= Sales – Variable costs
	= £55.258m – (41.827m + 0.248m + 1.250m)
	= £11.933m
EBIT	= £4.833m
Operational gearing	= 11,933/4.833
	= 2.47

(ii) **Financial gearing** is measured by comparing a company's use of long-term debt finance relative to equity. The higher the proportion of debt finance, the higher the level of gearing. Financial gearing affects the sensitivity of the profit attributable to equity (profit after interest and tax) to changes in EBIT. Using debt as a source of finance commits a company to the payment of debt interest which, for any given level of operating profit, erodes the amount of profit attributable to equity investors. However, once operating profits are sufficient to cover the interest payments due, all additions to operating profit will be fully attributable to equity investors.

Textbooks contain a number of different formulae for financial gearing. They include the following alternatives:

(1) $\dfrac{\text{Long - term interest bearing debt + preference share capital}}{\text{Equity plus reserves}}$

(2) $\dfrac{\text{Long - term interest bearing debt + preference share capital}}{\text{Total long - term capital}}$

(3) $\dfrac{\text{Profit before interest}}{\text{Profit after interest}}$

A further variation on the formula might be applied which includes short-term interest bearing debt in the numerator. In this way financial gearing is then measuring the proportion of total borrowing relative to total capital, rather than just the proportion of long-term loans in the total capital base.

It is useful to note the differences between the formulae. The first two differ only in relation to the denominator, but this has the effect of altering the resulting figure for financial gearing. This can be illustrated by reference to Spender plc.

Using formula (1) in respect of the 20X0 financial statements.

$$\text{Financial gearing} = \frac{1{,}200}{12{,}452}$$

$$= 0.0964 \text{ or } 9.64\%$$

Using formula (2):

$$\text{Financial gearing} = \frac{1{,}200}{13{,}652}$$

$$= 0.0879 \text{ or } 8.799\%$$

The second figure is lower because the denominator is larger. This means that care must be taken in interpreting figures for financial gearing to ensure that there is consistency in the formula chosen for the calculation. Finally, applying formula (3), which uses figures from the profit and loss account (as opposed to the balance sheet), and so is more consistent with the operational gearing calculation done earlier, we get:

$$\text{Financial gearing} = \frac{\text{Profit before interest}}{\text{Profit after interest}}$$

$$= \frac{4{,}833}{4{,}506}$$

$$= 1.07$$

Formula (3) yields a very different result to the other two, and so serves to underline further the need for caution in interpretation of gearing figures.

Financial gearing is sometimes referred to as 'second tier' gearing because it affects the profit going to equity but not until the impact of operational gearing has already affected the level of EBIT. This means that if a company trades with a high level of operational gearing, EBIT is already highly sensitive to changes in sales revenue. If this is then combined with the potential for further erosion of the returns to equity as a result of large debt interest payments (caused by high financial gearing) then the overall risk to equity investors is high. This overall effect is most important to investors, and means that attention needs to be given to a company's level of operational and financial gearing in combination.

Spender's fixed costs (which are £7,100,000 excluding interest payments) equal over 12.5 % of sales, compared with the industry average of just 7%. The potential risk of this high operational gearing level lies in the sales volatility that is often associated with construction firms. The industry is very sensitive to the state of the economy, and an economic downturn can hit sales quite dramatically. Under such circumstances, and with an operational gearing level of 2.47, Spender plc could find that a 10% fall in sales from current levels would cause a drop of almost 25% in operating profit. It is worth noting, however, that this gearing level will come down next year as a result of increased sales and reduced fixed costs. It is probably in recognition of this sensitivity of profits to changes in sales that the company has chosen to keep its level of financial gearing relatively low at 1.07.

Spender's financial gearing cannot be compared with that of the industry because the relevant information is not available. The lower level helps to limit the potential impact of sales changes on the profit available to equity, and so limits the overall risk to equity investors. Nonetheless, Spender plc must be regarded as a somewhat risky choice for equity investors and the example clearly demonstrates how a company needs to think about how it mixes its levels of financial and operating gearing in such a way as to limit the risk to equity shareholders.

(b) The additional working capital required is expected to rise in line with sales (note 6 in the question), i.e. growth of 15%.

To estimate the required increase in working capital, the net current asset figure in the balance sheet should be adjusted to exclude the overdraft and VAT bill, plus tax and dividends payable. Only stocks plus debtors minus trade creditors should be affected by the increase in sales volume.

	£000	£000
Net current assets in balance sheet		7,852
Add back:		
Overdraft	2,000	
VAT bill	450	
Corporation tax payable	1,352	
Dividends payable	1,520	
		5,322
Adjusted working capital figure		13,174

Working capital needed in 20X1 = 1.15 × (Net current assets in 20X0)

= 1.15 (£13.174 million)

= £15.15 million.

This represents an increase of £1.98 million (i.e. £13.174 × 0.15).

In addition to the capital expenditure investment of £7 million, this gives an extra funding requirement of £8.98 million. This may be raised either from external or internal sources. Internal funding will come from operations and the anticipated cash flow from operations can be estimated from the profit and loss account for 20X0 and the additional information in the question.

The profit and loss account for 20X0 shows cash inflows from operations equal to £4.956 million (i.e. £4.506 million plus £450,000 VAT), and after adjusting for depreciation this gives an operating cash flow of £5.391 million. The net cash available for investment within the business can thus be calculated as follows:

	£000	£000
Operating profit, 20X0		4,833
Depreciation		435
Cash from operations		5,268
Cash outflows		
Tax	(1,352)	
Interest payments	(327)	
Dividends	(1,520)	
Other payments	(2,500)	
		(5,699)
Net reduction in cash		(431)

The total funding requirement equals £8.98 million. In 20X0, the company would not have been able to meet any of this funding requirement from its operating activities. This suggests that in 20X1, it might be unable to meet any of its additional funding requirements from operating cash flows. (Note. The estimate excludes any allowance for additional cash required to pay higher debenture interest due to new borrowing, or the dividends planned for 20X1 - although these may be funded out of future profits.)

(c) In considering whether to replace short-term with long-term borrowing, Spender plc needs to look at the current structure of its balance sheet and its forecast capital requirements. The current level of financial gearing in the company is relatively low. Converting short- into long-term borrowing will affect the level of financial gearing slightly as calculated in (a)(1), and (a)(2), but the impact on the gearing measure in (a)(3) will depend upon relative short-term and long-term interest rates. The main factors that Spender plc need to consider are the need for flexibility in access to short-term funding and the relative cost and risk of alternative funding sources.

The **overdraft facility** offers the advantage of flexibility, but the cost is relatively high if the funds are borrowed on a semi-permanent basis. In other words, if Spender plc does not expect to utilise its overdraft except for brief periods throughout the year, it may be prudent and cheaper to retain it. On the other hand, if the overdraft is being used to finance 'permanent' working capital within the business, and Spender plc is regularly borrowing at close to the overdraft limit, then it may be prudent to convert the borrowing into a long-term loan. **As a general rule, long-term finance is slightly cheaper**, and given that the company is already having to raise funds for other purposes, the marginal cost of raising an additional £2 million would be small. As a general principle, it is a good idea for companies to **divide working capital requirements into temporary and permanent**, with the funding for these being short-term or long-term respectively. The forecasts suggest that Spender plc will be experiencing rising sales, and an associated high level of cash generation, although this will be linked to a related increase in its need for working capital. By converting the overdraft into a long-term loan, the company can leave itself renewed access to short-term borrowing whilst reducing the average cost of its working capital funding by an increased use of long-term money. The only time when it might not be sensible to convert the overdraft is if economic forecasts suggested that interest rates are expected to fall dramatically in the near future. In such a case, it would make sense to wait until interest rates had bottomed out before converting the overdraft.

(d) Number of shares currently in issue = 8 million (i.e. £4m/£0.50).

EPS in 20X0 = 39.4 pence (i.e. £3.154m/8m).

Dividend per share in 20X0 = 19 pence (i.e. £1.520 million/8 million).

In comparing a rights issue and a debenture issue as alternative funding sources, it is important to take account of the effect of each alternative on the returns to ordinary shareholders, and the level of risk to those shareholders. It is reasonable to assume that if we are asking shareholders to accept a higher level of risk (operational or financial) then they will expect to receive an increase in their returns in compensation. The two alternative methods of funding affect only the level of financial risk in the company. The debenture issue will increase the level of financial gearing whilst the rights issue will reduce the level of financial gearing. As at December 20X0 the financial gearing of Spender Construction was 1.07. In selecting the most appropriate source of funding, therefore, consideration must be given as to whether such changes would be acceptable to the equity shareholders. A comparison of the forecast EPS under both types of funding is useful in assessing the likely shareholder response. Care must be taken, however, in interpreting the forecast, because only one year's data is available.

Forecast profit and loss account, Spender Construction,
Year ending 31 December 20X1

		With debenture issue	*With rights issue*
		£000	£000
Turnover	(£55,258 × 1.15)	63,547	63,547
Cost of sales	0.98 × (£41,827 × 1.15)	47,139	47,139
Gross profit		16,408	16,408
Selling and dist'n costs	(£248 × 1.15) + 100	385	385
Administration costs	(1,250 × 1.15) + (7,000 – 500)	7,938	7,938
Operating profit		8,085	8,085
Interest charges	(10% of 1,200) + 280 + (10% of 7,000)	1,100	400
Profit before tax		6,985	7,685
Corporation tax (30%)		2,096	2,306
Profit after tax		4,889	5,379
Dividend	25p × 8,000/ 25p × 9,333	2,000	2,333
Retained profit		2,889	3,046

Assuming debenture is issued:	*Assuming rights issue*
Forecast EPS,	*Forecast EPS,*
Year ending 31 December 20X1	*Year ending 31 December 20X1*
EPS = 4,889/8,000 = 61.1 pence	EPS = 5,379/9,333 = 57.6 pence
Change in EPS = 55.1% growth	Change in EPS = 46.2% growth

The figures show that if the sales targets are achieved, the **EPS will grow faster if debenture financing is selected**, but in both instances the growth is substantial. This is largely because profits are already sufficiently high to meet the interest payments required and so, helped substantially by other changes, such as the fixed cost savings, all increases in profit (net of tax) can accrue to equity investors. The rights issue generates a smaller EPS because the number of shares in issue has been increased by 1.33 million, and so the equity earnings are shared more widely. In either case the shareholders benefit from a growth of EPS which exceeds the rate of growth of sales. However, if sales were to fall, then EPS would fall at a rate greater than the drop in sales, again because of the leverage effect. This risk from additional borrowing must be acknowledged and explained to shareholders.

If shareholders are looking for rapid growth of earnings, it is marginally preferable to fund the investment with the debenture issue. However the **effect** of this choice **on shareholder risk** needs to be taken into account, because Spender's financial gearing will be increased by the debenture issue. Whether shareholders will accept the higher risk or not depends to some extent on industry and economic forecasts. If the outlook for the construction industry is good, then shareholders are likely to accept such a proposal; conversely if the future prospects look poor then the rights issue is the safer choice. The attractiveness of the higher returns from using debenture finance needs to compensate for the marginal additional risk created by the issue, and given that the use of debentures yields an EPS 6% greater than if the rights issue is made then it is likely that this is the case.

In addition to financial considerations, Spender plc should also take into account the **organisational aspects of the two financing alternatives**, including the speed of issue, issue costs, and prevailing stock market conditions. Rights issues will tend to be slower to arrange and complete than a debenture issue, but rights do offer the advantage that the issue costs may be kept low as it is not a requirement (though it is usual practice) for them to be underwritten. At the same time, debentures may be easier to sell if the stock market is volatile or on a bear run.

In conclusion, the debenture issue should be the chosen source of funding if market forecasts indicate rising future sales and earnings. The rights issue should be the chosen source of finance if the directors believe that shareholders are highly risk averse, and would prefer to avoid any additional financial gearing, and that stock market conditions are favourable to such an issue.

(e) **Dividend cover** is calculated by dividing the profit available to equity by the total dividend payable, and it measures the extent to which equity investors can view their dividend as being 'secure'. As the level of cover rises, so does the security of the dividend, inasmuch as equity investors can still expect there to be sufficient profit available to pay the dividend. A high dividend cover offers a reasonable certainty that dividend levels can be maintained, but it should also lead investors to question how the retained profits are being utilised. By definition, a high dividend cover implies that a large proportion of profits are being retained within the business, and unless these funds are being invested wisely, the equity investor may be better off if the cash is paid out to shareholders, who can then re-invest it elsewhere to earn a better rate of return.

For Spender plc, the forecast profit available to equity (from (d)) if the debentures are issued equals £4.889m and the dividend forecast for the year is £2m. This gives a dividend cover of:

4.889/2 = 2.44 times.

This means that over half of the profit is being retained for re-investment. If the re-investment can be expected to maintain the profit growth achieved between 20X0 and 20X1, then investors have little to worry about. If, however, Spender plc gives little indication of how it intends to use this money, then shareholders should be concerned that dividend cover is perhaps a little high.

69 STADIUM EATS

Key answer tips

In part (a) there are 10 marks, so you need to spend a little time thinking of various issues that may be discussed. You have very little detail in the profit and loss account (indeed, this is one point to raise), so you are expected to look at the broad figures - level of turnover, margins etc - and then comment on the feasibility of achieving these for a brand new enterprise, and possible impact on the existing business. Some of your criticisms cannot be taken into account when redrafting the profit and loss, but some sensible assumptions are needed as regards turnover and margins to produce revised (lower) figures.

Part (b) gives you a chance to display your general knowledge of gearing before having to relate it to the scenario. Don't stint on your explanation of the meaning of capital gearing - the marks allow you to give a little detail about different definitions and which types of debt may be included etc. You then need to consider the impact of high gearing levels on both lenders and equity investors.

In part (c) you need to apply what you have discussed in general terms in (b) to the data and circumstances of the question. Make it clear which definition of gearing you are using in your calculations. You cannot come to any firm conclusions without any benchmarks for comparison, but you can discuss particular aspects of the restaurant business that may affect the impact of the gearing level.

In part (d) you can initially recall your sources of finance 'checklist', but before writing about any of them, you must think whether they will apply in this particular context. And don't forget the all important source - equity - that appears to be perhaps most appropriate in this case.

In part (e) there are two parts to this requirement - a general discussion on the AIM, followed by the specific factors to be considered in obtaining a listing. The latter actually carries more marks, and should not be skimped on.

(a) The forecast covers only the first trading year. This is unlikely to be representative of the longer-term trading position of the business, and a forecast over a three- to five-year period would be more appropriate.

The question indicates that the forecast is loosely based on the current Stadium Eats figures. There would in fact appear to have been some questionable assumptions made in constructing the forecast.

Firstly, a sales target of £600,000 (well in excess of the current sales of £425,000) might be considered rather ambitious for the first year. It is unrealistic to assume sales will be close to equivalent to those of the original restaurant within such a short time. Furthermore, it may be that some customers simply switch from eating at Stadium Eats to eating at the new location. The forecast makes no mention of the sales for the overall operation, and the possible interdependence of sales between the two outlets.

The figures given in the forecast are lacking in any detail. There is insufficient information and no comparative data to show sales trends over time. It is impossible to learn anything about the costs of the restaurant from the information given. A detailed breakdown of costs by type, and over time, would be very helpful. The operating profit margin is difficult to appraise without further information on the average rate for similar restaurant businesses, but seems excessive when compared with the margin currently achieved. A forecast cash flow would also be useful.

The forecast may also be criticised for failing to take account of the likely need to employ new managerial staff to take responsibility for the existing outlet, in order to free up the partners to concentrate on the new site.

Working on sales in Stadium Eats at present, annual turnover is equal to £2,833 per cover (£8,500 × 50 weeks/150 covers). The estimate for the new restaurant is equal to £3,333 per cover per annum (£600,000/180 covers). Taking a pessimistic view, sales of perhaps just £1,500 per cover per annum might be assumed, and this would give a turnover of only £270,000, instead of the forecast £600,000.

The current operating profit margin is 11%. If this margin is achieved on the forecast sales of £600,000, operating profit would be just £66,000, as compared to the £135,000 figure for operating profit that is in the forecast. This figure assumes management drawings are maintained at just £22,000 each.

Re-working the forecast to use an adjusted sales figure, and maintaining the 11% net margin gives:

	£
Sales	270,000
Operating profit	29,700
Less interest	(18,000)
Profit before tax	11,700

In practice, it is likely that the lower turnover (compared with the existing outlet) will lead to a reduction in net margin, leading to an even lower operating profit and lower profit before tax. If the margin is reduced to 10%, the operating profit (on sales of £270,000) would be £27,000, and the profit before tax just £9,000.

This is a great deal lower than the forecast, and significantly alters the potential viability of the business; hence the need for a longer term forecast set of figures.

(b) **Capital gearing** refers to the extent to which a company is funded by fixed return finance as opposed to equity. Two different formulae may be used when measuring capital gearing.

Formula 1

Capital gearing = Debt plus preference share capital/Equity

This measures the ratio of fixed return capital to equity finance within a business.

Formula 2

An alternative formula, commonly used, measures the proportion of fixed return capital in relation to the total capital of a business. The formula is as follows:

Capital gearing = Debt + preference share capital/Total long-term capital

In both cases, debt may be measured as either long-term debt, or all interest bearing debt. Clearly the gearing level will vary depending on the formula selected, and the type of debt included, but in all cases the level of gearing rises as the proportion of fixed return finance increases. It is not possible to specify a precise dividing line between high gearing and low gearing. Gearing is a relative measure, and should be assessed in terms of the gearing levels of comparable companies in the same business sector. Companies in different industrial sectors may exhibit very different levels of capital gearing.

The level of gearing is of interest to a bank that is lending to a business, because it reflects the extent to which the owners of the business are risking their own capital relative to that of the bank. At the same time, the bank will recognise that increased loan finance, which is not matched by an increase in equity investment, will lead to an increase in capital gearing. As the level of debt increases, if sales figures decline or are static, businesses may find it increasingly difficult to meet the interest payments due on the debt. The bank will therefore look for an increase in cash flows from operations to help to pay any incremental interest due on new borrowing. One problem, however, is that gearing does not measure cash flows.

The equity investor should be cautious of highly-geared companies, because the return on equity in such a business will be very sensitive to changes in profit before interest. When gearing is high, and interest payments are also high, a dramatic fall in the profit before interest figure may result in a collapse in the profit attributable to equity. Equally, a large rise in pre interest profit may lead to a surge in the profit attributable to equity, if earnings were already more than sufficient to meet interest payments. In summary, high gearing is of concern to the equity investor because it increases the volatility of the return on equity.

(c) **Using the first formula for capital gearing:**

Long-term debt/ Equity = 195/176 = 1.108 or 110.8%

or

Interest-bearing debt/ Equity = 195/176 = 1.108 or 110.8%

In this case, the absence of short-term interest-bearing debt means that the gearing calculation gives the same result for both calculations.

Alternatively, using the second formula:

Long-term debt/Total long-term capital = 195/371 = 0.526 or 52.6%

or

Interest-bearing debt/Total long-term capital = 195/371 = 0.526 or 52.6%

As before, the fact that long-term debt is the only form of interest bearing debt results in the same value for gearing using either definition.

The gearing level appears quite high, inasmuch as debt is a significant source of funding for the business, although the bulk of the debt is of a long-term nature and is secured against property. The restaurant business is a volatile one, subject to changing tastes, and sales volatility needs to be taken into account when analysing financial gearing. For most businesses in a volatile market, the risk of falling sales means that high levels of debt can leave a business facing difficulties in meeting its interest payments. The restaurant business, however, is cash generating when compared with other types of business that are dependent on credit sales. In view of this, the new restaurant should have fewer problems in servicing interest payments. Nonetheless, if the owners wish to limit their risk, it may be advisable to reduce the level of gearing to below one (depending on the formula used), so that a sharp drop in sales would not threaten the long-term survival of the business. It is often the case that banks will only be prepared to lend to small businesses on the basis of 'matching funds' i.e. £100 loan per £100 equity. As the gearing is in this case already over one, the owners would be unable to increase their borrowing if the matched funds approach was used.

The adjusted profit and loss account given in answer to (a) shows interest cover is poor. This would serve to confirm that gearing is uncomfortably high.

Furthermore, the figures do not reveal the true level of indebtedness and risk for the proprietors, who are in fact borrowing £75,000 in order to purchase their equity stake. For them the company is a very risky venture.

(d) The accounts clearly indicate that the business should seek out new equity investors, rather than further borrowing. However, the ease of attracting such investors will depend on the forecast profitability and medium-term growth potential of the business. In order to attract investors, Stadium Eats would need to prepare a Business Plan which included detailed profit and loss forecast, balance sheet forecast and cash flow forecast, together with information on company strategy and marketing plans. Such a plan could then be studied by potential investors, in order to make their own estimates of the potential of the business, and the risk that they would be taking in buying an equity stake.

Possible sources of such finance might include Business Angels, Venture Capital Trusts or wealthy relatives/individuals looking to obtain tax relief via an Enterprise Investment Scheme. It is possible that Stadium Eats could encourage customers to sign up as investors in return for discount vouchers on meals. Business Angels will be individuals who are used to dealing with small businesses, and might have some expertise to offer. Some Business Angels will request a seat on the Board of Directors in order to monitor the progress of their investment. Venture Capital Funds vary widely in size, from small regional funds (often part financed by local authorities) through to large-scale funds operating as investment trusts, and raising investment finance through the issue of shares to the general public.

Equity is not the sole source of funding which that might be available. If the restaurant is located in an economic development area, such as an inner city or rural community, then there may be job creation grants/soft loan funds provided by local or central government. In certain areas, a limited amount of grant finance is also available via the European Union.

(e) AIM is the Alternative Investment Market, which is a junior stock market operated by the London Stock Exchange. AIM serves as the market place in the UK where smaller companies can raise equity capital. The issue costs and annual registration fees are much lower than for the main stock exchange, and the investors are more likely to be looking for higher risk investments. As relatively new and fast growing businesses, many AIM companies choose to retain a large proportion of their profits, and so they offer low dividend yields to potential investors. The attraction of such investments lies in the potential for substantial capital gains if the business is successful.

Amongst the factors to be considered when seeking a stock market quotation are:

- Does the company need a large-scale injection of equity?
- Public quotation involves greater reporting requirements and openness.
- A stock market quotation increases take-over risks, because shareholdings are more widely spread.
- The owners are likely to see a reduction in the scale of their shareholding, and perhaps lose overall control.
- Are growth rates sufficient to give potential investors their required rate of return?

70 WATER SUPPLY SERVICES PLC

(a) Rental costs based on projected sales. Sales growth at 15% per annum.

Period:	*1*	*2*	*3*	*4*	*5*
Demand (units):	110,000	126,500	145,475	167,296	192,391
Existing capacity:	80,000	80,000	80,000	80,000	80,000
Extra capacity required:	30,000	46,500	65,475	87,296	112,391
Number of machines required:	1	2	2	2	3
Rental costs (£):	22,000	44,000	44,000	44,000	66,000

Unit variable costs

	£/unit
Labour (45+64)	109.00
Material A costs	23.85
Material B costs (5 x 12·45)	62.25
Variable overheads	10.00
Unit variable costs	205.10

Incremental cash flow schedule:

Year:	*0*	*1*	*2*	*3*	*4*	*5*
Units:		110,000	126,500	145,475	167,296	192,391
Incremental units:		30,000	46,500	65,475	87,296	112,391
	£000	£000	£000	£000	£000	£000
Variable costs (at £205.10 per unit)		(6,153)	(9,537)	(13,429)	(17,904)	(23,051)
Additional fixed costs					(50)	(50)
Machine rentals		(22)	(44)	(44)	(44)	(66)
Allowable costs		(6,175)	(9,581)	(13,473)	(17,998)	(23,167)
Incremental revenue (allowable costs + 25%)		7,719	11,976	16,841	22,498	28,959
Capital costs	(7,500)				(30)	
Working capital	(1,158)	(638)	(730)	(849)	(969)	4,344
Net cash flow	(8,658)	906	1,665	2,519	3,501	10,136
Discount factor at 20%	1.000	0.833	0.694	0.579	0.482	0.402
PV	(8,658)	755	1,156	1,459	1,688	4,075
NPV	**+ 475**					

Decision: project is worthwhile

Tutorial note: workings for working capital

Year	*15% of sales value*	*Total working capital*	*Increase in working capital*
1 (start of year 0)	15% of 7,719	1,158	1,158
2 (start of year 1)	15% of 11,976	1,796	638
3 (start of year 2)	15% of 16,841	2,526	730
4 (start of year 3)	15% of 22,498	3,375	849
5 (start of year 4)	15% of 28,959	4,344	969
6 (start of year 5)		0	(4,344)

(b) **Report**

To: Board of Directors

From: Accountant

Date: xx/xx/xx

Subject: **Aspects of capital investment appraisal**

Limitations of the five-year period of analysis

A number of limitations to the analysis potentially arise:

1 The approach does not take account of future benefits/costs after five years either continuing or new.

2 No information on contract length from the Water Authorities, which may be longer than five years.

3 Other, cheaper, resources may be available over a longer period e.g. it may be cheaper to buy machines rather than rent them.

4 Analysis does not take account of the potential for physical site capacity increases that may become available after five years.

Problems and difficulties associated with forecasting

We have relied to a great extent on the forecasting of data in order to provide an evaluation of the proposal. Not all the components are forecast: for example, we will know that we are able to recover agreed costs. However, to the extent that components are forecast, there exists the **potential for error** in our evaluation which, of course, leads to uncertainty in our conclusions. In particular, the following problems are evident at this stage:

1 Uncertainty increases with the length of time forecast. That is, the further into the future, the less able we are to predict with accuracy because our initial assumptions may be wrong and small errors at the beginning magnify subsequently as the forecast becomes increasingly irrelevant to what is actually happening to the key variable in question. For example, we may have not predicted general inflation rates correctly, and this could have a large impact on our labour costs.

2 Project complexity: The more variables we have to forecast, the less likely we are to be accurate. This problem has an unknowable outcome if there are a large number of variables to forecast, the uncertainty concerning the two components can have two effects:

- The larger the number of components to forecast, the greater the difficulty in determining project outcome. Forecasting so many components can lead to errors because the scale of the problem is large.
- By forecasting many components, we assume a relationship between the components which is also a forecast. This relationship may change. For example, the relationship of production variable overheads to units produced may change. Currently, they are related to the amount of materials used. If we use forecasts based on these assumptions, then we also assume that the relationship between materials used and overheads absorbed is constant. This may not be the situation if the type of materials change.

3 The background information may change. What happens, for example, if a new competitor enters the market? This effect will be alleviated to the extent that we have an agreed contract. There are other factors that could have a significant effect, given enough time to materialise. For example, technological change could have an impact on our industry. In particular, social change may be relevant if consumers begin to demand even higher quality water supplies, which would inevitably affect our costs.

4 There is always the random component that could distort our forecasts. However, an alternative view would suggest that such random components are really an admission of lack of skill in forecasting. The best forecasters attempt to anticipate all eventualities.

Choice of an appropriate discount rate

The difficulty with choosing a discount rate rests on whether the correct rate for the risk/return has been derived. A number of factors are relevant here.

1 The position of the Water Authorities as single customer. The business is potentially at risk if the Water Authorities choose to look elsewhere for their water supplies. This may mean that a higher discount rate is more appropriate.

2 The financing of the capacity expansion. This may have an impact on the discount rate if the debt/equity mix of the company is significantly altered. A number of factors are relevant here:

(a) Higher gearing is likely to induce higher costs of equity.

(b) Higher equity financing may reduce the cost of equity, but increase the overall WACC if we move off our minimum WACC.

3 A lower discount rate may be more appropriate to the extent that a long-term contract implies secure income streams.

4 Different components of the cash flows may have different variability and it may therefore not be appropriate to discount them all at the same rate.

Any non-quantifiable factors you feel might influence the decision to accept the proposal

Net present value methods are only assessments of factors that we can quantify. There may be non-quantifiable factors that also have an impact on any decision we make. Some of these may be:

1 It is important to keep our only customer happy and therefore a high standard of general service is important.

2 Future contracts are likely to depend on agreeing to the proposal. Hence, future benefits may emerge which are currently hard to quantify.

3 The continuance of the existing business relationship with the Water Authorities may position the company to expand and provide water to other sectors of the economy.

4 The existing and proposed contracts secure continued employment for personnel. This is important in a labour market that may be experiencing shortages and where key personnel are difficult to replace.

(c) In year 5, demand will be 192,391 units.

In year 6, demand will be 15% higher:

1.15 × 192,391 = 221,250 units.

Hence, the 1st quarter forecast is based on:	221,250
Average demand per quarter is therefore (× 3/12):	55,312
Applying the 1st quarter adjustment of – 8% gives:	
(– 8% × 55,312)	(4,425)
Hence, demand in the 1st quarter is projected to be:	50,887

The difficulty faced by the company is that the demand level is beyond its capacity of 200,000 units. It is reasonable to assume steady water production throughout the year, in which case maximum output capacity for the 1st quarter is only 50,000 units.

(d) (i) **Components of the linear equation:**

816,000: This might represent the initial level of fixed costs

205.1: This represents the impact of a change in the variable x. In cost equations such as the one indicated, x would normally represent the level of output and, hence, for every unit change in output, total costs will rise by £205.1.

x: This is likely to represent the number of units produced.

(ii) As outlined in the question, fixed costs are not constant over all activity levels. In fact, it would be more appropriate to describe them as stepped fixed costs. When costs are described as stepped-fixed they are constant only over a range of output, but make step changes at certain points in capacity. The problems for estimation of fixed costs under such circumstances are two-fold:

– The equation does not take into account capital investment required which will be occasional, as in the question, and assumes the costs incurred will be continuous (or annual as in the question): the linear equation cannot deal with non-yearly costs in an easy manner.

– Ascertaining an appropriate absorption rate for overheads which, in itself, is a forecast.

ACCA marking scheme

			Marks
(a)		Unit forecasts	2
		Rental costs	2
		Incremental units	1
		Unit variable costs	3
		Variable cost cash flows	1
		Fixed cost cash flows	1
		Revenues	3
		Capital costs	1
		Working capital	3
		Use of correct discount factors	1
		Correct NPV	1
		Investment decision	1
			20
(b)		1 mark each for detailed points, limitations of 5 years	up to 4
		Up to 2 marks each for difficulties with forecasting	up to 8
		Up to 2 marks each for discount rate problems	up to 8
		1 mark each for non-quantifiable factors	up to 4
		Maximum marks available	20
(c)		Projection of year 6 demand	1
		Quarterly adjustment	1
		1st quarter projection	1
		Comment	2
			5
(d)	(i)	1 mark each for explanation of each component	up to 2
	(ii)	1 mark for each point made	up to 3
		Marks available	5
Total			50

71 TOWER RAILWAYS PLC

(a) **Data**

After-tax discount rate (%)	10
Tax rate (%)	30
Contribution/sales ratio (%)	35
Therefore variable costs as a proportion of sales (%)	65
Occupancy rate (%)	60
Number of carriages	8
Passenger numbers per carriage	55
Number of trips	10
Average price per passenger (£)	12
Annual days travelling/operating	340

Assumption: It is assumed that tax cash flows occur in the same year as the benefit, allowance or cost to which they relate.

Capital allowances calculations, Year to:	*31 Dec X3*	*31 Dec X4*	*31 Dec X5*	*31 Dec X6*	*31 Dec X7*
	£000	£000	£000	£000	£000
Tax written down value	5,000	3,750	2,812	2,109	1,582
Writing down allowance (25%)	1,250	938	703	527	
Sale proceeds					500
Balancing allowance					1,082
Tax saving (30%)	375	281	211	158	325

Capital projections

	Year 0	*Year 1*	*Year 2*	*Year 3*	*Year 4*
	£000	£000	£000	£000	£000
Initial investment and proceeds	(5,000)				500
Capital allowances	375	281	211	158	325
Net capital flows	(4,625)	281	211	158	825
Discount factor at 10%	1.000	0.909	0.826	0.751	0.683
PV of capital flows	(4,625)	256	174	119	563
NPV of capital flows	**(3,513)**				

Projected annual revenue = 60% occupancy × 8 carriages × 55 passengers (carriage capacity) × £12 ticket price × 10 trips per day × 340 days = £10,771,200.

Annual operating cash surplus, years 1 – 5

	£000
Expected revenue	10,771
Variable costs (65%)	(7,001)
Contribution	3,770
Additional fixed costs (cash spend)	(1,000)
Incremental net cash income, pre-tax	2,770
Tax (30%)	(831)
Post-tax annual cash flows	1,939

Loss of revenue from long-standing contract

= £250,000 each year, before tax, in perpetuity

= £175,000 each year after tax in perpetuity.

The Present Value of £1 each year in perpetuity at a discount rate of 10% = £1/0.10 = £10, i.e. the discount factor for the perpetual annual cash flow is 10.

Years	*Cash flow item*	*Cash flow* £000	*Discount factor at 10%*	*Present value* £000
1 - 5	Post-tax additional profits	1,939	3.791	7,351
1 in perpetuity	Post-tax loss of revenue	(175)	10.000	(1,750)
				5,601
	PV of capital cash flows			(3,513)
	NPV of project			2,088

Decision: The contract is worthwhile

(b) The project will cease to be viable if the NPV falls by more than £2,088,000 and becomes negative.

This would happen if the Present Value of the annual operating profits fell by more than £2,088,000. A reduction in the average price charged would affect revenue and annual contribution, but would not affect fixed costs.

On the basis of the estimates in part (a), the expected annual contribution is £3,770,000 before tax. After tax, this is (× 70%) £2,639,000.

The discount factor at 10% for years 1 – 5 is 3.791.

In the estimates in part (a), the contribution for the five years, allowing for tax, therefore has a present value of:

£2,639,000 × 3.791 = £10,004,449.

If this value fell by £2,088,000, it would fall in percentage terms by (2,088,000/10,004,449) × 100% = 20.87%.

To reduce the NPV to zero, given no other changes in the estimated values, would therefore require a fall in price of about 20.87% or £2.50, from £12 to £9.50.

(c) (i)

	£000
PV of capital cash flows (given in the question)	(9,220)
PV of lost annual revenue in perpetuity	(1,750)
PV of extra operating profits, as estimated in (a)	7,351
NPV of the project for part (c)	(3,619)

A similar analysis can be made as in part (b), except that we need to calculate the occupancy rate at which the project would just break even. This requires an increase in the PV of extra operating profits in years 1-5 by at least £3,619,000.

The PV of the after-tax additional contribution was calculated, on the basis of the original estimates, as £10,004,449 (see above). For these to increase by £3,619,000 would mean an increase in percentage terms of (3,619/10,004.449) × 100% = over 36%.

Given no other changes in the estimates, this would require an **increase in the occupancy rate** from 60% to (60 × 1.36) 81.6%, say 82%.

(ii) The PV of the annual post-tax additional annual operating profits of £1,939,000 for years 1-5 is £7,351,000 (see earlier).

If the project could continue after year 5 earning additional post-tax cash flows of £1,939,000 each year, the project would achieve an NPV of 0 when the PV of the operating profits is (£7,531,000 + £3,619,000) = £10,970,000.

Given annual post-tax operating profits of £1,939,000, these would have a PV of £10,970,000 when the cumulative annual discount factor at 10% is (10,970,000/1,939,000) 5.658.

Examining the DCF annuity table under the 10% column for a figure closest to 5.658 we find the project length, expressed in whole years, should be at least 9 years long (at 9 years the annuity figure is 5.759).

(d) **REPORT**

Circulation: Chairman, Tower Railways

Author:

Date: xx/xx/xx

Subject: **Business Risk for Tower Railways plc**

Introduction

In the light of the possibility of an extension to the contract to services the main railway line this report makes an assessment of the background and specific risk relating to the project.

What is meant by business risk

1 **Basic description***:* Risk is related to the lack of certainty of future outcomes and is fundamentally related to decision making, such as the project proposed, in that business decisions are always taken against a background of risk. Because of that, it becomes important to understand the risk exposure that exists. At a basic level risk is positively associated with return in that the higher the return we expect from a project, the higher the degree of risk it is likely to be exposed to.

2 **Chance and probability***:* Risk is associated with chance or probability in ways that allow us to quantify the degree of risk we face. This is particularly relevant to businesses that face variability in projected outcomes, for example, so that a fairly clear idea can be formed of the profit impact of risk. In the contract extension facing Tower Railways, project outcome has been assessed using NPV techniques that assume cash flows are certain (without risk). However the cash flows are dependent on projections of future passenger occupancy, prices charged, implicit zero inflation, the relation of variable costs to sales, discount rates, constant tax rates and so on. In fact, every component of the calculation is subject to risk, because we cannot be certain of ensuring that the figures we use will actually arise when the time comes or even at the time we project. Under such circumstances, we can only estimate the most likely figures and the most likely times, and accept that we may be wrong on either or both counts.

3 **Time***:* Risk is also related to the length of time the projections extend. There is an important distinction at this point between constant risk and increased exposure. For example, we may assume that passenger occupancy stays constant at 60% and we may feel that there is a risk associated with being wrong in this project by a factor of –1% or + 1% each year. Whilst risk might remain constant at + or -1% each year, it is feasible that after five years, projected passenger occupancy could be less than 55% over 65%. Compounding effects of risk on risk over successive periods means that risk exposure grows without having to alter the risk percentage faced.

4 **Negative and positive variability***:* Another important point relates to risk being both a good or bad thing. Risk, in the context of NPV projections, relates to variability of returns, both positive and negative. Thus, while you may not welcome negative variability in income, you would welcome it in relation to costs. Thus, risk is not only related to unwelcome outcomes, although it is often misperceived as such.

5 **Uncertainty***:* Risk can also arise but may be unforeseen. This is perhaps the most important aspect in that, whilst we may be able to anticipate variability in income, we may not anticipate fully the risk we are exposed to or the form it will take (variability in sales revenues may be more than we anticipate for example). This is the hardest aspect of risk to judge.

Methods of estimating the degree of business risk

Because risk affects decisions in such a fundamental way, businesses attempt to estimate risk as a way of putting in place contingency plans and/or evaluating if the project is likely to produce a profitable outcome. This is usually incorporated into NPV decisions in a number of ways:

1 **Sensitivity analysis***:* This is one method which is widely used by which an assessment may be made of how responsive a project's NPV is to changes in its components. Thus, an idea may be gained of to what extent prices charged for a good or service have to reduce by before a zero NPV is produced. This technique can be applied to any cost, including initial capital costs, and also to

the discount rate. Sensitivity is normally expressed as a percentage. Some of the difficulties associated with the techniques are as follows:

- The analysis can only deal with changes in one key factor at a time. It cannot deal with multiple changes in NPV components which may well arise.
- No idea is given in sensitivity analysis of the likelihood of occurrence of a key variable changing to the extent to produce a zero NPV. In other words, it measures the percentage change required to produce a catastrophic result, but does not indicate if this has a low, medium or high chance of occurring.
- As with any risk assessment, sensitivity analysis is only a guide. It cannot tell managers how important such a risk exposure is to the company. In order to assess this, the attitude of the managers to risk needs to be determined. In other words, a high return/high risk company will want to be exposed to more risk than a low return/low risk company.

Examiner's note

Discussions of CAPM and Certainty Equivalents could be included in this list. Whilst beyond the syllabus, appropriate references to these subjects would have been rewarded.

---

2 **Probability analysis:** This approach attempts to use measures which indicate just how variable cash flows are. It addresses one of the key criticisms of the sensitivity approach, in that it provides an idea of how much variability is likely, whereas sensitivity analysis indicates the room for manoeuvre without an assessment of the likelihood that any such event will arise. Probability analysis is essentially a weighted average approach, where the averages are determined by pre-set probabilities. By doing this, expected cash flows emerge based on the most likely outcomes. The degree of variability of the expected outcomes may be estimated from the standard deviation of the net present value. It is in this calculation that we at least get some idea of the degree of risk a project is exposed to, which can be expressed in terms of a range of NPVs. The important drawback of this approach is that a good idea of what probability weights to use must first be established. This can never be determined with 100% accuracy for project cash flows that arise in the future simply because the future is uncertain and so are the probabilities.

3 **Decision trees:** This is similar to a probability approach, in that it relies on weighting future cash flows by probabilities to arrive at an overall average. The distinctive feature of decision trees is that certain cash flow outcomes can be made contingent on certain previous ones arising. Decision trees are most useful in expressing, in a systematic manner, the different project outcomes that may emerge. Formally, the technique is no different to that of using compound probabilities and hence the criticisms of probabilities apply here also.

4 **Simulation models:** This method allows management to vary changes in the different cash flows simultaneously. As such it gives an idea of the variability in project cash flows overall by allowing changes in many of the outcomes. It can only give an idea, since the number of changes allowed can be quite large and, when compounded together, the number of different combinations become unmanageable in terms of trying to interpret what is going on. The key advantage of this technique is that it allows an idea of the most likely range of project outcomes that could possible emerge. However, the technique requires many computations to be carried out.

Methods of reducing business risk

Risk can only be reduced to the extent that management can control events. Risks associated with uncontrolled events cannot be manipulated. There are a variety of ways the management can respond to risky situations:

- Undertake short payback projects. This is related to the fact that risk exposure increases with time because of its compounding effect even though the degree of risk may remain constant (this point is explained above).
- Avoid risky projects. If riskless projects are undertaken then only a risk free return could be expected. This may not satisfy shareholders.
- Ensure proper evaluations of risk are undertaken so that unnecessary exposure to risk is avoided.
- Employ risk avoidance project selection strategies. Management should not undertake high risk projects simultaneously, which might produce undesirable risk exposure to the business as a whole.
- Combine projects to diversify risk.

ACCA marking scheme

			Marks	
(a)	Calculation of capital allowance		3	
	Omission of apportionment overheads		1	
	Projected revenues		2	
	Variable costs		1	
	Incremental overheads		1	
	Tax on net revenues		1	
	NPV of revenues		1	
	NPV of lost contribution net of tax		2	
	Capital investment and disposal		1	
	Incorporation of capital allowances in cash flow		1	
	NPV of capital flows		1	
	Total NPV of new project		1	
	Use of correct discount factors		1	
	Investment decision		1	
				18
(b)	Calculation of correct sensitivity			4
(c)	(i)	Calculation of increase in occupancy	4	
	(ii)	Calculation of increase in contract length	4	
				8
(d)	Up to 2 marks each for detailed points on what is meant by risk		6	
	Up to 3 marks each for detailed points relating to estimating risk		12	
	Up to 2 marks each for detailed points on to how to reduce risk		6	
	Presentation and quality of argument		2	
	Maximum available		26	
	Maximum awarded			20
Total				50

72 AMBER PLC

(a) ***Tutorial* note:** The train company provides a daily return service, so there are two single journeys each day.

The expected number of passengers per journey using the service is dependent on the demand at each particular exchange rate.

At €1.52/£1: expected demand	= (500 + 460 + 420)/3
	= 460
At €1.54/£1: expected demand	= (550 + 520 + 450)/3
	= 506.67 (rounded)
At €1.65/£1: expected demand	= (600 + 580 + 500)/3
	= 560

The expected demand is therefore:

= (0.2) (460) + (0.5) (506.67) + (0.3) (560)

= 92 + 253.33 + 168

= 513.33 per train journey

= 1,026.67 per day (outward and return journeys).

(b) ***Workings***

45% of passengers use the catering service, spending £4.50 per head on average. Two journeys are run daily, for 360 days per year. This gives:

Annual revenue = 0.45 × 1,026.67 × £4.50 × 360
= £748,440

Daily revenue = £748,440/360 = £2,079 per day (= less than £2,200 per day).

		£
Variable costs		
Direct material (55% of revenue)	= (0.55) (£748,440)	411,642
Variable overhead (12% of revenue)	= (0.12) (£748,440)	89,813
Total variable costs		501,455
Fixed costs		
Labour: Year 1	= (0.10) (£748,440)	74,844
Rising by 5% per year; this gives:		
	Year 2: £78,586	
	Year 3: £82,516	
	Year 4: £86,641	
	Year 5: £90,973	
Purchase/store management and insurance	= 0.05 (£748,440)	37,422

With out-sourcing
If the service is out-sourced, there will be a saving of (£18,000 + £3,000) = £21,000 in purchasing/store management and insurance costs:

Purchase and insurance with out-sourcing (£37,422 - £21,000)	16,422
Contract cost per year = £250 per day × 360 days	90,000

Gross catering receipts are less than £2,200 per day on average, therefore the 5% commission does not apply.

Cash flows: in-house option

Year	*1*	*2*	*3*	*4*	*5*
	£	£	£	£	£
Sales	748,440	748,440	748,440	748,440	748,440
Variable costs	(501,455)	(501,455)	(501,455)	(501,455)	(501,455)
Contribution	246,985	246,985	246,985	246,985	246,985
Labour costs	(74,844)	(78,586)	(82,516)	(86,641)	(90,973)
Purchase and insurance	(37,422)	(37,422)	(37,422)	(37,422)	(37,422)
Asset purchase/sale	-	(500,000)	-	-	280,000
Net cash flow	134,719	(369,023)	127,047	122,922	398,590
Discount factor at 12%	0.893	0.797	0.712	0.636	0.567
Present value	120,304	(294,111)	90,457	78,178	226,001

Net present value = £220,829

Cash flows: contract out option

Year	*0*	*1*	*2*	*3*	*4*	*5*
	£	£	£	£	£	£
Contract fee payable		(90,000)	(90,000)	(90,000)	(90,000)	(90,000)
Asset sale	650,000					
Fixed costs	-	(16,422)	(16,422)	(16,422)	(16,422)	(16,422)
Net cash flow	650,000	(106,422)	(106,422)	(106,422)	(106,422)	(106,422)
Discount factor at 12%	1.000	0.893	0.797	0.712	0.636	0.567
Present value	650,000	(95,035)	(84,818)	(75,772)	(67,684)	(60,341)

Net present value £266,350

This option thus offers an NPV which is £45,521 greater than the in-house option, which means that profits could be increased by contracting out the catering service.

Contracting out the catering service is thus the preferred alternative and it is recommended that Amber plc accept the tender from the outside supplier.

(c) The financial effect can be assessed by comparing the present value of the additional costs incurred with the present value of the incremental contribution.

Workings

Additional staff training cost each year	£10,000
Discount factor at 12% for years 1 - 5	3.605
Present value of the additional training expense	£36,050
The additional contribution amounts to 10% per year for years 1 - 5	£24,699 each year
Discount factor at 12% for years 1 - 5	3.605
Present value at 12% per year	£89,040

The net present value of the additional investment in staff training is therefore £89,040 less £36,050. This means that the net present value can be increased by £52,990 by retaining the service in-house, but increasing demand via improved services.

This additional net present value is greater than the £45,521 that can be achieved by switching to an outside provider for the catering service. The decision to contract out is therefore changed.

However, Amber plc must be wary of the fact that the difference between the in-house and the contracted-out service is only £7,469 i.e. (£52,990 - £45,521). The advantage is therefore relatively insignificant. Perhaps more importantly, if demand can be increased by as much as ten per cent for the relatively small investment of £10,000 per year (less than 2% of current variable costs), this suggests that Amber plc should perhaps look more closely at the possible opportunities for increasing the contribution from the in-house catering service, before choosing to contract out. If demand is very sensitive to both price and quality, it may require little investment to make the catering service very profitable.

The gains from investing internally, however, must be weighed against the potential gains to be earned from higher demand for a contracted-out service. The additional information shows that the company will receive 5% of gross sales receipts once daily sales exceed £2,200. At present sales are at £2,079 and so, if the external contractor was able to raise demand by 10%, Amber plc would receive 5% of the new annual revenue i.e. £41,164 without incurring any additional expense. The choice, therefore, of whether to use the outside supplier or keep the service in-house is very much dependent on the anticipated levels of future demand.

(d) The **main limitation of making demand forecasts** lies in the fact that their **reliability is unknown.** Most forecasts are based on a mix of historical information and expectations in relation to relevant influential variables. For example, the exchange rate forecasts, where the highest probability is attached to a rate of €1.54/£1, is likely to be based on the statistical pattern of historical exchange rates (including the standard deviation) such that €1.54/£1 constitutes the most frequently-observed rate. This does not necessarily mean, however, that the rate will be similar in the future – history does not always repeat itself.

Another limitation relates to the **nature of the data being forecast**. Weather forecasts are notoriously unreliable, because nature is such an uncontrollable force. Even if the UK weather has been hot, on average, for the past five years, this does not imply that this will be the case in the future. The factors which dictate the weather are uncontrollable and consequently to a large degree unpredictable.

The forecast also runs into problems because it **seeks to link two unrelated variables**. The state of the weather is totally independent of the exchange rate, and vice versa, and they can only be linked in the way suggested by the table if the range of alternative observations is restricted. This is ultimately a distortion of a reality which is far more complex.

(e) There are numerous **non-financial factors** which may be relevant to a decision to contract out, and the type of factors are likely to be dependent on the process/service which is the subject of the decision. Amongst the most important of the non-financial considerations will be the impact of any decision on the company's **competitive position**. For example, in the case of Amber plc, if the on-train catering facility is of a sufficiently high standard, it may attract new clientele to use their trains, thereby giving Amber plc a competitive advantage. The opposite may also be the case. In other words, the **strategic impact of a decision** needs to be taken into account, in addition to the directly measurable financial effects.

Another factor that should be taken into account is the question of **management control over service quality**. Once a service moves 'out of house', the only control mechanism that remains with the purchasing company might be a variety of penalties, the extreme one being termination of the contract. If the service remains inside the company, it may be easier to change things in response to changing customer needs. In other words, contracting out may be linked to a reduction in the level of management control.

Staff morale might be affected by contracting out, and any such possible effects should be carefully considered. Staff in departments that remain in-house might begin to feel threatened and view their service as the next on the 'hit list' for external contracting. It is important for managers to help allay such fears, and make clear the criteria on which any future outsourcing decisions will be based.

Other non-financial factors which may be useful to consider include:

- Environmental effects, such as changes in food packaging policies
- The terms of any contract for outside supply, and the willingness of the supplier to respond to changes in market demand as and when necessary
- The capability of the business to manage the external supply process. If a large number of contracts are in place, this can possibly become a logistical headache.

73 SPRINGBANK PLC

(a) ***Working W1***

Calculation of tax benefits of capital allowances

Year	*Tax written-down value of asset*	*Writing down allowance – WDA (25%)*	*Tax saving due to WDA (30%)*
	£	£	£
1	3,000,000	750,000	225,000
2	2,250,000	562,500	168,750
3	1,687,500	421,875	126,563
4	1,265,625	316,406	94,922
5	949,219		284,766

(balancing allowance in Year 5)

These figures for tax savings will be rounded to the nearest £1,000.

Calculation of net present value of proposed investment

Year	0	1	2	3	4	5
	£000	£000	£000	£000	£000	£000
Sales		2,750	2,750	2,750	2,750	2,750
Production costs		(1,100)	(1,100)	(1,100)	(1,100)	(1,100)
Admin/dist'n expenses		(220)	(220)	(220)	(220)	(220)
Net revenue		1,430	1,430	1,430	1,430	1,430
Tax payable at 30%		(429)	(429)	(429)	(429)	(429)
Tax benefits from WDAs (W1)		225	169	127	95	285
Working capital	(400)					400
Machinery	(3,000)					
Project cash flows	(3,400)	1,226	1,170	1,128	1,096	1,686
Discount factor at 12%	1.000	0.893	0.797	0.712	0.636	0.567
Present value	(3,400)	1,095	932	803	697	956

The net present value is approximately £1,083,000.

This analysis makes the following assumptions:

(1) The first tax benefit occurs in Year 1, the last tax benefit occurs in Year 5

(2) Cash flows occur at the end of each year.

(3) Inflation can be ignored.

(4) The increase in capacity does not lead to any increase in fixed production overheads.

(5) Working capital is all released at the end of Year 5

(b) ***Tutorial note:*** The method of reaching a solution depends on whether it is assumed that the working capital investment varies with the volume of sales, or whether it is a fixed amount at £400,000. The solution here makes the assumption, preferred by the examiner, that the investment in working capital varies with the volume of sales.

Solution

Some costs and benefits would be fixed amounts. These are the cost of the investment and the tax benefits from the writing down allowances. The present value of these tax benefits is as follows.

Year	*Tax benefit (see (W1))*	*Discount factor at 12%*	*Present value*
	£000		£000
1	225	0.893	200.9
2	169	0.797	134.7
3	127	0.712	90.4
4	95	0.636	60.4
5	285	0.567	161.6
			648.0

After-tax profit from units sold

Variable administration and distribution expenses per unit = 220,000/5,500 = £40 per unit

Net revenue from additional units sold, before tax = £500 – £200 – £40 = £260 per unit.

Net revenue from additional units sold, after tax = 70% of £260 = £182.

Let the volume of annual sales be V units.

The present value of after-tax profits from selling V units each year for 5 years (years 1 – 5) = £182V × 3.605 (at a discount rate of 12%).

Working capital

It is assumed that the amount of working capital investment varies with the volume of annual sales.

Incremental working capital per unit = 400,000/5,500 = £72.73 per unit.

The net present value of the working capital investment is therefore:

Year	*Cash flow*	*Discount factor at 12%*	*Present value*
	£000		£000
0	(72.73V)	1.000	(72.73V)
5	72.73V	0.567	41.24V
Net PV of cost			31.49V

The NPV of the project is zero when:

(3,000,000) + 648,000 + 656.11V – 31.49V = 0

624.62V

= 2,352,000

V = 3,765 units.

Current annual sales are 10,000 units (£5,000,000/£500).

To achieve breakeven will therefore require an increase in annual sales of 37.65% (3,765/10,000).

This is about 32% (1,735/5,500) less than the expected increase in sales volume.

(c) (i)

The current gearing of Springbank plc	=	(3.5m/4m) × 100	=	87.5%
Total debt after issuing £3.4m of debt	=	3.5m + 3.4m	=	£6.9m
New level of gearing	=	(6.9m/4m) × 100	=	172.5%
				£
Current annual debenture interest	=	3.5m × 0.10	=	350,000
Current interest on overdraft	=	400,000 – 350,000	=	50,000
Annual interest on new debt	=	3.4m × 0.08	=	272,000
Expected annual interest				672,000

Current profit before interest and tax				£1.5m
Current interest cover	=	1.5m/0.4m	=	3.75 times

With the investment, annual profits before tax will increase by £1.43 million (see answer (a)).

Assuming straight-line depreciation, **additional depreciation** = £600,000 per year (£3,000,000/5 years).

Current profit before interest and tax	=	(1.5 + 1.43 – 0.6) m		£2.33m
Expected interest cover	=	2.33m/0.672m	=	3.47 times

This is lower than the current interest cover, assuming no change in overdraft interest.

Thus, Springbank's **gearing** is expected to rise from slightly below the sector average of 100% to significantly more than the sector average. Springbank's **interest cover** is likely to remain at a level lower than the sector average of four times, and will be slightly reduced assuming no change in overdraft interest.

(ii) **Ratio calculations**

	20X1		*20X2*	
ROCE	1,750/7,120	24.6%	1,500/7,500	20%
Net profit margin	1,750/5,000	35%	5,000/7,500	30%
Asset turnover	5,000/7,120	0.70	5,000/7,500	0.67
Current ratio	2,000/1,280	1.56	2,150/1,150	1.87
Quick ratio	1,000/1,280	0.78	980/1,150	0.85
Stock days	365 ×1,000/3,000	122 days	365 × 1,170/3,100	138 days
Debtors ratio	12 × 900/5,000	2.2 months	12 × 850/5,000	2 months
Sales/working capital	5,000/720	6.9	5,000/1,000	5
Debt/equity	3,500/3,620	96.7%	3,500/4,000	87.5%
Interest cover	1,750/380	4.6	1,500/400	3.75

The **return on capital employed** of Springbank has declined as a result of both falling net profit margin and falling asset turnover: while comparable with the sector average of 25% in 20X1, it is well below the sector average in 20X2. The problem here is that turnover has remained static while both cost of sales and investment in assets have increased.

Despite the fall in profitability, both **current ratio** and **quick ratio** have improved. This is due mainly to the increase in stock levels and the decline in current liabilities, the composition of which is unknown. However, the current ratio remains below the sector average. The increase in both stock levels and **stock days**, together with the fact that stock days is now 53% above the sector average, may indicate that current products are becoming harder to sell, a conclusion supported by the failure to increase turnover and the reduced profit margin. The expected increase in sales volume is therefore likely to be associated with a new product launch, since it is unlikely that an increase in capacity alone will be able to generate increased sales. There is also the possibility that the static sales of existing products may indicate that sales will decline in the future.

The decrease in the **debtors' ratio** is an encouraging sign, but the interpretation of the decreased **sales/working capital ratio** is uncertain. While the decrease could indicate less aggressive working capital management, it could also indicate that trade creditors are less willing to extend credit to Springbank, or that stock management is poor.

The **gearing** of the company has fallen, but only because reserves have been increased by retained profit. The **interest cover** has declined since interest has increased and operating profit has fallen. Given the constant long-term debt, the increase in interest, although small, could indicate an increase in overdraft finance.

Ratio analysis offers evidence that the financial performance of Springbank plc has been disappointing in terms of sales, profitability and stock management. It may be that the management of Springbank see the increase in capacity as a cure for the company's declining performance.

(iii) Since the investment has a positive NPV it is acceptable in financial terms. The danger highlighted by the analysis of recent financial performance is that existing sales may generate a declining contribution towards meeting interest payments in the future. However, sensitivity analysis shows the proposed expansion is robust in terms of sales volume, since a 31% - 32% reduction below the forecast increase in sales is needed to eliminate the positive NPV. The proposed expansion is therefore acceptable, but the choice of financing is critical.

Springbank should be able to meet future interest payments if the cashflow forecasts for the increase in capacity are sound. However, no account has been taken of expected **inflation**, and both sales prices and costs will be expected to change. There is also an underlying **assumption of constant sales volumes**, when changing economic circumstances and the actions of competitors make this assumption unlikely to be true. More detailed financial forecasts are needed to give a clearer indication of whether Springbank can meet the additional interest payments arising from the new debentures. There is also a danger that managers may focus more on the short-term need to meet the increased interest payments, or on the longer-term need to replace the machinery and redeem the debentures, rather than on increasing the wealth of shareholders.

Financial risk has increased from a balance sheet point of view and this is likely to have a negative effect on how financial markets view the company. The cost of raising additional finance is likely to rise, while the increased financial risk may lead to downward pressure on the company's share price. The current debentures represent 54% of fixed assets and after the new issue of debentures, this will rise to 73% of fixed assets. The assets available for offering as security against new debt issues will therefore decrease, and continue to decrease as fixed assets depreciate.

No information has been offered as to the **maturity of the new debenture issue**. If the matching principle is applied, a medium term maturity of five to six years is indicated. However, the 10% debentures are due for redemption in 20X7 and it would be unwise to have two significant redemption calls so close to each other.

On the basis of the above discussion, careful thought needs to be given to the maturity of any new issue of debentures and it may be advisable to use debt finance to meet only part of the financing need of the proposed capacity expansion. Alternative sources of finance such as equity and leasing should be considered.

(d) Financing the investment by an issue of ordinary shares could offer several advantages to Springbank plc. Gearing would fall to 47% (3.5/7.4), less than half of the sector average of 100%, rather than increasing to significantly more than the sector average. Interest cover would increase to 5.8 (2.33/0.4) from 3.75, compared to a sector average of 4. The financial risk faced by the company would thus be reduced, making it a more attractive investment prospect on the stock market. This could have a positive effect on the company's share price.

Ordinary shares do not carry a commitment to make regular payments such as interest on debt, giving Springbank plc a degree of flexibility in rewarding shareholders in financial terms. This must be balanced against the common desire of shareholders for a regular and increasing dividend.

Ordinary shares are permanent capital since they do not need to be repaid. Springbank plc would thus avoid the need to find funds for redemption that would arise if it issued debentures.

Because the fixed assets of the company would increase but its burden of long-term debt would be unchanged, Springbank would find it easier to raise additional debt in the future. This could be useful when the need arises to redeem the existing debentures in 20X7.

ACCA marking scheme			
			Marks
(a)		Calculation of capital allowances	2
		Calculation of tax benefits	1
		Calculation of net revenue	1
		Calculation of tax on net revenue	1
		Inclusion of tax benefits	1
		Treatment of working capital	1
		Capital investment	1
		Calculation of project cash flows	1
		Use of correct discount factors	1
		Calculation of NPV	1
			11
(b)		Formulation of algebraic solution	1
		Calculation of sales volume giving zero NPV	2
		Expression of volume change in relative terms	1
			4
(c)	(i)	Calculation of current gearing	1
		Calculation of expected gearing	1
		Calculation of current interest cover	1
		Calculation/discussion of expected interest cover	2
		Comparison with sector averages	1
			6
	(ii)	Calculation of relevant ratios	8
		Comment on recent financial performance	5
			13
	(iii)	Comment of acceptability of expansion	2
		Ability to meet future interest payments	2
		Maturity of new debentures	2
		Financial Risk and asset backing	2
		Comment on acceptability of proposed finance	2
			10
(d)		Up to 2 marks for each detailed advantage	6
Total			50

74 SASSONE PLC

(a) **Planning direct material usage variance:**

10,000 × (5.0 – 5.3) × 7.50 = £22,500 (A)

Operational direct material usage variance:

[(10,000 × 5.3) – 54,400] × 7.50 = £10,500 (A)

If the Production Director is correct in his claim that the standard material usage needs to be revised to 5.3 kg/unit, then 68% of the direct material variance of £33,000 is due to the use of an out-of-date standard. The Production Director is therefore correct in stating that most of the variance is due to an out-of-date standard, but he cannot avoid responsibility for the operational usage variance of £10,500.

Standards need to be revised regularly in order that they remain relevant for costing and control purposes. The Production Director's claim must be investigated and the material usage standard revised if the claim is found to be true and a revision is deemed to be necessary.

Providing planning and operational variances as a result of ex post variance analysis will enable more accurate assessment f managerial performance by identifying controllable and uncontrollable variances. Managers cannot be held responsible for uncontrollable variances, whether positive or negative in nature. Providing planning and operational variances will also reduce the frequency of revisions to standards.

(b) **Machine One**

Year	*0*	*1*	*2*	*3*	*4*	*5*
	£	£	£	£	£	£
Initial investment	(238,850)					
Maintenance		(10,000)	(13,000)	(16,000)	(19,000)	(22,000)
11% discount factor	1.000	0.901	0.812	0.731	0.659	0.593
	(238,850)	(9,010)	(10,556)	(11,696)	(12,521)	(13,046)

Present value of costs = £295,679

Annuity factor for five years at 11% = 3.696

Equivalent annual cost = 295,679/3.696 = £80,000 per year

Machine Two

Year	*0*	*1*	*2*	*3*	*4*
	£	£	£	£	£
Initial investment	(215,000)				
Maintenance		(10,000)	(15,000)	(20,000)	(25,000)
11% discount factor	1.000	0.901	0.812	0.731	0.659
	(215,000)	(9,010)	(12,180)	(14,620)	(16,475)

Present value of costs = £267,285

Annuity factor for four years at 11% = 3.102

Equivalent annual cost = 267,285/3.102 = £86,165 per year

Machine One should be bought as it has the lowest equivalent annual cost.

(c) **Sales volume reaches the maximum capacity of the new machine in Year 4.**

Year	*1*	*2*	*3*	*4*	*5*
	£	£	£	£	£
Sales revenue	312,000	432,000	562,500	702,000	
Marginal cost	(243,300)	(337,600)	(438,500)	(547,200)	
Fixed cost	(10,600)	(11,236)	(11,910)	(12,625)	
Maintenance	(10,000)	(15,750)	(22,050)	(28,941)	
Taxable cash flow	48,100	68,214	90,040	113,234	
Taxation		(14,430)	(20,464)	(27,012)	(33,970)
WDA tax benefit		16,125	12,094	9,070	27,211
Net cash flow	48,100	69,909	81,670	95,292	(6,759)
Discount factors	0.901	0.812	0.731	0.659	0.593
Present values	43,338	56,766	59,701	62,727	(4,008)

	£
Sum of present values	218,594
Initial investment	215,000
Net present value	3,594

The positive NPV indicates that the investment in Machine Two is financially acceptable, although the NPV is so small that there is likely to be a significant possibility of a negative NPV.

Workings

Year	*1*	*2*	*3*	*4*
Selling price (£/unit)	10.40	10.82	11.25	11.70
Sales (units/yr)	30,000	40,000	50,000	60,000
Sales revenue (£/yr)	312,000	432,800	562,500	702,000

Year	*1*	*2*	*3*	*4*
Marginal cost (£/unit)	8.11	8.44	8.77	9.12
Sales (units/yr)	30,000	40,000	50,000	60,000
Marginal cost (£/yr)	243,300	337,600	438,500	547,200

Year	*1*	*2*	*3*	*4*
Maintenance (£/yr)	10,000	15,000	20,000	25,000
Inflated cost (14/yr)	10,000	15,750	22,050	28,941

Writing down allowances and tax benefits

	Allowances	*Benefits*
	£	£
Year 1: 215,000 × 0.25 =	53,750	16,125
Year 2: 161,250 × 0.25 =	40,312	12,094
Year 3: 120,938 × 0.25 =	30,234	9,070
	124,296	
Year 4: (215,000 – 124,296) =	90,704	27,211
	215,000	

(d) Total taxable cash flow = (48,100 + 68,214 + 90,040 + 113,234) = £319,588

Total depreciation = £215,000

Total accounting profit = 319,588 – 215,000 = £104,588

Average annual accounting profit = 104,588/4 = £26,147

Average investment = 215,000/2 = £107,500

Return on capital employed = 100 × 26,197/107,500 = 24.3%

ROCE of 24.3% is slightly less than the target ROCE of 25%, indicating that buying the machine is not acceptable with respect to this criterion. However, evaluation using the net present value approach is preferred for investment advice.

(e) The objectives to which organisational strategy relates depend on the relative power of different stakeholders associated with the company, and on whether objectives are imposed on the organisation by, for example, government or other legislation. Since it is unlikely that the objectives of different stakeholders will coincide, conflict will arise between corporate objectives and management must decide on the extent to which conflicting objectives can be met. In this case, 55% of the company's shares are in the hands of institutional investors and so this shareholder group, if it acts in concert, can wield considerable power over the organisational strategy of Sassone plc. In practice shareholder groups are likely to be fragmented and this fragmentation will reduce the power of Sassone plc's institutional investors.

The primary financial objective of a company is usually stated to be the maximisation of shareholder wealth and Sassone plc has declared publicly that this is one of its objectives. Returns to shareholders can be measured in terms of dividend yield and capital growth, reflecting the attention paid by investors to dividends and increasing share prices. Both dividend yield and capital growth can be measured over a standardised holding period in order to assess shareholder returns.

Some of the institutional shareholders of Sassone have complained that annual dividend payments have not increased at an acceptable rate due to expenditure on environmentally-friendly and socially acceptable projects. This represents a conflict between a financial objective (shareholder wealth maximisation) and a non-financial objective (social welfare). The claim is that unnecessary expenditure has reduced the amount of profits paid out as dividends. It is important for Sassone plc to find the extent to which this view is shared by other institutional shareholders, given the relative size of this shareholder grouping.

This conflict between objectives cannot be resolved by rational argument. It is possible that Sassone plc's support for environmentally-friendly and socially acceptable projects has generated a positive image in the minds of its customers, resulting in increased sales, but this effect cannot be quantified readily. Alternatively, it is possible that sales would be lower if Sassone plc did not support environmentally-friendly and socially acceptable projects, since such behaviour may be expected by its customers. The institutional investors' complaint may therefore be short-sighted, although a comparison between Sassone plc and its competitors may show that its expenditure on socially acceptable and environmentally-friendly projects is larger than necessary. However, the benefit of such projects may arise only in the long term, whereas the complaint by institutional investors indicates a short-term focus.

One of the roles of company managers is therefore to seek to resolve or reduce any conflict between corporate objectives. The fact that institutional investors have threatened to vote against the re-appointment of directors at the next Annual General Meeting signifies that they are resolved to seek change, although in practice they may be unable to gather sufficient votes to achieve their objective. However, company managers must maintain a good relationship with institutional investors, if only because they may wish to seek investor support for a rights issue in the future, and it is likely the complaint will be investigated and an amicable solution found. The key task of management may be to persuade institutional investors to adopt a longer-term view.

(f) When considering the incremental increase in sales arising from the purchase of the new machine, it was assumed that product costs remained constant in real terms over the life cycle of the product. In fact, the life cycle of the product was ignored and all of the engineering components produced were treated as being identical. In reality, each kind of engineering component is likely to go through the stages of the product life cycle: introduction, growth, maturity and decline. Higher costs are likely to be incurred at the start of the product life cycle due to product development, marketing and promotion. During the growth stage, sales volumes increase and unit cost consequently decreases. During the maturity stage, unit cost initially continues to fall as developmental and promotional costs are recovered and scale economies continue to grow, but eventually competition on price and product differentiation begin to reduce profitability. In the decline stage, sales volumes fall and unit cost increases, further reducing profitability and leading to abandonment or replacement of the product concerned.

Most costing systems report product costs on a periodic basis (e.g. monthly or annually) and fail to track product profitability over the product life cycle. Life cycle costing accumulates actual costs over the product life cycle and allocates research, development, promotion and marketing costs to specific products rather than treating them as general overhead costs. In this way, a clearer picture of estimated life cycle costs and product profitability is gained, and actual life cycle costs can be monitored and compared to budgeted life cycle costs for cost control purposes.

Product pricing should reflect the need to recover costs over the product life cycle. Initially, prices may be set at a level that reflects the captive nature of the initial market (since competitors may not exist), while also considering the need to persuade potential customers to substitute the new product for existing products. During the maturity stage, product prices will decline as companies struggle to maintain market share in the face of increasingly fierce competition. Product prices will continue to fall in the decline stage as the product becomes obsolete and replacements are developed. Sassone plc could incorporate these considerations into the pricing of the engineering components it sells, particularly the need to keep prices competitive during the maturity and decline stages.

Target costing considers the price that ought to be charged in order to achieve a desired market share for a given product and uses this, together with the desired profit margin, as the basis for determining product cost. Target costing can therefore take account of the life cycle of the product rather than just production costs. For new products, the product development team can use this product cost as a target to be met when the product is launched. If the target cost differs from the expected actual cost, the product development team can seek ways to achieve the desired target cost, for example by product and process design. This approach could be useful to Sassone plc since it would discover what product price was needed to achieve the desired market share for a given engineering component, rather than simply adding a mark-up to expected actual cost, and it could use the derived target cost as a way of controlling costs and increasing profitability.

ACCA marking scheme		
		Marks
(a)	Planning variance	1
	Operational variance	1
	Discussion of Production Director's views	2
		4

(b)	Equivalent annual cost of machine 1	3
	Equivalent annual cost of machine 2	2
	Selection of lowest equivalent annual cost	1
		6
(c)	Sales volume	1
	Sales revenue	2
	Marginal costs	2
	Maintenance costs	1
	Incremental fixed costs	1
	Taxation	2
	Capital allowances and tax benefits	4
	Net cash flow	1
	Discount factors	1
	Net present value	1
	Comment	2
		18
(d)	Average annual accounting profit	1
	Average investment	1
	Return on capital employed	1
	Comment on findings	1
		4
(e)	Discussion of stakeholders and objectives	3-4
	Discussion of conflict between objectives	4-5
	Discussion relating to Sassone plc	2-3
		10
(f)	Discussion of life cycle costing	3-4
	Discussion of target costing	3-4
	Link to Sassone plc	1
		8
Maximum		50

75 ARG CO

(a) NPV calculation for Alpha and Beta

Year	*1*	*2*	*3*	*4*
	£	£	£	£
Sales revenue	3,585,000	6,769,675	6,339,000	1,958,775
Material cost	(1,395,000)	(2,634,225)	(2,466,750)	(761,925)
Fixed costs	(1,000,000)	(1,050,000)	(1,102,500)	(1,157,625)
Advertising	(500,000)	(200,000)	(200,000)	
Taxable profit	690,000	2,885,450	2,569,750	39,225
Taxation	(172,500)	(721,362)	(642,438)	(9,806)
WDA tax benefit	250,000			
Fixed asset sale				1,200,000
WC recovery				1,000,000
Net cash flow	767,500	2,164,088	1,927,312	2,229,419
Discount factors	0.885	0.783	0.693	0.613
Present values	679,237	1,694,481	1,335,626	1,366,634

	£
Sum of present values	5,075,978
Initial investment	3,000,000
Net present value	2,075,978

The positive NPV indicates that the investment is financially acceptable.

Workings

Alpha sales revenue

Year	*1*	*2*	*3*	*4*
Selling price (£/unit)	31.00	31.93	32.89	33.88
Sales (units/yr)	60,000	110,000	100,000	30,000
Sales revenue (£/yr)	1,860,000	3,512,300	3,289,000	1,016,400

Beta sales revenue

Year	*1*	*2*	*3*	*4*
Selling price (£/unit)	23.00	23.69	24.40	25.13
Sales (units/yr)	75,000	137,500	125,000	37,500
Sales revenue (£/yr)	1,725,000	3,257,375	3,050,000	942,375
Year	*1*	*2*	*3*	*4*
Sales revenue (£/yr)	3,585,000	6,769,675	6,339,000	1,958,775

Alpha direct material cost

Year	*1*	*2*	*3*	*4*
Material cost (£/unit)	12.00	12.36	12.73	13.11
Sales (units/yr)	60,000	110,000	100,000	30,000
Material cost (£/yr)	720,000	1,359,600	1,273,000	393,300

Beta direct material cost

Year	*1*	*2*	*3*	*4*
Material cost (£/unit)	9.00	9.27	9.55	9.83
Sales (units/yr)	75,000	137,500	125,000	37,500
Material cost (£/yr)	675,000	1,274,625	1,193,750	368,625
Year	*1*	*2*	*3*	*4*
Material cost (£/unit)	1,395,000	2,634,225	2,466,750	761,925

(b) The evaluation assumes that several key variables will remain constant, such as the discount rate, inflation rates and the taxation rate. In practice this is unlikely. The taxation rate is a matter of government policy and so may change due to political or economic necessity.

Specific inflation rates are difficult to predict for more than a short distance into the future and in practice are found to be constantly changing. The range of inflation rates used in the evaluation is questionable, since over time one would expect the rates to converge. Given the uncertainty of future inflation rates, using a single average inflation rate might well be preferable to using specific inflation rates.

The discount rate is likely to change as the company's capital structure changes. For example, issuing debentures with an interest rate of 9% is likely to decrease the average cost of capital.

Looking at the incremental fixed production costs, it seems odd that nominal fixed production costs continue to increase even when sales are falling. It also seems odd that incremental fixed production costs remain constant in real terms when production volumes are changing. It is possible that some of these fixed production costs are stepped, in which case they should decrease.

The forecasts of sales volume seem to be too precise, predicting as they do the growth, maturity and decline phases of the product life-cycle. In practice it is likely that improvements or redesign could extend the life of the two products beyond five years. The assumption of constant product mix seems unrealistic, as the products are substitutes and it is possible that one will be relatively more successful. The sales price has been raised in line with inflation, but a lower sales price could be used in the decline stage to encourage sales.

Net working capital is to remain constant in real terms. In practice, the level of working capital will depend on the working capital policies of the company, the value of goods, the credit offered to customers, the credit taken from suppliers and so on. It is unlikely that the constant real value will be maintained.

The net present value is heavily dependent on the terminal value derived from the sale of fixed assets after five years. It is unlikely that this value will be achieved in practice. It is also possible that the machinery can be used to produce other products, rather than be used solely to produce Alpha and Beta.

(c) ARG Co currently has £50m of fixed assets and long-term debt of £10m. The issue of £3m of 9% debentures will increase fixed assets by £2m of buildings and machinery. There seems to be ample security for the new issue.

Interest cover is currently 5.1 (4,560/900) which is less than the sector average, and this will fall to 3.9 (4,560/(900 + 3m × 9%)) following the debenture issue. The new products will increase profit by £440,000 (£690,000 – £250,000 of depreciation), increasing interest cover to 4.3 (5,000/1,170). Although on the low side and less than the sector average, this evaluation ignores any increase in profits from current activities. Interest cover may not be a cause for concern.

Current gearing using debt/equity based on book values of 32% (10,000/30,900) will rise to 42% (13,000/30,900) after the debenture issue. Both values are less than the sector average and ignore any increase in reserves due to next year's profits. Financial risk appears to be at an acceptable level and gearing does not appear to be a problem.

The debentures are convertible after eight years into 20 ordinary shares per £100 debenture. The current share price is £4.00, giving a conversion value of £80. For conversion to be likely, a minimum annual growth rate of only 2.83% is needed ((5.00/4.00)0.125 – 1). This growth rate could well be exceeded, making conversion after eight years a likely prospect. This analysis assumes that the floor value on the conversion date is the par value of £100: the actual floor value could well be different in eight years' time, depending on the prevailing cost of debt.

Conversion of the debentures into ordinary shares will eliminate the need to redeem them, as well as reducing the company's gearing.

The current share price may be depressed by the ongoing recovery from the loss-making magazine publication venture. Annual share price growth may therefore be substantially in excess of 2.83%, making the conversion terms too generous (assuming a floor value equal to par value on the conversion date). On conversion, 600,000 new shares will be issued, representing 23% (100 × 0.6m/2.6m) of share capital. The company must seek the views and approval of existing shareholders regarding this potential dilution of ownership and control.

The maturity of the debentures (12 years) does not match the product life-cycle (four years). This may be caution on the part of the company's managers, but a shorter period could be used.

It has been proposed that £1 million of the debenture issue would be used to finance the working capital needs of the project. Financing all working capital from a long-term source is a very conservative approach to working capital financing. ARG Co could consider financing fluctuating current assets from a short-term source such as an overdraft. By linking the maturity of the finance to the maturity of the assets being financed, ARG Co would be applying the matching principle.

(d) Calculation of ABC recovery rates

Cost driver	*Alpha*	*Beta*	*Total*	*Cost*	*Recovery rate*
Floor area (m^2)	3,500	6,500	10,000	£505,000	£50.50/m^2
Labour hours	10,000	15,000	25,000	£300,000	£12/hr
Inspections	3,000	3,750	6,750	£67,500	£10/test
Orders	3,000	1,500	4,500	£67,500	£15/order
Maintenance hours	625	1,875	2,500	£26,000	£10.40/hr
Set-ups	120	50	170	£34,000	£200/set-up

Activity-based cost apportionment

Fixed cost	£	*Alpha*	*Beta*
Power, heating, etc.	505,000	176,750	328,250
Salaries	300,000	120,000	180,000
Inspection costs	67,500	30,000	37,500
Order processing	67,500	45,000	22,500
Maintenance	26,000	6,500	19,500
Set-up costs	34,000	24,000	10,000
	1,000,000	402,250	597,750

Fixed costs for Alpha = 402,250/60,000 = £6·70
Fixed costs for Beta = 597,750/75,000 = £7·97

ARG Co uses a cost plus pricing system and appears from the information provided to use a mark-up of 50% on total cost. The revised total costs for Alpha and Beta are £18.70 and £16.97. Applying a 50% mark-up gives selling prices of £28.05 and £25.45 respectively. On this basis Alpha is over-priced and Beta is under-priced. However, the selling price should also reflect the best price obtainable in the market. This might be higher or lower than any of the prices based on total cost.

(e) ARG Co will be concerned to protect the sterling value of its expected dollar receipt. The quoted forward rates show that the dollar is weakening against sterling, so that the sterling value of $500,000 dollars will have fallen in three months. ARG Co can enter into a contract now with a bank to exchange its expected dollar receipt in three months time at the current forward rate. Such a contract is called a forward exchange contract and is binding on both the bank and ARG Co. By agreeing to an exchange at the current forward rate, the company will be protected against any further deterioration in the sterling-dollar exchange rate. The sterling value arising from the contract will be $500,000/1.8174 = £275,118.

(f) A bill of exchange is a means of payment initiated by an exporter. It is signed (accepted) by an importer, signifying agreement to pay the amount on the face of the bill. This payment may either be on demand (sight bill) or on a mutually agreed future date (term bill).

The risk associated with overseas debtors is reduced by bills of exchange since these bills are a liquid short-term financial asset. They can be discounted (sold at less than face value) to a bank in order to provide advance payment of the amount due to be received from overseas debtors. A smaller discount will be charged if the bill of exchange is confirmed (countersigned) by the importer's bank.

Bills of exchange can be also used in conjunction with documentary letters of credit (also known as documentary credits) to reduce export credit risk even further.

ACCA marking scheme		
		Marks
(a)	Sales revenue	4
	Material costs	4
	Fixed costs	1
	Advertising	1
	Taxation	2
	Capital allowance tax benefit	1
	Fixed asset sale	1
	Working capital recovery	1
	Present values	1
	Net present value and comment	1
		17
(b)	Assumptions regarding economic variables	2
	Fixed costs	1
	Sales volume	1
	Working capital	1
	Terminal value	1
		6
(c)	Evaluation and discussion should consider:	
	Security available	
	Interest cover	
	Gearing	
	Convertibility	
	Maturity	8
(d)	ABC recovery rates	3
	Fixed costs using ABC	4
	Total costs, selling prices and discussion	4
		11
(e)	Explanation of need to hedge receipt	2
	Sterling value of forward hedge	2
		4
(f)	Bills of exchange and risk reduction	2
	Discounting bills of exchange	2
		4
Total		50

76 BFD CO

Key answer tips

Part (a) asks for a NPV calculation. The first consideration is how to set out your answer as there are cash flows for the first four years and annuities for t=5-∞ and t=1-10. These can be incorporated as separate calculations or you could have had columns for flows 0,1,2,3,4,5-10 and 11-∞. This latter approach would have made part (c) slightly easier. Either way you needed to be particularly careful when calculating the tax flows given the lack of a delay.

In part (b) it is vital that issues are applied to the scenario, making reference to specific figures where possible.

Part (c) is tricky as the calculation to part (a) needs adjusting to remove the impact of cash flows for t= 11-∞.

Part (d) requires a structured approach to ensure a wide range of issues is covered, so a little time spent planning would have been a goo d idea. Where possible the impact of the loan should be quantified – for example, with the impact on gearing.

In part (e) you are asked to calculate the variances using both marginal and absorption costing so you need to prepare a standard cost under both systems. The required discussion is on the relative values so should be limited to explaining the difference, if any, rather than wider issues such as explaining the causes of the variances.

(a) Net present value evaluation of proposed investment:

	2005/6	*2006/7*	*2007/8*	*2008/9*
	£000	£000	£000	£000
Sales revenue	1,800	2,160	2,340	2,520
Variable costs	850	1,020	1,105	1,190
Contribution	950	1,140	1,235	1,330
Fixed costs	450	450	450	450
Net cash flow	500	690	785	880
Taxation	125	173	196	220
After-tax cash flow	375	517	589	660
12% discount factors	0.893	0.797	0.712	0.636
Present values	335	412	419	419

	£
Sum of present values	1,585,000
PV of tax benefits	423,750
PV of cash flows after Year 4 =	3,498,000
	5,506,750
Less initial investment	3,200,000
Net present value	2,306,750

Workings

	2005/6	*2006/7*	*2007/8*	*2008/9*
Sales volume (units)	100,000	120,000	130,000	140,000
Selling price (£/unit)	18.00	18.00	18.00	18.00
Sales revenue (£)	1,800,000	2,160,000	2,340,000	2,520,000
Variable costs (£/unit)	8.50	8.50	8.50	8.50
Variable costs (£)	850,000	1,020,000	1,105,000	1,190,000

Fixed costs = 4.50 × 100,000 = £450,000 per year

Annual writing down allowance = 3,000,000/10 = £300,000

Annual writing down allowance tax benefits = 25% × 300,000 = £75,000

Ten-year annuity factor at 12% = 5.650

Present value of writing down allowance tax benefits = 75,000 × 5.650 = £423,750

Year 4 value of year 5 after-tax cash flows in perpetuity = 660,000/0.12 = £5,500,000

Present value of these cash flows = 5,500,000 × 0.636 = £3,498,000

(b) From a net present value perspective the proposed investment is acceptable, since the net present value (NPV) is large and positive. However, a large part of the present value of benefits (63%) derives from the assumption that cash flows will continue indefinitely after Year 4. This is very unlikely to occur in practice and excluding these cash flows will result in a negative net present value of approximately £1.2m. In fact the proposed investment will not show a positive NPV until more than seven years have passed.

Before rejecting the proposal, steps should be taken to address some of the limitations of the analysis performed.

Inflation

Forecasts of future inflation of sales prices and variable costs should be prepared, so that a nominal NPV evaluation can be undertaken. This evaluation should employ a nominal after-tax cost of capital: it is not stated whether the 12% after-tax cost of capital is in nominal or real terms. Sales price is assumed to be constant in real terms, but in practice substitute products are likely to arise, leading to downward pressure on sales price and sales volumes.

Constant fixed costs

The assumption of constant fixed costs should be verified as being acceptable. Sales volumes are forecast to increase by 40% and this increase may result in an increase in incremental fixed costs.

Constant working capital

The assumption of constant working capital should be investigated. Net working capital is likely to increase in line with sales and so additional investment in working capital may be needed in future years. Inflation will increase required incremental working capital investment.

Taxation and capital allowances

The assumptions made regarding taxation should be investigated. The tax rate has been assumed to be constant, when there may be different rates of profit tax applied to companies of different size. The method available for claiming capital allowances should be confirmed, since it is usual to find a different method being applied to buildings compared to that applied to machinery, whereas in this case they are the same.

Machine replacement

The purchase of replacement machinery has been ignored, which seems unreasonable. Future reinvestment in new machinery will be needed and this will reduce the net present value of the proposed investment. Technological change is also possible, bringing perhaps new manufacturing methods and improved or substitute products, and these may affect the size of future cash flows.

Changes in technology

Technological change is also possible, bringing perhaps new manufacturing methods and improved or substitute products, and these may affect the size of future cash flows.

Financing

The method of financing the proposed investment should be considered. It may be that leasing will be cheaper than borrowing to buy, increasing the net present value and making the project more attractive. The amount of the investment is large compared to the current long-term capital employed by BFD Co and the after-tax cost of capital is likely to change as a result. A lower cost of capital would increase the NPV.

(c) The offer for the manufacturing rights is for a ten-year period.

Annual after-tax cash flow after Year 4 = £660,000

Present value of this cash flow over six years at 12% = 660,000 × 4.111 = £2,713,260

Present value of post Year 4 cash flows = 2,713,260 × 0.636 = £1,725,633

Sum of present values over 4 years	1,585,000
PV of tax benefits	423,750
PV of cash flows from Year 5 to Year 10 =	1,725,633
	3,734,383
Less initial investment	3,200,000
Net present value	534,383

This net present value is equivalent to an annual benefit of 534,383/ 5.650 = £94,581

The after-tax value of the offer of £300,000 per year for 10 years = 300,000 × 0.75 = £225,000

In the absence of other information, the offer should be accepted.

An alternative approach is to calculate the present value of the offer:

300,000 × 0.75 × 5.650 = £1,271,250

Since this is greater than the NPV of investing by £737,867, the offer should be accepted.

Alternative answer to parts (a) and (c)

Narrative	*0*	*1*	*2*	*3*	*4*	*5–10*	*11–∞*
Sales		1,800	2,160	2,340	2,520		
Var costs		(850)	(1,020)	(1,105)	(1,190)		
Fixed costs		(450)	(450)	(450)	(450)		
		500	690	785	880		
Tax		(125)	(173)	(196)	(220)		
		375	517	589	660	660	660
Invest	(3,200)						
Tax re WDAs		75	75	75	75	75	
Net cash flow	(3,200)	450	592	664	735	735	660
DF@12%	1	0.893	0.797	0.712	0.636	0.636 × 4.111	0.322 × 1/0.12
PV	(3,200)	402	472	473	467	1922	1,771

NPV = £2,307k

NPV (excluding t=11-∞) = 2,307 – 1,771 = £536k

(d) **REPORT**

To: The Board of BFD Co

From: Finance Director

Date:

Subject: Proposal to seek £3.2 million of Debt Finance

1. **Introduction**

This report considers whether seeking £3.2 million of debt finance is likely to be successful in the light of our current financial position and recent financial performance.

2. **Sector Data**

I have obtained some benchmark data relating to companies active in our business sector. The sector data applies to the current year and may not be applicable in previous years.

3. **Analysis of Financial Data**

Analysis of our financial statements gives the following results.

	2002/3	*2003/4*	*2004/5*	*Sector value*
Turnover growth	31%	53%		
Cost of sales growth	33%	63%		
Net profit margin	19%	17%	12%	9%
Interest cover	165	17	9	15
Sales/net working capital	4.7	6.2	9.5	
Stock days	104	130	116	85
Debtor days	56	91	98	75
Creditor days	69	95	90	70

	2002/3	*2003/4*	*2004/5*	*Sector value*
Current ratio	2.2	1.4	1.2	2.1
Quick ratio	0.9	0.7	0.6	0.8
Gearing (debt/equity ratio)	4%	33%	54%	40%

Note: Gearing calculations are based on our average overdraft, as our company has no long-term debt. This seems a reasonable approach to calculating gearing, since our overdraft is a large and increasing one.

Workings

	2002/3	*2003/4*	*2004/5*
Annual interest at 6% (£)	3,000	34,000	70,000
Overdraft (£)	50,000	567,000	1,167,000
Trade creditors (£)	400,000	733,000	1,133,000

4. **Comment on Financial Position and Performance**

BFD Co has experienced rapid growth in turnover since its formation three years ago, but it has been unable to maintain net profit margin, which has fallen from 19% in 2002 to 12% in 2004. On a positive note, our net profit margin is higher than the sector average, but this may also indicate that a further decrease may arise.

Our growth in turnover has not been matched by growth in long-term finance. Apart from the original equity investment made by the founder directors, growth in long-term finance has been through retained earnings alone. Our company has increasingly relied on short-term finance and over the three-year period the overdraft has grown from £50,000 to £1,167,000. From a financial risk point of view, gearing has increased from 4% to 54% and interest cover has declined from 165 times to nine times. Both ratios are currently worse than the comparable sector average. The average period of time in which we settle with trade creditors has grown from 69 days to 90 days compared to a sector average of 70 days.

The average amount of credit extended by the sector is 75 days but our debtors' ratio has grown from 56 days to 98 days. This has increased the amount of working capital finance we need, as has the growth in stock days from 104 days to 116 days compared to a sector average of 85 days. Funds which are tied up in stocks and debtors decrease profitability.

There is further bad news in the area of working capital management since both our current ratio and quick ratio are less than the current sector average, having declined in each of the past two years.

5. **Effect of Additional Debt Finance on Current Financial Position**

Debt finance of £3.2m would increase gearing on a book value basis from 54% to 203% ((1,167 + 3,200)/2,150), which is five times the sector average. If the overdraft is ignored in calculating gearing it would still be four times the sector average at 158% (3,400/2,150). Assuming interest at a fixed rate of 8%, our interest cover would fall from 9 times to 1.8 times (630/(272 + 70)). This is a dangerously low level of interest cover. We would need to assess whether we could offer security for a loan of this size.

6. **Chances of Success in Application for Debt Finance**

I must advise you that there are signs of overtrading in our recent financial statements and our company is approaching its overdraft limit of £1.25 million. We will need to obtain further long-term finance regardless of whether our application for a £3.2 million bank loan is successful.

I note that no further equity investment is available from the current directors. It may be in our best interests to address our overall long-term financing needs rather than seeking finance only for the proposed investment in Product FT7 manufacture. Our overall long-term financing need is greater than £3.2 million.

It is my opinion, based on our recent financial performance, our current financial position, and the effect of such a large amount of debt on our capital structure, that an application for a £3.2 million bank loan would not be successful and that alternative sources of finance should be sought. I would be pleased to advise on these if the Board requested.

Yours sincerely,

A.N. Accountant

(e) Calculation of standard contribution and standard profit

		£
Selling price		18.00
Direct material	7.00	
Direct labour	1.50	8.50
Standard contribution		9.50
Selling price		18.00
Direct material	7.00	
Direct labour	1.50	
Fixed production overhead	4.50	13.00
Standard profit		5.00

Sales price variance (marginal costing) = ((18.20 – 8.50) – 9.50) × 110,000

= (9.70 – 9.50) × 110,000 = £22,000 (F)

Sales price variance (absorption costing) = ((18.20 – 13.00) – 5.00) × 110,000

= (5.20 – 5.00) × 110,000 = £22,000 (F)

There is no difference between the two sales price variances because this variance depends upon the difference between actual selling price and standard selling price and not on the costing system employed in calculating it.

Sales volume profit variance (marginal costing) = (110,000 – 100,000) × 9.50 = £95,000 (F)

Sales volume profit variance (absorption costing) = (110,000 – 100,000) × 5.00 = £50,000 (F)

The sales volume profit variances are different, even though the volume difference is the same, because standard contribution (marginal costing) has a different value to standard profit (absorption costing), since marginal costing excludes production overheads from product cost while absorption costing includes them.

ACCA marking scheme		
		Marks
(a)	Sales revenue	1
	Variable costs	1
	Contribution	1
	Fixed costs	2
	Taxation of operating cash flows	2
	Present value of income	1
	Present value of capital allowance tax benefits	3
	Present value of cash flows after year 4	3
	Initial investment and working capital	1
	Net present value	1
		16
(b)	Acceptability of proposed investment	2–3
	Discussion of additional information	4–5
	Maximum	7
(c)	PV of post Year 4 after-tax cash flows	2
	NPV of investing over ten years	1
	Present value comparison of offer with investing	2
	Discussion and conclusion	1
		6
(d)	Financial analysis	7–8
	Discussion	8–9
	Report format	1
	Maximum	16
(e)	Sales price variances	1
	Sales volume variances	2
	Discussion	2
		5
Total		50

Section 5

JUNE 2006 EXAM QUESTIONS

SECTION A – THIS ONE QUESTION IS COMPULSORY AND MUST BE ATTEMPTED

1 MERTON PLC

The following financial information relates to Merton plc, a supplier of photographic equipment and film services to the film industry.

Profit and loss accounts for years ended 30 April

	2006	*2005*	*2004*
	£m	£m	£m
Turnover	160.0	145.0	132.0
Cost of sales	120.0	105.3	95.7
	40.0	39.7	36.3
Operating expenses	30.0	26.0	23.5
Operating profit	10.0	13.7	12.8
Interest	3.6	3.3	3.3
Profit before tax	6.4	10.4	9.5
Taxation	1.9	3.1	2.8
Profit after tax	4.5	7.3	6.7
Dividends	1.5	1.7	1.6
	3.0	5.6	5.1
Share price at 30 April:	£2.70	£5.11	£4.69

Balance sheets as at 30 April

		2006			2005	
	£m	£m	£m	£m	£m	£m
Fixed assets			45			35
Current assets						
Stock		36			32	
Debtors		41			24	
Cash		1			16	
		78			72	

	2006			2005		
	£m	£m	£m	£m	£m	£m
Current liabilities						
Trade creditors	17			11		
Overdraft	8			1		
	—			—		
		25			12	
		—				
Net current assets			53			60
			—			—
Total assets less current liabilities			98			95
Long-term liabilities						
10% debentures 2008		13			13	
8% debentures 2013		25			25	
		—			—	
			38			38
			—			—
			60			57
			—			—
Capital and reserves						
Ordinary shares (50 pence par)			10			10
Reserves			50			47
			—			—
			60			57
			—			—

Notes:

All sales are on credit. Merton currently pays interest on its overdraft at an annual rate of 4%, although this rate is variable.

Shareholders of Merton plc have been alarmed by the company's recent announcement that it intends to cut the total dividend for the year. The announcement, which was released on 1 June 2006, also said that Merton plc is considering expanding into the retail camera market, as a result of which it expects future share price growth and dividend growth to be at least 8% per year. Following the announcement, the company's share price fell from £2.70 to £2.45 (on an ex dividend basis) where it has remained.

The Board of Merton plc has not announced how it plans to finance the proposed expansion into the retail camera market, but it believes that the additional capital needed would be at least £19 million. It also believes that the expansion will generate an after-tax return of 9% per year. The newly-appointed Finance Director has suggested a rights issue to finance the proposed expansion, but he is concerned that the recent fall in the company's share price may cause many shareholders to decide against taking up their rights. Merton plc has not issued any new shares for the last three years.

The Finance Director believes that a rights issue would be a 1 for 2 rights issue at a 20% discount to the current share price. The rights issue would be underwritten by the issuing house for a fee of £300,000.

The Finance Director decided when taking up his appointment that substantial improvement was needed in the area of working capital management and asked the factoring subsidiary of a major bank to provide a quotation for non-recourse factoring. The factor has indicated that it would require an annual fee of 0.5% of sales. It would advance Merton plc 80% of the face value of sales at an interest rate 1% above the current overdraft rate. It expects the average time taken by debtors to pay to fall immediately to 75 days, with a reduction to no more than the average for the sector within two years.

The Finance Director has also been assured that bad debts, currently standing at £500,000 per year, would fall by 80%. Savings in current administration costs of Merton plc of £100,000 per year would be achieved as a result of factoring.

The Finance Director has collected the following average data for the media sector:

Return on capital employed	12%	Stock days	100 days
Gross profit margin	25%	Debtor days	60 days
Net profit margin	8%	Creditor days	50 days
Interest cover	8 times	Current ratio	3.5 times
Gearing (debt/equity using book values)	50%	Quick ratio	2.5 times

Required:

(a) Using appropriate ratios and financial analysis, comment on:

(i) the view of the Finance Director that substantial improvement is needed in the area of working capital management of Merton plc; **(10 marks)**

(ii) the recent financial performance of Merton plc from a shareholder perspective. Clearly identify any issues that you consider should be brought to the attention of the ordinary shareholders. **(15 marks)**

(b) Determine whether the factoring company's offer can be recommended on financial grounds. Assume a working year of 365 days and base your analysis on financial information for 2006. **(8 marks)**

(c) Calculate the theoretical ex rights price per share and the net funds to be raised by the rights issue, and determine and discuss the likely effect of the proposed expansion on:

(i) the current share price of Merton plc;

(ii) the gearing of the company.

Assume that the price–earnings ratio of Merton plc remains unchanged at 12 times. **(11 marks)**

(d) Calculate the ex dividend share price predicted by the dividend growth model and discuss the company's view that share price growth of at least 8% per year would result from expanding into the retail camera market. Assume a cost of equity capital of 11% per year. **(6 marks)**

(Total: 50 marks)

SECTION B – TWO QUESTIONS ONLY TO BE ATTEMPTED

2 FINANCIAL OBJECTIVES

(a) Discuss the nature of the financial objectives that may be set in a not-for-profit organisation such as a charity or a hospital. **(8 marks)**

(b) Explain the meaning of the term 'Efficient Market Hypothesis' and discuss the implications for a company if the stock market on which it is listed has been found to be semi-strong form efficient. **(9 marks)**

(c) Discuss the difficulties that may be experienced by a small company which is seeking to obtain additional funding to finance an expansion of business operations. **(8 marks)**

(Total: 25 marks)

3 ASH PLC

Ash plc recorded the following actual results for Product RS8 for the last month:

Product RS8	2,100 units produced and sold for £14.50 per unit
Direct material M3	1,050 kg costing £1,680
Direct material M7	1,470 kg costing £2,793
Direct labour	525 hours costing £3,675
Variable production overhead	£1,260
Fixed production overhead	£4,725

Standard selling price and cost data for one unit of Product RS8 is as follows.

Selling price	£15.00
Direct material M3	0.6 kg at £1.55 per kg
Direct material M7	0.68 kg at £1.75 per kg
Direct labour	14 minutes at £7.20 per direct labour hour
Variable production overhead	£2.10 per direct labour hour
Fixed production overhead	£9.00 per direct labour hour

At the start of the last month, 497 standard labour hours were budgeted for production of Product RS8. No stocks of raw materials are held. All production of Product RS8 is sold immediately to a single customer under a just-in-time agreement.

Required:

(a) Prepare an operating statement that reconciles budgeted profit with actual profit for Product RS8 for the last month. You should calculate variances in as much detail as allowed by the information provided. **(17 marks)**

(b) Discuss how the operating statement you have produced can assist managers in:

(i) controlling variable costs;

(ii) controlling fixed production overhead costs. **(8 marks)**

(Total: 25 marks)

4 SINE LTD

Sine Ltd produces a single product, Product DG, and is preparing budgets for the next three-month period, July to September. The current cost data for Product DG is as follows.

		£
Direct Material X	1.5 kg at 3.50 per kg	5.25
Direct Material P	2.0 kg at 4.50 per kg	9.00
Direct labour	12 minutes at £8.00 per hour	1.60
Variable production overhead	£1.00 per unit	1.00
Fixed production overhead	£3.00 per direct labour hour	0.60
		17.45

Sine Ltd experiences seasonal changes in sales volumes and forecast sales for the next four months are expected to be as follows.

Month	*July*	*August*	*September*	*October*
Sales (units)	30,000	35,000	60,000	20,000

It has been decided that opening stocks of finished goods in August and September must be 20% of the expected sales for the coming month. Closing stocks of finished goods in September must be 10% of the expected sales in October. Stocks of finished goods at the start of July are expected to be 4,000 units. Opening stocks of finished goods in July are valued at £69,800.

There will be 30,000 kg of Material X and 40,400 kg of Material P in stock at the start of July. These stocks will be bought in June at the current prices per kilogram for each material. Further supplies of Material X and Material P will need to be purchased for the higher prices of £3.80 per kg for Material X and £4.80 per kg for Material P due to supplier price increases. Opening stocks of each material will remain at the same level as the start of July.

In any given month, any hours worked in excess of 8,000 hours are paid at an overtime rate of £12.00 per hour.

Sine Ltd operates a FIFO (first in, first out) stock valuation system.

Required:

(a) Prepare the following budgets for July, August and September and in total for the three-month period:

(i) Production budget, in units;

(ii) Material usage budget, in kilograms;

(iii) Production budget, in money terms. **(10 marks)**

(b) Calculate the value of the closing stocks of finished goods at the end of the three-month period, and the value of cost of sales for the period. **(3 marks)**

(c) Discuss the ways in which budgets and the budgeting process can be used to motivate managers to endeavour to meet the objectives of the company. Your answer should refer to:

(i) setting targets for financial performance;

(ii) participation in the budget-setting process. **(12 marks)**

(Total: 25 marks)

5 CHARM PLC

Charm plc, a software company, has developed a new game, 'Fingo', which it plans to launch in the near future. Sales of the new game are expected to be very strong, following a favourable review by a popular PC magazine. Charm plc has been informed that the review will give the game a 'Best Buy' recommendation. Sales volumes, production volumes and selling prices for 'Fingo' over its four-year life are expected to be as follows.

Year	1	2	3	4
Sales and production (units)	150,000	70,000	60,000	60,000
Selling price (£ per game)	£25	£24	£23	£22

Financial information on 'Fingo' for the first year of production is as follows:

Direct material cost	£5.40 per game
Other variable production cost	£6.00 per game
Fixed costs	£4.00 per game

Advertising costs to stimulate demand are expected to be £650,000 in the first year of production and £100,000 in the second year of production. No advertising costs are expected in the third and fourth years of production. Fixed costs represent incremental cash fixed production overheads. 'Fingo' will be produced on a new production machine costing £800,000. Although this production machine is expected to have a useful life of up to ten years, government legislation allows Charm plc to claim the capital cost of the machine against the manufacture of a single product. Capital allowances will therefore be claimed on a straight-line basis over four years.

Charm plc pays tax on profit at a rate of 30% per year and tax liabilities are settled in the year in which they arise. Charm plc uses an after-tax discount rate of 10% when appraising new capital investments. Ignore inflation.

Required:

(a) Calculate the net present value of the proposed investment and comment on your findings. **(11 marks)**

(b) Calculate the internal rate of return of the proposed investment and comment on your findings. **(5 marks)**

(c) Discuss the reasons why the net present value investment appraisal method is preferred to other investment appraisal methods such as payback, return on capital employed and internal rate of return. **(9 marks)**

(Total: 25 marks)

Section 6

ANSWERS TO JUNE 2006 EXAM QUESTIONS

SECTION A

1 MERTON PLC

Key answer tips

It is important that you read the whole question before starting – e.g. some students started trying to calculate the share price in c) using DVM, when this was required in d).

Part (a) is, in some respects, standard ratio analysis. The main danger is that ratios are calculated but not discussed. Always try to discuss inter-relationships between ratios and bring in industry comparatives.

(i) Key points to watch out for:

– Start with the context e.g. growth

– Deal with individual components - don't forget to look at cash!

– Pull it together via the operating cycle

– Conclude!

(ii) Don't just calculate "investor" ratios – shareholders will be interested in profitability and financing strategy as well.

Part (b) is a relatively standard calculation but is time pressured to do it twice and discuss the conclusions.

In part (c) underwriting the issue ensures that 10 million new shares are issued. Use this to calculate the net funds raised rather than the "at least 19 million" comment given.

In part (d) the calculations are easy but interpreting them is more tricky as they indicate zero growth. Some students just assumed that they had got the answer wrong in the exam.

(a) (i) **Discussion of working capital management**

The Finance Director believes that substantial improvement in the area of working capital is needed. It should be noted that turnover increased by 10.3% in 2006 and 9.8% in 2005, so an increase in working capital to support this growth is to be expected. This discussion will focus on the year ending 31 April 2006, but balance sheets for earlier periods would allow a more complete analysis.

Stock management

The average stock days for the sector are 100 days and Merton plc has marginally improved stock days from 111 days in 2005 to 110 days in 2006. The increase in stock (12.5%) is similar to the increase in cost of sales (14%)

and therefore greater than the increase in turnover (10.3%). The reasons why the stock days are higher than the sector, and the reason why stock has increased at a greater rate than turnover, should be investigated. There may be no cause for concern in the area of stock management.

Debtor management

The increase in debtors of 71% is much greater than the increase in turnover (10.3%) and it is therefore not surprising to find that debtor days have deteriorated from 61 days in 2005 to 94 days in 2006. This compares unfavourably with the sector average of 60 days, which the factoring company believes is achievable for Merton plc. It is possible that the increase in turnover has been achieved in part by relaxing credit terms, but poor management of debtors is also a possibility.

Cash management

The cash balance has declined from £16m to £1m due to financing an increase in current and fixed assets. The optimum level of cash needs to be found from cash flow forecasts and the expected transactions demand for cash. The increased reliance on overdraft finance is unwelcome, since the company is now carrying a total of £46m of debt and incurring annual interest of £3.6m: it is not clear how this debt is going to be repaid. Comments on the cash management of Merton plc are not very useful in the absence of benchmark data.

Creditor management

Merton plc is just over the sector average creditors ratio of 50 days, having experienced an increase in creditor days from 38 days to 52 days. This is not a cause for alarm, unless the increasing trend continues due to the company's increasing reliance on short-term financing. In fact, taking full advantage of offered trade credit is good working capital management, in the absence of any incentives for early settlement.

Operating cycle and other ratios

The operating cycle of Merton plc has lengthened from 134 days to 152 days and remains greater than the operating cycle for the sector, which is 110 days (100 + 60 – 50). If the debtor days were reduced from 94 days to 60 days, the current operating cycle would fall to 118 days, which is similar to the sector average.

The current ratio of 3.1 times is less than the sector average of 3.5 times, but in 2005 it was almost twice the sector average at 6 times. This could indicate that in 2005 the company was holding too much cash (£16m), but cash reserves might have been built up in preparation for the purchase of fixed assets, which have increased substantially.

The movement from a substantial cash surplus to a substantial overdraft has been the main factor causing the quick ratio to decline from 3.3 times to 1.7 times, substantially below the sector average of 2.5 times.

Working capital financing

Merton plc is increasingly relying on short-term finance from trade credit and a large overdraft. An increase in long-term finance to support working capital is needed. It would be interesting to know what limit has been placed on the overdraft by the lending bank.

Conclusion

Only in the area of debtor management is there clear evidence to support the Finance Director's view that substantial improvement was needed in the area of working capital management. It is possible that this could be achieved by accepting the factor's offer. Attention also needs to be directed toward the company's financing strategy, which from a working capital perspective has become increasingly aggressive.

Analysis of key ratios and financial information

	2006		*2005*	
Stock days	(365 × 36/120) =	110 days	(365 × 32/105.3) =	111 days
Debtor days	(365 × 41/160) =	94 days	(365 × 24/145) =	60 days
Creditor days	(365 × 17/120) =	52 days	(365 × 11/105.3) =	38 days
Current ratio	(78/25) =	3.1 times	(72/12) =	6.0 times
Quick ratio	(42/25) =	1.7 times	(40/12) =	3.3 times
Operating cycle	(110 + 94 – 52)	152 days	(111 + 61 – 38)	134 days
Turnover/NWC	160/53 =	3.0 times	145/60 =	2.4 times

Growth rates:	*2006*		*2005*	
Turnover	160/145 =	10.3%	145/132 =	9.8%
Cost of sales	120/105.3 =	14.0%	105.3/95.7 =	10.0%
Operating expenses	30/26.0 =	15.4%	26.0/23.5 =	10.6%
Stock	36/32 =	12.5%		9.8%
Debtors	41/24 =	71%		

(ii) **Discussion of financial performance**

It is clear that 2006 has been a difficult year for Merton plc. There are very few areas of interest to shareholders where anything positive can be found to say.

Profitability

Return on capital employed has declined from 14.4% in 2005, which compared favourably with the sector average of 12%, to 10.2% in 2006. Since asset turnover has improved from 1.5 to 1.6 in the same period, the cause of the decline is falling profitability. Gross profit margin has fallen each year from 27.5% in 2004 to 25% in 2006, equal to the sector average, despite an overall increase in turnover during the period of 10% per year. Merton plc has been unable to keep cost of sales increases (14% in 2006 and 10% in 2005) below the increases in turnover. Net profit margin has declined over the same period from 9.7% to 6.2%, compared to the sector average of 8%, because of substantial increases in operating expenses (15.4% in 2006 and 10.6% in 2005). There is a pressing need here for Merton plc to bring cost of sales and operating costs under control in order to improve profitability.

Gearing and financial risk

Gearing as measured by debt/equity has fallen from 67% (2005) to 63% (2006) because of an increase in shareholders' funds through retained profits. Over the same period the overdraft has increased from £1m to £8m and cash balances have fallen from £16m to £1m. This is a net movement of £22m. If the overdraft is included, gearing has increased to 77% rather than falling to 63%.

None of these gearing levels compare favourably with the average gearing for the sector of 50%. If we consider the large increase in the overdraft, financial risk has clearly increased during the period. This is also evidenced by the decline in interest cover from 4.1 (2005) to 2.8 (2006) as operating profit has fallen and interest paid has increased. In each year interest cover has been below the sector average of eight and the current level of 2.8 is dangerously low.

Share price

As the return required by equity investors increases with increasing financial risk, continued increases in the overdraft will exert downward pressure on the company's share price and further reductions may be expected.

Investor ratios

Earnings per share, dividend per share and dividend cover have all declined from 2005 to 2006. The cut in the dividend per share from 8.5 pence per share to 7.5 pence per share is especially worrying. Although in its announcement the company claimed that dividend growth and share price growth was expected, it could have chosen to maintain the dividend, if it felt that the current poor performance was only temporary. By cutting the dividend it could be signalling that it expects the poor performance to continue. Shareholders have no guarantee as to the level of future dividends. This view could be shared by the market, which might explain why the price-earnings ratio has fallen from 14 times to 12 times.

Financing strategy

Merton plc has experienced an increase in fixed assets over the last period of £21m and an increase in current assets of £10m. These increases have been financed by a decline in cash (£15m), an increase in the overdraft (£7m) and an increase in trade credit (£6m). The company is following an aggressive strategy of financing long-term investment from short-term sources. This is very risky, since if the overdraft needed to be repaid, the company would have great difficulty in raising the funds required.

A further financing issue relates to redemption of the existing debentures. The 10% debentures are due to be redeemed in two years' time and Merton plc will need to find £13m in order to do this. It does not appear that this sum can be raised internally. While it is possible that refinancing with debt paying a lower rate of interest may be possible, the low level of interest cover may cause concern to potential providers of debt finance, resulting in a higher rate of interest. The Finance Director of Merton plc needs to consider the redemption problem now, as thought is currently being given to raising a substantial amount of new equity finance. This financing choice may not be available again in the near future, forcing the company to look to debt finance as a way of effecting redemption.

Overtrading

The evidence produced by the financial analysis above is that Merton plc is showing some symptoms of overtrading (undercapitalisation). The board are suggesting a rights issue as a way of financing an expansion of business, but it is possible that a rights issue will be needed to deal with the overtrading problem. This is a further financing issue requiring consideration in addition to the redemption of debentures mentioned earlier.

Conclusion

Ordinary shareholders need to be aware of the following issues.

1. Profitability has fallen over the last year due to poor cost control
2. A substantial increase in the overdraft over the last year has caused gearing to increase
3. It is possible that the share price will continue to fall
4. The dividend cut may warn of continuing poor performance in the future
5. A total of £13m of debentures need redeeming in two year's time

6. A large amount of new finance is needed for working capital and debenture redemption Appendix: Analysis of key ratios and financial information

	2006		*2005*		*2004*	
Gross profit margin (%)	(40.0/160)	25.0	(39.7/145.0)	27.4	(36.3/132)	27.5
Net profit margin (%)	(10.0/160)	6.2	(13.7/145)	9.4	(12.8/132)	9.7%
Interest cover (times)	(10/3.6)	2.8	(13.7/3.3)	4.1	(12.8/3.3)	3.9
Earnings per share (pence)	(4.5/20)	22.5	(7.3/20)	36.5	(6.7/20)	33.5
Dividend per share (pence)	(1.5/20)	7.5	(1.7/20)	8.5	(1.6/20)	8.0
Dividend cover (times)	(4.5/1.5)	3	(7.3/1.7)	4.3	(6.7/1.6)	4.2
Price-earnings ratio (times)	(270/22.5)	12	(511/36.5)	14	(469/33.5)	14

	2006		*2005*	
ROCE (%)	(10/98)	10.2	(13.7/95)	14.4
Asset turnover (times)	(160/98)	1.6	(145/95)	1.5
Gearing (%)	(38/60)	63	(38/57)	67
Gearing (with overdraft, %)	(46/60)	77	(39/57)	68
Growth rates:				
Cost of sales	120/105.3 =	14.0%	105.3/95.7 =	10.0%
Operating expenses	30/26.0 =	15.4%	26.0/23.5 =	10.6%

(b) **Evaluation of offer made by factoring company**

	£	£
Current level of debtors	41,000,000	
Proposed level of debtors = £160m × 75/365 =	32,876,712	
Decrease in debtors	8,123,288	
Saving in overdraft interest = £8,123,288 × 0.04 =	324,931	
Reduction in bad debts = £500,000 × 0.8 =	400,000	
Reduction in administration costs	100,000	
		824,931
Interest cost of advance = £32,876,712 × 0.8 × 0.01 =	263,014	
Annual fee of factor = 0.005 × £160m =	800,000	
		1,063,014
Net cost of factoring		238,083

The factor's offer is not financially acceptable on the basis of this analysis.

However, the factor believes that debtors' days can be reduced to the sector average of 60 days over two years, so the analysis can be repeated using this lower value.

	£	£
Current level of debtors	41,000,000	
Proposed level of debtors = £160m × 60/365 =	26,301,370	
Decrease in debtors	14,698,630	

	£	£
Saving in overdraft interest = £14,698,630 × 0.04 =	587,945	
Reduction in bad debts = £500,000 × 0.8 =	400,000	
Reduction in administration costs	100,000	
		1,087,945
Interest cost of advance = £26,301,370 × 0.8 × 0.01 =	210,411	
Annual fee of factor = 0.005 × £160m =	800,000	
		1,010,411
Net benefit of factoring		77,534

On this basis, the factor's offer is marginally acceptable, but benefits will accrue over a longer time period. A more accurate analysis, using expected levels of turnover and forecast interest rates, should be carried out.

(c) Rights issue price = 2.45 × 0.8 = £1.96

Theoretical ex rights price = ((2 ×2.45) + (1 × 1.96))/3 = 6.86/3 = £2.29 New shares issued = 20m × 1/2 = 10 million

Funds raised = 1.96 × 10m = £19.6 million

After issue costs of £300,000 funds raised will be £19.3 million

Annual after-tax return generated by these funds = 19.3 × 0.09 = £1,737,000 New earnings of Merton plc = 1,737,000 + 4,500,000 = £6,237,000 New number of shares = 20m + 10m = 30 million New earnings per share = 100 × 6,237,000/30,000,000 = 20.79 pence

New share price = 20.79 × 12 = £2.49

The weaknesses in this estimate are that the predicted return on investment of 9% may or may not be achieved: the price-earnings ratio depends on the post investment share price, rather than the post investment share price depending on the price-earnings ratio; the current earnings seem to be declining and this share price estimate assumes they remain constant; in fact current earnings are likely to decline because the overdraft and annual interest are increasing but operating profit is falling.

Expected gearing = 38/(60 + 19.3) = 47.9% compared to current gearing of 63%. Including the overdraft, expected gearing = 46/(60 + 19.3) = 58% compared to 77%.

The gearing is predictably lower, but if the overdraft is included in the calculation the gearing of the company is still higher than the sector average. The positive effect on financial risk could have a positive effect on the company's share price, but this is by no means certain.

(d) The dividend growth model calculates the ex div share price from knowledge of the cost of equity capital, the expected growth rate in dividends and the current dividend per share (or next year's dividend per share). Using the formula given in the formulae sheet, the dividend growth rate expected by the company of 8% per year and the decreased dividend of 7.5p per share:

Share price = (7.5 × 1.08)/(0.11 – 0.08) = 270p or £2.70

This is the same as the share price prior to the announcement (£2.70) and so if dividend growth of 8% per year is achieved, the dividend growth model forecasts zero share price growth. The share price growth claim made by the company regarding expansion into the retail camera market cannot therefore be substantiated.

In fact, a lower future share price of £2.49 was predicted by applying the current price-earnings ratio to the earnings per share resulting from the proposed expansion. If this estimate is correct, a fall in share price of 7% can be expected.

The share price predicted by the dividend growth model of £2.70 would require an after-tax return on the proposed expansion of 11.66%, which is more than the 9% predicted by the Board. The current return on shareholders' funds is 7.5% (4.5/60), but in 2005 it was 12.8% (7.3/57), so 11.66% may be achievable, but looks unlikely.

Since the market price fell from £2.70 to £2.45 following the announcement, it appears that the market does not believe that the forecast dividend growth can be achieved.

ACCA marking scheme			
			Marks
(a)	(i)	Ratio calculations and financial analysis	5–6
		Discussion of working capital management	5–6
		Maximum	10
	(ii)	Ratio calculations and financial analysis	8–9
		Discussion of financial performance	7–8
		Maximum	15
(b)		Reduction in debtors and overdraft interest	2
		Decrease in bad debts and administration costs	1
		Interest cost of advance	1
		Factor's fee	1
		Net cost of factoring and comment	1
		Analysis and comment on average debtors' days	3
		Maximum	8
(c)		Rights issue price	1
		Theoretical ex rights price per share	1
		Net funds raised	1
		New earnings	1
		New earnings per share	1
		New share price	1
		Discussion of predicted share price	2
		Expected gearing	1
		Discussion	2
			11
(d)		Calculation of ex div share price	2
		Comparison with pre-announcement share price	1
		Comparison with earnings-based prediction	2
		Discussion	1
			6
Total			50

2 FINANCIAL OBJECTIVES

Key answer tips

For the well prepared students this should be a very straightforward question.

(a) In the case of a not-for-profit (NFP) organisation, the limit on the services that can be provided is the amount of funds that are available in a given period. A key financial objective for an NFP organisation such as a charity is therefore to raise as much funds as possible. The fund-raising efforts of a charity may be directed towards the public or to grant-making bodies.

In addition, a charity may have income from investments made from surplus funds from previous periods. In any period, however, a charity is likely to know from previous experience the amount and timing of the funds available for use. The same is true for an NFP organisation funded by the government, such as a hospital, since such an organisation will operate under budget constraints or cash limits. Whether funded by the government or not, NFP organisations will therefore have the financial objective of keeping spending within budget, and budgets will play an important role in controlling spending and in specifying the level of services or programmes it is planned to provide.

Since the amount of funding available is limited, NFP organisations will seek to generate the maximum benefit from available funds. They will obtain resources for use by the organisation as economically as possible: they will employ these resources efficiently, minimising waste and cutting back on any activities that do not assist in achieving the organisation's non-financial objectives; and they will ensure that their operations are directed as effectively as possible towards meeting their objectives. The goals of economy, efficiency and effectiveness are collectively referred to as value for money (VFM). Economy is concerned with minimising the input costs for a given level of output. Efficiency is concerned with maximising the outputs obtained from a given level of input resources, i.e. with the process of transforming economic resources into desires services. Effectiveness is concerned with the extent to which non-financial organisational goals are achieved.

Measuring the achievement of the financial objective of VFM is difficult because the non-financial goals of NFP organisations are not quantifiable and so not directly measurable. However, current performance can be compared to historic performance to ascertain the extent to which positive change has occurred. The availability of the healthcare provided by a hospital, for example, can be measured by the time that patients have to wait for treatment or for an operation, and waiting times can be compared year on year to determine the extent to which improvements have been achieved or publicised targets have been met.

Lacking a profit motive, NFP organisations will have financial objectives that relate to the effective use of resources, such as achieving a target return on capital employed. In an organisation funded by the government from finance raised through taxation or public sector borrowing, this financial objective will be centrally imposed.

(b) The term 'Efficient Market Hypothesis' (EMH) refers to the view that share prices fully and fairly reflect all relevant available information[1]. There are other kinds of capital market efficiency, such as operational efficiency (meaning that transaction costs are low enough not to discourage investors from buying and selling shares), but it is pricing efficiency that is especially important in financial management.

Research has been carried out to discover whether capital markets are weak form efficient (share prices reflect all past or historic information), semi-strong form

[1] Watson, D. and Head, A. (2004) *Corporate Finance: Principles and Practice*, 3rd edition, FT Prentice Hall, p.35

efficient (share prices reflect all publicly available information, including past information), or strong form efficient (share prices reflect all information, whether publicly available or not). This research has shown that well-developed capital markets are weak form efficient, so that it is not possible to generate abnormal profits by studying and analysing past information, such as historic share price movements. This research has also shown that well-developed capital markets are semi-strong form efficient, so that it is not possible to generate abnormal profits by studying publicly available information such as company financial statements or press releases. Capital markets are not strong form efficient, since it is possible to use insider information to buy and sell shares for profit.

If a stock market has been found to be semi-strong form efficient, it means that research has shown that share prices on the market respond quickly and accurately to new information as it arrives on the market. The share price of a company quickly responds if new information relating to that company is released. The share prices quoted on a stock exchange are therefore always fair prices, reflecting all information about a company that is relevant to buying and selling. The share price will factor in past company performance, expected company performance, the quality of the management team, the way the company might respond to changes in the economic environment such as a rise in interest rate, and so on.

There are a number of implications for a company of its stock market being semi-strong form efficient. If it is thinking about acquiring another company, the market value of the potential target company will be a fair one, since there are no bargains to be found in an efficient market as a result of shares being undervalued. The managers of the company should focus on making decisions that increase shareholder wealth, since the market will recognise the good decisions they are making and the share price will increase accordingly. Manipulating accounting information, such as 'window dressing' annual financial statements, will not be effective, as the share price will reflect the underlying 'fundamentals' of the company's business operations and will be unresponsive to cosmetic changes. It has also been argued that, if a stock market is efficient, the timing of new issues of equity will be immaterial, as the price paid for the new equity will always be a fair one.

(c) Small businesses face a number of well-documented problems when seeking to raise additional finance. These problems have been extensively discussed and governments regularly make initiatives seeking to address these problems.

Risk and security

Investors are less willing to offer finance to small companies as they are seen as inherently more risky than large companies. Small companies obtaining debt finance usually use overdrafts or loans from banks, which require security to reduce the level of risk associated with the debt finance. Since small companies are likely to possess little by way of assets to offer as security, banks usually require a personal guarantee instead, and this limits the amount of finance available.

Marketability of ordinary shares

The equity issued by small companies is difficult to buy and sell, and sales are usually on a matched bargain basis, which means that a shareholder wishing to sell has to wait until an investor wishes to buy. There is no financial intermediary willing to buy the shares and hold them until a buyer comes along, so selling shares in a small company can potentially take a long time. This lack of marketability reduces the price that a buyer is willing to pay for the shares. Investors in small company shares have traditionally looked to a flotation, for example on the UK Alternative Investment Market, as a way of realising their investment, but this has become increasingly expensive. Small companies are likely to be very limited in their ability to offer new equity to anyone other than family and friends.

Tax considerations

Individuals with cash to invest may be encouraged by the tax system to invest in large institutional investors rather than small companies, for example by tax incentives offered on contributions to pension funds. These institutional investors themselves usually invest in larger companies, such as stock-exchange listed companies, in order to maintain what they see as an acceptable risk profile, and in order to ensure a steady stream of income to meet ongoing liabilities. This tax effect reduces the potential flow of funds to small companies.

Cost

Since small companies are seen as riskier than large companies, the cost of the finance they are offered is proportionately higher. Overdrafts and bank loans will be offered to them on less favourable terms and at more demanding interest rates than debt offered to larger companies. Equity investors will expect higher returns, if not in the form of dividends then in the form of capital appreciation over the life of their investment.

ACCA marking scheme

		Marks
(a)	Financial objectives related to funding	2–3
	Value for money	3–4
	Other financial objectives	2–3
	Maximum	8
(b)	Explanation of Efficient Market Hypothesis	2
	Discussion of forms of market efficiency	3–4
	Implications of Efficient Market Hypothesis	3–4
	Maximum	9
(c)	Risk	2
	Marketability of ordinary shares	2
	Tax considerations	2
	Cost	2
		8
Total		25

3 ASH PLC

Key answer tips

For part (a) the question gives no indication whether materials M3 and M7 are substitutes, so it is unclear whether separate usage or mix and yield variances should be calculated. The key here is to state your assumption and keep going.

In part (b) after describing the control process (especially management by exception), try to comment on specific variances and likely action. You could have developed this aspect of your answer more:

e.g. material M3 – the adverse price variance should direct managers to investigate why prices are higher than expected. This could involve reviewing whether it is the result of market conditions (uncontrollable) or poor purchasing (controllable).

(a) **Operating statement for Product RS8 for the last month**

		£	
Budgeted gross profit (W1)		18,339.3	
Sales volume profit variance (W2)		258.3 (A)	
Actual sales at standard profit		18,081.0	
Sales price variance (W3)		1,050.0 (A)	
Actual sales less standard cost		17,031.0	
Cost variances	£ *Favourable*	£ *Adverse*	
Direct material M3			
Price variance (W4)		52.5	
Usage variance (W5)	325.5		
Direct material M7			
Price variance (W6)		220.5	
Usage variance (W7)		73.5	
Direct labour			
Rate variance (W8)	105.0		
Efficiency variance (W9)		252.0	
Variable production overhead			
Expenditure variance (W10)		157.5	
Efficiency variance (W11)		73.5	
Fixed production overhead			
Expenditure variance (W12)		252.0	
Volume variance (W13)		63.0	
	430.5	1,144.5	714.0 (A)
Actual gross profit (W14)			16,317.0

Workings

Number of units of RS8 budgeted to be produced in period = 497 × 60/14 = 2,130 units

Calculation of standard profit per unit:	£
Direct material M3 = 0.6 × 1.55 =	0.93
Direct material M7 = 0.68 × 1.75 =	1.19
Direct labour = 7.20 x 14/60 =	1.68
Variable production overhead = 2.10 × 14/60 =	0.49
Fixed production overhead = 9.00 × 14/60 =	2.10
Total cost	6.39
Selling price	15.00
Standard gross profit per unit	8.61

(W1) Budgeted gross profit = 2,130 × 8.61 = £18,339.3

(W2)	Sales volume profit variance = (2,130 – 2,100) × 8.61 =	£258.3 (A)
(W3)	Sales price variance = (15.0 – 14.5) × 2,100 =	£1,050.0 (A)
(W4)	Material M3 price variance = (1.55 × 1,050) – 1,680 =	£52.5 (A)
(W5)	Material M3 usage variance = ((2,100 × 0.6) – 1,050) × 1.55 =	£325.5 (F)
(W6)	Material M7 price variance = (1.75 × 1,470) – 2,793 =	£220.5 (A)
(W7)	Material M7 usage variance = ((2,100 x 0.68) – 1,470) × 1.75 =	£73.5 (A)

Mix and yield variances may be offered instead of usage variances:
Actual quantity in actual proportions = (1,050 × 1.55) + (1,470 × 1.75) = £4,200
Actual quantity in standard mix = (1,181.25 × 1.55) + (1,338.75 × 1.75) = £4,173.75
Standard mix for actual yield = (1,260 x 1.55) + (1,428 x 1.75) = £4,452

Direct material mix variance = £4,173.75 – 4,200 = £26.25 (A)
Direct material yield variance = 4,452 – 4,173.75 = £278.25 (F)

The sum of the mix and yield variances is the same as the sum of the usage variances

(W8)	Direct labour rate variance = (7.2 × 525) – 3,675 =	£105.0 (F)
(W9)	Direct labour efficiency variance = ((2,100 ×14/60) – 525) × 7.2 =	£252.0 (A)
(W10)	Variable overhead expenditure variance = (2.1 × 525) – 1,260 =	£157.5 (A)
(W11)	Variable overhead efficiency variance = ((2,100 × 14/60) – 525) × 2.1 =	£73.5 (A)

Budgeted fixed production overhead = 497 × 9 = £4,473

(W12) Fixed production overhead expenditure variance = 4,473 – 4,725 = £252.0 (A)

Standard hours for actual production = 2,100 x 14/60 = 490 hours

(W13) Fixed production overhead volume variance = (490 – 497) × 9 = £63.0 (A)

Fixed production overhead efficiency and capacity variances may be offered:
Budgeted standard labour hours = 497 hours
Actual labour hours = 525 hours Standard labour hours for actual production = 2,100 × 14/60 = 490 hours

Fixed production overhead efficiency variance = (490 – 525) × 9 = £315 (A)
Fixed production overhead capacity variance = (497 – 525) × 9 = £252 (F)

The efficiency and capacity variances sum to the fixed production overhead volume variance

(W14) Actual gross profit calculation	£
Direct material M3	1,680
Direct material M7	2,793
Direct labour	3,675
Variable production overhead	1,260
Fixed production overhead	4,725
	14,133
Sales revenue = 2,100 x 14.50 =	30,450
	16,317

(b) **Controlling variable costs**

The first step in the process of controlling costs is to measure actual costs. The second step is to calculate variances that show the difference between actual costs and budgeted or standard costs. These variances then need to be reported to those managers who have responsibility for them. These managers can then decide whether action needs to be taken to bring actual costs back into line with budgeted or standard costs. The operating statement therefore has a role to play in reporting information to management in a way that assists in the decision-making process.

The operating statement quantifies the effect of the volume difference between budgeted and actual sales so that the actual cost of the actual output can be compared with the standard (or budgeted) cost of the actual output. The statement clearly differentiates between adverse and favourable variances so that managers can identify areas where there is a significant difference between actual results and planned performance. This supports management by exception, since managers can focus their efforts on these significant areas in order to obtain the most impact in terms of getting actual operations back in line with planned activity.

In control terms, variable costs can be affected in the short term and so an operating statement for the last month showing variable cost variances will highlight those areas where management action may be effective. In the short term, for example, managers may be able to improve labour efficiency through training, or through reducing or eliminating staff actions which do not assist the production process. In this way the adverse direct labour efficiency variance of £252, which is 7.3% of the standard direct labour cost of the actual output, could be reduced.

Controlling fixed production overhead costs

In the short term, it is unlikely that fixed production overhead costs can be controlled. An operating statement from last month showing fixed production overhead variances may not therefore assist in controlling fixed costs. Managers will not be able to take any action to correct the adverse fixed production overhead expenditure variance, for example, which may in fact simply show the need for improvement in the area of budget planning. Investigation of the component parts of fixed production overhead will show, however, whether any of these are controllable. In general, this is not the case[2].

Absorption costing gives rise to a fixed production overhead volume variance, which shows the effect of actual production being different from planned production. Since fixed production overheads are a sunk cost, the volume variance shows little more than that the standard hours for actual production were different from budgeted standard hours[3]. Similarly, the fixed production overhead efficiency variance offers little more in information terms than the direct labour efficiency variance. While fixed production overhead variances assist in reconciling budgeted profit with actual profit, therefore, their reporting in an operating statement is unlikely to assist in controlling fixed costs.

ACCA marking scheme		
		Marks
(a)	Standard gross profit per unit	1
	Budgeted production	1
	Budgeted gross profit	1
	Sales volume profit variance	1
	Sales price variance	1
	Material price variances	2
	Material usage variances	1
	Material mix and yield variances	1
	Labour rate variance	1
	Labour efficiency variance	1
	Variable overhead expenditure variance	1

[2] Drury, C. (2004) *Management and Cost Accounting,* 6th edition p. 745–6
[3] Drury, C. (2004) *Management and Cost Accounting,* 6th edition, p. 751

	Variable overhead efficiency variance	1
	Fixed overhead expenditure variance	1
	Fixed overhead volume variance	2
	Fixed overhead efficiency and capacity	1
	Actual gross profit	1
	Operating statement format	1
	Maximum	17
(b)	Controlling variable costs	5-6
	Controlling fixed costs	3-4
	Maximum	8
Total		25

4 SINE LTD

Key answer tips

Part (a) is, in many respects, a normal budgeting question so, as always, the key is to use a sensible layout and to watch that you don't overrun your time allocation.

For part (b) the answers should follow on from a) if your layout permits.

Part (c) is standard bookwork. It may be best to do it to time first before starting the calculations.

(a) **Production budget (units)**

Month	*July*	*August*	*September*	*Total*
Sales (units)	30,000	35,000	60,000	125,000
Closing stock (units)	7,000	12,000	2,000	2,000
	37,000	47,000	62,000	127,000
Opening stock (units)	4,000	7,000	12,000	4,000
Production (units)	33,000	40,000	50,000	123,000

Material usage budget (kg)

Month	*July*	*August*	*September*	*Total*
Material X (kg)	49,500	60,000	75,000	184,500
Material P (kg)	66,000	80,000	100,000	246,000

Production Budget (money terms)

	£	£	£	*Total* (£)
Material X	179,100	228,000	285,000	692,100
Material P	304,680	384,000	480,000	1,168,680
Labour	52,800	64,000	88,000	204,800
Variable production overhead	33,000	40,000	50,000	123,000
Fixed production overhead	19,800	24,000	30,000	73,800
	589,380	740,000	933,000	2,262,380
Cost per unit	£17.86	£18.50	£18.66	

Workings

Material X used in July = (30,000 × 3.50) + (19,500 × 3.80) = £179,100

Material X used in August = 60,000 × 3.80 = £228,000

Material X used in September = 75,000 x 3.80 = £285,000

Material P used in July = (40,400 × 4.50) + (25,600 × 4.80) = £304,800

Material P used in August = 80,000 × 4.80 = £384,000

Material P used in September = 100,000 × 4.80 = £480,000

Labour paid in July = 33,000 × (12/60) = 6,600 × 8.00 = £52,800

Labour paid in August = 40,000 × (12/60) = 8,000 × 8.00 = £64,000

Labour hours in September = 50,000 × (12/60) = 10,000 hours

Labour paid in September = (8,000 × 8.00) + (2,000 × 12.00) = £88,000

(b) Opening stock of finished goods = £69,800

Closing stock of finished goods = 2,000 × 18.66 = £37,320

Cost of sales for three-month period = 69,800 + 2,262,380 – 37,320 = £2,294,860

(c) **Examiner's Note:**

The topic of managerial motivation and budgeting has been a subject of discussion for a number of years. There are links here to the topics of performance measurement and responsibility accounting. Discussion should be focused on the area of budgets and the budgeting process, as specified in the question.

Setting targets for financial performance

It has been reasonably established that managers respond better in motivation and performance terms to a clearly defined, quantitative target than to the absence of such targets. However, budget targets must be accepted by the responsible managers if they are to have any motivational effect. Acceptance of budget targets will depend on several factors, including the personality of an individual manager and the quality of communication in the budgeting process.

The level of difficulty of the budget target will also influence the level of motivation and performance. Budget targets that are seen as average or above average will increase motivation and performance up to the point where such targets are seen as impossible to achieve. Beyond this point, personal desire to achieve a particular level of performance falls off sharply. Careful thought must therefore go into establishing budget targets, since the best results in motivation and performance terms will arise from the most difficult goals that individual managers are prepared to accept[4].

While budget targets that are seen as too difficult will fail to motivate managers to improve their performance, the same is true of budget targets that are seen as being too easy. When budget targets are easy, managers are likely to outperform the budget but will fail to reach the level of performance that might be expected in the absence of a budget.

One consequence of the need for demanding or difficult budget targets is the frequent reporting of adverse variances. It is important that these are not used to lay blame in the budgetary control process, since they have a motivational (or planning) origin rather than an operational origin. Managerial reward systems may need to reward almost achieving, rather than achieving, budget targets if managers are to be encouraged by receiving financial incentives.

[4] Otley, D. (1987) *Accounting Control and Organizational Behaviour*, Heinemann, p.43

Participation in the budget-setting process

A 'top-down' approach to budget setting leads to budgets that are imposed on managers. Where managers within an organisation are believed to behave in a way that is consistent with McGregor's Theory X perspective, imposed budgets may improve performance, since accepting the budget is consistent with reduced responsibility and avoiding work.

It is also possible that acceptance of imposed budgets by managers who are responsible for their implementation and achievement is diminished because they feel they have not been able to influence budget targets. Such a view is consistent with McGregor's Theory Y perspective, which holds that managers naturally seek responsibility and do not need to be tightly controlled. According to this view, managers respond well to participation in the budget-setting process, since being able to influence the budget targets for which they will be responsible encourages their acceptance. A participative approach to budget-setting is also referred to as a 'bottom-up' approach.

In practice, many organisations adopt a budget-setting process that contains elements of both approaches, with senior management providing strategic leadership of the budget-setting process and other management tiers providing input in terms of identifying what is practical and offering detailed knowledge of their area of the organisation.

ACCA marking scheme		
		Marks
(a)	Production budget (units)	2
	Material usage budget	1
	Material X costs	1
	Material P costs	1
	Direct labour costs	2
	Variable production overhead cost	1
	Fixed production overhead cost	1
	Presentation	1
		10
(b)	Closing stock of finished goods	1
	Cost of sales	2
		3
(c)	Up to 3 marks for each detailed point made	12
Total		25

5 CHARM PLC

Key answer tips

This should have been the most popular question on the paper.

In (a) fixed costs should be included, being incremental. Layout is important anticipating part b).

Part (b) is made much easier if your layout for a) showed net annual cash flows.

Part (c) is standard bookwork so do it first.

(a) **Calculation of NPV of 'Fingo' investment pro**ject

Year	*1*	*2*	*3*	*4*
	£000	£000	£000	£000
Sales revenue	3,750	1,680	1,380	1,320
Direct materials	(810)	(378)	(324)	(324)
Variable production	(900)	(420)	(360)	(360)
Advertising	(650)	(100)		
Fixed costs	(600)	(600)	(600)	(600)
Taxable cash flow	790	182	96	36
Taxation	(237)	(55)	(29)	(11)
	553	127	67	25
CA tax benefits	60	60	60	60
Net cash flow	613	187	127	85
Discount at 10%	0.909	0.826	0.751	0.683
Present values	557.2	154.5	95.4	58.1

	£000
Present value of future benefits	865.2
Initial investment	800.0
Net present value	65.2

Workings

Fixed costs in year 1 = 150,000 × 4 = £600,000 and since these represent a one-off increase in fixed production overheads, these are the fixed costs in subsequent years as well.

Annual capital allowance (CA) tax benefits = (800,000/4) × 0.3 = £60,000 per year

Comment

The net present value of £65,200 is positive and the investment can therefore be recommended on financial grounds. However, it should be noted that the positive net present value depends heavily on sales in the first year. In fact, sensitivity analysis shows that a decrease of 5% in first year sales will result in a zero net present value. (Note: candidates are not expected to conduct a sensitivity analysis)

(b) **Calculation of IRR of 'Fingo' investment project**

Year	*1*	*2*	*3*	*4*
	£000	£000	£000	£000
Net cash flow	613	187	127	85
Discount at 20%	0.833	0.694	0.579	0.482
Present values	510.6	129.8	73.5	41.0

	£000
Present value of future benefits	754.9
Initial investment	800.0
Net present value	(45.1)

Internal rate of return = 10 + [((20 – 10) × 65.2)/(65.2 + 45.1)] = 16%

Since the internal rate of return is greater than the discount rate used to appraise new investments, the proposed investment is financially acceptable.

(c) There are many reasons that could be discussed in support of the view that net present value (NPV) is superior to other investment appraisal methods.

NPV considers cash flows

This is the reason why NPV is preferred to return on capital employed (ROCE), since ROCE compares average annual accounting profit with initial or average capital invested. Financial management always prefers cash flows to accounting profit, since profit is seen as being open to manipulation. Furthermore, only cash flows are capable of adding to the wealth of shareholders in the form of increased dividends. Both internal rate of return (IRR) and Payback also consider cash flows.

NPV considers the whole of an investment project

In this respect NPV is superior to Payback, which measures the time it takes for an investment project to repay the initial capital invested. Payback therefore considers cash flows within the payback period and ignores cash flows outside of the payback period. If Payback is used as an investment appraisal method, projects yielding high returns outside of the payback period will be wrongly rejected. In practice, however, it is unlikely that Payback will be used alone as an investment appraisal method.

NPV considers the time value of money

NPV and IRR are both discounted cash flow (DCF) models which consider the time value of money, whereas ROCE and Payback do not. Although Discounted Payback can be used to appraise investment projects, this method still suffers from the criticism that it ignores cash flows outside of the payback period. Considering the time value of money is essential, since otherwise cash flows occurring at different times cannot be distinguished from each other in terms of value from the perspective of the present time.

NPV is an absolute measure of return

NPV is seen as being superior to investment appraisal methods that offer a relative measure of return, such as IRR and ROCE, and which therefore fail to reflect the amount of the initial investment or the absolute increase in corporate value. Defenders of IRR and ROCE respond that these methods offer a measure of return that is understandable by managers and which can be intuitively compared with economic variables such as interest rates and inflation rates.

NPV links directly to the objective of maximising shareholders' wealth

The NPV of an investment project represents the change in total market value that will occur if the investment project is accepted. The increase in wealth of each shareholder can therefore be measured by the increase in the value of their shareholding as a percentage of the overall issued share capital of the company. Other investment appraisal methods do not have this direct link with the primary financial management objective of the company.

NPV always offers the correct investment advice

With respect to mutually exclusive projects, NPV always indicates which project should be selected in order to achieve the maximum increase on corporate value. This is not true of IRR, which offers incorrect advice at discount rates which are less than the internal rate of return of the incremental cash flows. This problem can be overcome by using the incremental yield approach.

NPV can accommodate changes in the discount rate

While NPV can easily accommodate changes in the discount rate, IRR simply ignores them, since the calculated internal rate of return is independent of the cost of capital in all time periods.

NPV has a sensible re-investment assumption

NPV assumes that intermediate cash flows are re-invested at the company's cost of capital, which is a reasonable assumption as the company's cost of capital represents the average opportunity cost of the company's providers of finance, i.e. it represents a rate of return which exists in the real world. By contrast, IRR assumes that intermediate cash flows are reinvested at the internal rate of return, which is not an investment rate available in practice,

NPV can accommodate non-conventional cash flows

Non-conventional cash flows exist when negative cash flows arise during the life of the project. For each change in sign there is potentially one additional internal rate of return. With non-conventional cash flows, therefore, IRR can suffer from the technical problem of giving multiple internal rates of return.

ACCA marking scheme		
		Marks
(a)	Sales revenue	1
	Material costs	1
	Variable production costs	1
	Advertising	1
	Incremental fixed costs	2
	Taxation	1
	Capital allowance tax benefits	1
	Discount factors	1
	Net present value	1
	Comment	1
		11
(b)	Net present value	1
	IRR	3
	Comment	1
		5
(c)	Up to 2 marks for each detailed point made	9
Total		25